T0299889

The Global Economic Crisis and the Developing World

The world economy is currently in the throes of a global economic crisis reminiscent of the great depressions of the 1930s and the 1870s. As back then, the crisis has exposed the major structural imbalances in financial and credit markets in addition to global trade, forcing many governments, developed and developing, to impose debilitating austerity measures that are exacerbating the structural weaknesses that caused the crisis in the first place.

This crisis has erupted at a time when the global economy is integrated, intertwined and interdependent as perhaps never before in history. Thus, the impact of this crisis which originated in the advanced industrial countries can be felt sharply in the developing world, which is already grappling with its own internal constraints and structural barriers to sustained development. Emergent debates about resurgent protectionism, currency wars and alternative reserve currencies suggest that the global economy has entered a phase of heightened geo-economic and political change which will transform the development "equation" in varied and diverse ways. Indeed, the economic and financial crisis is but one element of the global transition, given what is referred to as the "triple crisis" of finance, development and environment with challenges like climate change that underscore the limits of the global economy.

It is imperative at this time that development economists and policy-makers should engage with two crucial points: the implications of these changes for the developing world, and the prospects for "development" for the majority of people in the developing world. This volume offers historical insights into the origins of the contemporary crisis, as well as detailed analyses of the financial and trade dimensions, and an assessment of the technological and innovation context along with perspectives on the implications for unemployment and gender imbalances. The volume also looks at the scenario for big developing countries, with a focus on South Africa, in addition to small developing states, with reference to the Caribbean. The volume provides a wide variety of angles and approaches with which the discussion on the global economic crisis and its impact on the developing world can be approached in a methodologically and analytically rigorous manner.

Ashwini Deshpande is Professor of Economics at the Delhi School of Economics, University of Delhi, India.

Keith Nurse is Director of the Shridath Ramphal Centre for International Trade Law, Policy and Services at the Cave Hill Campus (Barbados) of the University of the West Indies.

Routledge studies in development economics

The Global Economic Crisis and the Developing World

Implications and prospects for recovery and growth

Edited by
Ashwini Deshpande and Keith Nurse

Routledge
Taylor & Francis Group

LONDON AND NEW YORK

First published 2012
by Routledge
2 Park Square, Milton Park, Abingdon, Oxon OX14 4RN

Simultaneously published in the USA and Canada
by Routledge
711 Third Avenue, New York, NY 10017

Routledge is an imprint of the Taylor & Francis Group, an informa business

© 2012 Selection and editorial matter, Ashwini Deshpande and
Keith Nurse; individual chapters, the contributors

The right of Ashwini Deshpande and Keith Nurse to be identified as the
authors of the editorial material, and of the authors for their individual
chapters, has been asserted in accordance with sections 77 and 78 of the
Copyright, Designs and Patents Act 1988.

All rights reserved. No part of this book may be reprinted or reproduced or
utilised in any form or by any electronic, mechanical, or other means, now
known or hereafter invented, including photocopying and recording, or in
any information storage or retrieval system, without permission in writing
from the publishers.

Trademark notice: Product or corporate names may be trademarks or
registered trademarks, and are used only for identification and explanation
without intent to infringe.

British Library Cataloguing in Publication Data
A catalogue record for this book is available from the British Library

Library of Congress Cataloging in Publication Data
The global economic crisis and the developing world: implications and
prospects for recovery and growth/edited by Ashwini Deshpande and
Keith Nurse.
   p. cm.
   1. Developing countries–Economic conditions–21st century.
   2. Developing countries–Economic policy–21st century.
   3. Global Financial Crisis, 2008–2009. I. Deshpande, Ashwini, 1965–
   II. Nurse, Keith.
   HC59.7.G56323 2012
   330.9172′4–dc23   2011045400

ISBN: 978-0-415-67128-6 (hbk)
ISBN: 978-0-203-11943-3 (ebk)

Typeset in Times New Roman
by Wearset Ltd, Boldon, Tyne and Wear

Contents

Figures

Tables

Contributors

Aldo Caliari is the Director of the Rethinking Bretton Woods Project at the Washington-based Center of Concern. He has a Masters in International Policy and Practice from George Washington University (2007), with a focus on economics and finance. He also holds a Masters degree from the Washington College of Law, American University, on International Legal Studies (2000), where he was honored with the Outstanding Graduate Award. He has been staff at the Center of Concern since 2000, where he has focused on global economic governance, debt, international financial architecture, human rights in international economic policy, and linkages between trade and finance policy. He has done considerable public speaking for a variety of audiences that range from popular workshops to academia and closed government briefings. He has edited three books on linkages between trade and finance, and one on regional and global liquidity arrangements. Other writings of his have been featured in books, academic and specialized journals, and the media. He has been a consultant to several intergovernmental organizations – such as UNCTAD, UNDP, UN DESA and the Office of the High Commissioner for Human Rights – in addition to governments, civil society networks and foundations.

Elisa Calza is a research assistant within the Unit of Innovation and ICT of the Division of Production, Productivity and Management at the UN Economic Commission for Latin America and the Caribbean (ECLAC). Having graduated in Economics from the Universitá Bocconi (Milan, Italy), she also obtained a MA in Development Economics at the University of Sussex (UK) in 2008. Her research activities focus on innovation and development, STI policies and institutions, industrial development and new technologies.

Mario Cimoli is the Director of the Division of Production, Productivity and Management at the UN Economic Commission for Latin America and the Caribbean (ECLAC). He gained his DPhil at the SPRU (University of Sussex) with a thesis that analyses the effect of technological gaps and trade on growth in developing economies; since 1992 he has been Professor of Economics at the University of Venice (Ca'Foscari). In 2004 he was appointed Co-Director (with Giovanni Dosi and Joseph Stiglitz) of two task forces:

Industrial Policy and Intellectual Property Rights Regimes for Development (Initiative for Policy Dialogue, Columbia University, New York). He makes speeches and writes and publishes books and articles on economics issues, including industrial as well as science, technology and innovation related topics. The following works are remarkable and stand out: *Innovation and Economic Development: the Impact of Information and Communication Technologies in Latin America* (Edward Elgar, 2010); *Industrial Policy and Development, The Political Economy of Capabilities Accumulation* (Oxford University Press, 2009) (with G. Dosi and J.E. Stiglitz (eds); 'Structural Change and the BOT Constraint: Why did Latin America fail to converge?' (*Cambridge Journal of Economics*, 2010); 'Global Growth and Implicit Reciprocity: A structuralist perspective' (*Cambridge Journal of Economics*, 2010); 'Elites e inercia estructural en América Latina: una nota introductoria de la Economía Política del Desarrollo' (*Journal of Economic Issues*, 2008); *La apertura comercial y la brecha tecnológica en América Latina: Una trampa de bajo crecimiento* (with J.A. Ocampo, eds), *Más allá de las reformas, dinámica estructural y vulnerabilidad macroeconómica* (Stanford University Press, 2005); *Structural Reforms, Technological Gaps and Economic Development: A Latin American Perspective* (with J. Katz, Industrial and Corporate Change, Oxford, 2003); and *Developing Innovation System: Mexico in the Global Context* (Pinter Publishers, 2000).

Vanessa da Costa Val Munhoz received a BA in economics from the Federal University of Minas Gerais, Brazil (2003), an MA in economics from the Federal University of Uberlândia, Brazil (2006) and a PhD in economics from the Federal University of Minas Gerais, Brazil (2010). Vanessa da Costa Val Munhoz works as a professor of economics at the Federal University of Uberlândia, Brazil. Her main areas of interest are macroeconomics, international finance, the Post-Keynesian approach, capital flows, external vulnerability and volatility. She has been awarded grants from the Institute for Applied Economic Research (IPEA-2005) and the Brazilian Federal Council of Economics (COFECON-2006 and 2010). She has published Brazilian journal articles and a chapter of a book, and works in the proceedings of conferences.

Ashwini Deshpande is Professor of Economics at the Delhi School of Economics, University of Delhi, India. Her PhD and early publications were on the international debt crisis of the 1980s. Subsequently, she has been working on the economics of discrimination and affirmative action issues, with a focus on caste and gender in India, as well as on aspects of the Chinese economy: the role of FDI in the reform process, regional disparities and gender discrimination. She has published extensively in leading scholarly journals. She is the editor of *Boundaries of Clan and Color: Transnational Studies of Intergroup Disparity* (with William Darity, Jr), Routledge, London, 2003; *Globalization and Development: A Handbook of New Perspectives*, Oxford University Press, New Delhi, 2007 (hardcover) and 2010 (paperback); *Capital Without Borders: Challenges to Development*, Anthem Press, UK, 2010 (hardcover) and 2011 (paperback). Her latest book is *Grammar of Caste: Economic Discrimination in Contemporary India*, Oxford University Press, 2011. She received the EXIM Bank award for her outstanding dissertation in 1994, and the 2007 VKRV Rao Award for Indian economists under forty-five.

Bill Freund has a PhD from Yale University in history, achieved in 1971. He has taught in the USA, Nigeria and Tanzania, and from 1985 to 2004 was Professor and Head of Department, Economic History, University of Natal. He is currently teaching in the Corporate Strategy and Industrial Development Programme, University of the Witwatersrand, Johannesburg, South Africa. His best-known books are *The Making of Contemporary Africa*, first published in 1984, and *The African City: A History* (Cambridge University Press, 2007).

Özge Izdeş holds a BA and an MA in Economics from Istanbul University, and started a second MA in Economic History (ATA) at Bhosphorus University, which was terminated by her PhD in Economics at the University of Utah, Salt Lake City. She has worked with the International Working Group on Gender, Macroeconomics and International Economics (GEM-IWG) on conference organization and research projects since 2006. She has taught economics at Istanbul University, the University of Utah and Kadir Has University, and is currently teaching at Arel University. She is the author of a number of articles on economic crises, gender and employment, labor market transformations, poverty, women and the economy. She is an active participator in the Women's Movement in Turkey, and is especially active in campaigns on gender and labor. Recently she has been working on employment-oriented development strategies. She is a member of the American Economic Association (AEA), Women's Labor and Employment Initiative (the KEIG Platform), IAFFE, the GEM-IWG, ASSA, EEA and URPE.

Jason Jackson is a PhD Candidate in the Political Economy of Development at the Massachusetts Institute of Technology. He has an AB in Economics from Princeton University, an MSc in Development Economics from the University of London School of Oriental and African Studies and an MPA from the Harvard Kennedy School. He has won fellowships from the Social Sciences Research Council in the US and the Overseas Development Institute in the UK, and has worked on issues of social and economic development with a variety of private, non-governmental and international organizations in the Caribbean, South Africa and the United States.

Jessica Jones is a Research Consultant with the Shridath Ramphal Centre for International Trade Law, Policy and Services, University of the West Indies, Cave Hill Campus, Barbados. As a Consultant for the International Organization for Migration (IOM), Jessica Jones has authored manuals providing policy advice to strengthen technical capacity in migration management for the Government of Trinidad and Tobago. Jessica Jones has also worked with the IOM Headquarters in Geneva, interning with the Migration Policy, Research and Communication Department, on projects relating to Migration, Climate Change and Environmental Degradation, Migration and Development, and Labor Mobility. Holding an advanced degree in International Relations from the University of the West Indies, Jessica Jones is also an alumna of the Graduate Institute of International Studies (HEI, now IHEID), Geneva, Switzerland and the Comparative Regional Integration programme of the Centre for European Integration Studies (ZEI), Germany. Jessica Jones is the Project Manager of the IDRC-funded project examining "Strategic Opportunities in Migration Management for the Caribbean: Brain Circulation, Diasporic Tourism and Investment", for which a key outcome has been the documentary *Forward Home: The Power of the Caribbean Diaspora.*

Gilberto Libânio received a BA in economics from the Federal University of Minas Gerais, Brazil (1994), an MA in economics from the Federal University of Rio de Janeiro, Brazil (1998), and a PhD in economics from the University of Notre Dame, USA (2006). He works as a professor of economics at the Federal University of Minas Gerais, Brazil. His main areas of interest are macroeconomics, central banking, growth theory and international finance, with a regional focus on Latin America. He has been awarded grants and fellowships from the Kellogg Institute for International Studies, the University of Notre Dame, the Global Development Network, and the National Council for Scientific and Technological Development (CNPq, Brazil), among others. Gilberto Libânio is the author of *Three Essays on Aggregate Demand and Growth* (VDM Verlag, 2009), and has published journal articles, chapters of books and book reviews in Brazil, the UK and the USA.

Seeraj Mohamed is an academic economist and writer with more than twenty years' experience working on economic, industrial and finance development issues. He has been active in the research and formulation of economic policies for a democratic South Africa since democracy in 1994. He is Director of the Corporate Strategy and Industrial Development Research Programme at the University of the Witwatersrand (Wits University), where he also has been involved in designing and teaching new postgraduate degrees and courses in the School of Economic and Business Sciences. He is a member of the Executive Committee of the Global Labour University (GLU) at Wits University, and teaches a core course in the GLU Masters programme. Seeraj was appointed Special Advisor to the South African Minister of Trade and Industry in 2010. He also advises the South African Labour Movement on economic policy issues, and is a member of the Economist Advisory Panel of Cosatu – the country's largest trade union federation. He is a member of the Board of Directors of the Development Fund of the Development Bank of Southern Africa. He is involved in a number of progressive international networks working on economic development and finance. For example, since 2009 he has been a member of the Economist Advisory Council of the Task Force on Global Financial Integrity, an international coalition of more than fifty international civil society organizations and governments working together to address inequalities in the global financial system. He is a frequent commentator on the South African and global economy, and has written a weekly column called Global Account for the business magazine *Engineering News* and the website www.Polity.org.za since 2002. He attended the Cambridge Advanced Programme on Rethinking Development Economics (CAPORDE) in 2003, now teaches in the African Programme on Rethinking Development Economics (APORDE) in South Africa, and has participated in their alumni conferences, the Annual Conference on Development and Change.

Luiz M. Niemeyer is currently Associate Professor at the Economics Department of the Catholic University of Sao Paulo (PUC-SP) and Faculdades Campinas (FACAMP). He has PhD in Economics from the New School University (2000). In 2005, he was a Visiting Professor at Denver University – Graduate School of International Studies. In 2003, he was Deputy Director of the Third Cambridge Advanced Program on Rethinking Development Economics. Luiz has published several articles in Brazil, and a book, *Brazil's External Debt in the 1990s in a Historical Perspective: The Role of Short-term Portfolio Investment and the Shifting Character of the Brazilian State during Debt Crises*, which is available in English through University Microfilm, Ann Arbor, MI. His research areas are international finance, economic development, and monetary economics.

Keith Nurse is director of the Shridath Ramphal Centre for International Trade Law, Policy and Services at the Cave Hill Campus (Barbados) and currently holds the World Trade Organization Chair at the University of the West Indies (UWI). Keith is one of the founding members of the recently established World Economics Association and has served on the advisory board of several international organizations, such as the World Trade Organization Chairs programme, the OECD Knowledge Networks and Markets project, the ACP Intra-Regional Observatory on Migration and the OAS Inter-American Cultural Policy Observatory. He is on the advisory board of academic institutions like the MA in Technology Governance at the University of Tallinn, Estonia and the Diploma for Advanced Studies in Trade Negotiations and Governance, University of Geneva. He has served on the editorial board of the academic journal *Tourism and Cultural Change* and the *Anthem Press Other Canon Series*. He is the author of *Heritage Tourism in the Caribbean* (Caribbean Tourism Organization 2008), *Festival Tourism in the Caribbean* (Inter-American Development Bank 2003) and *The Caribbean Music Industry* (Caribbean Export Development Agency 2003). Keith has published several scholarly articles on the trade policy dimension of the clothing, banana, tourism, climate change, diaspora, copyright and creative industries. He is also the co-editor of *Caribbean Economies and Global Restructuring* (Ian Randle Publishers 2002) and *Globalization, Diaspora and Caribbean Popular Culture* (Ian Randle Publishers 2005) and co-author of *Windward Islands Bananas: Challenges and Options under the*

Single European Market (Freidrich Ebert Stiftung 1995). He is also the executive producer of the documentary *Forward Home: The Power of the Caribbean Diaspora* which is an outcome of the IDRC funded project entitled Strategic Opportunities in Caribbean Migration.

Annalisa Primi has been an economist at the OECD (Paris, France) since 2009. From 2003 to February 2009 she worked for the United Nations Economic Commission for Latin America and the Caribbean (CEPAL), in Santiago. Her areas of expertise are innovation policy, industrial policy and intellectual property for development. She earned a Masters degree at the University of Pavia (Italy) in International Cooperation and Economic Development, and a degree in Economics of Institutions and Financial Markets at the University of Tor Vegata (Rome, Italy). She has a record of official and academic publications and extensive experience in technical assistance to governments on innovation and industrial policy.

Sebastián Rovira is Economic Affairs Officer within the Unit of Innovation and New Technologies of the Division of Production, Productivity and Management at the UN Economic Commission for Latin America and the Caribbean (ECLAC). Between 2006 and 2007, he was consultant for the Unit of Industrial Development at ECLAC. He obtained his degree in Economics at the Universidad de la República Oriental del Uruguay and has an MA in Economics from the Universitá degli Studi di Siena (Italy), where he is currently a PhD candidate in Economics. His main research interests concern economic development, innovation and industrial dynamics, structural change and ICT.

Leandro Serino is an economic analyst at Aerolineas Argentinas. He has been a researcher and assistant professor of economics at the Institute of Sciences, University of General Sarmiento, Argentina, and between 2008 and 2010 he collaborated with the Ministry of Economy and Public Finances in Argentina in relation to the international crisis and the development of an applied CGE model. Serino obtained his PhD from ISS-EUR in 2009 for an applied analysis of alternative policies to encourage productive diversification in wage-goods exporting countries. His research interests are development economics theory, international finance and applied macroeconomics.

Mehdi Shafaeddin is a development economist with a DPhil degree from the University of Oxford, the former head of the Macroeconomics and Development Policies Branch of the United Nations Conference on Trade and Development (UNCTAD), and the author of *Trade Policy at the Crossroads. The Recent Experience of Developing Countries* (Palgrave Macmillan, 2005) and *Competitiveness and Development* (Anthem Press, forthcoming). He has authored many articles in international journals on trade and development issues, and the development of China, Africa and oil-exporting countries. He was, until recently, an international consultant affiliated with the Institute of Economic Research, University of Neuchatel, Switzerland, and runs a training course on Building-up Competitive Industrial Capacity.

David Tennant, PhD, is a senior lecturer in Economics at the University of the West Indies, Mona Campus, and was previously an economist in the Jamaican Ministry of Finance and Planning. He has a strong background in quantitative and qualitative research methodologies. His areas of specialization include: Financing Development in Emerging Markets; Financial Crises; Micro, Small and Medium Enterprise (MSME) Development; and Pensions Reform. He has published papers in journals such as *The Journal of Economics and Business*; *The Journal of International Financial Markets, Institutions and Money*; *World Development*; *Applied Economics*; *Applied Financial Economics*; *The Journal of Developing Areas; Empirical Economics Letters; The Journal of Economic Issues*: and *Social and Economic Studies*.

Fiona Tregenna is an associate professor in the Department of Economics and Econometrics at the University of Johannesburg, South Africa. She holds a PhD in Economics from the University of Cambridge, a Masters degree in Economics from the University of Massachusetts (Amherst), and earlier degrees from the Universities of the Witwatersrand and Natal (now KwaZulu-Natal) in South Africa. In the past she has worked for, among others, the National Labour and Economic Development Institute, the Congress of South African Trade Unions, universities in South Africa and abroad, and as a consultant to various research institutes and international organizations. Her research has been published or is forthcoming in journals including *The Review of Political Economy*; *The Cambridge Journal of Economics*; *Applied Economics*; *The International Review of Applied Economics*; *The South African Journal of Economics*; *Development Southern Africa*; *The European Journal for the History of Economic Thought*; *The Review of African Political Economy*; and *Industrial and Corporate Change*, as well as a number of book chapters. Fiona has presented her research at conferences and seminars in the United States, Brazil, Japan, Greece, Finland, Chile, Cuba, Turkey, Spain, India, China, Switzerland, Ghana, The Netherlands, the United Kingdom and elsewhere.

1   Global economic crisis and the developing world

An introduction

Ashwini Deshpande and Keith Nurse

This introduction is being written at a time when the "Occupy Wall Street" movement is in its third week and continues to gather momentum in the United States of America. On the other side of the Atlantic, European leaders have delayed by two weeks the summit to finalize the bailout plan for Greece and the wider eurozone debt crisis. And to add more drama to the sequence of events, the cover story of this week's issue of *The Economist* is entitled "Be Afraid", with the tagline stating "unless politicians act more boldly, the world economy will keep heading towards a black hole" (*The Economist*, 2011). Also of note is the passing of the US Senate bill aimed at punishing China and other countries that the US deems are undervaluing their currencies. The Chinese response through its official news agency Xinhua stated that the "US legislation was reminiscent of the Smoot-Hawley tariff act in 1930 that is widely credited with worsening the Great Depression" (*Financial Times* 2011a).

In an unrelated but topical bit of trade news it is reported that Chinese exports, now considered a barometer for the health of the global economy, fell in September by seventeen percentage points – the biggest drop since 2009 – due in large part to the decline in orders from the EU and the US, China's biggest export markets (*Financial Times* 2011b). Coupled with this is the latest employment news that the global economy has lost twenty million jobs since the outbreak of the financial and economic crisis in 2008, and that a further twenty million jobs could disappear by the end of 2012 based on current trajectories (ILO/OECD 2011). The specter of rising unemployment, declining consumer demand (and confidence), reduced investor confidence and constricting government spending are the key challenges facing the recovery effort after the furor of bank bailouts, stimulus packages and debt restructuring that defined the policy response in the immediate aftermath of the financial and economic crisis.

There is now a foreboding sense that the volatile mix of fiscal austerity, rising social discontent and political gamesmanship may lead to the further growth of low-intensity protectionism, or worse yet, the return of beggar-thy-neighbor policies (e.g. currency wars), thereby further threatening the already fragile global economic recovery. As the prospects of a double-dip recession become more evident and the predictions of sustained recovery fade there is increasing recognition that the global economy is in the throes of a global economic crisis reminiscent of the great depressions of the 1930s and possibly that of the 1870s and 1820s. As such, the current crisis should be seen not just as a period of financial and economic instability but as a more fundamental shift in the geo-economic and political moorings of the contemporary global economy (see Nurse 2010). For example, Gourevitch, in his seminal work on comparative responses of five governments (United States, United Kingdom, France, Germany and Sweden) in the advanced economies during international economic crises, noted that each of the previous crises exhibited similar tendencies, such as there was in each case a major downturn in a regular investment/business cycle; a major change in the geographical distribution of production, and, lastly a significant growth of new products and new productive processes (Gourevitch 1986).

What is observable in the contemporary conjunctural shift has been the significant shift in economic power away from the advanced economies towards the emerging and developing world. For instance, the share of global GDP of the G7 countries dropped from 50 percent in 1990 to 40 percent by 2008 while the share of the G20 emerging economies rose from 11 percent to 17 percent in the same time period (Canuto and Yufa Lin 2011). It is also critical to note that the main source of growth in the global economy has come from emerging economies followed by developing countries, generally.

The growth performance and the prospects for recovery are uneven and largely dependent on the trade structures of the respective developing countries (see Table 1.1). The economies most severely affected are the net food and energy importers, on account of the rise in food and energy prices in global markets. The countries worse affected are the small and island economies due to the high dependence on imports in these areas. Exporters of manufactured goods also suffered during the downturn depending on the extent of their exposure to the advanced economies that are in a recession. Exporters of fuel and exporters of minerals and other mining products experienced the most favorable terms of trade, followed by the exporters of agricultural products.

Trade in international services, a sector where many developing countries are highly dependent, was also impacted by the economic downturn, as reflected in data for 2009. Travel and transport, which together account for half of the world trade in services, had respective declines of 9 and 16 percent. The next most

Table 1.1 Income gains or losses from the terms of trade of selected developing and transition economies, by trade structure, 2002–2010 percentage of GDP

	2002–2007	*2008*	*2009*	*2010*
Exporters of manufactures	−0.9	−2.6	1.8	−1.0
Fuel exporters	4.6	7.7	−10.5	5.0
Exporters of minerals and other mining products	3.0	−4.4	−1.0	4.6
Exporters of agricultural products	0.2	1.6	−0.5	1.0

Source: UN World Economic Situation and Prospects, 2011: 51.

negatively affected sectors were personal, cultural and recreational services (11 percent), financial services (16 percent) and construction services (20 percent). The only areas that experienced growth were trade in computer and information services (3 percent) and royalties and licence fees (19 percent) (United Nations 2011a).

In total, world trade took a major and unprecedented hit, with a decline of minus 11 percent in 2009. The last time world trade fell by this much was during the Great Depression of the 1930s (see Figure 1.1). However, data and analysis of the global trade imbalances (GTIs) suggest that the trade problem is structural rather than episodic, showing that the average annual growth of GTIs for the period 1990 to 2007 was 11 percent as compared to 1 percent in the prior two decades (Freund 2011). From this standpoint, rebalancing current account imbalances is a critical feature of the post-crisis policy framework if sustainable growth is to be achieved (Serven and Nguyen 2011). Achieving coordination in this arena is no mean task, given the divergence of perspectives from the key actors. For example, the US points to the under-valued Chinese currency, whereas China and the other emerging economies argue that the greater distortion is the excessive quantitative easing, particularly in the US (United Nations 2011b).

From a regional perspective, an analysis of the growth performance in the last few years provides a very compelling picture of the unfolding context of growth and recovery. As Figure 1.1 illustrates, overall world output experienced a major

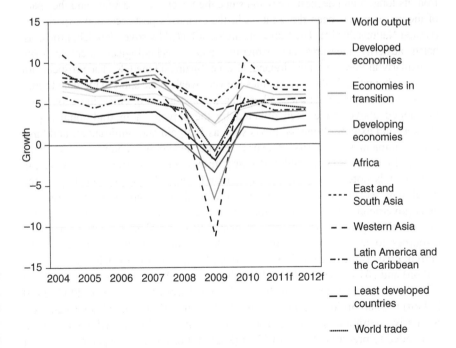

Figure 1.1 Growth of world output, by region, 2004–2012 (source: UN 2010, 2011).

drop-off of minus 2.0 percent in 2009, with a recovery of 3.6 percent in 2010. The advanced economies had a below-average performance, with a decline of minus 3.5 percent and a slight recovery of growth in 2010 of 2.3 percent. Developing countries, on the other hand, only had a decline to 2.4 percent, rebounding to 7.1 percent in 2010 and thereby returning to pre-crisis peaks. The success of this group is largely determined by the strong export performance of East and South Asia, namely China and India, which have been averaging output growths of 10 percent and 8 percent, respectively, over the 2004–2010 period. Africa's average was closer to 5 percent, whereas Western Asia and Latin America and the Caribbean hover around 4 percent.

What Figure 1.1 depicts is what has been described as the "two-speed global recovery" process and the sustained imbalance between surplus and deficit countries. Several emerging economies, namely China, Brazil and India, have built healthy foreign exchange reserves on the basis of solid export performance that generated strong current account positions. As for the larger emerging economies, they have been able to rely on large and relatively under-tapped domestic markets or to switch to South–South trade to ride out the slump in external demand from the OECD countries in recent years.

On the other side of the equation are the advanced economies that have been mired in low growth with rising unemployment, faltering consumer spending and high debt levels along with widening trade and reserves deficits. The US, whose prospects are slightly better than that for Europe and Japan, "has been on the mend from its longest and deepest recession since the Second World War" and the "pace of the recovery has been the weakest in the country's post-recession experience" (United Nations 2011c). The Eurozone area is affected by sovereign debt problems, harsh austerity measures and structural and/or technological unemployment, particularly in Portugal, Italy, Ireland, Greece, Spain and the UK. The prospects for growth rebounding in these economies are very weak in the short to medium term.

Most developing countries, other than the fast-growing emerging economies mentioned above, have been affected by the slowdown in traditional export markets and external financial flows such as FDI, aid and remittances, and have had to implement austerity measures. Some developing countries have been buoyed by increased commodity demand, from China in particular. However, in general it is noted that poverty, hunger and inequality are on the rise in the developing world, in part as a result of the depth of the austerity measures that most governments have been required to implement. It is also important to note that developing countries continue to hemorrhage massive amounts of financial resources to the advanced economies. One of the presumed benefits of the current crisis is the decline of net transfers of financial resources in 2009 (–$545 billion) and 2010 (–$557 billion) from the peak of –$881 billion in 2007. On the other hand, net private capital flows rebounded from the slump in 2008 ($110 billion) to $386 billion in 2009 and $659 billion in 2010 (United Nations 2011d). Similarly, remittances, which also took a dip in 2009 to US$309 billion, rebounded to pre-crisis levels in 2010 ($325 billion) and are expected to rise in 2011 to $349 billion (Mohapatra *et al.* 2011).

These shifts have created a new global social redistribution of income quite unlike the post-World War II model, where the North Atlantic economies were the principal drivers of economic growth that provided the demand push behind late twentieth-century economic development. While the growth of the emerging economies like the BRICS has been rapid, the largest share of global GDP still comes from the G7 economies and the former countries are still very reliant on these markets.

This scenario raises the question of where the new source of world demand and consumption will come from to propel the global economy out of the downturn. Most economies in Latin America, the Caribbean, Africa, the Middle East and Asia, given their levels of external indebtedness, high unemployment and general impoverishment, are not to be that source. On the positive side, one of the potential new engines of growth is the global middle class in emerging economies, and this target group has become far easier to tap into with the growth of global media and the Internet economy. However, is this demand sufficient to compensate for the fall-off in demand from the advanced economies? In effect, the unfolding context is one where workers in the G20 are producing goods and services for markets that are severely constrained in the current global economic crisis. More fundamentally, the situation relates to the tendency for world production to outstrip world consumption during the latter phases of an economic downturn (see Mandel 1984, Wallerstein 1984).

The combination of these structural shifts in the global economy establishes the basis for major instability as the existing international economic regime is challenged by the weight of unrealistic expectations within and across countries. As such, the difficulties of generating consensus among the major economies and the inadequacy of a unified global policy response make for a dangerous economic and political context. Ben Bernanke, chairman of the US Federal Reserve, at the Sixth European Central Bank Central Banking Conference in Frankfurt, Germany in November 2010, argued along similar lines. The following quotation from him is worth highlighting because it captures both the historical dimension of the current crisis as well as the risks of uncoordinated rebalancing of the contemporary global economy:

> As currently constituted, the international monetary system has a structural flaw: It lacks a mechanism, market based or otherwise, to induce needed adjustments by surplus countries, which can result in persistent imbalances. This problem is not new. For example, in the somewhat different context of the gold standard in the period prior to the Great Depression, the United States and France ran large current account surpluses, accompanied by large inflows of gold. However, in defiance of the so-called rules of the game of the international gold standard, neither country allowed the higher gold reserves to feed through to their domestic money supplies and price levels, with the result that the real exchange rate in each country remained persistently undervalued. These policies created deflationary pressures in deficit countries that were losing gold, which helped bring on the Great

Depression. The gold standard was meant to ensure economic and financial stability, but failures of international coordination undermined these very goals. Although the parallels are certainly far from perfect, and I am certainly not predicting a new Depression, some of the lessons from that grim period are applicable today. In particular, for large, systemically important countries with persistent current account surpluses, the pursuit of export-led growth cannot ultimately succeed if the implications of that strategy for global growth and stability are not taken into account.

(Bernanke 2010)

Regardless of the contending perspectives, it is undeniable that the burgeoning protest movements, on both sides of the North Atlantic and in the South, capture public outrage at the fact that a large share of the working classes (the industrial workers, the middle classes and so forth) are paying a debilitating and unequal price for the crisis, as unemployment and inequality continue to remain high and expand. The advanced economies continue to have slow growth, and the policy initiatives are principally focused on imposing stronger austerity measures, rather than stimulating productive economic activity which has the potential to create jobs, boost living standards and significantly mitigate economic hardship. These same economies, however, are constrained by ballooning fiscal deficits and worrisome debt-to-GDP ratios on account of the fall in tax revenue and the burden of bank bailouts and stimulus packages.

The competition between short-term fiscal austerity measures and longer-term growth and expansion policies reminds us that in hard economic times policy debate and political experimentation is at its sharpest and most controversial (Gourevitch 1986). It is also noteworthy that the global economic crisis has erupted at a time when the global economy is integrated, intertwined and inter-dependent as perhaps never before in history. Thus, the impact of this crisis that originated in the advanced industrial countries can be felt sharply in the developing world, which is already grappling with its own internal constraints and structural barriers to sustained development. It is on this basis that Krugman (2008) argues "the spread of the financial crisis to emerging markets makes a global rescue for developing countries part of the solution to the crisis."

Emergent debates about resurgent protectionism, currency wars and alternative reserve currencies suggests that the global economy has entered a phase of heightened geo-economic and political change which will transform the development "equation" in varied and diverse ways. Indeed, the economic and financial crisis is but one element of the global transition, given what is referred to as the "triple crisis" of finance, development and environment with challenges like climate change that underscore the limits of the global economy. It is imperative at this time that development economists and policy-makers should engage with two crucial questions: the implications of these changes for the developing world and the prospects for "development" for the majority of people in the developing world. This volume hopes to contribute to this engagement.

The scope of the book

This is the third volume to emerge from the rigorous academic research and lively discussions among young scholars associated with the Annual Conference on Development and Change (ACDC). The ACDC is an international network of heterodox *young* scholars, mainly development economists, but not exclusively, as it includes sociologists and non-academic practitioners as well. The network has had four conferences, and this volume contains selected chapters from the fourth conference, which was held in Johannesburg in April 2010. Space constraints prevented us from including all the papers presented; we hope this selection showcases the wide variety of angles and approaches with which participants approached the discussion on the global economic crisis and its impact on the developing world. The book is divided into six parts, with one of the parts turning the spotlight on South Africa, given that the conference was held there.

Part I: Insights from history

The first part takes a historical view of some components of globalization and their impact on the developing world. There is also an attempt to understand the current crisis as a part of a longer history of crises. In the opening essay, Mehdi Shafaeddin examines the link between trade liberalization, industrialization and development. Trade liberalization, variously defined as a package consisting of removal of quantitative restrictions on imports, easing (or, in some cases, removal) of import tariffs, removal of export taxes and subsidies, and a general outward orientation, is one the key pillars of neo-liberal prescriptions and is assumed to bring unmitigated benefits and gains from trade, especially for developing countries. Shafaeddin argues for not making this an orthodoxy, and suggests that trade policy should be one of the core ingredients of industrial and development policies. Under this arrangement of integrated and complementary policies, trade liberalization could be used, selectively and gradually, to ensure that industries achieve competitiveness and higher levels of efficiency through technological upgrading. On the other hand, if trade liberalization is seen as an orthodox mantra and as a magic cure, and hence undertaken rapidly and across-the-board and when the industrial foundation of the domestic economy is not ready to take advantage of the opportunities that it offers, the result could be de-industrialization and unemployment. In some cases, it could lock countries into production and export of primary commodities or natural resource-based, extractive industries, or into labor-intensive production, low in the value chain.

Shafaeddin finds that the historical evidence on the performance of successful early and late industrializers is not supportive of the unmitigated benefits of rapid and across-the-board trade liberalization. He shows how Britain protected its industries for nearly 200 years before opening them up to external competition. He recognizes that late industrializers do not have the luxury of time, that they are tremendous pressure to catch up, especially given the reservoir of technology that is already available in the developed world. Also, he demonstrates how the policy space for developing countries has shrunk dramatically, an argument made elsewhere by Chang (2002). For several developing countries, specifically the least developed countries, the inability to resist rapid trade liberalization has not only failed to boost economic growth but also resulted in de-industrialization (defined as the ratio of Manufacturing Value Added to Gross Domestic Product). In the newly industrializing economies of East Asia, since trade liberalization was gradual and selective, undertaken after these countries had reached a level of industrial maturity, the effects were more favorable.

The chapter focuses on the contrasting experiences of Mexico and China to demonstrate two alternative paths to trade liberalization with dramatically different consequences. Mexico was the poster-boy for the neo-liberal school, with rapid and across-the-board liberalization. In contrast, China pursued a more gradual path, using functional and targeted government intervention, focused on "learning-by-doing" and on enhancing capabilities of domestic firms in strategic sectors. More importantly, China's case illustrates the use of trade policy as an integral part of a larger policy framework, rather than as an end in itself.

Keith Nurse's chapter argues that as the world battles yet another "bone-crushing recession" (quote from Krugman, 2008: 181), we need to take a longer view of the crisis by looking at the historical trends in booms and recessions of capitalism. If capitalist development is marked by long-term cyclical trends, then in retrospect, we can argue that this recession was imminent, not a "blip on the curve of ... business as usual". Nurse discusses the analysis of W. Arthur Lewis who suggests that Kondratieff cycles (long waves of forty to sixty years) can provide the key to understand the dynamics of growth in the core economies (the engines of growth); the changes in the terms-of-trade between agriculture and industry and the consequent changes in the core–periphery relations. Nurse suggests that we need to understand and be aware of the consequences of the crisis, in terms of institutional changes, relocation of industries to the periphery as well as the impact on the periphery, as the "engine of growth", namely the core economies, slows down. The premise of the engine-of-growth theory is that countries already on the escalator pull others along as well. However, this logic would break down in the recessionary or downswing phase of the long cycle.

In view of these long-term tendencies, Lewis' argument is that countries of the periphery could either follow the example of the core and engage in industrial deepening and upgrading, or rely on international trade for commodity export. Nurse draws our attention to the fact that Lewis had shown how the former option is open to the relatively large developing countries, like India or China, but not really to smaller economies or the "tropical world". The implications for developing countries in the context of the current economic crisis are clear: if countries rely on trade as the engine of growth, they are bound to suffer significant decline of output, employment and export revenues during downswings, which are inevitable features of capitalist growth over the long run. Nurse's chapter provides detailed empirical evidence on these propositions in the context of the current crisis, in addition to discussing the rise of new centers of economic activity (as witnessed by the rise of China) and the consequent shift in the global balance of power.

Continuing the historical discussion, Bill Freund discusses the dependency theory in view of the African experience during colonialism and thereafter. He argues that contrary to the experience of other colonies (and of Lenin's analysis), African colonies, barring exceptions, were not targets for metropolitan investment, as their societies could not absorb profitable large-scale investments. Thus, the continent by and large specialized in export of raw materials, much in line with the dependency arrangements (another manifestation of which were the imperial preference arrangements), and was thus drastically hit by the precipitous decline in prices during the 1930s depression. However, large parts of Africa were still characterized by largely self-sufficient peasants, basically outside the purview of the colonial/cash economy. Some African economies were abundant in gold and these were able to enjoy unprecedented prosperity, in contrast to agriculture-based societies.

All things considered, Freund argues that the Great Depression meant "lost years" for Africa, where investment and infrastructure suffered, and there emerged a view that development would need to be in focus in order to realize the economic potential of the continent. Turning to the current crisis, Freund argues that the African depression, characterized by disinvestment, de-industrialization and a roll back of the state, began far earlier, and that perhaps the entire last quarter of the twentieth century qualifies for that title, as most economies were not able to find a sustainable growth path. Freund discusses the turn-around in the first decade of the twenty-first century, especially in mineral-based economies, where he suggests that the rise of newly economically powerful countries like China, which have contributed to the rise of the multi-polar world, could have played a role in this turn around. He also suggests that this crisis should be seen as an opportunity rather than simply a disaster, as it presents an chance to break down the uni- or bi-polar world and move towards the creation of a multi-polar world. His chapter ends with a discussion of South Africa, which links directly to Part III which is specifically on South Africa.

Part II: The finance and trade dimension

Vanessa da Costa Val Munhoz and Gilberto Libânio examine the vital and hotly debated issue of comprehensive capital controls: should developing countries introduce capital controls? Would that not act as disincentive for entry of foreign capital? Could it be that too much capital might have an adverse macroeconomic impact on the host economy? Mainstream orthodoxy militates against the idea of any kind of control on the movements of private foreign capital. However, after the Asian crisis of 1997 this discussion re-emerged on the international scene, and several economists have argued that controls on inflows of foreign capital could reduce vulnerability of these economies to financial instabilities. In the wake of the sub-prime crisis, the urgency of regulating capital flows (whether domestic or foreign) cannot be overstated.

The chapter provides an in-depth review of the literature on capital controls and makes a cogent argument in favor of capital controls as a means of reducing vulnerability, of providing greater autonomy for monetary policy and a greater ability for the host country to manipulate exchange rates. It goes on to discuss definitions and concepts of capital controls – very important in understanding the nuances of the debate. In an empirical analysis of fifty-three countries between 1987 and 2007, the authors test for whether capital flows are able to explain the high exchange-rate volatility and loss of monetary policy autonomy. The idea is to examine if the macroeconomic impact of excessive volatility of financial flows can justify a position in favor of capital controls. They find that for the sample of countries without capital controls, their hypothesis is valid (and for the sample of countries with capital controls, the relationship between capital inflows and exchange rates is weakened). Thus, the authors make a strong case for the adoption of capital controls. Seeraj Mohammed's chapter, in Part V, demonstrates the validity of their argument in the context of South Africa.

Aldo Caliari's chapter argues that while the bulk of the policy response to the crisis has focused on the financial measures, the trade dimensions of the crisis tend to be overlooked, except for measures intended to limit protectionism and restore trade finance. This chapter links to the points made by Shafaeddin in the first part of the book, and argues for looking at trade and trade policy as an integral part of a wider development strategy. Coming after decades of reform in developing countries that placed export-led growth as the central paradigm, Caliari examines the role of trade in developing economies during the boom and recession phases and makes two observations. The first is that focus on an improved export performance, without an equal emphasis on the mechanisms by which such exports would yield increased and stable financial gains to the source countries, cannot take the developing countries very far. The second is that the success of a trade-led development model hinges not so much on market access or on trade policy reforms per se, but on redrawing the role of trade in developing country economies and its linkages to a number of external and internal financial structures in those economies. For instance, he points out that sub-Saharan Africa delivered its peak export performance of the last three decades between 2003 and 2008, a period that registered no movement in the WTO Doha Round. This would seem to suggest that lack of market access is not really the central issue it appears to be in official responses, except maybe at the margins.

His main suggestion is that trade can be and ought to be seen as a development finance tool; a tool that helps countries weather, rather than place them at the mercy of, financial cycles. He makes the plea that, therefore, the crisis could be seen as an opportunity to address longstanding issues that have prevented developing countries from a more beneficial trade engagement in the global economy, not only during crises but during more benign times, when it is business as usual.

Leandro Serino's chapter argues that even though Latin America and several other developing countries have not been as badly hit as during some earlier phases, the crisis has affected them through different mechanisms. Some developing countries, especially those implementing inflation-targeting regimes and more integrated into the web of global financial markets (e.g. Peru and Colombia), suffered from the reversal of capital flows as uncertainty spread out and institutional investors decided to move to "safe" financial assets. For several other developing countries, the effects of the crisis have been felt through the trade channel.

The most important channel has been the collapse of world trade between the second half of 2008 and the beginning of 2009. Second, developing countries have been affected through falling external demand, as industrialized economies went into recession and, in spite of the good performance of China, world output contracted in 2009. An additional and "paradoxical" mechanism through which the recent crisis has impacted developing countries has been the fast recovery (and sustained expansion) observed in primary commodity prices, which, after falling strongly, increased by 20 percent in US dollar terms between March 2009 and the time of writing, according to the Index of Primary Commodity Prices elaborated by Argentina's Central Bank. This, a priori, constitutes a positive external shock for natural-resource exporting countries (which many developing countries are), and this is linked in part to expansionary monetary policies that rich economies have put in place to overcome the crisis.

This chapter discusses the impact of all these changes on the economic performance of Argentina. This is an interesting case because the country, first, is a primary commodity exporter, and second, has been implementing a stable and competitive exchange rate regime in recent years. The strategy underpinning both these factors is to promote its non-traditional tradable sector and diminish the vulnerability of the economy to the moods of international financial markets. This analysis focuses on two connected transformations. One is the recovery of the expected 2010 world output growth on the basis of a continuous supportive policy stance and given that persistent vulnerabilities do not undermine the recovery process. The other transformation focuses on the rebound in primary commodity prices and associated improvements in the price of Argentina's traditional exports. Using the analytical framework of a structuralist CGE model, the chapter shows that for Argentina these two effects are positive shocks which are likely to be expansionary. However, Serino argues for an expansionary fiscal policy to make sure there is life after what he calls the "Great Recession".

Part III: The technology and innovation dimension

This part looks at two key issues in the contemporary development challenge: the costs and benefits of bio-fuel production, and the relationship between technology, industrial policies and the process of creative destruction and economic policies.

Luiz Niemeyer examines, through the lens of Brazilian ethanol production, the costs and benefits of renewable fuels such as ethanol. Brazil has the natural resource base to produce ethanol (given the large volume of sugarcane production), and indeed renewable fuels such as ethanol are being promoted as viable alternatives to fossil fuels. However, Niemeyer shows how conventional cost–benefit analysis of ethanol production, which declares it viable, disregards important negative environmental impacts. First, the economic viability of the ethanol production depends strongly on sustained stable oil prices, which are outside the control of Brazil or, for that matter, any ethanol-producing country. Second, he demonstrates a strong negative impact on water quality, as the effluents from ethanol production are discharged into rivers and streams. Third, there are naturally competing claims on the use of water and ethanol, contributing to the increasing competition among different types of water users. Fourth, the production and processing of sugarcane for ethanol production has deleterious effects on air quality – another factor which is not taken into account by the conventional cost–benefit analysis. Fifth, there are trade-offs between food and sugarcane production, with land and other agricultural resources which could be used for the production of food being used for ethanol. This has serious implications for food security for millions of Brazilians.

Thus, if these costs were to be accounted for, it is not clear that ethanol production would be viable. What is needed is a discussion of priorities in the use of scarce resources. The demand for ethanol emanates from the top 20 percent of the income distribution – the car owners. The competing claims over the same resources would fulfill the needs of the remaining 80 percent. The challenge is to put the latter high enough on the development agenda such that policy-makers reassess their priorities.

Mario Cimoli, Elisa Calza, Annalisa Primi and Sebastián Rovira discuss the role of technology and industrial policies specifically in the context of the Latin American response to the global crisis. As they demonstrate, the region has been, relatively speaking, less adversely affected than some other parts of the world. However, they argue that the crisis will nevertheless have important micro-economic consequences on the strategies adopted by firms, on the production structure, on the re-adaptation of learning processes and so forth. In addition, the region has already been dealing with the consequences of the absence of industrial policy; and of the weakness in product diversification and the development of more knowledge-intensive sectors and related technological capabilities. They argue, therefore, that the region should take the crisis as a cue to return to policies aimed at building technological capacities and an industrial structure geared towards more competitive technology-intense sectors. They draw up a very useful "out-of-crisis roadmap". While their analysis is based on the Latin American experience, their conclusion clearly has far-reaching validity.

Part IV: The gender and employment dimension

There is ample evidence suggesting that the impact of economic crises is not neutral in its consequences, and particularly that it affects men and women differently. This view is part of a wider feminist scholarship which argues that the way in which economies and institutions function, not necessarily during a crisis, is gendered. According to this view, gender discrimination is not an aberration but a systemic phenomenon. Izdeş, trained in the feminist tradition, offers this alternative view in her analysis of employment patterns in Turkey. Since the financial liberalization in 1989, Turkey has been through three financial crises (1994, 1999 and 2001) and a significant economic contraction in 1991. The crisis-prone structure, together with high and persistent unemployment, contributes to the strikingly low female labor-force participation and employment.

Özge Izdeş argues that, a priori, female employment could be favorably or unfavorably impacted by a crisis. Favorable segmentation would occur when increasing female employment during a downswing could either be due to women workers' concentration in less volatile jobs, or to substitution of cheaper female workers for male workers (the substitution hypothesis), or maybe to a combination of the two. Similarly, women may be disproportionately shed because of the vulnerable positions they hold in the labor market (unfavorable segmentation). Decomposition of changes in female employment across cycles allows us to distinguish segmentation (favorable and unfavorable) from the buffer (gender-specific characteristics of women's participation make them more disposable in times of crisis) and the substitution cases.

She finds that, for Turkey, different crises have seen different effects on gendered pattern of employment. In the first round of the unemployment cycle following the 2001 crisis, the burden of the crisis seems to have fallen on male workers. However, persistent and high unemployment disproportionately affected women workers in the second round of the unemployment cycle from 2003 onwards. Overall, in the 2001 crisis women's share of employment decreased, and women who preserved their jobs and made small employment gains were in the less cyclically sensitive sectors or occupations (favorable segmentation). Her analysis points to the need for a nuanced analysis and the willingness to recognize that just as "one size fits all" is not the right dictum for policy, it might not be the correct way of understanding the impact of crises either. Effects may vary across time and space, and only rigorous research can pinpoint these differences and help formulate policies accordingly.

Jason Jackson's chapter provides a framework to think more broadly about the gendered impacts in the trade and production sphere during economic crises. Despite important differences across countries and regions, Jackson argues that women tend bear a disproportionate share of the burden arising from economic crises due to their gendered responsibilities in households and the community, as well their often-tenuous employment security and limited access to formal unemployment benefits. The chapter points towards regional variation by comparing the effects of the crisis across sub-Saharan Africa, South Asia, the Caribbean and the Pacific. It shows that, regardless of region, developing countries have been affected by the crisis through similar channels: contracting global demand for exports and declining commodity prices, falling tourism arrivals and revenue, as well as declining remittances and increased pressure on already weak fiscal positions. However, while the mechanisms of transmission have been similar, differences in local social and economic structures have resulted in important variations in the ultimate effect of the crisis. In line with Izdeş' contribution, this chapter argues for recognizing the diversity in outcomes and provides a macroeconomic policy framework that demonstrates how government interventions aimed at promoting a recovery can be re-engineered to target vulnerable groups – such as low-income women-headed households – and hence provide more broad-based benefits from stimulus plans and other recovery efforts.

Part V: The scenario for big developing states – the case of South Africa

The two chapters in this part can be linked to Bill Freund's chapter in the first part of the book, whose historical overview has a special section on South Africa. The special focus on South Africa in this volume stems simply from the fact that it was the host country for the conference. Seeraj Mohammed's chapter suggests that despite the reasonable GDP rate of growth of 5 percent per annum, the South African economy was already in a crisis before the onset of the global financial crisis. Unemployment had been over 20 percent for a decade; decline in manufacturing employment suggests de-industrialization and there is clear evidence of debt-driven consumption. The global crisis accelerated unemployment and further aggravated the domestic economic crisis. As mentioned above, Mohammed's chapter provides support to the da Costa Val Munhoz–Libânio argument in Part II by showing how the rapid growth of short-term capital flows can have various undesirable effects on the host economy: currency appreciation, adversely affecting the competitiveness of exports; and increased credit used not for productive investment, but for debt-driven consumption and for speculation in financial and real estate markets. Of course, the crisis would not be as deep as it is had it not been for some inherent weaknesses of the industrial structure (e.g. an industrial sector centered on mineral extraction), which the chapter discusses.

Fiona Tregenna's chapter focuses on inequality and unemployment during the growth and recovery process in South Africa. This is a country with one of the highest levels of inequality in the world, which is rooted in the country's apartheid history. However, seventeen years of democracy have not enabled a lowering of inequality rates, with some studies suggesting that these might have gone up in recent years. In this context, an increase in unemployment during the crisis, ceteris paribus, would result in an increase in inequality, even with the caveat that unemployment is only one of the drivers of inequality. It is too soon to empirically examine the role of the global crisis in explaining inequality in South Africa. However, the trends outlined by Tregenna are instructive and revealing, as she analyzes the relative contributions of unemployment and earnings dispersion to inequality using both static and dynamic decomposition methods.

Tregenna's analysis, covering the period 2001–2007, finds that not only is there a very strong relationship between unemployment and overall income inequality (not surprising given that overall income inequality is calculated for both the employed and unemployed), but also that there is a strong relationship between income inequality *among the employed* and unemployment. Using dynamic decomposition, Tregenna divides the overall period into two parts: the first where both unemployment and inequality were increasing (2001–2002), and the second, the period in which both were falling (2002–2007). During the first period, in which both unemployment and inequality rose, increases in the unemployment rate accounted for 77 percent of the increase in earnings inequality within the labor force. Both unemployment and inequality fell in the second period, with the decrease in the unemployment rate explaining 72 percent of the decrease in inequality. These results highlight the huge importance of the unemployment rate in explaining earnings inequality, during both rises and falls of inequality and unemployment.

Part VI: The scenario for small developing states – the Caribbean

Through this part we try to redress the imbalance in several publications, including in the heterodox tradition, of marginalizing (perhaps unwittingly) the smallest and in many ways the most vulnerable countries in the global economy. We have two chapters on the Caribbean region. The first, by David Tennant, focuses on Jamaica and how firms there responded to early warning signals of financial and economic turmoil. The ability to recognize early warning signals as well as mechanisms to cope with them is important, as they help cushion the adverse impact of the crisis. He finds that the unresponsiveness of some Jamaican businesses to the early warning signs of the crisis, along with immediate reactions of other firms to lay off workers and reduce the use of local inputs, however, contributed to a 21.7 percent increase in the number of unemployed persons in the Jamaican labor force between 2007 and 2009. This, along with substantial underemployment, made it more difficult for the Jamaican economy to navigate through the downturn. His analysis fits in neatly with the previous two chapters, as his empirical results indicate that businesses which are more likely to immediately resort to laying off workers are those that experience a decrease in the availability of credit and a reduction in the prices of their goods, thus once again underscoring the importance of traditional financial and trade linkages in the international transmission of crises.

Jessica Jones' chapter examines the impact of the global crisis on remittances to the Caribbean region, which are an important component of the balance of payments of the region. Data clearly show that remittances have fallen substantially as a result of the crisis. Moreover, unemployment and a lack of job opportunities will compel some workers to return home to the Caribbean. Since return migration is one of the factors upon which remittance flows are dependent, Jones investigates if the Caribbean can benefit from return migration as a way to mitigate the slowdown in remittances. She examines remittance data from several Caribbean countries, looking at the dynamics of migration in the region. Her results suggest that remittances, which declined across the board for the Caribbean Community (CARICOM) member states, fluctuating sharply for some countries after the crisis, have leveled off but are unlikely to stabilize at pre-crisis rates in the near future. Further, due to the global nature of the crisis, significant risks remain for remittance flows to the Caribbean, thus making the problem of external financing significant and going beyond the short term.

She examines each country in the region separately, and thus provides for a rich and nuanced understanding. Given the lack of policy space and high levels of international integration, she argues for the need to balance short-term economic stabilization measures with long-term strategies for sustainable growth. One such strategy would be to take advantage of any return migration which may accompany the global economic downturn and recovery. She suggests that even if the volume of return migration turns out not to be that substantial, the measures that would need to be put in place to encourage people to resettle would enhance the region's long-term prospects for research and development, facilitating easy investment by those who remain overseas, and may actually have a sustained multiplier effect on encouraging return migration.

We hope not only that this collection contributes to the growing volume of academic literature on the global crisis, but that the analysis contained in these pages is useful in the urgently needed dialogue towards alternative policies.

References

Bernanke, B.S. (2010). "Rebalancing the Global Recovery". Speech at the Sixth European Central Bank Central Banking Conference, Frankfurt, Germany, November 19.

Canuto, O. and Yifu Lin, J. (2011). "Introduction", in M.K. Nabli (ed.), *The Great Recession and Developing Countries: Economic Impact and Growth Prospects*. Washington, DC: The World Bank, p. 9.

Chang, H.-J. (2002). *Kicking Away the Ladder – Development Strategy in Historical Perspective*. London: Anthem Press.

Financial Times (2011a) "China bill passes, currency falls", October 12.

Financial Times (2011b) "China's trade growth slows", 13 October.

Freund, C. (2011). "Rebalancing Trade after the Crisis", in M. Haddad and B. Shepherd (eds), *Managing Openness: Trade and Outward-Oriented Growth after the Crisis*. Washington, DC: The World Bank, pp. 41–54.

Gourevitch, P.A. (1986). *Politics in Hard Times: Comparative Responses to International Economic Crises*. Cornell Studies in Political Economy. Ithaca, NY: Cornell University Press.

ILO/OECD (2011) *Short-Term Employment and Labour Market Outlook and Key Challenges in G20 Countries*. A statistical update for the G20 Meeting of Labour and Employment Ministers, Paris, 26–27 September.

Krugman, P. (2008). *The Return of Depression Economics and the Crisis of 2008*. London: Penguin Books, p. 187.

Mandel, E. (1984). "Explaining Long Waves of Capitalist Development" In: C. Freeman (ed.), *Long Waves in the World Economy*. London: Frances Pinter, pp. 195–201.

Mohapatra, S., Ratha, D. and Silwa, A. (2011). "Remittance Flows Recover to Pre-crisis Levels". Outlook for Remittance Flows 2011–13: Migration and Development Brief 16, May.

Nurse, K. (2010). "Development: Unthinking the Past", *NACLA* 4 March [republication of 2003 article].

Serven, L. and Nguyen, H. (2011). "Global Imbalances: Past and Future", in M. Haddad and B. Shepherd (eds), *Managing Openness: Trade and Outward-Oriented Growth after the Crisis*. Washington, DC: The World Bank, pp. 27–40.

The Economist (2011) "Be afraid", 1 October, p. 13.

United Nations (2011a). *World Economic Situation and Prospects 2011*. New York, NY: United Nations, p. 61.

United Nations (2011b). *World Economic Situation and Prospects 2011*. New York, NY: United Nations, p. 35.

United Nations (2011c). *World Economic Situation and Prospects 2011*. New York, NY: United Nations, p. 3.

United Nations (2011d). *World Economic Situation and Prospects 2011*. New York, NY: United Nations, pp. 69–74.

Wallerstein, I. (1984). "Long Waves as Capitalist Process." *Review* 7(4): 559–574.

Part I

Insights from history

2 Trade liberalization, industrialization and development[1]

The experience of recent decades

Mehdi Shafaeddin

1 Introduction

> *We cannot go back to the past. But neither should we fail to recognize the failures of the present.*
>
> (Stiglitz, 2005: 32)

Is trade liberalization conducive to industrialization and development? The purpose of this chapter is to argue that trade liberalization is necessary for industrialization if it is regarded as part and parcel of a package of dynamic and flexible trade and industrial policies, and is undertaken at the right time, gradually and selectively. More importantly, trade policy should be an ingredient of a comprehensive set of industrial and development policies and measures to enhance the capabilities of firms for establishing industries, making them efficient and upgrading them. By contrast, if trade liberalization is undertaken prematurely, rapidly and uniformly – i.e. across the board – it will lead to de-industrialization and unemployment; it will lock the country in specialization in production and export of primary commodities and, at best, natural-resource based products and/ or labour-intensive assembly operations.

We will first review the background to, and features of, the trade liberalization hypothesis (TLH). To examine the validity of the TLH, we will then shed some light on the historical experience of the successful early and late industrializers, in section 3. Subsequently, we will refer, in section 4, to the results of trade liberalization forced on colonies during the colonial era. The increased need for infant-industry support in the case of late industrializers and the characteristics of trade liberalization during recent decades, as compared with the colonial era, will be studied in sections 5 and 6. Section 7 will be devoted to the examination of available evidence on the result of trade liberalization in more recent decades. In section 8, the contrasting experiences of China and Mexico will be examined. The final section will conclude the study and discuss the policy implications of our findings for developing countries.

2 The trade liberalization hypothesis: background and features

The dominant views of scholars on trade and industrial policies have gone through considerable changes since the Great Depression of the 1930s, shifting from one extreme to the other. The Great Depression led to beggar-my-neighbour policies in industrialized countries of the time, and across-the-board import substitution in developing countries. Nevertheless, import substitution as an official trade and industrial policy of developing countries only began following the Second World War. During this period until the early 1980s two tendencies were observed.

The first was the one observed in East Asian countries following the initial experience of the Republic of Korea. Facing a severe balance-of-payments constraint around 1958, Korea began to stimulate exports of manufactured goods. With experiencing some success in export expansion, the combination of import substitution and export promotion became the official policy of the Korean government till around the mid-1990s, when the industrial structure of the country became more or less consolidated. Learning from Japan, the country began a process of dynamic trade policy resembling the flying-geese model, by which it initially restricted imports of some consumer goods but left imports of intermediate inputs and machinery relatively free. Subsequently, it gradually liberalized imports of those consumer goods and tried to penetrate the international market. To do so, the government provided some export subsidies. Meanwhile, it embarked on import substitution of some imported intermediate products used in the established industries. When such industries reached the stage of maturity, it began liberalizing them, and ventured into machinery manufacturing and heavy industries by providing these sectors with government support. This dynamic process of mixed import substitution/export penetration and upgrading of the industrial structure continued till more recent decades (see Shafaeddin, 2005a; Lall, 1996; Huang, 2002; Amsden, 1989).

A somewhat similar, although not necessarily exactly the same, process took place in a few other East Asian countries/territories, i.e., Singapore, Hong Kong and Taiwan, Province of China (together with Korea, these countries made up the so-called "gang of four").

In the meantime, many developing countries continued a long process of "traditional import substitution" – i.e. across-the-board protection – as against temporary infant-industry protection as an element of a dynamic trade policy. These countries gradually faced balance-of-payments problems, which intensified after the oil price rise of 1973–1974 and the subsequent debt crisis.

In the early 1970s, Little et al. (1970), confusing the infant-industry argument with "traditional import substitution" and misinterpreting the Prebisch thesis on industrialization, attributed the success of the "gang of four" to an "outward-oriented industrial strategy" (see also Baldwin, 1969). Subsequently, a number of other neoliberals, such as Krueger (1974, 1978), Balassa (1980, 1989) and Bhagwati (1978), put forward strong arguments against the infant-industry thesis and presented their "trade liberalization hypothesis". Thus across-the-board trade liberalization became an ingredient of conditionalities in the Structural Adjust-ment Programmes (SAPs) and Stabilization Programmes (SPs) of the interna-tional financial institutions (IFIs) in the early 1980s. In the early 1990s the IFIs went further by propagating the "Washington Consensus" initiated by John Williamson (1990).

2.1 Elements and features of the trade liberalization hypothesis

While the views expressed by various neoliberals and neoliberal institutions are not exactly the same, one may outline the common elements of the trade liberali-zation hypothesis as follows:

- removal of import quotas, import licences and other quantitative restrictions, or their initial replacement with tariffs;
- subsequent reduction of the level and dispersion of import tariff rates;
- devaluation of the national currency in order to compensate for the removal of protection or remedy over-valuation of the exchange rate;
- removal of export taxes and subsidies; and
- privatization of ownership of productive firms.

Emphasis was placed on outward orientation and market orientation, uniformity of the nominal tariff structure, and universality of the hypothesis (i.e. universal appli-cability of the TLH). Outward orientation, it was argued, requires neutrality of incentives for production for both the domestic and international markets. Market orientation implies the lack of (or minimal) government intervention in the economy and in the flow of trade. Uniformity of the nominal tariff structure would imply the need for across-the-board trade liberalization of various sectors and indus-tries. The ultimate goal is zero tariff rates for all activities. Nevertheless, a low and across-the-board tariff rate of 10–20 per cent is exceptionally accepted, for revenue purposes, by some neoliberals. Similarly, it is argued that devaluation will provide uniform incentives for all tradables (Krueger, 1978: Chapter 4). Universality implies that the hypothesis is applicable to all developing countries, irrespective of their level of development and industrial capacity, and to each country over time.

Neoliberals seem to regard trade liberalization as an end per se, rather than a means to industrialization and development. Some neoliberals argue, in fact, that developing countries should undertake unilateral trade liberalization even if developed countries do not do so (Corden, 1993; see also Kowalski et al., 2009)!

Even when some government intervention is accepted, it is to "enable" or "facilitate" a country's "current comparative advantage" (read: static compara-tive advantage) rather than achieving dynamic comparative advantage and devel-opment (see, for example, Justin Lin in Lin and Chang, 2009). Williamson (1990: 19), advocate of the "Washington Consensus", has confessed that "none of the ideas spawned by ... development literature ... plays an essential role in motivating the Washington Consensus..."

2.2 The philosophy behind the trade liberalization hypothesis

The TLH is based on the assumption that trade liberalization leads to static and dynamic efficiency gains through stimulating investment, export expansion and GDP growth as well as export and output diversification in favour of manufactured goods (Bhagwati, 1988: 36; Krueger, 1980; World Bank, 1987: 21–22). In the particular case of the World Bank, in more recent years the Bank has admitted the failure of across-the-board liberalization, the risk in indiscriminate opening of the capital account, the importance of "country specificities" in drawing up policies, and a superior performance of countries which have not followed orthodox policies. For example:

> In retrospect, it is *clear* [our italics] that in the 1990s we often mistook efficiency gains for growth. The "one size fits all" policy reform approach to economic growth and the belief in "best practices" exaggerated the gains from improved resource allocation and their dynamic repercussions, and proved to be both *theoretically incomplete and contradicted the evidence* [our italics]. Expectations that gains in growth would be won entirely through policy improvements were unrealistic. Means were often mistaken for goals – that is, improvements in policies were mistaken for growth strategies, as if improvements in policies were an end in themselves.
>
> (World Bank, 2005: 11)

Yet in the end the Bank recommends "across-the-board", uniform and "accelerated" trade and financial liberalization, significant devaluation, deregulation of domestic and foreign investment, etc. (see World Bank, 2005 and Shafaeddin, 2006a for more details).

The philosophy behind the TLH is the theory of static comparative cost advantage, although sometimes lip service is paid to the dynamic issues. Such a philosophy has also been the basis of conditionalities imposed on developing countries, not only by the IFIs but also by developed countries directly, through multilateral (World Trade Organization [WTO]), regional and bilateral trade agreements, and practices of donors since the early 1980s. In the negotiations for Economic Partnership Agreements (EPAs), for example, the European Union (EU) demands trade liberalization by the African, Caribbean and Pacific (ACP) countries (most of which are some of the least-developed countries) on a reciprocal basis and tries to impose "WTO-plus" conditions on them.

Has trade liberalization led to export expansion and diversification? Has it stimulated investment and growth of manufacturing value added (MVA) and GDP?

3 The experience of successful industrializers[2]

The historical evidence on the performance of successful early and late industrializers is not supportive of the TLH. In fact, their experience, including that of

Great Britain as the first industrializer, indicates that, with the exception of Hong Kong, Province of China, all have gone through an infant-industry phase. Hong Kong was a city territory; moreover, its ability to upgrade its industrial structure was limited. While different countries did not follow exactly the same path, all learned from the experience of others; the USA learned from Great Britain, Germany from the USA, Japan from Germany and the Republic of Korea from Japan, etc. (Shafaeddin, 1998). In all cases, functional and selective government intervention was not confined to trade; the state also intervened through other means, directly and indirectly, to encourage savings, to promote investment, to develop agriculture and the necessary institutions and infrastructure, and to provide facilities for training. Foreign direct investment (FDI) was also used and targeted to specific areas to enhance industrialization. In all cases, including Great Britain, industrialization began on a selective basis, although to different degrees, and continued in the same manner until the industrial sector was consolidated. When their industries matured, the industrial countries began to liberalize, also selectively and gradually.

In all cases, industrialization was supported by attention to and growth in agricultural production. The Corn Laws in Great Britain (see below) and protection of rice production in Japan and other East Asian countries are only two examples.

Premature trade liberalization, whether by early industrializers, by colonies or, in more recent decades, by developing countries, has been disappointing. In the particular case of the USA, when it tried to liberalize prematurely in 1847–1861, the industrial sector suffered and the country had to revert to protectionism.

All main early industrializers tried to open the markets in other countries when their industrial sector matured by using tariffs as a tool of bargaining in trade negotiations, or even by force or political pressure (see below).

3.1 The particular case of Great Britain as the first industrializer

The literature on the use of infant-industry support by such countries as the USA, Germany, France, Japan, the Republic of Korea, etc., which industrialized after Great Britain, is ample. But it is interesting to note that, contrary to the contention of some famous classical and neoclassical economists such as Adam Smith and Alfred Marshall, Great Britain, the first early industrializer, also undertook infant-industry protection.

Marshall (1920) attributed the industrialization of the country to the industrial revolution, cultural issues related to "the spirit of economic nationality ... patriotism ... [and] pride in their [Englishmen's] work" (ibid.: 32), and the introduction of the policy of free trade around the 1860s (ibid.: 10, 89). Smith (1776) maintained that Great Britain achieved industrialization despite its protectionist policies. The historical evidence contradicts these views (see Box 2.1).

Box 2.1   Great Britain, the first industrializer

The beginnings of the process of industrialization in Great Britain can be traced back a couple of centuries before the Industrial Revolution of the eighteenth century, although the latter accelerated the process. By around 1700, industrial production already accounted for about 20 per cent of the country's total income. Trade restrictions begun by Elizabeth I (1553–1603) sharply increased in 1690 and continued until around the 1860s. "As of 1820, Great Britain showed the highest rate of tariffs on imports of manufactured goods (50 per cent) in Europe" (Shafaeddin, 2005b: 157 and Table 7.2).

The country's industrialization process has some features in common with those of other successful early and late industrializers. Protection was selective, and trade policy was dynamic and flexible. Protection started with woollen and cotton cloths and iron, and eventually extended to shipbuilding and restrictions on transportation through the Navigation Act (1651). The agricultural sector was also protected through the Corn Law of 1434, followed by the Corn Bounty Act (1614–1689) and the Corn Law of 1815. The government prohibited the sale of imported grain to millers, unless the home price exceeded a certain limit. Moreover, exports of some products, such as wheat, were subsidized.

The government also intervened extensively, particularly after 1760, in other areas: to encourage savings, investment and scientific activities; to develop infrastructure, roads, waterways and railways; to provide facilities for training; to establish necessary institutions, etc. The Bank of England was established in 1694; small and provincial banks, banking houses and private banks were established in 1716; saving banks were established in 1798. To encourage investment, the law of partnership was passed, joint stock companies were initiated, insurance services were developed and the stock market was created.

When Great Britain consolidated its industrial base, after over two centuries of protection, the government began reducing its tariffs gradually, over a period of nearly 30 years, beginning in 1833. The Corn Law and Navigation Act were abolished in 1846 and 1849, respectively, before a policy of free trade took hold (around 1850–1860). Further, the nature of government intervention changed in other areas. Many ineffective regulations were abolished between 1760 and 1850. Around the early nineteenth century the government began to take a more positive role in the economy, but its intervention did not cease even after the 1850s (Deane, 1965: 232).

Source: Based on Shafaeddin (2005b: 156–165)

---

4 The impact of forced trade liberalization imposed on colonies

Free trade policy was forced on colonies, semi-colonies and independent countries through the so-called "5 per cent rule" and "unequal" bilateral treaties, mostly during the first half of the nineteenth century. Under the 5 per cent rule, 5 per cent was the maximum tariff rate allowed on any item imported by colonies of Great Britain. When a country did not submit, military force was employed (e.g. the imposition of the Opium War of 1839–1842 on China). To deprive the colonies of new technology, Britain prohibited exportation of machinery to, and its use in, the colonies until the 1830s. High-value-added manufacturing activities were outlawed in the colonies and exports of competing items from colonies to England were banned. Instead, production of primary products was encouraged (Chang, 2005a).

The result of the forced liberalization was sluggish growth, de-industrialization and destruction of handicrafts of the colonies (Bagchi, 1982: 32–39). The Latin American countries modified their commercial policies from 1880 onwards, while some other countries did so between 1913 and the Great Depression of 1929 (Bairoch, 1993: 41–42 and Chapter 8). As can be seen in Table 2.1, during the height of compulsory liberal trade regimes (1800–1880) growth in per capita income was negative in the Third World. Only after 1880, when the Third World began to gradually regain its policy autonomy, did the per capita income of the group begin to accelerate (see also Chang, 2005b: 30–34). Generally speaking, "in all parts of the developing world economic growth accelerated after the end of imperialism" (ibid.: 32). Growth also accelerated during 1950–1980 as the remaining colonial territories gained independence and were able to implement their own trade policies.

The de-industrialization effect of the forced liberal trade policy imposed on the Third World was between 85 and 95 per cent; i.e. in the absence of trade liberalization the size of the manufacturing sector of the Third World would have been 85 to 95 per cent larger (Bairoch, 1993: 88). For example, in the case of the Indian textiles sector, it is estimated that the de-industrialization effect was equal to the destruction of between 55 and 75 per cent of national consumption around 1870–1880, and 95 to 99 per cent in 1880–1900 (Bagchi, 1982: 32–39, 82–83; Chang, 2005b: 61).

5 The increased need for infant-industry support in late industrializers

In the case of Great Britain, the process of infant-industry support lasted over 200 years before the country consolidated its industrial structure. By contrast, to

Table 2.1 Annual average growth rates[a] in per capita GNP, 1800–1980

Period	Third World[b]	Developed countries
1800–1830	−0.2	0.6
1830–1870	0	1.1
1870–1880	0	0.5
1880–1890	0.1	0.9
1890–1900	0.2	1.7
1900–1950	0.45	1.34
1950–1980	1.7	3.4

Source: Based on Bairoch (1993): 53 and Chang (2005): 30–40.

Notes
a Three-year average.
b Excluding China.

be able to catch up, the time pressure on late industrializers has increased over time, particularly during recent decades (Shafaeddin, 2005b). The more backward is a country, the greater is the need for acceleration of the process of industrialization in order to catch up with the early industrializers – yet the wider will be its competence gap. While the need for government intervention in the process of industrialization has increased, the policy space of the latecomers has shrunk. To begin with, the pace of technological development has accelerated and the technological gap between the industrial countries and the late industrializers has grown. In the case of Great Britain, the emergence of new technology was dependent on invention, which was a slow process. For the late industrializers, some technology is already available elsewhere. Therefore, there is a need for application, adaptation or imitation of the existing technology. But the technology is not available readily and freely. Further, as the pace of technological development accelerates and technology becomes more complicated, the longer will be the period needed for technological learning (see, for example, Lall, 2004).

Second, during the industrial revolution firms were relatively small. Over time, the size of established firms of industrial countries has enlarged, international market power has become more and more concentrated, and thus monopoly and oligopoly power has increased in the international market. Large established firms enjoy the advantages of increasing returns to scale. Barriers to entry for newcomer firms have increased, inter alia, because of the strategic behaviour of large firms which can exercise their Schumpeterian "creative destruction".

Third, the combination of the time pressure, technological gap, capital intensity of production and large scale of operations increases the need for investment and savings, thus putting pressure on consumption. At the same time, population growth and change in tastes due to the appearance of foreign goods increase demand for luxury consumption, reducing the savings necessary for investment (Gerschenkron, 1962).

Fourth, even if the required savings were available, the higher the rate of growth needed for catching up, the faster would be the required rate of social, institutional and infrastructural changes, and hence the greater the need for government intervention to deal with these issues.

In more recent decades, the risks of investment by new firms have also increased. According to Lazonick (1991), a newcomer firm faces risks related to productive uncertainty (the risk related to the development of a product and the utilization of productive capacity) as well as competitive uncertainty (related to the rivalry of established firms such as transnational corporations [TNCs]). One can add risks related to the fallacy of composition (Blecker and Razmi, 2008), development of protectionism in the main international markets, increased exposure to world demand and increased frequency of booms and busts during international business cycles, and volatility in the foreign exchange market.

FDI provides marketing channels to international markets, but the objectives of the TNCs are different from the development objectives of the host countries, and their contribution to development is limited unless they are managed. Even then, they can only supplement the capabilities of local firms.

The increase in risks requires the provision of higher rewards (expected income) for newcomer firms. In other words, the newcomer firms need more support and a greater degree of nurturing than before. Yet the policy space of developing countries has declined, for the reasons mentioned below.

6 The characteristics of trade liberalization during recent decades

One can draw an analogy between the trade liberalization during recent decades and that imposed on colonies during the eighteenth and nineteenth centuries. For example, when Great Britain consolidated its industrial base and enjoyed technological supremacy, the government opened its market to imports. Meanwhile, it tried to open up the markets of its colonies to its exports through the so-called unequal treaties (1810–1850) and the 5 per cent rule, together with equal taxes imposed on their domestically produced goods. If a trade treaty was not accepted by a country, it was forced on it by war (e.g. the Opium Wars imposed on China). All colonies were forced to give preference to products of the mother country (Bairoch, 1993: 41–43). The Fair Trade League Act of 1881 (through which retaliatory import taxes were imposed on imports of manufactured goods from colonies) was used as an instrument of reciprocity to open up the markets of other countries. Further, as mentioned earlier, England prohibited exports of machinery to the colonies.

During recent decades, developed countries have sought to open the markets of developing countries by other means. For example, according to Peter Mandelson, then EU Trade Commissioner, "The aims of our trade policy should be to achieve better market access for European goods and services worldwide" (Mandelson, 2005). He has repeated this statement in different forms many times on various occasions (see Curtis, 2006). Thus developing countries have been pushed, through the SAPs and SPs of the World Bank and International Monetary Fund (IMF) and through bilateral trade agreements, to open their markets (Chang, 2005a: 10; Shafaeddin, 1998). Towards this end, the unequal treaties of old were replaced by "unequal trade agreements" and letters of credit, and denial of loans or financial aid by IFIs and donors took the place of military intervention. For example, according to EU officials, "poor countries will receive EU aid and improved treatment on trade if they sign up to deepening liberalization" (Curtis, 2006: 3). Reciprocity is now imposed on low-income countries through EPAs rather than through the Fair Trade League Act. When 10 per cent import duties are allowed in exceptional cases for fiscal reasons, it is also recommended that a 10 per cent value-added tax be imposed on the sale of similar domestically produced goods. Production of high-value-added products in developing countries is not prohibited, but it is constrained by unfair competitive pressure from imports, and hampered by tariff peaks and escalation and arbitrary and unjustified anti-dumping and countervailing measures (Shafaeddin, 2010). Exports of machinery are not prohibited, but transfer of technology to developing countries is restricted through the WTO Agreement on Trade-Related Aspects of Intellectual Property Rights (TRIPS). Further, severe loss of policy space is experienced by developing countries through such other WTO agreements as the Agreement on Trade-Related Investment Measures (TRIMs), General Agreement on Trade in Services (GATS) and the Agreement on Subsidies and Countervailing Measures (see Shafaeddin, 2010). Summarizing the impact of the first three agreements (TRIPS, TRIMs and GATS), Wade (2005) concludes that "With a touch of hyperbole the agreements could be called a slow-motion Great Train Robbery". Even more policy space will be lost if the demands of developed countries during the ongoing Doha Round of multilateral trade negotiations are met and the EPAs, with their "WTO-plus" conditions, come into effect. In fact, if the EPAs are finalized it will be the last nail in the coffin of the industrial sectors of ACP countries which are at early stages of development (see Oxfam, 2008; Shafaeddin, 2010).

In short, in recent decades the means of pressure on developing countries to liberalize across the board, universally, and most often prematurely, have been economic rather than political or military. But the result has been the same as that during the colonial era: de-industrialization of countries at early stages of industrialization. We will return to this issue below.

7 Recent experience in trade liberalization[3]

While across-the-board import substitution and prolonged protection have led to inefficiency and failure, the experience of developing countries in implementing the TLH during recent decades has also been disappointing. However, the neoliberals and the neoliberal-oriented institutions try to convince us to the contrary (see, for example, Sachs and Warner, 1995).[4] The studies undertaken by the neoliberals suffer from many methodological problems. In fact, the results of cross-sectional studies undertaken by other scholars have revealed little or no evidence that there was any statistically significant correlation between trade openness and economic growth in recent decades (Rodriguez and Rodrik, 1999; Rodrik, 1997; Wacziarg and Welch, 2003; Moguillansky and Bielschowsky, 2001; Di Maio, 2008). More importantly, UNDP (2003) finds a positive correlation between a country's tariff rate and growth rate for the 1990s. There is also some evidence that trade liberalization has led to de-industrialization of low-income countries, particularly in sub-Saharan Africa (Bennell, 1998; Shafaeddin, 1995; Noorbakhsh and Paloni, 2000; Thoburn, 2002).[5]

According to Stiglitz (2005: 31): "Today the inadequacies of Washington Consensus reform [in general] are apparent…" He maintains that stabilization policies do not ensure either growth or stability; the benefits of trade liberalization are questionable, particularly as "workers move from low-productivity jobs to unemployment" instead of moving to high-productivity jobs; capital market liberalization does not necessarily lead to faster growth and exposes the countries to higher risks; privatization often leads to higher prices of utilities; and the adverse social consequences of wrong policies imposed on developing countries have been seen in many countries (ibid.: 16–18).

The results of our own studies on the experience of developing countries in trade liberalization are mixed, depending on the stage of industrialization of the country which undertakes liberalization and the way it has been done. We have studied a sample of fifty developing countries for the period 1980–2000. Then, we repeated the analysis for the period 2000–2004 in order to examine the possible impact of the lag between liberalization and economic performance as well as the degree of vulnerability of the countries during the economic slowdown in the early years of the decade (Shafaeddin, 2006a, 2006b). The study for the 1980–2000 period shows that twenty countries experienced rapid expansion of exports of manufactured goods. In several countries, mostly East Asian newly industrializing economies (NIEs), rapid export growth was also accompanied by fast expansion of industrial supply capacity (MVA) and upgrading. In these countries, after they had reached a certain level of industrial maturity, trade liberalization took place gradually and selectively. By contrast, the performance of the remaining countries, mostly in Africa and Latin America (majority cases), was not satisfactory. These countries embarked, in the main, on a process of structural reform in the 1980s, including uniform, across-the-board and often premature trade liberalization. They further intensified their liberalization efforts in the 1990s. Consequently, half of the sample countries, mostly low-income ones, have faced de-industrialization. In cases where manufactured exports grew extremely fast, such as Mexico, MVA did not accelerate and little upgrading of the industrial base took place. In the 1990s Mexico achieved an annual average manufactured export growth rate of about 30 per cent, yet its corresponding growth rate of MVA did not exceed 4 per cent, as against an average of 7.5 per cent for Malaysia, Thailand, Indonesia and Singapore (Shafaeddin, 2005b: Table 2.1) and its own MVA growth rate of about 7 per cent in the 1960s.

In the case of low-income countries, the example of Ghana is telling. Despite two decades of reform, Ghana's annual average growth in MVA was significantly negative during the 1990s (−3.5 per cent). Further, the liberalization efforts did not encourage exports of manufactured goods beyond some wood-processing, the production capacity of which in the late 1990s remained in fact below the level of the mid-1970s (ibid.: 46–48). Although the country's growth performance has somewhat improved in subsequent years, mainly due to high commodity prices, the sustainability of growth is questionable as investment has not picked up much.

The reform programmes designed by IFIs failed to stimulate private investment, particularly in the manufacturing sector; the ratio of investment to GDP fell even in cases where the inflow of FDI was considerable, including Mexico and a number of other Latin American countries. While trade liberalization changed the structure of incentives in favour of exports, the balance between risk and return shifted away from the manufacturing sector in favour of non-tradable activities and speculation in property. In contrast to traditional import-substitution strategy, the outward-orientation strategies reduced the incentive for investment in the manufacturing sector due to the reduction in its profit margin resulting from competitive pressure from imports. At the same time, it increased the risks of investment for the reasons mentioned earlier.

Generally speaking, in the "majority cases", trade liberalization has led to the development and reorientation of the industrial sector in accordance with static comparative advantage. Resource-based industries and some labour-intensive activities, such as assembly operations, expanded in most countries and little upgrading took place. In fact, some labour-intensive industries also shut down, leading to significant layoffs as resources did not shift to new activities, except for shifts to resource-based and speculative activities, as predicted by neoliberals.

The performance of two categories of industries in the particular case of Latin America was, however, exceptional: industries that were near maturity and/or that had been dynamic during the import-substitution era. Both categories continued to be dynamic in terms of production, exports and investment. The aerospace industry of Brazil is an example; it was near the stage of maturity after years of nurturing, and benefited from trade liberalization as the competitive pressure from imports made it more efficient despite the initial difficulties it encountered (Shafaeddin, 2006b).

The result of the study of the same sample countries for the period 2000–2004 indicated that the differential performance of the "minority group" in general continued, in relation not only to the "majority group" but also to its own performance during the 1990s. Further, the majority group, particularly Mexico, Costa Rica and low-income countries, showed more vulnerability to global slowdown. Export processing zones (EPZs) are responsible for the bulk of the exports of Mexico and Costa Rica (see also Paus, 2005, on Costa Rica). Other countries which also have concentrated on EPZs, by liberalizing FDI, have not fared much better than Costa Rica and Mexico. One example is Mauritius, which has not only been unable to upgrade its production and export structure, but also experienced a slowdown in its pace of export growth (Shafaeddin, 2009). Only China is an exception; in particular, its performance stands out as compared with Mexico. The contrasting experiences of the two countries require closer attention, as they share many similarities but also differ in their policy performance and the role of government (see below).

On the basis of the aforementioned studies, we have concluded that "where there is a correlation between export growth and output growth [manufactured goods], a causal relation goes from output to exports rather than the other way round" (Shafaeddin, 2006a).[6] This is particularly true in the case of low-income countries such as least developed countries (LDCs).

7.1 Least developed countries

LDCs are at the early stages of industrialization. Hence, one would expect, based on the experience of other countries (Chenery and Syrquin, 1985), that the share of MVA in their GDP should have increased during the past couple of decades.

Yet, premature trade liberalization during the 1980s and early 1990s was accompanied by de-industrialization in most LDCs (Shafaeddin, 1995, 1996). The neoliberals' response is that low-income countries should intensify trade liberalization in order to improve their performance (IMF, 2001). Has the situation improved during the following period when trade liberalization has in fact intensified in these countries, particularly in African LDCs (Shafaeddin, 2009: Table 11)? The data indicate that de-industrialization has also intensified since 1990.

We have taken the MVA/GDP ratio as an indicator of the degree of industrialization. Table 2.2 shows that on average the ratio in LDCs has declined between 1990 and 2006, influenced mainly by the performance of African LDCs. Nevertheless, the average figure for Asian LDCs is heavily influenced by the performance of Bangladesh, Cambodia and Laos. When these countries are excluded, the ratio for Asian LDCs declines from 12.9 per cent in 1990 to 10 per cent in 2006. Furthermore, de-industrialization seems more pronounced in countries which are, relatively speaking, at earlier stages of industrialization. Thus, 78 per cent of countries which show a decrease in their MVA/GDP ratio over the same period figure among those with MVA/GDP ratios of less than 10 per cent in 2005–2006 (based on Tables 2.2 and 2.3). The corresponding figure for countries which show an increase in the ratio is 63 per cent. Moreover, on the basis of the same sources, out of twenty-four countries which do not show a decline, two countries show no change (Eritrea, Sao Tome and Principe), five register a marginal change of 0.1 per cent (Djibouti, Ethiopia, Gambia, Haiti and Madagascar), and a few others record minor changes of 0.2 per cent (Guinea and Togo), 0.3 per cent (Somalia and Sudan) and 0.6–0.9 per cent (Uganda, Tanzania and Yemen). Such small changes over more than a decade cannot be regarded as progress in industrialization.

Note that the increases in the MVA/GDP ratio cannot be necessarily attributed to trade liberalization in all cases. Countries with noticeable increases in the ratio include Cambodia (10.6 per cent), Equatorial Guinea (9.3 per cent),

Table 2.2 Changes in the share of MVA in GDP of LDCs[a] (1990–2006)

Year	All	LDCs			Other developing countries[b]	
		Asia	Africa[c] and Haiti	Islands	All	Major exporters of manufactured goods
1990	10.5	12.1	9.7	6.1	22.5	25.6
2000	10.2	13.2	7.7	6.4	23.2	27.1
2006	9.8	13.8	7.5	6.4	24	28.5

Source: Shafaeddin (2009), based on UNCTAD (2008a: Table 8.3.2).

Notes
a All variables are in current terms.
b Excludes LDCs.
c 10.7 for 1980.

Table 2.3 Changes in the share of MVA in GDP of LDCs (2005–2006)

MVA/GDP (per cent)	Asia		Africa		All LDCs	
	Increased	*Decreased*	*Increased*	*Decreased*	*Increased*	*Decreased*
Less than 5	–	5	5	3	5	8
5–10	3	2	7	8	10	10
10–15	–	–	4	3	4	3
15–20	2	–	2	2	4	2
20–21	1	–	–	–	1	–
Total	6	7	18	16	24	23
Per cent in total number for each region	46	54	53	47	51	49

Source: Calculated by the author, based on UNCTAD (2008b: Table 3).

Mozambique (8.5 per cent), Liberia (8.1 per cent), Laos (5.4 per cent), Afghanistan (4.7 per cent), Myanmar (1.8 per cent) and Bangladesh (1.5 per cent). Nevertheless, with the exception of Equatorial Guinea and the latter two countries, all are among special cases which had suffered from low capacity utilization in the initial period due to a war or internal conflict. Equatorial Guinea enjoyed expansion of oil revenues, and the increases in the ratios for Bangladesh and Myanmar are relatively small. In fact, if the ratio for 2006 is compared with that of 1980, it declined slightly in the case of Myanmar and remained the same for Bangladesh (UNCTAD, 2008a: Annex Table 5).

Generally speaking, the degree of de-industrialization will become even more evident if one compares the MVA/GDP ratios for 2006 with 1980 or 1970. In the first case, twenty-five out of forty countries for which data are readily available show a decline in the ratio, and two cases show no change (based on UNCTAD, 2008a: Annex Table 5). Again, the exceptional cases mentioned above figure in the list of countries where the ratio went up. The results of omparison with the 1970s will be even more dramatic (see also Jomo and von Arnim, 2008: Table 7).

While a number of factors, including structural weaknesses, may have contributed to de-industrialization, the influence of premature liberalization cannot be denied (Shafaeddin, 2006a, 2009). During the past two to three decades, quantitative trade restrictions have been eliminated and tariff rates have been reduced drastically. In particular, tariffs on imports of manufactures have been reduced significantly, ranging from 33.5 per cent to 83.2 per cent (Shafeddin, 2009: Table 14).

8 The comparative experience of China and Mexico[7]

As mentioned earlier, among countries with some industrial base the performance of China in particular stands out as compared with Mexico. Their comparative performance provides a good opportunity for testing the neoliberals' hypothesis vis-à-vis developmentalists. In 1978, MVA accounted for 44 per cent of Mexico's GDP; the ratio was around 40 per cent for China around 1980. Both countries started opening up their economies to foreign trade and FDI, and reforming their economies more or less around the early 1980s. Mexico, however, intensified its trade liberalization through the General Agreement on Tariffs and Trade (GATT) (1986) and North American Free Trade Agreement (NAFTA) (1995) and relied heavily on market forces in general; it is regarded as a champion of trade liberalization and economic reform (Moguillansky and Bielschowsky, 2001). China's trade, financial, capital and labour market reforms continued in the 1980s and 1990s; it acceded to the WTO in 2001. Export processing zones have been mainly responsible for export expansion in both countries.

During 1980–2000, Mexico registered considerably faster expansion of exports of manufactured goods than China, but, unlike in the case of China, such rapid expansion was not associated with acceleration of growth of MVA and GDP. Further, in contrast with China, its rapid growth of exports could not be sustained after 2000; the ratio of investment to GDP fell; public investment was cut and domestic private investors hardly responded positively to liberalization. Unlike in China, FDI crowded out domestic investment and the trade balance ratio for its manufacturing sector ([exports − imports]/exports) deteriorated (for details, see Pizarro and Shafaeddin, 2010); little increase in value added and upgrading has taken place in its export processing zones. There has also been a shift to resource-based industries and less risky activities (than productive activities), such as residential construction (Shafaeddin, 2005c: 50–52 and Table 3.3). In comparison, China has developed comparative advantage in production of non-electronic capital/technology-intensive products (mostly produced by state-owned enterprises [SOEs]) and in exports of assembled electronic products. Unlike Mexico, it has improved its comparative advantage in production of components and finished items of electronic products and other intermediate goods.

In short, Mexico has intensified its static comparative advantage and its prospects for rapid growth of exports of manufactured goods are slim. By contrast, China has managed to upgrade its industrial structure to achieve dynamic comparative advantage accompanied by rapid growth of exports and MVA. What has China done which Mexico has not?

8.1 Differences in policies of the two countries

In a nutshell, the answer to the above question lies in the two countries' different approaches to trade and industrial policies as well as learning. Mexico followed the recommendation of neoliberals who are proponents of market-led industrialization, rapid and across-the-board liberalization and "learning by trading". It was assumed that the market would take care of research and development (R&D), technological development, learning through trade and FDI. By contrast, China pursued a strategy advocated by neo-developmentalists and the proponents of "capability-building theory" who stress gradual and experimental liberalization,

Table 2.4 Development of China's national innovation system

Policy	Dominant feature	Year established
Key technology R&D programme	Encouraging efforts in key technology	1982
Resolution on reform of S&T system (CCCP)	Adopting flexible system on R&D management	1985
Sparkle system 5	Promoting basic research in agriculture	1985
863 programme	High-tech promotion	1986
Torch programme	High-tech communication, high-tech zones	1988
National S&T achievements spreading programme	Promoting product communication	1990
National engineering technology research centre programme	Technology transfer and communication research	1991
Climbing programme	Promoting basic research	1992
Endorsement of UAEs by SSTCC	Promoting university and industry linkage	1992
S&T progress law	Technology transfer, S&T system reform	1993
Decision on accelerating S&T progress (CCCP)	Promoting URI-industry linkage	1995
Law for promoting commercialization of S&T achievements	Regulating the commercialization of S&T	1996
Super 863 programme	Commercialization, breakthrough in key areas	1996
Decision on developing high-tech industrialization	Encouraging technology innovation and commercialization	1999
Guidelines for developing national university science park	Accelerating the development of university science parks	2000

Source: Gallagher and Shafaeddin (2010: Table 4). Based on Zhong and Yang (2007).

functional and targeted government intervention, "learning by doing" and development of capabilities of domestic firms, particularly in technology.

More specifically, unlike Mexico, the Chinese government targeted some strategic industries, particularly information technology (IT) industries (in 1986), through SOEs or government support for private firms, while it was also responsive to market forces. The government developed an institutional framework for science and technology (S&T) development, a national system of innovation and learning through R&D and training. It also provided some incentives to TNCs and directed them to specific activities.

A sophisticated system of national innovation, for basic research as well as R&D, was developed, as is shown in Table 2.4. The Chinese Academy of Science, Ministry of Information Technology and four other ministries were involved in providing guidance to S&T development. Universities, research institutes, public and private enterprises, including foreign firms, were also involved. The 1986 "863 programme", 1988 "Torch programme", 1992 "climbing programme", 1995 "decision on accelerating scientific and technological progress", and 1996–2000 and 2001–2005 Five-Year Plans targeted development and intensification of technology and provision of training for six high-tech industries as well as energy. Some technology parks were also established for the purpose; commercialization of technology was encouraged. By 2003, 18,669 R&D institutes had been established. As is shown in Table 2.5, expenditure on R&D expanded considerably faster in China than in Mexico. The share of business enterprises in China's total R&D expenditure also increased from 43.3 per cent in 1996 to over 68 per cent in 2004.[8] By contrast, in the case of Mexico it increased only from over 22 per cent in 1996 to about 32 per cent in 2004 (Gallagher and Shafaeddin, 2010: Table 5, based on Zhong and Yang, 2007 and UNESCO, online database on R&D expenditure).Although foreign enterprises have become more active in R&D in China as compared with Mexico (see below), national enterprises took the lead in technological development.

According to World Bank sources, each year more patents are filed in China than in the whole of Latin America. More importantly, as late as 2002, 112,103 patents were granted to Chinese firms as against 20,296 granted to foreign firms (MOST, 2006).

Table 2.5 Expenditure on R&D in Mexico and China (1996–2005)

		Share in GDP	*Per capita ($)*
Mexico	1996	0.31	22.4
	2004	0.41	40.4
China	1996	0.57	15.7
	2005	1.34	89.6

Source: UNESCO online database on R&D expenditure.

Note
GDP is in PPP.

8.2 *The role of the government in developing capabilities of domestic firms*

In addition to its direct involvement in R&D activities, the Chinese government provided a high level of support for tertiary education, training and skills development. For example, in 2005 the number of graduates in the field of S&T was over 1,000 per million of population; government expenditure on tertiary education per student was equal to 90 per cent GDP per capita, as against 48 per cent for Mexico (World Bank, 2008). In the field of training, the number of graduates from vocational schools increased from 79,000 in 1978 to 1,700,000 in 2005, when there were 198,566 vocational schools in the country.

To develop the capabilities of domestic firms, a division of labour was established between private firms and SOEs. The objective of the former was to exploit short-term opportunities for profit-making. The latter concentrated on long-term goals through development of new products while benefiting from the "National Science and Technology Diffusion" programme and Export Development Fund (Gallagher and Shafaeddin, 2010, based on Li and Xia, 2008).

Chinese firms also cooperated with TNCs, particularly in R&D. In the case of Mexico, FDI was negatively correlated with R&D. *Maquiladora* (foreign) firms provided few linkages with, and technological spillovers to, domestic firms (Pizarro and Shafaeddin, 2010). Further, a large number of Mexican firms were closed down as a result of their inability to compete with TNCs. For example, in the IT industry alone thirteen important domestic firms were closed (Gallagher and Shafaeddin, 2010: Table 13, based on Woo, 2001 and Rivera Vargas, 2002). In the case of China, TNCs have become increasingly involved in R&D as they were provided incentives and initially made to engage in participation with national firms (Walsh, 2003). Eventually, many TNCs established R&D facilities in China; the number of foreign-firm R&D centres is estimated to have reached anywhere between 120 and 400 in 2003 (Walsh, 2003: xiv).

As the capabilities of the Chinese domestic firms were enhanced, in contrast to Mexico, FDI crowded in domestic investment. But FDI was basically managed not only by directing it to targeted industries, but also by other means. For example, initially, licensing FDI was conditioned on transfer of technology. In 2001 this condition was dropped, but various incentives were provided to TNCs to get them engaged in R&D.

The IT industry was designated as a "pillar" strategic industry of China in 1988 (MOST, 2006). Top TNCs in the IT industry (IBM, HP, Toshiba and Compaq) were invited to form joint ventures with local firms such as Legend, Great Wall, Tonture and Star. The condition was that the TNCs transfer technology to the joint venture and engage in training. Further, the government decided to invest over $120 billion in the IT industry by the end of 2005 (Walsh, 2003: 71). As a result, around 2005, the IT firms engaged in R&D in China included four foreign-owned, twenty-two joint-venture and thirteen privately owned domestic firms and SOEs (Gallagher and Shafaeddin, 2010: Table 12). As domestic firms developed their own capabilities, supported directly by the government, the TNCs became more willing to transfer technology. By 2000, Legend emerged as the biggest seller of PCs in the Asia-Pacific region and China. After acquiring IBM's PC business in 2005, it became the world's third largest PC maker (Spooner, 2005). Domestic manufacturers together have dominated 70 per cent of the domestic PC market (Walsh, 2003: 108). Founder, Datang and Huawei became giant firms in laser typesetting and electronic publishing, 3G (TD-SCDMA) technology, and telecommunications, respectively. China has developed its own brand of mobile phone and high definition disc players (see Fan *et al.*, 2007). IT products have become major exports; in 2007–2008, electronic products constituted the country's top three export items.[9]

9 Concluding remarks and policy implications

Mexico and China have followed different approaches to trade liberalization and industrialization. Mexico, following the neoliberal approach, relied on market forces and has been regarded as a champion of trade liberalization. In particular, the government believed in learning technological development mainly through trade and relying on TNCs. By contrast, China has attempted a gradual and experimental approach to trade liberalization, and meanwhile has continued nurturing technological development through measures and policies to develop the technological capabilities and skills of domestic firms. It has targeted IT and a number of other industries, embarked on institutional development and created a national system of innovation for technological development. Thus it has managed to increase domestic value added in these industries which started, like in Mexico, through assembly operations. China also continued its rapid growth of exports, MVA and GDP after joining the WTO. By contrast, Mexico has achieved little in building up the capabilities of domestic firms, increasing value added in exports and growth of MVA and GDP. Furthermore, the country has become more vulnerable to external factors than China, as was evident during the recent financial crisis, despite the fact that its exports-to-GDP ratio (28.5) in 2008 was far smaller than that of China (37.8).[10] In 2005, Mexico depended on the US market for over 85 per cent of its exports and 54 per cent of all its imports. Since the early 2000s, many TNCs have been relocating their plants from Mexico to China.

The performance of China is consistent with the literature on capability-building theory and the views of proponents of neo-developmentalism (e.g. Wade, 1990; Amsden, 2000; Paus and Gallagher, 2008; Chang, 2005a; Shafaeddin, 2005b; Lall, 2004).

9.1 Can the experience of China be replicated by other countries?

China's impressive success in enhancing the capabilities of its domestic firms raises the question of whether its experience can be replicated by other developing countries. Although development policy is country-specific, as the socio-economic features of various countries are different and the experience of a country cannot be generalized, certain lessons can be learned from China's experience as compared with that of Mexico. First, trade policy cannot be considered in isolation from industrial and other development policies of a country. In particular, there is a need for industrial policy (Lall, 2004; Rodrik, 2004, 2007; Wade, 1990, 2007; Shafaeddin, 2006c; Di Maio, 2008).

Second, capability-building of domestic firms is crucial for industrialization, but the market alone is not capable of developing such capabilities in various categories of developing countries as well as within one country over time. Developing countries can be classified into three categories: those with little industrial capacity, such as low-income African and other least developed countries; those with some industrial capacity developed during the import-substitution era, such as Brazil; and those with a considerable industrial base which have also successfully penetrated the international market, such as the East Asian NIEs. The main problem of the first group is to establish production capacities; that of the second group is to make existing production capacities efficient and penetrate international markets. The burning issue for the third group is to upgrade their industrial structure. Market forces alone are not adequate to deal with any of these issues. The capabilities of government should be developed to formulate and implement policies for capability-building at the firm level.

Third, trade and industrial policies should be not only development-oriented and country-specific, but also selective, mixed, flexible, performance-linked, dynamic and predictable (Shafaeddin, 2005a). The flexibility and dynamism of trade policy can be exemplified by changes in the structure of tariffs during the course of industrialization, as shown in the self-explanatory Table 2.6.

Trade and industrial policies should also be supplemented by the development of what I call "non-price factors" (see below), and development of

Table 2.6 Evolution of average tariffs for various groups of industries at different phases of industrialization

Phase	RB&LI	LT	MT	HT	Manufactures (average)
I	20	0	0	0	5
II	10	40	0	0	12.5
III	0	30	50	0	20
IV	0	20	40	40	25
V	0	10	30	40	20
VI	0	0	15	25	10
VII	0	0	5	15	5
VIII	0	0	0	0	0

Source: Akyüz (2005: 27).

Notations:
RB: Resource-based industries
LI: Labour-intensive industries
LT: Low-technology-intensive industries
MT: Medium-technology-intensive industries
HT: High-technology-intensive industries

agriculture in order to enhance the supply of wage goods. Further, provision of incentives should be linked to the satisfactory performance requirements, i.e. incentives should be provided in exchange for performance, and support should be temporary and time-bound. In addition, FDI should be managed and targeted to areas which can contribute to meeting the development objectives of the host country.

Fourth, regarding "non-price factors", the process of industrialization requires "COU-Ps-INs" (Shafaeddin, 2005a, 2010b). COU stands for: Create capacity, Operate it efficiently and Upgrade the industrial structure. To do so incentives are necessary but not sufficient. There is a need for a number of INs and Ps. The INs include INvestment, INput, INfrastructure (not only transport and communication but also other facilities such as marketing channels, distribution network, etc.), INstitutions, INnovation and INformation (Streeten, 1987). We use "information" here in the wide sense of the term, which includes knowledge, science, R&D as well as market information which requires investment in human resources through education, skills development and training.

The Ps stand for Political stability, Predictability of policies, Participatory Politics, Pressure for Performance, Public–Private Partnership, respect for Property rights and, last but not least, Production capabilities of local firms in the value chain and Productivity. Here, we use "production capabilities" in a wider sense than supply capabilities; thus it includes such factors as organizational issues, which also contribute to productivity, marketing, etc.

There are also two INs which are to be avoided. These are instability in exchange rates and inflation, which are largely related to agricultural development, control of capital flows and macroeconomic policies.

Development of food production and other wage goods is essential, particularly during the early stages of industrialization, in order to ease the pressure on the balance of payments and inflationary tendencies, thus contributing to the competitiveness of manufactured goods in the internal and international markets.

Of course, implementation of the trade policy framework outlined above is constrained by WTO rules. However, there is still some room to manoeuvre under the WTO rules, particularly for least developed countries. This is so, provided developing countries do not lose their remaining policy autonomy through bilateral and regional agreements (Rodrik, 2004; Di Maio, 2008; Amsden, 2000), including EPAs, and do not submit to conditionalities of IFIs and excessive liberalization proposals put forward by developed countries in the Doha Round NAMA (non-agricultural market access) negotiations on trade in manufactured goods and in the EPAs (Shafaeddin, 2010). "What constrains sensible industrial policy is largely the willingness to adopt it, not the ability to do so" (Rodrik, 2004: 32).

There is nevertheless a need for some changes in the WTO rules to make them development-friendly. For this purpose, as well as in the EPA, NAMA and other trade negotiations, developing countries should follow a bottom-up rather than a top-down approach. In other words, instead of agreeing with some issues in such negotiations without having been clear about their own trade and industrial policies (as was the case during the earlier Uruguay Round trade talks), they should be clear about their trade and industrial policies before going to the negotiating table (see Shafaeddin, 2005a, for details). The aftermath of the recent global economic crisis, which saw intensive intervention of developed countries in the market, provides a good opportunity for developing countries to bring up the limitations of market forces in the process of industrialization and development and argue in favour of different trade and industrial policies, and thus a different international trading system. Neither the WTO rules nor the theory of static comparative cost advantage is god-given.

Notes

1 This is the text of a keynote speech delivered at the Fourth ACDC (Annual Conference on Development and Change) in the University of Witwatersrand, Johannesburg, South Africa in April 2010. It is mainly based on the earlier work of the author as listed in the references.
2 This and the following chapter are based mainly on Shafaeddin (2005b: 156–162).
3 This chapter is based mainly on Shafaeddin (2006a, 2009).
4 See also various literature by the World Bank and IMF, particularly World Bank (1987, 1993). For a brief survey, see Shafaeddin (2006b).
5 For a survey, see Shafaeddin (2006b).
6 It is interesting to note that in an unusual recent paper, a staff member of the IMF also concluded that out of seventy-one "so-called" export-led growth episodes, twenty-four cases "are more likely to be characterized by 'growth driving exports'" (Yang, 2008: 1).
7 Based mainly on Gallagher and Shafaeddin (2010).
8 The total number of people engaged in this activity increased from 804,000 in 1996 to 1,152,617 in 2004, and the share of the business community in the number of personnel engaged increased from 46 per cent to 60 per cent over the same period (UNESCO, online database on R&D expenditure).
9 Based on UNCTAD (2008a), *Handbook of Statistics 2009*, Table 3.2.D.
10 Based on UNCTAD, ibid., Table 8.3.1.

Acknowledgement

A slightly different version of this chapter also appeared in M. Shafaeddin (2011) *Trade Liberalization, Industrialization and Development: The Experience of Recent Decades*, Penang, Malaysia: Third World Network, and it is reproduced with the information and permission of the Third World.

References

Akyüz, Y. (2005) "The WTO Negotiations on Industrial Tariffs: What Is at Stake for Developing Countries?", paper presented at a workshop on "NAMA Negotiations and Implications for Industrial Development in Developing Countries", Geneva, 9 May 2005.
Amsden, A.H. (1989) *Asia's Next Giant: South Korea and Late Industrialization*, New York, NY: Oxford University Press.
Amsden, A.H. (2000) "Industrialization under New WTO Law", paper prepared for UNCTAD X, High-level Round Table on Trade and Development: Directions for the Twenty-First Century, Bangkok, 12 February 2000.

Bagchi, A.K. (1982) *The Political Economy of Underdevelopment*, Cambridge: Cambridge University Press.

Bairoch, P. (1993) *Economic and World History*, Brighton: Wheatsheaf.

Balassa, B. (1980) "The Process of Industrial Development and Alternative Development Strategies", World Bank Staff Working Paper No. 438, World Bank.

Balassa, B. (1989) "Outward Orientation", in H.B. Chenery and T.N. Srinivasan (eds), *Handbook of Development Economics*, Vol. 2, Amsterdam: North Holland, pp. 1645–1689.

Baldwin, R.E. (1969) "The Case Against Infant-Industry Tariff Protection", *Journal of Political Economy*, 77(3): 295–305.

Bennell, P. (1998) "Fighting for Survival: Manufacturing Industry and Adjustment in Sub-Saharan Africa", *Journal of International Development*, 10(5): 621–637.

Bhagwati, J. (1978) *Foreign Trade Regimes and Economic Development: Anatomy and Consequences of Exchange Control Regimes*, Cambridge: Ballinger Publishing Company.

Bhagwati, J. (1988) "Export-Promoting Trade Strategy: Issues and Evidence", *World Bank Research Observer*, 3(1): 27–57.

Blecker, R.A. and Razmi, A. (2008) "The Fallacy of Composition and Contractionary Devaluations: Output Effects of Real Exchange Rate Shocks in Semi-Industrialised Countries", *Cambridge Journal of Economics*, 32(1): 83–109.

Chang, H.-J. (2005a) "Policy Space in Historical Perspective – with Special Reference to Trade and Industrial Policies", paper presented at the Queen Elizabeth House 50th Anniversary Conference "The Development Threats and Promises", Queen Elizabeth House, Oxford University, 4–5 July 2005.

Chang, H.-J. (2005b) *Why Developing Countries Need Tariffs: How WTO NAMA Negotiations Could Deny Developing Countries' Right to a Future*, Geneva: South Centre.

Chenery, H.B. and Syrquin, N. (1985) *Patterns of Development 1950–1970*, Oxford: Oxford University Press.

Corden, W.M. (1993) "Round Table Discussion", in J. de Melo and A. Panagariya (eds), *New Dimensions in Regional Integration*, Cambridge: Cambridge University Press for Centre for Economic Policy Research, pp. 457–460.

Curtis, M. (2006) "Forcing Trade Liberalization on the Poor", UK Watch, www.ukwatch.net/article/1261.

Deane, P. (1965) *The First Industrial Revolution*, Cambridge: Cambridge University Press.

Di Maio, M. (2008) "Industrial Policy in Developing Countries: History and Perspectives", Universita Degli Studi Macerata, Discussion Paper No. 48.

Fan, P., Gao, X. and Watanabe, K.N. (2007) "Technology Strategies of Innovative Chinese Domestic Companies", *International Journal of Technology and Globalisation*, 3(4), 344–363.

Gallagher, K.P. and Shafaeddin, M. (2010) "Policies for Industrial Learning in China and Mexico", *Technology in Society*, 32(2), 81–99.

Gerschenkron, A. (1962) *Economic Backwardness in Historical Perspective*, Cambridge, MA: Harvard University Press.

Huang, Y. (2002) *Selling China: Foreign Direct Investment During the Reform Era*, New York, NY: Cambridge University Press.

IMF (International Monetary Fund) (2001) "Global Trade Liberalization and the Developing Countries", www.imf.org/external/np/exr/ib/2001/110801.htm.

Jomo, K.S. and von Arnim, R. (2008) "Economic Liberalization and Constraints to

Development in Sub-Saharan Africa", DESA Working Paper No. 67, United Nations Department of Economic and Social Affairs.

Kowalski, P., Lattimore, R. and Bottini, N. (2009) "South Africa's Trade and Growth", OECD Trade Policy Working Paper No. 91, Organization for Economic Cooperation and Development.

Krueger, A.O. (1974) "The Political Economy of the Rent-Seeking Society", *American Economic Review*, 64(3): 291–303.

Krueger, A.O. (1978) *Foreign Trade Regimes and Economic Development: Liberalization Attempts and Consequences*, New York, NY: National Bureau of Economic Research.

Krueger, A.O. (1980) "Trade Policy as an Input to Development", *American Economic Review, Papers and Proceedings*, 70: 288–292.

Lall, S. (1996) *Learning from the Asian Tigers*, London: Macmillan.

Lall, S. (2004) "Reinventing Industrial Strategy: The Role of Government Policy in Building Industrial Competitiveness", G-24 Discussion Paper No. 28, United Nations Conference on Trade and Development.

Lazonick, W. (1991) *Business Organization and the Myth of the Market Economy*, New York, NY: Cambridge University Press.

Li, S. and Xia, J. (2008) "The Roles and Performance of State Firms and Non-State Firms in China's Economic Transition", *World Development*, 36(1).

Lin, J. and Chang, H.-J. (2009) "Should Industrial Policy in Developing Countries Conform to Comparative Advantage or Defy It? A Debate Between Justin Lin and Ha-Joon Chang", *Development Policy Review*, 27(5): 483–502.

Little, I.M.D., Scitovsky, T. and Scott, M. (1970) *Industry and Trade in Some Developing Countries*, Oxford: Oxford University Press.

Mandelson, P. (2005) Speech of 15 February 2005, cited in Curtis (2006).

Marshall, A. (1920) *Industry and Trade*, London: Macmillan.

Moguillansky, G. and Bielschowsky, R. (with Pini, C.) (2001) *Investment and Economic Reform in Latin America*, Santiago: ECLAC.

MOST (2006) *National High Tech R&D Program (863 Program)*, Ministry of Science and Technology of the People's Republic of China, Beijing.

Noorbakhsh, F. and Paloni, A. (2000) "The De-industrialisation Hypothesis, Structural Adjustment Programmes and the Sub-Saharan Dimension", in H. Jalilian, M. Tribe and J. Weiss (eds), *Industrial Development and Policy in Africa: Issues of De-industrialisation and Development Strategy*, Cheltenham: Edward Elgar, pp. 107–136.

Oxfam (2008) "Partnership or Power Play? How Europe Should Bring Development into Its Trade Deals with African, Caribbean, and Pacific Countries", Oxfam Briefing Paper No. 110.

Paus, E. (2005) *Foreign Direct Investment, Development and Globalization: Can Costa Rica Become Ireland?* London: Palgrave.

Paus, E. and Gallagher, K.P. (2008) "Missing Links: Foreign Investment and Industrial Development in Costa Rica and Mexico", *Studies in Comparative International Development*, 43(1).

Pizarro, J. and Shafaeddin, M. (2010) "The Evolution of Value Added in Assembly Operations: The Case of China and Mexico", *Journal of Chinese Economic and Business Studies*, 8(4): 373–397.

Rivera Vargas, M.I. (2002) *Technology Transfer via University–Industry Relationship: The Case of the Foreign High Technology Electronics Industry in Mexico's Silicon Valley*, London: RoutledgeFalmer.

Rodriguez, F. and Rodrik, D. (1999) "Trade Policy and Economic Growth: A Skeptic's Guide to Cross-National Evidence", NBER Working Paper No. 7081, National Bureau of Economic Research.

Rodrik, D. (1997) "Trade Policy and Economic Performance in Sub-Saharan Africa", paper prepared for the Swedish Ministry for Foreign Affairs.

Rodrik, D. (2004) "Industrial Policy for the Twenty-First Century", KSG Faculty Research Working Paper Series RWP04–047, John F. Kennedy School of Government, Harvard University.

Rodrik, D. (2007) "Normalizing Industrial Policy", Harvard University.

Sachs, J. and Warner, A. (1995) "Economic Reform and the Process of Global Integration", *Brookings Papers on Economic Activity*, No. 1.

Shafaeddin, M. (1995) "The Impact of Trade Liberalization on Exports and GDP Growth in Least-developed Countries", *UNCTAD Review*, January, 1–6.

Shafaeddin, M. (1996) "Risk of Further Marginalization of Sub-Saharan Africa in International Trade", *Journal of Developing Societies*, XII(2): 254–274.

Shafaeddin, M. (1998) "How Did Developed Countries Industrialize? The History of Trade and Industrial Policy: The Case of Great Britain and the USA", UNCTAD Discussion Paper No. 139, United Nations Conference on Trade and Development.

Shafaeddin, M. (2005a) "Towards an Alternative Perspective on Trade and Industrial Policies", *Development and Change*, 36(6): 1143–1162.

Shafaeddin, M. (2005b) *Trade Policy at the Crossroads: The Recent Experience of Developing Countries*, New York, NY: Palgrave Macmillan.

Shafaeddin, M. (2005c) "Friedrich List and the Infant Industry Argument", in K.S. Jomo (ed.), *The Pioneers of Development Economics: Great Economists on Development*, London: Zed Books.

Shafaeddin, M. (2006a) "Does Trade Openness Favour or Hinder Industrialization and Development?", paper presented at the Technical Group Meeting of the Intergovernmental Group of Twenty-Four on International Monetary Affairs and Development (G-24), Geneva, 16–17 March 2006.

Shafaeddin, M. (2006b) "Trade Liberalization and Economic Reform in Developing Countries: Structural Change or De-industrialization?", in A. Paloni and M. Zanardi (eds), *The IMF, the World Bank and Policy Reform*, London: Routledge.

Shafaeddin, M. (2006c) "Is Industrial Policy Relevant in the 21st Century?", Keynote Address presented at the International Conference on "New Approaches to the Design of Development Policies", organized by the Arab Planning Institute (API), Beirut, 20–21 March 2006. Published by the API as Special Paper No. 2 (2006).

Shafaeddin, M. (2009) "The Impact of the Global Economic Crisis on Industrialization of Least Developed Countries", Institute of Economic Research, University of Neuchatel, www2.unine.ch/irene/page14695.html.

Shafaeddin, M. (2010) "The Political Economy of WTO with Special Reference to NAMA Negotiations", *European Journal of Development Research*, 22(2): 175–196.

Smith, A. (1776) *An Inquiry into the Nature and Causes of the Wealth of Nations* (reprint, Modern Library, New York, 1937, edited by Cannan, E.).

Spooner, J.G. (2005) "New Lenovo takes shape", CNet News, 3 March.

Stiglitz, J.E. (2005) "Development Policies in a World of Globalization", in K.P. Gallagher (ed.), *Putting Development First: The Importance of Policy Space in the WTO and IFIs*, London: Zed Books, pp. 15–32.

Streeten, P.P. (1987) "Structural Adjustment: A Survey of the Issues and Options", *World Development*, 15(12): 1469–1482.

Thoburn, J. (2002) "Could Import Protection Drive Manufacturing Exports in Africa?", in D. Belshaw and I. Livingstone (eds), *Renewing Development in Sub-Saharan Africa: Policy, Performance and Prospects*, London: Routledge, pp. 285–296.

UNCTAD (United Nations Conference on Trade and Development) (2008a) *Handbook of Statistics*, Geneva: United Nations.

UNCTAD (2008b) *The Least Developed Countries Report 2008*, Geneva: United Nations.

UNDP (United Nations Development Programme) (2003) *Human Development Report 2003*, New York: United Nations.

Wacziarg, R. and Welch, K.H. (2003) "Trade Liberalization and Growth: New Evidence", NBER Working Paper No. 10152, National Bureau of Economic Research.

Wade, R. (1990) *Governing the Market: Economic Theory and the Role of Government in East Asian Industrialization*, Princeton, NJ: Princeton University Press.

Wade, R. (2005) "What Strategies Are Viable for Developing Countries Today? The World Trade Organization and Shrinking of Development Space", in K.P. Gallagher (ed.), *Putting Development First: The Importance of Policy Space in the WTO and IFIs*, London: Zed Books, pp. 80–101.

Wade, R. (2007) "Rethinking Industrial Policy for Low Income Countries", paper presented at the African Economic Conference, organized by the African Development Bank and UNECA, Addis Ababa, 15–17 November 2007.

Walsh, K. (2003) *Foreign High-Tech R&D in China: Risks, Rewards, and Implications for US–China Relations*, Washington, DC: The Henry L. Stimson Centre.

Williamson, J. (ed.) (1990) *Latin American Adjustment: How Much Has Happened?* Washington, DC: Institute for International Economics.

Woo, G. (2001) "Hacia la integracion de pequenas empresas en la industria electronica de Jalisco: dos casos de estudio", in E. Dussel (ed.), *Claroscuros: Integracion Exitosa de las Pequenas y Medianas Empresas en Mexico*, Mexico City: Editorial Jus.

World Bank (1987) *World Development Report*, Washington, DC: World Bank.

World Bank (1993) *East Asian Miracle: Economic Growth and Public Policy*, Washington, DC: World Bank.

World Bank (2005) *Economic Growth in the 1990s: Learning from a Decade of Reform*, Washington, DC: World Bank.

World Bank (2008) *World Development Indicators*, Washington, DC: World Bank.

Yang, J. (2008) "An Analysis of So-Called Export-Led Growth", IMF Working Paper WP/08/220, International Monetary Fund.

Zhong, X. and Yang, X. (2007) "Science and Technology Policy Reform and Its Impact on China's National Innovation System", *Technology in Society*, 29: 317–325.

3 The slowing down of the engine of growth

Was W.A. Lewis right about global economic crises and the impact on the peripheries?

Keith Nurse

1 Introduction

The contemporary economic and financial crisis in the global economy – the great depression of 2008 and 2009 and the ongoing instability and threat of double dip recession – has surprised many analysts and opened up the field of economics to much criticism. The current economic downturn was not predicted by mainstream economic theories, or by short-term and intermediate-term theories of business cycles. According to Krugman, in the past decade or two there had emerged a view that modern-day economics had tamed the problem of crises associated with business cycle fluctuations and recessions. In his latest book, *The Return of Depression Economics and the Crisis of 2008*, Krugman argues against such thinking and makes the point that:

> Fifteen years ago hardly anybody thought that modern nations would be forced to endure bone-crushing recessions for fear of currency speculators, and that major advanced nations would find themselves persistently unable to generate enough spending to keep their workers and factories employed. The world economy has turned out to be a much more dangerous place than we imagined.
>
> (2008: 181)

> Essentially it means that for the first time in two generations, failures on the demand side of the economy – insufficient private spending to make use of available productive capacity – have become the clear and present limitation on prosperity for a large part of the world.
>
> (2008: 182)

The failure in mainstream economics has stimulated renewed but marginal interest in the theories of long-term, large-scale cycles, or waves of capitalist development. In circumstances of this sort, the late Ernest Mandel (1984: 195) made the point that "it is amusing that the long waves of capitalist development also produce long waves in the credibility of long-wave theories, as well as additional long waves of these theories themselves".

The literature on long waves generally credits N.D. Kondratieff, the Russian economist who headed the Conjuncture Institute in Moscow during the 1920s, with the discovery of long-wave or cyclical like patterns in the world-economy estimated to last some fifty to sixty years. Based on data from the 1780s, the beginning of the Industrial Revolution in Europe, Kondratieff mapped long waves by means of price data, theorizing that price fluctuations and economic development were correlated in a broad sense. For instance, Kondratieff (1984: 103) argues that:

> During the period of a rising wave in the long cycles, the intermediate capitalist cycles are characterized by the brevity of depressions and the intensity of the upswings. During the period of a downward wave in the long cycles, the picture is the opposite.

Since Kondratieff's contribution, several theories on long waves have emerged, but their explanations as to the causality of cyclical rhythms still remain quite disparate. According to Delbeke (1984: 3–11), the main theoretical explanations on long waves can be categorized into the following:

- innovation theories (Mensch, 1979; Schumpeter, 1939; Van Duijin, 1984) relating long waves to the clustering of innovations;
- capital accumulation theories (Kondratieff, 1984; Mandel, 1975), considering changes in capital accumulation as the causal dynamic;
- the labour theory (Freeman, Clark and Soete 1982) relating technical change to levels of employment; and
- the terms of trade approach by Rostow (1978), whose main focus is on the movement of relative prices of raw materials and foodstuffs.

As can be seen, each approach emphasizes different causal factors in their analysis. Wallerstein (1984: 568), in his essay on "Long Waves as Capitalist Process", notes, however, that there is some complementarity in these different approaches in that "they all assert that there is some process whereby over time there grows to be a significant discrepancy between some supply and some demand, and that this process is structural, not conjunctural". Delbeke (1984: 10), in a survey of the long-wave literature, suggests as well that, given the complexity of the phenomenon, an emphasis should be placed on multicausality rather than monocausality by integrating the varied explanations on long waves.

Delbeke (1984: 5) also makes the criticism that the "major lacuna of most long-wave theories is their neglect of demand as an important engine in long-wave movement, their emphasis being largely focused on supply-oriented dynamics". Another major criticism of long-wave theories is their virtual neglect of the periphery of the world economy, and its role in long-wave movement.[1]

W.A. Lewis provides a useful corrective to this lacuna through his attempt to explain the long-term and cyclical trends in the global economy especially as it applies to peripheral areas. In his historical and empirical work he observed that there were cyclical shifts in growth rates. So, for example, in his Nobel Prize lecture he makes the point that:

> The extraordinary growth rates of the two decades before 1973 surprised everybody. We knew that the world economy experiences long swings in activity; that world trade, for example, grew faster between 1830 and 1873 than it grew between 1873 and 1913, that is to say, between 4 and 5 percent before 1873, compared with between 3 and 4 percent after 1873. But a jump to 8 percent was inconceivable.
>
> Since 1973 the growth rate of world trade has halved, and nobody knows whether this is temporary or permanent. But most of our economic writing continues to assume implicitly that a return to eight per cent is only just around the corner.
>
> (Lewis, 1980: 555)

Lewis utilizes the Kondratieff (1984) price swing as one of the key methodological approaches to explain the cyclical shifts in growth rates in the world economy. He specifically focuses on the Kondratieff price swing to explain: (a) the dynamics of growth in the core economies, what he calls the "engine of growth"; (b) the change in the terms of trade between agriculture and industry; and (c) the consequent changes in core–periphery relations (1978: 27).

This aspect of Lewis' work has continued relevance but is relatively underexplored. Lewis is among a small group of analysts who have used long-wave theory to explain the changing role of the periphery in the world economy (Chase-Dunn, 1978; Nurse, 1998; Pamuk, 1982; Stewart, 1993; Suter, 1989; Wallerstein, 1980). The key focus of the chapter is on exploring the key insights from what can be described as Lewis' magnum opus, *Growth and Fluctuations 1870–1913* (1978). According to Tignor (2006), Lewis regarded this book as his most important scholarly work. In many respects it is the culmination of Lewis' quest to answer the problem of growth and development in the periphery.

2 The global economic crisis in historical perspective

The current global financial and economic crisis is not just a blip on the curve of what would otherwise be described as business as usual. Economic historians suggest that the current changes are indicative of a turning point in capitalist development similar to the systemic transformations that accompanied the economic crises of the 1820s, 1870s and 1930s (Delbeke, 1984; Lewis, 1978).

The current crisis relates to the fact that the global economy has been in a phase of massive structural changes, with a myriad of imbalances, for the past three decades or so. Contemporary global trade and economic development has been impacted by a number of shocks since the late 1970s and early 1980s, such as the Third World debt crisis, the Mexican peso crisis, the Japanese slowdown, the US savings and loan crash, the Russian ruble crisis, the Asian meltdown, the "dot.com" crash and the Argentinian financial crisis, to name the key events. The combination of these shocks explains why growth in the world economy and most national economies has been in a relative period of stagnation since the mid-1970s as compared with the prior period after the Second World War (Nurse, 2003).

These transformations in the global political economy are not without some antecedents. World history suggests that the current transformations point to a shift in the techno-economic, socio-political and institutional framework of global development similar to the systemic transformations that accompanied the economic downturns of the 1820s, 1870s and 1930s. For example, during the period from 1914 to 1945, the last time the world economy went through a cyclical economic downturn, there was a confluence of several dramatic political and economic developments: two world wars; the Russian and Chinese socialist revolutions; the Great Depression of the 1930s; the rise of fascism in Italy, German and Japan; the emergence of new social and economic policies in Keynesianism and state monopoly capitalism; and the replacement of British by US hegemony.

In an analogous crisis of the last quarter of the nineteenth century similar transformations occurred: the Great Depression of the 1870s; the decline of free trade and the rise of protectionism; the ascent of Germany and the United States as rivals to British hegemony; the rise of monopoly capitalism, classical imperialism and renewed colonialism; and the emergence of new state formations as a result of the American Civil War, the Italian unification, the formation of the German state, the Meiji restoration in Japan and the British North American Act establishing the Dominion of Canada.

From this perspective, contemporary convulsions in the global political economy cannot be viewed as unique in that they have several parallels, particularly with the period of the late nineteenth century. For instance, the relative decline of the US as hegemon and the shift to a multicentric geo-economic and political context (i.e. the rise of the BRICS and the shift from G7 to G20) are not unprecedented. Indeed, many of the dramatic transformations in technology (growth of the green economy and cloud technologies) as well as the social order (such as the revolutions in the Arab World and the anti-austerity protests in the US and Europe) have their historical antecedents. From an economic perspective, downturn phases are associated with Great Power trade rivalries, the resurgence of protectionism, technological revolutions, debt crises and new modes of peripheral specialization. However, it is important to note that periods of crisis or the downturn phase are not bad for all countries or all sectors, as elaborated in the following quote:

> What needs to be underlined most of all is that a downturn is a slowdown of activity, not a stoppage. It represents, in economic terms, a set of obstacles in the search for profit that, if you will, weeds out the capitalist sheep from the goats. The strong not only survive; they frequently thrive. For the

peripheries, therefore, a downturn in the world economy occasions both involution and evolution; both a seeming decline in the monetarization of economic activity and the emergence of new enterprises; both abandonment and restructuring or relocation; both a decline in their specialized role in the world economy and a deepening of it.

(Wallerstein, 1980: 129)

3 Downturns and the peripheries

Peripheral economies play multiple roles at different phases in the evolution of the long wave. In the upswing, the periphery first plays the role as supplier of raw material and basic inputs, then as a market for the new products and services, and lastly as a destination for mature technologies and industries. In the downturn phase of the long wave, the failure of this mode of peripheral industrialization becomes evident and sets up the conditions for high levels of leakage of capital to the core economies except for those peripheral countries that have upgraded and restructured their economies for global competitiveness.

Table 3.1 provides a synopsis of the key trends associated with each phase of the long wave and its impact on growth, investment and consumer demand in the core economies, as well as its implications for peripheral economies. The upswing phase (periods of expansion) is characterized as a time of prosperity, and rightly so, because profitability is high, employment and consumer demand are up, and there is economic growth. The good times also spread to the peripheral economies through trade, mainly through the importation of key agricultural and mineral commodities. This period of "good times" does not last forever, however, for there comes a point when what is produced cannot be sold, given existing world effective demand. Profitability declines, and investment demand and consumer demand contract as a period of stagnation becomes apparent.

From this perspective, the current phase in the world economy can be described as a downturn phase – a period of stagnation. The downturn phase has two sub-periods: recession and depression. It is suggested that the contemporary transformations are indicative of the latter, the depressionary stage, where there is little or no growth in the core economies. These periods of crisis stimulate transformational changes in the techno-economic and institutional structure of the world economy. For example, during the period from 1914 to 1945 – the last time the world economy went through a cyclical economic downturn – international demand for peripheral exports declined, the terms of trade deteriorated, the balance of payments became unfavourable and, ultimately, an outflow of capital to the core was effected through external debt and other mechanisms.

Lewis' thesis is that the "engine of growth" in the world economy results from the process of innovation and technological change in the core countries which generates growth, creates demand for inputs and pulls raw material and food imports from the peripheral areas. There is a cyclical dimension to this in that the upswing phase leads to increased investment in the periphery until the downturn arrives, which retards international demand for peripheral exports and

Table 3.1 Macroeconomic impact of long waves

	UPSWING (period of expansion)		DOWNTURN (period of stagnation)	
	Recovery	Prosperity	Recession	Depression
Growth in core economies	Increasing growth	Strong growth	Decreasing growth	Little or no growth
Investment demand	Increased replacement investment	Strong expansion of capital	Scale increasing investment	Innovation, rationalization, relocation
Consumer demand	Purchasing power seeks new outlets	Expansion of demand	Growth of new sectors	Growth at expense of savings
Impact on periphery	Economic re-specialization creates new export opportunities	Trade becomes the engine of growth	Traditional commodity exports decline	Terms of trade and balance of payments un-favourable

Source: Adapted from van Duijn (1984).

ultimately results in an outflow of capital through debt and other mechanisms. The "engine of growth" thesis is premised on "the proposition that the upward movement of those already on the escalator helps to pull more and more countries into the moving company" (1978: 16). This does not mean that all countries will benefit equally or will seize the opportunity.

What is described above relates specifically to the upswing phase where innovations emerge, forging the new techno-economic paradigm that leads to increased investment in the core with expanding demand for inputs from the periphery. Prosperity generated in the core proliferates to the periphery. However, much of the benefit of the new innovations that are applied to peripheral exports accrues to consumers in the core through lower prices and specifically to the traders in terms of higher profits. Consequently, when the downturn in the core economies arrives, international demand for peripheral exports declines, the terms of trade deteriorate, the balance of payments becomes unfavourable and ultimately an outflow of capital to the core is effected through external debt and other mechanisms.

Lewis maps the effect of the downswing phase on the periphery by relating tropical agricultural exports and total tropical exports to industrial production in the core countries over the period 1883–1965. Figure 3.1 shows industrial production in the core dipping first and having a knock-on effect on tropical exports and agricultural exports. It also shows that the decline in growth rates for the latter was more significant than that for industrial production and total tropical exports. The figure also shows that the recovery of growth for core industrial production was faster, with an almost ten-year lag for the peripheral exports. However, after 1937, peripheral exports jumped rapidly to catch up with the growth rate for core industrial production. In short, agricultural exports proved to be more vulnerable to the slump in global demand compared to core industrial production. As Lewis puts it,

> The intervening three and a half decades were for the tropics a period of disaster. First there was the First World War, culminating in the great slump of 1920. Then in the 1920s the terms of trade moved against tropical products. Then came the great depression of the 1930s with sharp curtailment of demand and even more adverse terms of trade. Finally there came the Second World War.
>
> (1978: 225)

> By the middle 1930s tropical development had come to a standstill. Private investment had ceased. Governments had cut back their budgets on education and welfare services, and with international investment paralysed, infrastructure could not be expanded.
>
> (1978: 227)

What Lewis has illustrated in Figure 3.1 is a pattern of stagnation and rejuvenation for the periphery over the Kondratieff long wave. Lewis' general

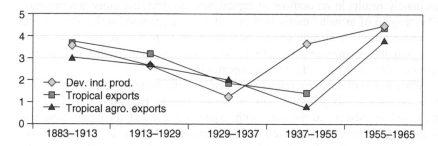

Figure 3.1 Rates of growth for core industrial production, tropical exports and agricultural exports (source: Lewis, 1978: 226).

argument is borne out by a long view of industrialization in the world economy. Figure 3.2 shows the shares in world manufacturing output by region from 1750 to 2002. In broad outline, it illustrates the relative decline in the periphery's share of manufacturing and the emergence of a "technology gap" between the Third World and the West after the 1840s on account of the de-industrialization of countries like India, China and Pakistan and the consequent rapid growth of industrialization in Europe and North America (Williamson, 2006). From the 1950s what is observed is the apparent re-industrialization of the periphery, largely reflected in the growth of China, South Korea, Taiwan, India, Brazil and a small group of exporters through technological and industrial upgrading. Other peripheral regions (e.g. South Asia, Latin America and the Caribbean, Africa, the Middle East) that applied more passive approaches to technological development have underperformed, as exemplified in declining shares of world manufacturing value added (UNIDO, 2005).

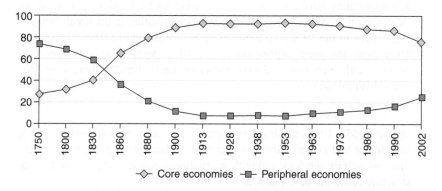

Figure 3.2 Shares of world manufacturing output by region, 1750–2002 (sources: Bairoch, 1982; UNIDO, 2005).

4 Options for the peripheries

The analysis and theoretical framework offered by Lewis provides an explanation for the fluctuations in growth over long historical periods and the impact on the peripheral regions. What we grapple with now is not the cyclical rhythms but the long-term secular trajectories of the global economy and the shifting roles of countries and regions.

Lewis argues that the industrialization of the core countries since the early nineteenth century presented two options to the peripheral areas: (1) "to follow the example of the core" and engage in industrial deepening and upgrading, or (2) to rely on international trade with the core and "develop by selling to expanding core markets" raw materials and commodities (1978: 158–159). The second option is viewed not as a stand-alone strategy but potentially as a catalyst for the first through graduating from commodity production to import substitution and, ultimately, export-oriented manufacturing. In summary, his argument is that the core countries contributed to the development of the countries at the periphery in three ways:

1   They offered a new and highly productive technology
2   The core countries contributed resources – specifically, capital and people
3   The core contributed its own markets (1978: 29–30).

The first option, Lewis argues, is only open to countries that "already had sizable industrial sectors", like India and China or the settler colonies like the US, Canada and Australia. The latter group, although originally commodity exporters, enjoyed significant economic surpluses on account of productivity improvements in agricultural production and resource-based industries. This success is in clear juxtaposition to the impact that trade in commodities had on the developing economies, or the "tropical world" as Lewis called it. For instance, Lewis shows that when commodity prices in 1913 are compared with prices in 1883, the temperate countries enjoyed far superior factoral terms of trade in commodities than did tropical countries. He notes:

> with the exception of sugar, all the commodities whose price was lower in 1913 than in 1883 were commodities produced almost wholly in the tropics. All the commodities whose prices rose over this thirty-year period were commodities in which the temperate countries produced a substantial part of total supplies.
>
> (1978: 189)

The divergence in performance of commodities production between core and peripheral economies is explained in part by the weak productivity gains in the "tropical countries" such that the terms of trade work against them. Lewis argues that the problem is not rooted in the products themselves, but in the productivity, labour regimes and social structure of accumulation in the respective economies. For example, he makes the point that if tea had been a temperate instead of a tropical crop, its price would have been perhaps four times as high as it actually was. And if wool had been a tropical instead of a temperate ... it would have been had for perhaps one-fourth of the ruling price.

(1978: 189)

This argument is one of the key planks of Lewis' thesis in the seminal article entitled "unlimited supplies of labour". He argues:

The contribution of the temperate world to the tropical world, whether in capital or knowledge, has in the main been confined to the commercial crops for export, where the benefit mainly accrues to the temperate world in lower prices. The prices of tropical commercial crops will always permit only subsistence wages until, for a change, capital and knowledge are put at the disposal of the subsistence producers to increase the productivity of tropical food production for home consumption.

(1954: 183)

What does all of this have to do with the current economic crisis? Lewis argues that for most peripheral economies the arrival of an economic downswing stalls development and may even reverse some of the gains of the prior period of growth and prosperity. In this regard he is very critical of those countries that rely principally on trade as a mechanism for development, especially where the factoral terms of trade are low. In short, he argues, "the tropics could not really hope to 'take off' until technological change became embedded in their way of life" (1978: 202). It is on this basis that Lewis concludes in his book *Growth and Fluctuations* that "the long-run engine of growth is technological change" and not trade "except in the initial period of laying development foundations" (1978: 245).

In effect, Lewis is arguing that the prospects for countries are largely determined by the development strategies that they have employed (industrial upgrading versus trade dependence), especially when the traditional "engine of growth" slows down, as is the case in the contemporary context. This issue is well articulated in Lewis' Nobel Prize lecture. He states that:

If a sufficient number of LDCs reach self-sustaining growth, we are into a new world. For this will mean that instead of trade determining the rate of growth of LDC production, it will be the growth of LDC production that determines LDC trade, and internal forces that will determine the rate of growth of production. Not many countries are ready to make this switch.

   It is not possible for all LDCs to make this switch and neither is it necessary, for if leading LDCs grow fast and import heavily, they will substitute to some extent for the former rapid growth of the MDCs. For those who use the language of center and periphery, this means that a number of countries leave the periphery and join the center.

The shadow on this picture is what happens to those LDCs whose best option has been to export raw materials to MDCs.... We have provided an escape for LDCs that can turn to exporting food or manufactures, but we have not assumed that the new core LDCs will substitute for the MDCs by drinking more coffee or tea, or using more rubber and jute. This solution therefore involves some hardships for the less adaptable LDCs, constrained by climate or by small size of their markets.

(1980: 562)

Lewis, in this passage, is highlighting the growth of the "new" engine of growth coming from the South and assessing the prospects for South–South trade as an alternative to the historical pattern of North–South trade. As such, the question at hand is whether the new engine of growth (for example, China, India and Brazil, the "Big South") will play a similar role to that of the traditional engine of growth (the OECD economies), which provided export markets for commodities from the peripheral economies. An examination of trade between China and Latin America and the Caribbean (LAC) illustrates both the emerging challenges as well as the opportunities.

5 The rise of the "South" – a new engine of growth?

One of the key transformations that has emerged from the global economic crisis has been the extent to which the recovery has been driven by emerging economies such as China, India and other East and South Asian economies. There is an emerging consensus that this represents a shift in the locus of growth in the global economy from the traditional North Atlantic sphere to Asia. The economies of North America and Europe are mired in debt and undergoing austerity measures of varying intensities, the worst affected being Portugal, Ireland, Greece and Spain, along with Italy, the UK and the US. Government and consumer spending, in addition to private sector investment, have been negatively affected by the slowdown in the growth rates in these economies. These economies have been operating at below-average world output levels for the past several years.

The largest share of growth in world output has come from the emerging markets and an increasing share of world trade is now South–South trade, up from 7 per cent in 1990 to 17 per cent in 2009. Asia accounts for 75 per cent of South–South commerce, with China dominating with 40 per cent of the total. China's dominance and rising trade surplus with its trading partners in the South has generated much concern about de-industrialization even among the larger economies like Brazil and South Africa. The problem is becoming widespread. For example, Mexico, which is the second largest trading partner of the US, has lost significant market share in competition to China. It is estimated that Mexico lost 250,000 jobs and over 300 maquiladoras between 2001 and 2003 (Loser, 2006: 7–8). The explanation is not just that of the cheaper wages of China; it is that the level of local value-added in manufacturing activity in Mexico is shallow and so is vulnerable to global competition. This is so for much of LAC, although Mexico is the worst case. Data for 2009 show that 97 per cent of manufacturing exports from Mexico, which account for 71 per cent of the national exports, are under direct threat from Chinese competition. The figures for LAC as a whole are slightly better, with 92 per cent of manufacturing exports under direct threat, which account for only 39 per cent of total regional exports (Gallagher, 2010: 6).

What accounts for this high level of vulnerability? It is argued by several analysts that the neoliberal policy agenda which dominated the ideological landscape in LAC encouraged investment in low-skilled and low value-added maquila-type activities as well as a deepening of commodity production and resource-based extraction. This is reflected in the trade pattern that LAC has with China. LAC trade with China is overwhelmingly in commodity- and resource-based exports (89 per cent in 1999 and 78 per cent in 2003) when compared with ASEAN exports to China, which are predominantly in medium- and high-technology goods (53 per cent in 1999 and 66 per cent in 2003) (UNCTAD, 2003).

In effect, LAC has become one of the key resource suppliers for China's industrialization thrust, with several LAC countries deepening their dependence on commodity and raw material exports. Recent estimates indicate that eight sectors and five countries account for over 80 per cent of all regional exports to China. The top export sectors are copper alloys from Chile, iron ore from Brazil, soybeans and soybean oils from Brazil and Argentina, ores and concentrates of base metals from Chile and Peru, crude petroleum from Brazil and Colombia, pulp and waste paper from Brazil and Chile, and feedstuffs from Peru and Chile (Gallagher 2010: 2).

The problem faced by LAC from the rise of China is mirrored in the context of Africa. Africa's exports to China rose from US$1,427.4 million in 1995 to US$42,282.1 million in 2009, while imports from China grew from US$2,493.7 million to US$47,724.6 million in the same period (Adekunle and Gitau, 2011). China's trade with African countries is very concentrated in terms of partners. Around 85 per cent of Africa's exports to China come from five oil-rich countries – Angola, Equitorial Guinea, Nigeria, the Republic of Congo and Sudan (Hansen, 2008; Adekunle and Gitau, 2011). Raw materials comprise the majority of Africa's exports to China, while high-value manufactured goods dominate its imports from that country (Renard, 2011; Adekunle and Gitau, 2011).

It is increasingly argued that China and Africa's trade relationship has implications not just for trade but also for the industrial policies of African countries. Some have argued that China's cheap exports could harm the infant-industry development and economic diversification prospects of African countries (Zafar, 2007; Ademola et al. 2009; Adekunle and Gitau, 2011). It is also argued that the influx of cheap Chinese goods crowds out non-Chinese exports, particularly imports from other African countries (Adekunle and Gitau, 2011). For example, Ghanaian furniture and clothing exporters and South African manufacturers are finding it increasingly difficult to compete with Chinese imports both in their own local market and in foreign markets (Kaplinsky and Morris, 2006).

What the above analysis illustrates is that the rise of China, India, Brazil and other industrial competitors – i.e. the rise of the "Big South" – is deepening commodity dependence in other peripheral countries and thereby reinforcing their traditional role in the international division of labour. In effect, what is evolving is a three-tiered global economy where the traditional core economies are in relative decline, the Big South is expanding to supplant some of the geo-economic and political prowess of the core, and the rest of the South is falling further behind due to weak competitiveness. As such, the decline in the manufacturing sector in Africa and LAC countries is symptomatic of a broader malaise. These observations point to the longstanding problem associated with extraverted development. In effect, the key challenge facing these regions is the historic legacy of persistent poverty exemplified in a mode of accumulation that perpetuates inequity and social injustice.

6 Conclusion

Lewis's theoretical framework for understanding how the periphery is incorporated into the world economy from one historical phase to another is a useful framework to explain and predict core–periphery relations in the contemporary economic crisis. By focusing on the terms of trade, Lewis is able to identify the key impacts for the periphery of cyclical shifts (i.e. upswings and downturns) in the world economy. His main argument is that the demand for peripheral exports is reliant on industrial production and consumer demand in the core, and that this is subject to cyclical swings of prosperity and stagnation. Thus, during a downturn peripheral countries can experience a massive reversal of fortunes compared to the upswing. However, downturns are not bad for all countries. It all depends on a country's level of dependence on core markets, and the technological and market sophistication of its exports. The countries that are the most affected during the downturn are those with a heavy reliance on core markets and with low value-added exports.

Lewis also provides a framework to understand longer-term trajectories in the global economy. For example, Lewis argued that the world economy had entered a phase of slower growth and that the traditional engine of growth had slowed down since the 1970s. He also predicted that the engine of growth would expand from just the core economies in North America, Europe and Japan to include the emerging countries like China, India, Brazil, and so on. The rise of the Big South is having a dramatic impact on the geo-economics of the world economy. One of the key trends is that the growth in competitiveness among the Big South has resulted in the growth of South–South trade and a reduction in the traditional North–South flow. Another key trend is that the manufacturing prowess of the Big South is resulting in a process of de-industrialization in regions like Africa and LAC. Consequently, South–South trade has increased commodity dependence among developing countries, particularly Africa and LAC regions where many sectors continue to provide basic inputs and services and operate at the low value-added end of global production chains. The problem is particularly evident in the manufacturing sectors. Lewis uses the term "tropical trade" to typify such production, which can be broadened to apply to a wide range of peripheral exports.

Note

1 This is a shortcoming in the literature admitted to in the preface of Freeman (1984).

References

Adekunle, B. and Gitau, C.W. (2011). *Illusion or Reality: Understanding the Trade Flow between China and Sub-Saharan Africa*. Retrieved from www.csae.ox.ac.uk/conferences/2011-EDiA/papers/046-Adekunle.pdf.

Ademola, O.T., Bankolea, A.S. and Adewuyia, A.O. (2009). *China–Africa Trade Relations: Insights from AERC Scoping Studies*. Retrieved from www.palgrave-journals.com/ejdr/journal/v21/n4/pdf/ejdr200928a.pdf.

Bairoch, P. (1982). "International Industrialization Levels from 1750 to 1980", *Journal of European Economic History*, 11(1&2).

Chase-Dunn, C. (1978). "Core–Periphery Relations: The Effects of Core Competition", in B. Kaplan (ed.), *Social Change in the Capitalist World Economy*. London: Sage, pp. 159–176.

Delbeke, J. (1984). "Recent Long-Wave Theories: A Critical Survey", in C. Freeman (ed.), *Long Waves in the World Economy*. London: Frances Pinter, pp. 1–10.

Freeman, C. (ed.) (1984). *Long Waves in the World Economy*. London: Frances Pinter.

Freeman, C., Clark, J. and Soete, L. (1982). *Unemployment and Technical Innovation*. London: Pinter.

Gallagher, K. (2010). China and the Future of Latin American Industrialization. Issues in Brief, Pardee Center. Retrieved from www.bu.edu/pardee/publications/issues-in-brief-no-18/.

Hansen, S. (2008). *China, Africa and Oil*. Retrieved from www.cfr.org/china/china-africa-oil/p9557

Kaplinsky, R. and Morris, M. (2006). *Dangling by a Thread: How Sharp are the Chinese Scissors?* Retrieved from http://asiandrivers.open.ac.uk/documents/Dangling_by_a_thread_Feb_06_%20final.pdf.

Kondratieff, N. (1984). *The Long Wave Cycle* (trans. G. Daniels). New York, NY: Richardson and Snyder.

Krugman, P. (2008). *The Return of Depression Economics and the Crisis of 2008*. London: Penguin Books.

Lewis, A. (1954). "Economic Development with Unlimited Supplies of Labour", *The Manchester School*, 22(2): 139–191.

Lewis, A. (1978). *Growth and Fluctuations 1870–1913*. London: Allen & Unwin.

Lewis, A. (1980). "The Slowing Down of the Engine of Growth" [The Nobel Lecture], *American Economic Review*, 70(4): 555–564.

Loser, C.M. (2006). *The Growing Economic Presence of China in Latin America*. Washington, DC: Inter-American Dialogue.

Mandel, E. (1975). *Late Capitalism*. London: New Left.

Mandel, E. (1984). "Explaining Long Waves of Capitalist Development", in C. Freeman (ed.), *Long Waves in the World Economy*. London: Frances Pinter, pp. 195–201.

Mensch, G. (1979). *Stalemate in Technology*. Cambridge, MA: Ballinger Press.

Nurse, K. (1998). "Third World Industrialization and the Reproduction of Underdevelopment", *Marronnage*, 1(1): 69–97.

Nurse, K. (2003). "Development: Unthinking the Past", *NACLA Journal*, 37.3: 29–35.

Pamuk, S. (1982). "World Economic Crises and the Periphery: The Case of Turkey", in E. Friedman (ed.), *Ascent and Decline in the World-System*. Beverly Hills, CA: Sage, 147–161.

Renard, M.F. (2011). *China's Trade and FDI in Africa*. Retrieved from www.afdb.org/fileadmin/uploads/afdb/Documents/Publications/WPS%20No%20126%20China%E2%80%99s%20trade%20and%20FDI%20in%20Africa.pdf.

Rostow, W.W. (1978). *The World Economy: History and Prospect*. New York, NY: Macmillan.

Schumpeter, J. (1939). *Business Cycles*, two volumes. New York, NY: Mc Graw-Hill.

Stewart, T. (1993). "The Third World Debt Crisis: A Long Waves Perspective", *Review* 16(2), 117–171.

Suter, C. (1989). "Long Waves in the International Financial System: Debt-Default Cycles of Sovereign Borrowers", *Review*, 12(1), 1–49.

Tignor, R. (2006). *W. Arthur Lewis and the Birth of Development Economics*. Princeton, NJ: Princeton University Press.

UNCTAD (2003). *Trade and Development Report 2003*. Geneva: United Nations.

UNIDO (2005). *Industrial Development Report 2005. Capacity Building for Catching-up: Historical, Empirical and Policy Dimensions*. Vienna: UNIDO Publication.

Van Duijin, J.J. (1984). "Fluctuations in Innovations Over Time", in C. Freeman (ed.), *Long Waves in the World Economy*. London: Frances Pinter.

Wallerstein, I. (1980). *The Modern World-System II: Mercantilism and the Consolidation of the European World-Economy, 1600–1750*. New York, NY: Academic Press.

Wallerstein, I. (1984). "Long Waves as Capitalist Process", *Review*, 7.4: 559–574.

Williamson, G.J. (2006). *Globalization and The Poor Periphery Before 1950*. London: MIT Press.

Zafar, A. (2007). *The Growing Relationship between China and Sub-Saharan Africa: Macroeconomic, Trade, Investment, and Aid Links*. Retrieved from www.relooney.info/SI_Oil-Politics/China_6.pdf.

4 Africa

Dependency and crisis; the Great Depression and the 2008 recession

Bill Freund

A generation ago the economic history of sub-Saharan Africa was shaken by the increasingly successful adaptation of dependency theory, with its platform in the experience of Latin America, to the African continent by writers such as Claude Ake, Colin Leys, Rhoda Howard and, above all, Samir Amin. (Ake 1981, Leys 1975, Howard 1978, Amin 1971) While there are some problems in making this adaptation work, it is certainly true that dependency theory in the cold light of day exposed the economic vision operative in European colonialism in Africa. The metropole and the colony were profoundly distinctive entities. The metropole retained financial autonomy and power, and was the seat of manufacture, research and innovation. The purpose of the colony was to provide raw materials, absorb export production and control strategic points. It might also, as in the case of the French empire, provide manpower for the metropolitan military. There were occasionally colonies that, in a world where free trade still had some purchase, traded primarily elsewhere than with the metropole, but these were problematic exceptions. It was true that Lenin's view that colonies were above all targets for investment is not very close to African historical reality. Such investment only worked where particular infrastructural projects or unusual resource troves could be found, such as the Suez Canal or the gold fields of South Africa.

This is because the African colonies were the site of distinct and historically very different societies which could not absorb and make profitable large-scale investments without massive internal changes. In some regions indigenous societies were pushed aside in favour of settler minorities, as in Algeria or Kenya, but while these minorities were far more adept than the natives at promoting capitalist production and monetarised economic activities, sponsoring them was costly, problematic politically, and required subsidisation that was also not necessarily very profitable. South Africa was the only important exception, and even in the early twentieth century that exception existed more in potential than in reality.

What was the impact of the Great Depression of the 1930s on this situation? Put simply, the metropole–colony link, which had expanded and found more purchase in the 1920s, was now significantly attenuated. African primary production brought into Africa dramatically lower prices. Thus, to take Nigeria: the value of exports fell from £17 million in 1929 to below £10 million in 1938, with corresponding falls in imports (Crowder 1973: 263). This was true of primary products but also, very remarkably, of industrial mineral products such as copper and tin as well. The impact on the Copper Belt, both on the Belgian Congo and on the Northern Rhodesia side of the border, was dramatic. In the case of Northern Rhodesia, this decline affected an industry that was just getting underway after quite significant investments in transport and infrastructure during the second half of the 1920s. Outside South Africa, it would for a long time be Africa's biggest mining zone (Perrings 1979, Higginson 1989).

It is true that the impact of this on Africans was limited, to the extent that Africans were still largely self-sufficient peasants able to withdraw from the colonial economy and its demands. In Kenya, for example, Bruce Berman reports that the African labour force shrank in size from 160,000 in 1929 to 132,000 in 1932, although it would reach new heights before the end of the next decade. (Berman 1990: 234) On both sides of the frontier, it was notable, and notably remarked on, that while many Africans withdrew from Elisabethville, Kitwe, Ndola, Broken Hill and other urban communities, not all did so. Some had become sufficiently absorbed through cultural practice and the ability to find a living in the interstices of these new towns that they now built their lives there and were no longer, in colonial parlance, *tribesmen.* For the continent as a whole, one can exaggerate the extent to which even the cash economy was totally dependent on *dependencista*-type relationships. A place as large as Nigeria in fact even at the height of the colonial era marketed a very large range of basic goods according to handicraft production structures and internal marketing networks. This was true as well, say, for the independent state of Ethiopia, and should not be underestimated anywhere.

However, the modern economy was significantly dependent on the colonial relationships established over the previous half-century with antecedents in the commerce of the pre-colonial era. Agricultural goods from Africa were in very poor shape throughout the 1930s, compounded in places by unfavourable weather conditions. Moreover, the situation was no better with livestock. Africans did often respond with attempts to produce more for the market in order to keep up their cash requirements, and there were some important attempts, notably on the Gold Coast, to withhold supplies in order to bring up producer prices. However, on the whole, their ability to compete with the interests of capitalist marketing firms, which responded to crisis by withdrawal, consolidation and the formation of market monopolies and organised pools, was poor (Hopkins 1973).

The situation with mineral production was somewhat different. Here prices at first fell even more radically, but by 1935 or so recovery was very well on the way and actual boom conditions began to prevail on the eve of war. A special case was gold production, which was fundamental to the South African economy. Here there was a turn to gold hoarding from the earliest phases of the Depression, which made gold mines profitable (in contrast to the crisis situation that followed the First World War a decade earlier). When South Africa and

Britain went off the gold standard in 1932, profitability was very tangible indeed and the whole urban economy took off dramatically to an unprecedented extent, including manufacturing (Table 4.1).[1]

Despite the continued backwardness of agriculture, conditions made it possible for the gold bonanza to become a platform for what I would argue was an important effort at the creation of a *developmental state*, notably under the Union government that was in power from 1939 to 1948 (Freund 2011). Elsewhere in Africa, too, those colonies with gold resources were able to rely on one source of unprecedented prosperity.

Priscilla Shilaro has recently explored the conditions for the consequences of the gold rush in Kakamega district, Kenya. In its eagerness to exploit this new source of wealth – briefly Kenya's main export – all the fine language of Kenya as a trusteeship run in the name of its native population was swept away like the week's rubbish (Shilaro 2008). An equivalent but less optimistically observed gold rush took place in southern Tanganyika. And, of course, the Gold Coast had some valuable gold resources. In Southern Rhodesia, gold had brought in 36 per cent of export value in 1929; by 1933 it had reached 66 per cent. Agricultural exports, 36 per cent of the whole in the peak year of 1927, had fallen to below 15 per cent in 1935 (Phimister 1988: 177).

In general, we could look at the 1930s and call them lost years for Africa: clearly investment and infrastructure suffered, social infrastructure included. In the 1920s, conviction had grown that something we can begin to identify as 'development' would be required if the continent was to realise any sort of economic potential. Existing routes to wealth were limited and drying up or involved crude exploitation that was unsustainable. At the very onset of the depression, this led to the proclamation of the Colonial Development Act by a short-lived Labour government in Britain, and the Maginot Plan, the so-called Great Colonial Loan, in France. Both were curtailed and largely aborted, however, for the next decade (Hopkins 1974: 261).

A second point to stress was the turn to protectionism in the form of imperial preference arrangements which represented, in a sense, the further refinement of dependency arrangements (Austen 1987: 203–204). In the conditions of the 1930s, however, these failed on the whole to bring about overall growth. The British share in imperial African commerce failed to increase and French efforts

Table 4.1 The South African economy viewed sectorally by value of production in pounds

	Agriculture	Mining	Industry
1920	£51.00	£51.90	£26.00
1928	£53.00	£50.30	£35.80
1933	£30.60	£56.40	£32.00
1939	£50.80	£81.50	£69.70
1945	£81.90	£95.90	£132.70

led at best, according to Jacques Marseille, to a not very happy marriage between African consumers without choices and protected French producers who were essentially backward and uncompetitive but reliant on the colonial markets (Marseille 1984). In Salazar's Portugal, the poor state of the colonies, according to Malyn Newitt, was to be mended first and foremost through economies to balance the budget – 'drastic economies were introduced, wages were cut, government-assisted immigration schemes were stopped and taxation and customs duties were increased' (Newitt 1981: 188).

However, it is also true that the smarter colonial officials were very frustrated by the onslaught of belt-tightening policies and continued to formulate plans, occasionally with the possibility of being carried out, for what we can begin to call development. Thus the French continued to put resources into the *Office du Niger* (van Beusekom 2002). The British and the French introduced cooperatives, *sociétés de prévoyance* and marketing boards to buy agricultural goods when prices were poor and hoard them until peasants could realise fairer returns (Hopkins 1973: 263ff.). It is also true that where white settlers, who represented powerful lobbies, were affected, the state moved in with a range of preferential policies to save their resources – notably in Kenya and in Southern Rhodesia, where the crops that white farmers grew, such as tobacco, were a disaster area (Berman 1990, Phimister 1988).

From this one can therefore sum up with the following results:

1   Disastrous prices for African commodities.
2   Lesser dependence than today, however, on marketized trade for survival.
3   Some withdrawal and some deeper involvement in markets.
4   A sharp difference between mineral and agricultural commodity patterns opening with time especially.
5   Market failure: the big companies with African interests reacted to the Depression by withdrawal and disinvestment, in contrast to what Africa needed. A further failure was the distance between colonial thinking and the real economy, e.g. trade in kola nuts and livestock in West Africa which actually had international ramifications.
6   A commitment to protectionism which was fairly ineffective, and to the possibility of state-led development which was not on for the moment but would blossom after the war. However, the colonial state was racially biased and often very ignorant of what development policies might work. For West Africa, for example, Tony Hopkins has written that 'at a time when Africans were looking for cost-reducing innovations and alternative exports, government policy was memorable chiefly for its failures, some of which were spectacular' (Hopkins 1974: 262). Among the examples Hopkins has given were the very expensive Office du Niger irrigation works in what is today Mali, which survived only due to the different social arrangements and crops that suited locals and certainly never produced much wealth, and the British insistence on responding to swollen shoot disease in cocoa trees by mass destruction of plants, a remedy which did no good.

The context of the recent shake-up in global markets has been very different from how things looked in the 1920s and 1930s in sub-Saharan Africa (Freund 2010). If one wants to search for an African Depression, the entire last quarter of the twentieth century is perhaps the most deserving of that name. Between 1980 and 2003, according to the Atlas method of calculating Gross National Income (which includes estimates of remittances from overseas), twenty-nine of forty-nine African countries with available figures experienced per capita income *decline* and three (Democratic Republic of Congo, Liberia and Sierra Leone) *absolute decline*. Only Egypt, Tunisia, Botswana, the island nations of Seychelles and Mauritius, plus the expanding oil producers, Angola and Equatorial Guinea, are estimated to have grown their economies by more than 50 per cent per capita over almost a quarter century – that is to say, at 2 per cent per annum.[2]

The first years after independence were marked by both continuations of neo-colonialism and experiments in structural transformation, sometimes underwritten from the outside under the impact of the Cold War. Developmental plans were not lacking; neither was state intervention in the economy discouraged, even in conservative countries. However, the failure to find a growth path that was sustainable was almost universal. The failure to achieve a discernible qualitative shift began to tell by the middle 1970s, as what the French are fond of calling the *Trente Glorieuses* [thirty glorious years] came to an end, accompanied by a decline in many commodity prices and an increasing reluctance, outside the colonial bargain, to provide Africa with grants rather than loans – loans which became increasingly difficult to repay after 1980. The 1980s, and even more the 1990s, were characterised by disinvestment, de-industrialisation and the imposition by funders of a common line focused on debt repayment and the chimerical insistence on rolling back the state. African governments were so dependent on aid donors that their capacity to formulate policies largely eviscerated. International trade advanced dramatically after a phase of sluggishness, but Africa became more and more marginal within its circuits as it focused on exchange within multinational corporation branches and in manufactured consumer products. Primary products lost value dramatically. States that tried to defy the run of the tide found themselves under new management – the so-called 'good governance agenda' – while some states effectively collapsed. This occurred, moreover, at a time when Africa was becoming more culturally integrated into the wider world. Populations grew very fast, albeit not in those countries most affected with AIDS; cities grew even faster without the capacity in any sense to make them more liveable or productive environments. Peasants started to experience 'deagrarianisation', in Bryceson and Jamal's words, and gave up on the cultivation of poorly rewarded cash crops for the international market (Bryceson and Jamal 1997). Some left the countryside and looked for survival in petty commerce and services – the so-called informal sector – while many found new homes outside the continent entirely. These Depression conditions were understood by Westerners to be the price borne by Africans unable to discipline their rulers or state agencies, and unable to compete effectively in world markets. In fact that understanding is still quite dominant despite the decline in Africa's ability and, more critically, the ability of ordinary Africans, even people in the countryside, to withdraw from the international market networks.

The long winter of African decline, however, experienced a turnaround as the new millennium arrived, and especially after c. 2003. By 2007 annual African GDP growth was estimated at the very fast clip of 6.1 per cent, and even when that fell to 4.9 per cent in 2008, no less than twenty-five countries on the continent were expanding GDP at 5 per cent or more.[3] The key element for this lay in very much better prices for African minerals, with oil now produced or going into production in more and more nations. The more fortunate countries re-acquired some bargaining capacity and the possibility of taking practical economic steps without having to rely on aid resources. This in turn has to do with the dramatic economic growth in China and more moderate, but still very significant, growth in other Asian countries with a correlative hunger for African raw materials. The poor prices that still obtain for many African cultivated crops matter (and in fact have not receded in the mode of the 1920s and 1930s in any case), but have to be seen in perspective in this context.

I want to finish by commenting on the current situation in Africa with some separate thinking about South Africa, sub-Saharan Africa's only industrialised country. The heart of the world economic recession since 2008 has been laid at the increasingly unregulated, increasingly 'shareholder value'-driven and increasingly management (as opposed to entrepreneur)-driven financial corporations which failed to find suitably lucrative outlets in Western countries to match the high GNP increases expected in the past twenty years, and placed money into less and less reliable alternatives. The Doha round of WTO talks, intended to further open world trade, collapsed. Financialisation and luxury spending provided rapid growth for a while, but have proved unsustainable. In the end it was the bursting of a US property boom that drove ahead a huge credit crisis with serious effects, in the short term at least, for the real economy. Global economic figures marked a downturn in GDP of 2.2 per cent in 2009, and a decline in world trade of 12.4 per cent.[4] Today, as tentative claims of the end to the recession typify newspaper coverage, if we look around it is striking that its impact has been remarkably different in different countries. Some European countries, such as Germany, France and the Netherlands, seem in much better shape despite lower projected growth rates than the least regulated market powers, such as the USA and Britain, with their dramatically unbalanced budgets. The return of growth may be stuttering, but the relatively generous social wage and regulated banking systems have prevented property crises on a really significant scale and cushion hard times.

By contrast, in what is termed the developing world, Africa included, demand for oil and minerals, while briefly slackening dramatically, has quickly recovered, and there are expectations for continued high growth figures, notably in the case of China despite the apparent Chinese dependence on Western markets. In contrast to that overall 2009 figure of economic decline globally of 2.2 per cent, the figure can be broken up into a steeper decline of 3.5 per cent in the developed world and an actual increase, however modest, of 1.9 per cent in the developing world. Citing *The Economist*, the USA is supposed to grow at a rate of 3.1 per cent in 2010 and 2.9 per cent in 2011, compared to Britain at 1.3 per cent and 2.1 per cent and the Eurozone at 1.2 per cent and 1.4 per cent, respectively. But India's growth is anticipated to be 7.7 per cent and 8.0 per cent and China's at 9.6 per cent and 8.1 per cent – spectacular figures by any historical standards. Recovery in many Asian countries has come quickly. Typical African rates bottomed at very low positive growth (2.5 per cent for oil-producing countries and 0.5 per cent for the rest in 2009) but are already improving, with better figures than those in the West, with the prediction of 4.3 per cent growth for 2010. In certain areas – for instance, decline in tourist revenues and in remittance income from African workers in Europe and America – African economies have felt the downturn, but the growing impact of demand for African mineral resources has cushioned the negative effect in many, probably most, places. Obviously, African banks were not in any position to invest significantly in Western speculative adventures in real estate or the like. Probably the most serious negative effect has been the reduction in credit available from the so-called Washington Consensus institutions and aligned organisations due to more pressing engagements elsewhere.

In truth, for most of Africa a perturbation of this magnitude in the world economy would have been a terrible disaster up to five or six years ago. Today this is much less the case, as noted above. The situation remains a considerably more positive one than in the past, and the scope for African governments to escape the debt trap and search for a way forward – a return to genuine development initiatives as opposed to band-aid poverty alleviation schemes – has increased. The world has become more multi-polar and the capacity for Africa to move forward greater, albeit with having lost any capacity to genuinely withdraw from the global market, as Samir Amin once hoped.

The figures so far suggest that the financial crisis of 2008 has intensified that shift to multi-polarity, although its effects will presumably be far more striking if these trends prevail in the course of another decade or two. In my view, the result is that it is more than before up to African leaders, intellectuals, social and political movements to deal with social, political and economic conditions internally that hold it back, although I see this as likely to be an extremely uneven and slow process. The growing success of Asian and, to a far more uneven extent, Latin American economies has meant that Africa is starting to look as though the catchy if unpleasant phrase of British economist Paul Collier shows more and more verisimilitude – the home of the 'bottom billion' (Collier 2007). If so, its problems are apt to be subject to a more and more intense gaze from within and without.

The case of South Africa is in some ways typically African, and in some ways atypical. The recent Copenhagen environmental conference was a particularly glaring window into its contradictions. On the one hand, South Africa wished to speak for Africa, obsessed with extracting whatever aid it could out of the apparent global climate situation. On the other, it was equally eager to be taken as a emerging BRIC power alongside Brazil, India and China, anxious to break into Western markets and identifying with initiatives not necessarily in the interest of poorer and weaker countries. Of course, it remains true that South Africa has a far more complex developed economy than anywhere else in sub-Saharan Africa despite the impressive amounts of wealth being garnered in oil-rich Angola and Nigeria. Despite the institution by and large of orthodox liberal macroeconomic policy after the end of apartheid, involving the reduction of what was not an especially high debt burden and the balancing of budgets, South Africa after 1994 can be said to have experienced very limited growth, deteriorating human welfare indicators due to the dramatic rise of AIDS sickness and death, and little foreign investment. An open economy meant the departure of several major previously dominant corporations at least in terms of site of registration as well as considerable disinvestment. If the 'rainbow nation' liked to see itself in the mirror as the 'flavour of the month', it was not in the end a flavour many purchased. Money would flow in and out of the country on the basis of superficial and untrue rumours, making monetary policy almost uncontrollable.

However, from 2001 South Africa too started to experience happier times, although it is notable that growth was lower than average for the African continent. Again the answer has been mineral purchases, both of gold – a declining resource – and of mounting alternatives such as platinum (now overtaking gold in value) and coal. Increasingly exports are aimed at Asia, although this process could go much further. Figures for growth and investment improved. However, the weaknesses of South Africa's industrial base have eaten into potential benefits. Only in the case of the car industry, stimulated by choices made in Germany and secondarily Japan, has an important industrial export emerged and with almost no local R&D component and quite limited local initiative to it. In better times, just as under *apartheid*, South Africans buy foreign goods and travel overseas to an extent that more than eats up the growth in exports. South Africa also experienced a credit boom which by 2008 left consumers heavily in the red, and a real-estate boom, partly rational due to the cheap undersold market of the latter part of the twentieth century but also no longer sustainable by that year. It is true that South Africa's financial sector is nevertheless not in crisis; being almost entirely in private hands with suitable management components of 'black empowerment deals' to please the state, the banks have not ceased to make money, and charge rates for services that more than make up for the country's security challenges to holders of money and property. It is interesting that mining-cum-bank dominated South Africa, whose economic history has strong elements in common with Australia and Canada, has joined those two countries in coming out of the crisis relatively well. The national economy is supposed to grow by 2.8 per cent in 2010 and 3.7 per cent in 2011. Back on Easy Street?

In fact, the situation is one that will only take the car back to a relatively sluggish growth path lane that is insufficient; it leaves South Africa with a massive residue of low-skill, impoverished people, and reliance on unpredictable sales of commodities put to use elsewhere. It does not help to solve the problem of a far more impoverished southern African region (Zimbabwe, Mozambique). There is a growing debate in government over the wisdom of so-called neo-liberalism and the dominance of financial markets. Whether this debate leads to initiatives that point South Africa more in the developmentalist direction rather than merely being a rich exporter of primary products (like Canada or Australia), with a successful service sector that hopes to buy off discontent through significant social benefit payments (admittedly, on a bigger scale, it has been argued, than virtually any other country at its income level), becomes more important as a question on the agenda.

However, it has to be said that that the recent global crisis – one that has particularly shaken the conservative global powers and is likely to hasten the breakdown of the bipolar world of rich and poor, powerful and powerless – is perhaps more an opportunity than a disaster. A consequence of the Great Depression of the 1930s was to make more apparent the need for what we now call development in Africa, based at least on every kind of infrastructure and investment, while postponing the possibilities for this on a significant scale. Today the ball is far more in the African court, and requires indigenous hands that can mould development in particular directions that are at once homespun and mesh with the international environment around us. I largely agree with the Economic Commission on Africa, which has stated recently that

> The current global economic crisis has demonstrated the vulnerability of Africa to the fortunes of the global economy. It has also demonstrated that Africa cannot rely on external sources to finance its development in a sustainable way. There is therefore a need for African countries to increase their efforts to mobilize domestic resources to finance development. In the final analysis, Africa's development is the responsibility of Africans, and the argument that Africa is a poor continent that cannot finance its own development is getting tired.
>
> (*Africa Economic Report* 2010)

Long ago, Japan used its specialised skills at manufacturing silk to help pay for the early modernisation process; this is how, in a very general sense, the promotion of mineral exports needs to be handled. Much of what is needed in fact at this time in the first instance in most of Africa is pretty basic; it concerns fundamental infrastructure and basic platform-building as a learning process. The real challenge is how to make the 'planet of slums', in Mike Davis' lugubrious phrase (Davis 2004), where a larger and larger percentage of Africans live, into more productive and enterprising spaces where the intensive interchanges of the so-called informal sector are put to diversified and growing use with better and better returns. However, the conditions for this, without wishing to see things through rose-tinted spectacles, are actually more propitious now than they have been for some time.

Notes

1 These figures and many other relevant tables can be found in *Union Statistics for Fifty Years* (Pretoria, 1960).
2 These estimates are taken from World Bank calculations supplemented with a consideration of the GNP figures of the *Africa Contemporary Record*, XIV, 1981–1982 (New York, NY: Africana).
3 Figures here and below are from *Africa Economic Report*, 2010.
4 Idem.

Bibliography

Africa: Economic Report 2010, Africa Focus Bulletin, 5 April, 2010 (100405).
Ake, C. (1981) *A Political Economy of Africa*, London: Longman.
Amin, S. (1971) *Neo-Colonialism in West Africa*, Harmondsworth: Penguin.
Austen, R. (1987) *African Economic History; Internal Development and External Dependency*, London: Heinemann.
Berman, B. (1990) *Control and Crisis in Colonial Kenya; The Dialectic of Domination*, London: Heinemann.
Bryceson, D. and V. Jamal (1997) *A Farewell to Farms; De-agrarianization and Employment in Africa*, Leiden: African Studies Centre.
Collier, P. (2007) *The Bottom Billion*, Oxford: Oxford University Press.
Crowder, M. (1973) *The Story of Nigeria*, 3rd edn, London: Faber.
Davis, M. (2004) *Planet of Slums*, London: Verso.
Freund, B. (2010) 'The Social Context of African Economic Growth 1960–2008', in V. Padayachee (ed.), *The Political Economy of Africa*, London: Routledge.
Freund, B. (2011) 'South Africa: The Union Years, Political and Economic Foundations 1910–48', in R. Ross, A. Kelk Mager and B. Nassen (eds), *Cambridge History of South Africa*, Vol. II, Cambridge: Cambridge University Press.
Higginson, J. (1989) *A Working Class in the Making; Belgian Colonial Labor Policy, Private Enterprise and the African Mineworker, 1907–51*, Madison, WI: University of Wisconsin Press.
Hopkins, A.G. (1974) *An Economic History of West Africa*, London: Longmans.
Howard, R. (1978) *Underdevelopment in Ghana*, London: Croom Helm.
Leys, C. (1975) *Underdevelopment in Kenya; The Political Economy of Neo-Colonialism*, London: Heinemann.
Marseille, J. (1984) *Empire colonial et capitalisme français; histoire d'un divorce*, Paris: Albin Michel.
Newitt, M. (1981) *Portugal in Africa; The Last Hundred Years*, London: C. Hurst.
Perrings, C. (1979) *Black Mineworkers in Central Africa*, London: Heinemann.
Phimister, I. (1988) *An Economic and Social History of Zimbabwe 1890–1948, Capital Accumulation and Class Struggle*, London: Longman.
Shilaro, P. (2008) *A Failed Eldorado; Colonial Capitalism, Rural Industrialization, African Land Rights in Kenya and the Kakamega Gold Rush 1930–52*, Lanham, MD: University Press of America.
van Beusekom, M. (2002) *Negotiating Development; African Farmers and Colonial Experts at the Office du Niger 1920–60*, Portsmouth, NH: Heinemann.

Part II

The finance and trade dimension

5 Reassessing capital controls

Theoretical perspectives and empirical evidence

Vanessa da Costa Val Munhoz and Gilberto Libânio

1 Introduction

By the mid-1990s many developing countries had removed capital controls, following the example of developed economies. Important criticisms on these types of controls arise from the emphasis on its costs, such as increased domestic interest rates and reduced access to international credit markets. That view is based on the idea that developing countries would benefit from the liberalization process by getting access to cheaper credit from developed markets, promoting growth and stability. As a consequence, advocates for capital market liberalization sparked a discussion regarding the need for liberalizing the flows of international capital.

However, after the experience of nearly a decade of crises, particularly with the Asia Crisis in 1997 and its spread throughout the world, the discussion on capital controls was re-stimulated, especially in emerging and developing countries. These countries are usually the most affected by the crises. Several economists have come to believe that controls on inflows of foreign capital could reduce the vulnerability of these economies to financial instabilities in the international market.

Although the behavior of international capital flows is a subject of great importance and very much in debate among economists since the financial crises of the 1990s, more recently the discussion about the negative impact of unregulated capital flows in developing countries has been more strongly rekindled. Discussion took place especially in academia, after the outbreak of the subprime crisis in the United States which reversed itself in the global crisis in 2008. Since then, political and academic environments have revived the debate about the effectiveness of temporary capital controls as a policy response to crises.[1] More broadly, following the crisis, policy-makers are also considering unfettered capital flows to be a benign phenomenon. The principal concern is that massive inflows can explode the risk of asset bubbles and leading exchange rate overshooting.

In this context, the main objective of this chapter is to examine the proposal of the introduction of more extensive capital controls. More specifically, it will examine the relationship between the free dynamics of capital flows and macroeconomic variables in several economies. From this analysis, if we find a negative relationship – that is, if the volatile movements of financial flows have negative impact on macroeconomic stability – we will indicate a favorable position to capital controls.

If the national and international macroeconomic literature has not yet reached a conclusion about an appropriate measure for analyzing the effectiveness of capital controls, we believe that empirical evidence showing that the complete freedom of capital flows generates a negative impact, particularly for developing economies, are enough to justify the relevance of capital controls. Moreover, we believe that the absence of empirical and theoretical approaches on the part of advocates of financial liberalization to justify the recurrence of economic/financial crises and its consequences for economies that suffer from capital flight reinforces the proposal.

The argument underlying this chapter is therefore that permanent capital controls are desirable for economic and political reasons. In addition to the prevention of speculative financial cycles and the chronic instability of exchange and interest rates, the controls facilitate industrial policies, increase employment and thus reduce social inequality.

The chapter is divided into three sections in addition to this introduction. After a brief presentation of arguments pointing to the defense of restrictions to unlimited capital flows (section 2), section 3 will present definitions, instruments and types of capital controls. Subsequently, we present an empirical study on the impact of the dynamics of financial flows (section 4). Equations relating the international capital flows to the levels of interest rate and exchange rate in a sample of fifty-three countries (including developed and developing countries) will be estimated using a dynamic model of panel data (Generalized Method of Moments [GMM]).

In sum, through a theoretical presentation and an empirical analysis, this chapter seeks to present consolidated and standardized arguments in favor of capital controls.

2   The defense of restrictions on (unfettered) capital flows

There is a vast literature analyzing the negative impact of a capital account operating freely across borders, even among the various theoretical approaches. Although the pro-liberalization bias remains, the IMF and authors typically from the orthodox field had begun to "flirt", indirectly and partially, with the Chilean-type of capital controls (on capital inflows). In fact, the Fund generally admits that limited and temporary controls deserve further study and attention.

Controls or capital flows management may be needed in order to avoid reversion of financial flows – the famous *sudden stop*, among other reasons detailed below. For Forbes (2007, 2008), capital controls could potentially reduce the costs of free capital movement, such as the appreciation of domestic currency, reduction of export competitiveness, the Dutch disease[2] and the inefficiency of investments due to market distortions.

Magud and Reinhart (2006) argue the following possible skills concerning the effectiveness of capital controls: (1) limit capital inflows, (2) change the composition of flows (especially the direction towards the long-term liabilities), (3) relieve pressures on the real exchange rate and (4) create greater autonomy for monetary policy through the proximity between the domestic and international interest rates. In this sense, capital controls are imposed on four basic fears: fear of appreciation, fear of hot money, fear of large inflows, and fear of loss of monetary autonomy.[3]

Through an analysis of thirty empirical studies on this topic and constructing two indicators of capital controls, Magud and Reinhart (2006) found the following results: the area where capital controls have greater success is in providing greater autonomy to monetary policy and changing the composition of capital inflows, while success in reducing the volume of inflows and the pressure in exchange rate had mixed results.

According to Carvalho and Sicsú (2004), the theoretical argument often stressed to support the imposition of controls is the existence of externalities and the absence of perfect and complete markets that generate inefficient market situations. In addition to this theoretical rationale, the authors mention reasons concerning the fundamental and radical uncertainties that surround transactions with financial and capital assets. Thus, the isolation of an economy in the face of external shocks and the autonomy for domestic economic policy would be the main goals to be achieved via the existence of capital controls.

Another point frequently and sometimes more intensely addressed by advocates of controls is the relationship between capital movements and exchange rates. The free movement of capital increases exchange rate volatility under floating exchange rates. During a crisis, herd behavior can cause an exchange rate overshooting. The sudden reversal of capital flows results in large depreciation of the nominal exchange rate, which tends to increase financial problems of domestic borrowers and to generate inflationary pressures. Thus, exchange rates can reach excessive levels in times of crisis, as it was the case in Brazil in 2002, deteriorating market expectations.

Among the benefits of capital controls, Oreiro (2006) also points to the increasing autonomy of economic policy, reduction in external vulnerability and the prevention of exchange rate appreciation resulting from large inflows of capital in emerging countries during booms in international financial markets. The consequence of the latter result is a positive contribution to the intertemporal equilibrium of balance of payments.

Grabel (2003a, 2003b) associates the international flows of private capital (IFPCs) with five risks: currency, flight, fragility, contagion and sovereignty risks.[4] Thus, the author argues that "regulation of IPCFs is a central component of what can be thought of as a 'developmentalist financial architecture', by which I mean a financial system that promotes equitable, stable and sustainable economic development" (Grabel, 2003a: 342).

Other arguments also raised by the advocates of restrictions on capital flows suggest the possibility of taxing the capital income, enabling the adoption of distributive tax policy – when preventing domestic agents from transfering resources to countries with lower taxes; and the possibility of being used as instruments of industrial policy to shape the structure of domestic supply – when encouraging inflows of foreign direct investment in specific sectors.

Epstein, Grabel and Jomo (2005: 6) propose capital management techniques (henceforth CMTs) "to refer to two types of complementary financial policies: policies that govern international private capital flows, called 'capital controls', and those that enforce prudential management of domestic financial institutions". From these, the authors suggest seven lessons:

1   CMTs can promote financial and monetary stability, macro- and microeconomic autonomy policy, stable long-term investment and sound current account performance.
2   The successful implementation of controls over a significant period of time depends on the presence of a sound policy environment and strong fundamentals (relative low debt ratio, moderate rates of inflation, sustainable fiscal balances and current account, consistent exchange rate policies).
3   There is synergy between CMTs and economic fundamentals.
4   Nimble and flexible capital is very desirable.
5   CMTs work better when they are coherent and consistent with the overall aims of the economic policy regime coherent and consistent with overall purposes of the economic policy regime, or better yet, when they are an integral part of a national economic vision.
6   Prudent regulations are generally an important complement to capital controls and vice versa.
7   There is not one type of CMT that works better for all countries, once there is variety of strategies.

Nevertheless, it is easy to find favorable arguments and positive effects of capital controls in developing economies; we can state that the results on the analysis of capital controls impact are still inconclusive. In regard to empirical evidence on capital controls, Carvalho and Sicsú (2004) pointed out some difficulties, such as the absence of an accepted measure of the control degree actually practiced in each economy, the multiplicity of objectives of controls and the difficulty of choosing the relevant variable for measuring the controls' effectiveness.

However, despite the problems of the database in which the empirical studies on the relationship between liberalization/growth are based, empirical evidence is much less favorable to removal of controls. That is, there is no evidence showing that costs of reducing the capital mobility outweigh the benefits. Many objections to this type of policy are guided by high ideological loads (Oreiro, 2006).

Forbes (2008) points out that the results on the analysis of capital controls are inconclusive due to five general reasons. First, it is extremely difficult to measure the opening of capital accounts and capture various types of capital controls in a simple measure which can be used for empirical analysis – a factor also noted in Carvalho and Sicsú (2004). Second, different types of capital flows and controls may have different effects on growth and other macroeconomic variables. Third, the impact of removing controls could depend on a variety of other factors that are difficult to catch in *cross-country* regressions, such as institutional factors, financial system, corporate governance, or even the sequence in which various controls are removed. Fourth, capital controls can be difficult to execute (especially for countries with developed financial markets); such that the same control can have different levels of effectiveness in different countries. Finally, many countries that removed their capital controls were found to have undergone both a range of reforms and structural changes, making it difficult to isolate the impact of removal of controls.

In the same way, Magud and Reinhart (2006) indicated that the literature on capital controls has at least four serious problems ("apple-to-orange problems"): (1) there is no unified theoretical framework to analyze macroeconomic consequences of controls; (2) there is significant heterogeneity between countries and the time of control measures implemented; (3) there are multiple definitions of what constitutes a "success" (capital controls are a single policy instrument, but there are several policy objectives); and (4) studies are marked by the lack of a common methodology. Furthermore, these methods are significantly overestimated for a couple of cases (Chile and Malaysia).

In an attempt to rescue some positive experiences with use of capital controls, then, five cases of countries that have adopted different types and instruments of controls, which are well differentiated by their form of insertion of country in the global economy, time of measures implementation and objectives sought, will be examined.

In Chile, an unremunerated reserve requirement (URR) was introduced in the 1990s with the following objectives: (1) to maintain the independence of monetary policy; (2) to avoid excessive appreciation of the real exchange rate; and (3) to moderate the construction of short-term speculative liabilities. However, there has been less evidence that the Chilean capital controls have depreciated the exchange rate (Edwards and Rigobon, 2005) but by the URR changed the composition of capital inflows, as shown in some studies (De Gregorio *et al.*, 2000; Edwards, 1999; Valdés-Prieto and Soto, 1998).

In Malaysia, the imposition of control measures on capital outflow, as the closure of the offshore market; the blocking of residents funds outflow; the imposition of commitments and limits for investment abroad; and the repatriation prevention of foreign investments portfolio already internalized by one year were effective in self-isolation of the contagion effect of the Asian financial crisis (Bastos *et al.*, 2006).

Meanwhile, in the mid-1990s Thailand imposed an application of unpaid reservation (the same URR above). While Ariyoshi *et al.* (2000) point out that these controls did not prevent capital outflows through alternative channels, since it created arbitrage opportunities with interest, Coelho and Gallagher (2010) indicate that the URR has reduced the overall volume of financial flows.

In China, capital controls involve detailed rules, managed by a complex of net of institutions and supervision of private decisions, which are oriented to minimize dependence on short-term funds. The aim, in this case, is to encourage the long-term inflow, particularly foreign direct investment, which can be effective due to the large amount of international reserves accumulated during the 1990s in this country. Ma and McCauley (2008) indicate that, in light of tight controls, Chinese authorities retain some degree of short-term monetary autonomy, despite the regime of fixed exchange rate to July 2005.

Clements and Kamil (2009), analyzing the case of Colombia, show that the impact of controls varies among different categories of inflows. The econometric results of this study generate some evidence that the controls were effective in reducing at least one category of capital inflows. Although indicating that there is no statistical evidence that capital controls have resulted in a more depreciated exchange rate, or reduced the exchange rate sensitivity to the differential in interest rates, authors found that capital controls have been successful in reducing foreign loans.

Therefore, it is clear that the debate on the effects and convenience of adopting capital controls continues to motivate new academic researches, due to the underlying issues still outstanding and the positive empirical evidence of the cases reported here. The scenario of the global financial crisis contributes to this trend by raising the discussion of more effective, practical and really able measures to contain the inevitable high speculation of international capital flows.

3 Definitions, types and instruments of capital controls

Capital controls can take different forms, and are basically defined as any restriction on capital movement across the borders of a country used upon the entry or the exit of foreign capital. Nevertheless, given the hybrid formats and types of instruments of controls, the issue about how setting the restriction of international capital flows, especially the speculative capital, generates controversy.[5] There are divergences with regard to temporality of controls – for example, whether they should be permanent or temporary in face of the impact of controls; the movement which they wish to control – that is, whether controls should be located on the entry and/or exit of capital; whether they should be selective or complete; and, especially, in what is regarded as success of capital controls. Here, we point out a divergence regarding what are considered to be effective capital controls. After an investigation of case studies of countries that have adopted some type of measure of capital controls, it is intended to show that the discussion on the effectiveness of capital controls should be qualified when it is about indirect restriction measures of inflow or outflow of capital, as well as the time the measure was adopted and whether it was an ex ante measure or ex post financial crisis.

Briefly, we base our definition of capital controls on effective measures, in the sense of being comprehensive, dynamic and intense on the restriction of capital flows. Thus, we still consider that controls should be based on exogenous instruments (before the explosion of a financial crisis, for example). For us, the proposal of capital controls should be the adoption of permanent controls of

Box 5.1 Types and instruments of capital controls

Types of capital controls

1 Control on capital inflows

Preventive character to avoid excessive attraction of capital in phases of abundant liquidity. It indicates a decision to select the more desirable volume and type of resource for countries.

2 Control on capital outflow

Emergency character (temporary) during liquidity crises, although it may also be part of a careful strategy of external insertion.

Instruments of capital controls

1 Direct or administrative

These are restrictions on the capital mobility in **quantitative** terms. Involve complete prohibitions or explicit limits (total or partial) that reduce the scope of the freedom of private management of portfolios. These administrative boundaries may restrict, in terms of values and prompts, both the exchange rate exposure of banks and companies as the leveraging local resources for exchange rate transactions for residents and/or non-residents, sometimes using the bureaucratic authorization procedures of private decisions. They include, therefore, administrative controls such as setting credit ceilings, price-interest, etc. They seek to affect directly the volume of relevant financial transactions across borders.

2 Indirect or priced

These are restrictions on the capital mobility in **qualitative** terms. Attempt to discourage capital inflows by increasing their costs, through tax disincentives, reserve requirements, multiple exchange rates, minimum collateral requirements and other mechanisms. They also include explicit or implicit tax of financial flows across borders (Tobin tax) and differential exchange rates for capital transactions, and thus market-based work, such as open market operations. It can affect prices, and volume of a given transaction. Tax collection, for example, can differ according to the characteristics of the capital flow to be charted.

Source: own elaboration.

capital, effectively limiting the inflows – particularly those that are speculative. In order to construct a more categorical defense of the adoption of such a policy, we propose to analyze empirically different macroeconomic scenarios in economies that have used or still use some restriction on international capital flows. Thereafter, we aim to draw a conclusion on this economic policy strategy.

Having an own delimitation of capital controls, we also show different types of capital controls. These can be based on quantity or prices, or even focusing only on the movement of entry into or exit of capital from one country. Moreover, capital controls can be targeted to different types of flows – such as bank loans, foreign direct investment or portfolio investment – or to different actors – such as companies, banks, governments or individuals (Forbes, 2008). For better analysis, Box 5.1 summarizes the types of controls and its instruments.

On the question of temporality of capital controls, restriction to the degree of financial integration can be considered a continuous development strategy, when recognizing costs superiority against the liberalization benefits; or temporary, when controls are seen as a necessary evil. In the latter case, Carvalho and Sicsú (2004) found that capital controls are seen as "patches" rather than legitimate policy options. Similarly, Oreiro (2006) suggests that if the purpose of controls is to allow the Central Bank to manage the interest rate without, however, producing massive inflows or outflows of capital which would generate a strong variation on the nominal exchange rate or on the level of international reserves – with reflections either on the current transactions balance or on the inflation rate – controls should be permanent and comprehensive (both on capital inflows and outflows). Thus, there is a range of discussions and dichotomies regarding to the operation, meanings and strategies of capital controls, which may lead to different conclusions. Here the purpose is only to show how controls can be adopted, considering the possibility of a favorable position toward controls after the empirical analysis and its results.

4 Empirical analysis

4.1 Methodological issues

Several papers dealing with the issue of capital controls examine the effects of instruments used for this policy on the volume and composition of capital flows, as well as on the dynamics of the exchange rate. The majority of them find no evidence that restrictions on capital mobility have moderated (or controlled) the appreciation of domestic currencies or increased the degree of independence of monetary policy. Under the same theme, in this section this chapter presents an alternative empirical analysis.

Given the enormous difficulty in choosing the relevant variable for measuring the controls efficiency and the endogenous determination of the degree of capital controls,[6] the main question here is different. We want to know which measures, or how strongly the free (or unrestricted) movements of international capital flows impact on the dynamics of exchange rates and interest in detriment of movements observed in the current transactions, particularly in developing economies. Thus, instead of analyzing the impact of measures to control capital, which would require additional effort in the creation or adaptation of some control index, we will analyze the impact of free dynamics of financial flows on the conduction of the macroeconomic policy.

For such analysis, we will observe a sample of advanced and emerging countries that experienced large capital inflows between 1987 and 2008, following Cardarelli *et al.* (2009). First, we will analyze the impact of the dynamics of capital flows on the total sample. Subsequently, we will analyze a restricted sample of countries that have adopted some type of capital controls.

Although this work has its own definition of what is considered an effective measure to control speculative capital flows, the present empirical analysis will consider those countries that have been concerned or worried about the large volatile capital movements. Thus, the examination of the countries' classification as (more or less) restrictive or non-restrictive on the movements of capital is not the objective of this work. The purpose here is to separate the countries analyzed into two groups: those that allow the free movement of capital flows, and those that limit (even to a lesser extent) these free movements.

Thus, the objective from this analysis is to test if the dynamics of capital flows explain movements in exchange and interest rates in emerging countries that have adopted some type of measure of capital controls. It is intended, more specifically, to test whether capital flows are able to explain the high exchange rate volatility and loss of monetary policy autonomy, which are more strongly verified in emerging economies. The overall aim is therefore to examine empirically if the macroeconomic impact of excessive volatility of financial flows justify a position in favor of capital controls.

The underlying hypothesis is that the negative impact on the exchange rate volatility and interest rate in developing countries should contribute to the discussion on the need for introduction of prudential measures to manage capital markets in developing countries.

Panel data estimations are performed in the econometric analysis. The models are estimated using a difference system – the Generalized Method of Moments – GMM (Blundell and Bond, 1998) and data from fifty-three countries. The selection of countries in the sample follows the results of Cardarelli *et al.* (2009). As indicated above, they identified episodes of large net private capital inflows to these countries.[7] The first wave of large capital inflows commenced in the early 1990s, and ended with the Asian crisis in 1997. The second one began in 2003, and ebbed in 2008 in the wake of global financial crisis. The periodicity is annual, and covers the period of these strong capital inflows over 1995 and 2008. In this way, we have for the model panel application $N = 53$ and $T = 14$.

Therefore, our chapter contributes to a large literature on the relationship between capital flows and macroeconomic policy in three dimensions. First, we, analyze a comprehensive sample of advanced and developing countries.[8] Second, we consider our set of criteria consistent because of the episodes of large capita inflows. For us, it is important to discuss proposals of comprehensive measures in order to control speculative financial flows in countries that receive large capital inflows. That is, it makes little sense to discuss these measures in countries that do not suffer from episodes of strong inflows and consequently outflows of foreign capital. Moreover, the empirical analysis proposal covers the most recent period, after the outbreak of the global financial crisis in 2008.

The data used are components of financial series as reported in the *International Financial Statistics* (2009) from the IMF and in the *World Development Indicators* (2007, 2008, 2009) from the World Bank.

The motivation for the use of GMM is the opportunity to take into account the following: (1) the time-series dimension of the data; (2) non-observable country-specific effects; (3) the inclusion of a lagged dependent variable among the explanatory variables; and (4) the possibility that all explanatory variables are endogenous.

The dynamic relations among variables can be captured by the estimator model from this methodology. The dynamic models of panel data from the GMM are defined by the presence of lagged dependent variable (in lags) among the explanatory variables. The explicit consideration of the dynamic element allows controlling for the possible existence of a correlation between past values of the dependent variable and contemporary values of other explanatory variables, thus eliminating potential sources of bias of the estimators associated with this type of correlation[9] (Baltagi, 2005).

The GMM method starts with the following equation:

$$Y_{it} = a + b_1 Y_{it-1} + b_2 X_{it} + v_i + u_{it}$$

The elimination of the country-specific (fixed effects) is obtained once we apply the first difference to the above equation, as follow:

$$\left(Y_{it} - Y_{it-1}\right) = b_1\left(Y_{it-1} - Y_{it-2}\right) + b_2\left(X_{it} - X_{it-1}\right) + \left(u_{it} - u_{it-1}\right)$$

$$\Delta Y_{it} = b_1 \Delta Y_{t-1} + b_2 \Delta X_{it} + \Delta u_{it}$$

With this transformation, the individual error v_i is removed (endogeneity cause), but other issues arise:

1   Autocorrelation of errors is introduced: $\Delta u_{it} = u_{it} - u_{it-1}$ e $\Delta u_{it-1} = u_{it-1} - u_{it-2}$ are correlated and have a common variable, u_{it-1}.
2   The endogeneity is introduced again: $\Delta Y_{it-1} = (Y_{it-1} - Y_{it-2})$ e u_{it-1} are correlated.

The use of instruments is required to deal with the possible endogeneity of the explanatory variables and the correlation between the new term of error and the lagged dependent variable, ΔY_{it-1}.

$Y_{it-2}, Y_{it-3}, \ldots$, are considered valid instruments. Estimating the dynamic panel model with first differences and using instrumental variables, we obtain consistent estimators. Moreover, it can dramatically improve efficiency.

Therefore, the problem of autocorrelation of errors is solved by the application of the GMM method (see Arellano and Bond, 1991), which is an estimation method of instrumental variables that take into account the autocorrelation of the errors. The empirical evidence presented in this work is based on the estimator resulting from this application, called system GMM.

Considered the joint validity of instruments, this two-step estimator is asymptotically efficient and robust to whatever patterns of heteroskedasticity and cross-correlation in the model's error component. For comparison, we present also the estimates performed with pooled OLS.

Based on this methodological presentation, regressions estimated are based on the following general specification:

$$y_{it} = \alpha y_{i,t-1} \beta x_{it}' + \varepsilon_{it} \tag{1}$$

$$\varepsilon_{it} = \mu_i + v_{it} \tag{2}$$

$$E[\mu_i] = E[v_i] = E[\mu_i v_i] = 0$$

Here, x_{it} is a vector of explanatory variables of size $1 \times K$ and β is the vector of coefficients, $K \times 1$, associated with these variables. The error component model, ε_{it}, is composed of two orthogonal components: a random idiosyncratic component v_{it} and individual fixed effects constant in time, μ_i.

4.2 Empirical results[10]

The regressions were estimated in two models, which are subdivided into two blocks of results. The first model (Model 1) has exchange rate (EXCHANGE) as dependent variable and includes as explanatory variables the following: lagged exchange rate (L.EXCHANGE), exchange rate regime dummy[11] (EXCHANGE_DUM), real interest rate[12] (REAL_INTEREST), current transactions balance (CA), and the movement of capital flows (CAPITALFLOWS).[13] Two control variables were also chosen: the level of international reserves (RESERVES) and the monetary aggregates (M2). The justification for using the first variable is due to the volume of international reserves which directly influence the possible interventions that monetary authorities perform in the exchange rate market. In turn, the choice of the latter variable (monetary aggregates) is due to the need to control the explanatory variable's influence on the exchange rate regarding the sterilization operations of the monetary authorities. Thus, the basic specification of this model is given by:

EXCHANGE = f (L.EXCHANGE, EXCHANGE_DUM, REAL_
INTEREST, CA, CAPITALFLOWS)

The descriptions of each variable and its data sources are reported in Appendix A. Estimates of the first block of results of this model were based on the complete sample, which includes fifty-three countries; for the second block, the sample was reduced to twelve countries (see Appendix B). The restricted sample includes only countries that have adopted some type of measure of capital controls. Thus, we tried to measure the effect of capital controls on the appreciation of the exchange rate. The descriptive statistics are reported in Appendix C.

The second model (Model 2) has the nominal interest rate (INTEREST) as dependent variable and includes as explanatory variables the following: lagged interest rate (L.INTEREST), exchange rate (EXCHANGE), movement of capital flows (CAPITALFLOWS) and external debt (EXTERNALDEBT). The specification of this model is given by:

INTEREST = f (L.INTEREST, EXCHANGE, CAPITALFLOWS, EXTERNALDEBT)

Here we adopt, in addition to the two control variables used in the first model, the international interest rate[14] (US_INTEREST) and a price index (INFLATION). Following the same application of the first model, the estimates of the first block of results were based on the complete sample, which includes fifty-three countries; and for the second block the sample was reduced to twelve countries. Thus, we tried to measure the effect of capital controls on the autonomy of monetary policy.

Before the estimates of the dynamic model GMM, we present preliminary estimates obtained with the estimator pooled OLS. From the analysis of Model 1 from Table 5.1, the coefficients of capital flows and current account balance are negative, indicating a negative impact on the exchange rate (decrease of this value). Moreover, these coefficients are statistically significant, considering 95 percent significance level. Turning to the estimation with the GMM system, the right column in Table 5.1 shows that the current account balance changes its sign, thus presenting positive and non-significant values, suggesting that only the dynamics of capital flows is important to explain the fluctuations in the exchange rate, with respect to the variables that represent the balance of payments (influence of the external sector in the domestic economies). The variable capital flow has a negative GMM estimator and strong statistical significance, although it assumes low value.

Thus, we can assume that financial flows influence the exchange rate appreciation. In other words, we are dealing with a negative impact of capital flows on the exchange rate. Therefore, if the exchange rate decreases when the capital flows increase (financial inflows) the exchange rate appreciates. Therefore, the exchange rate appreciates by 0.6 percent for each entry of U$1 million in foreign capital.

The exchange rate is also explained by the following variables: real interest rate, which assumed a negative result; the lagged exchange rate, which assumed a positive value; and the dummy of exchange rate regime, which also assumed a positive value. Thus, as we have suggested, the interest rate and financial flows have strong correlation with the level of the exchange rate when international capital flows are unfettered, following the international finance market.

Table 5.1 Results of Model 1 regressions (first block: large sample = 53 countries from 1995 to 2008)

Dependent variable: EXCHANGE (exchange rate, final period)

Independent variables	Pooled OLS	System GMM
L.EXCHANGE	1.032***	0.7163***
	(0.008)	(0.033)
EXCHANGE_DUM	60.939*	140.810*
	(33.17)	(78.850)
REAL_INTEREST	−1.942	−5.820***
	(1.25)	(2.440)
CA	**−0.002***	**0.002**
	(0.016)	(0.002)
CAPITALFLOWS	**−0.002***	**−0.006****
	(0.011)	(0.003)
RESERVES	−6e-5	0.001
	(6e-4)	0.001
M2	−2.64	−3.850
	(3.180)	6.640
_CONS	−25.322	
	(48.364)	
R^2	0.97	
Sargan Test (p value)		0.132
Arellano–Bond Test (Z calc.)		−6.87
Number of observations	394	394

Notes
a *** statistically significant at 1%; ** statistically significant at 5%; * statistically significant at 10%.
b Standard deviation of all independent variables in parentheses.
c Constant not reported in the GMM system method.

On the other hand, the results of the same model are different when we are dealing with the restricted sample. Regressions were estimated with the GMM system[15] for the restricted sample, which includes economies that have adopted some measure of restriction on capital flows. In this case, Table 5.2 shows that the capital inflows lose their significance in explaining the exchange rate variations as well as the real interest rate and the current account balance. Thus, the correlation between financial flows and exchange rate referred to above is weakened when we deal with countries that have adopted capital controls.

Based on this result, we can infer that changes in exchange rates are not explained by the dynamics of the international finance market, thus being less vulnerable to speculative movements, out of domestic authority control. Furthermore, the monetary aggregates (M2) variable presents a significant statistic, such that the role of Central Banks' intervention in the exchange rate market becomes important to determinate the level of the exchange rate. The Central Bank policy may be important to minimize the exchange rate volatility in countries that limit the dynamics of speculative capital flows.

Table 5.2 Results of Model 1 regressions (second block: restricted sample = 12 countries, from 1995 to 2008)

Dependent variable: EXCHANGE (exchange rate, final period)

Independent variables	Pooled OLS	System GMM
L.EXCHANGE	1.026***	0.757***
	(0.0203)	(0.412)
EXCHANGE_DUM	5.510	83.360***
	(28.72)	(32.712)
REAL_INTEREST	0.5542	0.3016
	(0.855)	(1.235)
CA	0.001	6e-4
	(0.001)	(0.002)
CAPITALFLOWS	−1e-4	9e-4
	(0.011)	(0.002)
RESERVES	−1e-4	−6e-4
	3e-4	7e-4
M2	−1.640	−6e-5**
	2.350	3e-5
_CONS	10.170	
	(42.60)	
R^2	0.97	
Sargan Test (p value)		0.129
Arellano–Bond Test (Z calc.)		−1.63
Number of observations	83	83

Notes
a *** statistically significant at 1%; ** statistically significant at 5%; * statistically significant at 10%.
b Standard deviation of all independent variables in parentheses.
c Constant not reported in the GMM system method.

In particular, estimates for the restricted sample show that the following variables were significant in explaining variations in the exchange rate: lagged exchange rate, dummy of exchange rate regime, and monetary aggregates (M2).

These results corroborate the favorable position in capital controls adoption. A lower appreciation of the exchange rate in response to massive capital inflows can help to reduce the vulnerability of an economy to sudden reversals, asset booms and busts.

Considering Model 2, the purpose is to analyze the movements of interest rates in order to capture the effects of the international capital flows on the dynamics. Our hypothesis is that there is a strong correlation between these two variables (interest rate and capital flows), since the interest rate is an instrument to attract financial inflows, especially in developing countries. On the other hand, we argue that this relationship is weakened when we analyze countries that counter surges in capital inflows in order to have more freedom to manage the interest rate. Thus, we measure the effect of capital controls in the autonomy of monetary policy. To accomplish the objective, we start with estimates for the complete sample, using a pooled OLS.

From Table 5.3, evidence from the pooled OLS estimator does not allow us to obtain significant results regarding the relationship between capital flows and interest rates. However, this relationship becomes extremely important when we observe the dynamic estimators by the GMM system.

The CAPITALFLOWS variable is strongly significant and presents negative sign. This shows that when there is capital flight (or a decrease in the volume of capital flows), the nominal interest rate increases. This result approximates with our argument that there is a loss of monetary autonomy when international capital flows are kept free from restrictions. It is necessary to increase the interest rate to minimize the intense outflows of foreign capital. It should be noted that in the case of developing economies, this reaction (high interest rate) is not effective in controlling the massive capital outflows in times of international economic crisis.

In this instance, other variables were also significant to explain variations in the interest rate, as follow: external debt, international interest rates, inflation,

Table 5.3 Results of Model 2 regressions (first block: large sample=53 countries, from 1995 to 2008)

Dependent variable: INTEREST (nominal exchange rate)

Independent variables	Pooled OLS	System GMM
L.INTEREST	0.396***	0.016
	(0.037)	(0.054)
EXCHANGE	−9e-5	0.001
	(1.9e-5)	(0.001)
CAPITALFLOWS	−1.8e-6	−4e-4***
	9e-5	(1e-4)
EXTERNALDEBT	9.8e-6	1e-4***
	1e-5	4e-5
US_INTEREST	−0.197	2.802***
	(0.357)	(0.313)
RESERVES	−1e-5	−2.5e-5***
	4e-5	(8e-5)
M2	7e-6	3.18e-7
	1e-6	(2.07e-7)
INFLATION	0.225***	0.035*
	(0.032)	(0.019)
_CONS	24.918***	
	(3.56)	
R^2	0.57	
Sargan Test (p value)		0.637
Arellano–Bond Test (Z calc.)		−2.85
Number of observations	297	297

Notes
a *** statistically significant at 1%; ** statistically significant at 5%; * statistically significant at 10%.
b Standard deviation of all independent variables in parentheses.
c Constant not reported in the GMM system method.

and international reserves variables. This indicates that a variation of external liabilities, or interest rate differentials, or domestic prices, or international reserves can push the countries into the trap of high interest rates needed to attract international capital.

In turn, the results for the restricted sample are more favorable than the results for the complete sample. Table 5.4 shows that the coefficient of CAPITAL-FLOWS becomes positive and not significant. In this case, only the lagged interest rate, among the explanatory variables, explains the dynamics of the nominal interest rate of countries that have adopted restrictive measures on capital flows. This may mean an increase of monetary policy autonomy for these countries.

Moreover, the importance of the differential of interest rate to the determination of the level of domestic interest rates should be noted. The domestic interest rate increase 1.82 percent for each increase of 1 percent on the US interest rate level. This shows how the developing countries are dependent on the monetary policy conduction of the central countries, particularly the US economy.

Table 5.4 Results of Model 2 regressions (second block: restricted sample = 12 countries, from 1995 to 2008)

Dependent variable: INTEREST (nominal interest rates)

Independent variables	Pooled OLS	System GMM
L.INTEREST	0.181***	0.190***
	(0.042)	(0.043)
EXCHANGE	7e-4	−0.002
	(0.001)	(0.003)
CAPITALFLOWS	8e-5	4e-5
	(1e-4)	1e-4
EXTERNALDEBT	2e-5	2e-5
	(1e-5)	3e-5
US_INTEREST	−0.831	1.826***
	0.623	0.524
RESERVES	−4e-4	−1e-4*
	(4e-5)	5e-5
M2	1e-5	8.28e-8
	(1e-5)	2.61e-7
INFLATION	−0.211***	0.055
	(0.062)	(0.042)
_CONS	26.863***	
	(0.621)	
R^2	0.61	
Sargan Test (p value)		0.359
Arellano–Bond Test (Z calc.)		−1.22
Number of observations	69	69

Notes
a *** statistically significant at 1%; ** statistically significant at 5%; * statistically significant at 10%.
b Standard deviation of all independent variables in parentheses;
c Constant not reported in the GMM system method.

Finally, we must emphasize the results of models' specification tests. Based on the results of the Sargan test (presented in tables results), it is observed that the instruments used in all models are appropriate. Meanwhile, the serial auto-correlation tests (Arellano–Bond tests) indicate that one cannot reject the null hypothesis of no second-order serial correlation in the differentiated error term, also in all models. Therefore, specifications are not rejected for equations of the exchange rate and interest rate.

From this empirical analysis, we can conclude, once again, about the need for imposing capital controls. By reducing the impact of speculative capital flows on the exchange and interest rates, restrictions on capital flows generate less pressure on the exchange rate market and result in higher monetary autonomy. The results have not allowed a conclusion about the different possible arrangements of controls in different economic situations. Nevertheless, we can conclude that there is extreme relevance in the introduction of tight restriction measures to counter the speculative capital flows. It is fair to highlight the capital controls' importance ahead of the negative results of the unfettered (unlimited) financial flows movements.

5 Concluding remarks

From analytical and empirical dimensions, the present chapter aims to contribute to the debate about capital controls, considered important to counter speculative capital flows. The volatility of capital flows is important because of the impact on domestic macroeconomic variables, such as exchange rate variability and interest rate flexibility.

The empirical analysis shows that economies which address concerns of large short-term inflows present financial accounts' results able to reduce pressures on exchange rate and to maintain monetary control through the management of the interest rate.

The econometric exercise performed in the chapter cannot make a conclusion about the most appropriate control type for each country. Country experiences have varied with many types of controls, depending largely on the motivation and nature of controls, and on country-specific characteristics such as the administrative capacity to implement them. However, if there is a clear difference in the behavior pattern of the relationship between capital flows versus exchange rates and capital flows versus interest rates in countries that have adopted measures with a restrictive bias, the importance and efficacy of these measures is clear. Therefore, the effort of this chapter has not been directed to understand and define the best measure for specific cases. Our purpose is only to corroborate the favorable position of measures able to restrict the high volatility of international capital flows.

The implications of such volatility for peripheral countries allow us to draw other conclusions. Brazil, in particular, has a potential vulnerability in the external front. This country has a huge amount of external debt and a balance of payments dominated by highly flexible and speculative financial flows. In this sense, the capital flight from Brazil, in moments of sudden change in the international investors' expectations, causes a loss of resources in the domestic economy and consequently causes serious implications to the economic performance in the long run. In order to counter large capital inflows after the global crisis, the Brazilian government imposed a temporary tax on inflows of short-term capital, as a response to the massive upswing in inflows in 2009. However, the capital account data in this country show that it didn't reduce the inflow through the capital market. The consequence was an appreciation of the Brazilian currency of over 30 percent on the dollar.

Therefore, it is important to deal with the impact of potentially destabilizing short-term capital flows in peripheral countries like Brazil. With this, we want to highlight the need for a toolkit to manage capital flows, which effectively inhibit the speculation of international investors. This could be achieved with an inflow control linked to an outflow control. Otherwise, the imposition of an unremunerated reserve requirement could be more effective. Moreover, the underlying perspective in this chapter suggests taxing financial flows through the imposition of limits and deposits for capital inflows; regulating banks' operations in foreign currency; as well as controlling the Securities, Commodities and Futures Exchange. These would be some possible strategies for the Brazilian economy. In sum, there is a need for a regular reassessment to ensure capital controls, and the administrative capacity to implement them.

Finally, this note also emphasizes that such measures should be complemented by other strategies to promote economic development, such as political stability, increased investment in gross formation of fixed capital, the incentive to export, and development policies towards the modification of structural problems of Brazilian balance of payments. These policies are relevant for the effectiveness of capital controls (either on inflow or capital outflow). International experience proves this important complementarity. Moreover, the discussion of capital controls is also a crucial topic for future empirical and theoretical researches. There is much space for discussions about the specifics of this issue.

Appendices

Appendix A: Description and source of data

Box 5.2 Description and source of data

EXCHANGE	Nominal Effective Exchange Rate, end of period (domestic currency units per US Dollar).	IFS (2009)
L.EXCHANGE	Lagged Nominal Effective Exchange Rate, end of period.	IFS (2009)
REAL_INTEREST	Real interest rate as reported by World Bank. Real interest rate is the lending interest rate adjusted for inflation as measured by the GDP deflator.	WDI (2007, 2008)
INTEREST	Nominal interest rate as reported by IMF. It is the money market rate (percent per annum).	IFS (2009)
L.INTEREST	Lagged Nominal interest rate.	IFS (2009)
CA	Current account (US$ million).	IFS (2009)
CAPITALFLOWS	Private Capital inflows as calculated by Cardarelli *et al.* (2009)* (US$ million).	IFS (2009)
RESERVES	International reserves: total reserve minus gold (US$ million).	IFS (2009)
M2	Monetary aggregates – M2 (US$ million).	IFS (2009)
US_INTEREST	International interest rate. It is the *Federal Funds Rate* (percent per annum).	IFS (2009)
EXTERNALDEBT	Total external debt. Total external debt is the sum of public, publicly guaranteed, and private non-guaranteed long-term debt, use of IMF credit, and short-term debt. Short-term debt includes all debt having an original maturity of one year or less and interest in arrears on long-term debt. Data are in current (US$ million).	WDI (2007, 2008)
INFLATION	Consumer price index. Index numbers (2005=100).	IFS (2009)

Notes

IFS = International Financial Statistics (International Monetary Fund – IMF, 2009). WDI = World Development Indicators (World Bank, 2007, 2008).

* The net private capital inflows series used in the paper are constructed in five steps. First, we calculate (net) foreign direct investment (FDI) taking direct investments into the recipient country and subtracting direct investments abroad. Second, we strip out assets that are classified under the monetary authority and the general government for each of the remaining categories: portfolio investments, financial derivatives, and other investments. We then do the same for liabilities, in effect yielding assets and liabilities that are private in nature. Third, these series of private assets and liabilities are netted, yielding net inflows for the three categories. Fourth, we add FDI to the net private portfolio investment, financial derivative, and other investment categories, yielding our definition of net private capital inflows.

Appendix B: Description of sample of countries

Complete sample

Australia, Canada, Denmark, Iceland, New Zealand, Norway, Spain, Sweden, Switzerland, Argentina, Brazil, Chile, Colombia, Costa Rica, Mexico, Paraguay, Peru, Uruguay, Venezuela, China, India, Indonesia, Korea, Kenya, Malaysia, Pakistan, Philippines, Singapore, Thailand, Vietnam, Bulgaria, Croatia, Czech Republic, Estonia, Hungary, Latvia, Lithuania, Poland, Romania, Russia, Slovak Republic, Slovenia, Ukraine, Albania, Algeria, Cyprus, Egypt, Israel, Malta, Morocco, Tunisia, South Africa and Turkey.

Restricted sample

Spain, Brazil, Chile, Colombia, Venezuela, China, India, Malaysia, Singapore, Thailand, Romania and Russia.[16]

Appendix C: Descriptive statistics

Table 5.A1 Model 1 – first block: complete sample

Variable	Mean	Std Dev.	Min	Max
EXCHANGE	608.83	2,360.561	0.05	16,977
EXCHANGE_DUM	1.31	0.46	1	2
REAL_INTEREST	8.07	12.36	−82.45	84.04
CA	556.32	17,643.89	−154,129	102,400
CAPITALFLOWS	7,173.20	29,792.47	−126,813.1	3,81479.1
RESERVES	26,532.6	433,60.86	241.05	466,750
M2	3,152,849	6,984,746	55.09	49,400,000

Table 5.A2 Model 1 – second block: restricted sample

Variable	Mean	Std Dev.	Min	Max
EXCHANGE	224.55	579.43	0.25	2,864.79
EXCHANGE_DUM	1.24	0.43	1	2
REAL_INTEREST	9.68	17.64	−35.31	77.68
CA	1,749.16	29,187.8	−154,129	102,400
CAPITALFLOWS	13,717.86	52,918.18	−126,813.1	381,479.1
RESERVES	56,565.75	67,847.1	1,526.27	466,750
M2	5,143,933	8,758,690	856.13	45,900,000

Table 5.A3 Model 2 – first block: complete sample

Variable	Mean	Std Dev.	Min	Max
EXCHANGE	608.83	2,360.561	0.05	16,977
US_INTEREST	4.02	1.75	1.12	6.23
INTEREST	11.04	14.44	0.01	190.42
CA	736.73	18,298.08	−154,129	129,469
CAPITALFLOWS	7,173.20	29,792.47	−126,813.1	381,479.1
EXTERNALDEBT	51,147.45	58,427.04	286.439	281,612.1
RESERVES	26,532.6	43,360.86	241.05	466,750
M2	3,152,849	6,984,746	55.09	4.59e+07
INFLATION	85.7	26.89	0.757	376.746

Table 5.A4 Model 2 – second block: restricted sample

Variable	Mean	Std Dev.	Min	Max
EXCHANGE	224.55	579.43	0.25	2,864.79
US_INTEREST	4.02	1.74	1.12	6.23
INTEREST	12.82	20.90	0.07	190.43
CA	1,749.16	29,187.8	−154,129	102,400
CAPITALFLOWS	13,717.86	52,918.18	−126,813.1	381,479.1
EXTERNALDEBT	90,861.01	71,327.3	6,832.09	281,612.1
RESERVES	56,565.75	67,847.1	1,526.27	466,750
M2	5,143,933	8,758,690	856.13	4.59e+07
INFLATION	84.17	28.53	3.61	175.88

Notes

1 Recently, the IMF published a paper recognizing that capital controls are again in the news. They highlighted the importance of such controls to achieve a less risky external liabilities structure and to reduce financial fragility (Ostry, Ghosh, Habermeier, Camon, Qureshi and Reinhardt, 2010).

2 The "Dutch disease" is associated with some degree of industrialization due to increased export revenues resulting from the discovery of mineral resources. The consequence of this discovery is the appreciation of domestic currency caused by a surge of capital inflows. The term was coined after the discovery of natural gas in the Netherlands in the 1970s. About the process of de-industrialization and the Dutch disease, see Palma (2008).

3 Ocampo and Palma (2008) add a fifth fear to justify the capital controls: the fear of an asset bubble.

4 To Grabel (2003b), the liberal model of financial integration makes national governments face constraints when implementing independent policies in the midst of international crises. This risk is common to emerging economies that receive foreign aid and are subject to the veto of political decisions.

5 Kawai and Takagi (2003) point out different types of capital controls based on the following rivalries: controls on inflows × controls on outflows, permanent controls × temporary controls; based-prices controls × administrative controls, and

imposition × controls effectiveness. Oreiro (2006) uses three criteria to differentiate between types of capital controls, namely the permanence degree of controls (temporary or permanent), the instrument used to control these flows (market controls and direct controls), and the type of movement to be controlled (outflow control and inflow controls).

6 Carvalho and Sicsú (2004) also highlight the complexity nature of available information on capital controls, as pointed in section 2 of this work.

7 In fact, the Cardarelli *et al.* (2009) study identified 109 episodes of large private capital inflows for fifty-two countries over the period 1987–2007. In our sample one country was added, Kenya, because of its experience with a rapid process of financial liberalization. We think its inclusion is interesting, to reinforce our purpose of comparing a sample of countries without restrictions on capital flows (considered most liberalized) with a sample of countries that have adopted restrictive measures to these flows. For details of countries in the sample, see Appendix B.

8 The sample of countries includes eight advanced countries and forty-five developing countries; see the list in Appendix B.

9 The endogeneity between the lagged dependent variable and the fixed effects components of the model error tends to generate an overestimation of the coefficient associated with the dynamic component, giving it a predictive power that actually belongs to the individual effects not observed.

10 The results in this section were obtained from the use of STATA 10 software. All estimates for the dynamic panel were performed using the command xtabond2 developed by Roodman (2009).

11 Assumes value = 1 for fixed exchange rate regime, and value = 2 for floating exchange rate regime. For these data we used the database of Ilzetzki *et al.* (2008), following the IMF's classification. The IMF ranks countries according to six different classifications of exchange rate regimes. For our purposes we assume only the classifications between fixed exchange rate and floating exchange rate, since we are not interested in analyzing the impact of different types of regimes on changes in the exchange rate.

12 In the first model we used the real interest rate instead of the nominal interest rate because this provides the important values of the interest rate that most directly influence the international capital flows, which, under our hypothesis, most explain the exchange rate appreciation in the face of huge capital inflows.

13 All equations include time dummies.

14 Following the empirical economic literature, the variable that best represents the international interest rate is the US economy interest rate, considered the safest economy for financial investments.

15 We omitted here the results obtained with the pooled OLS, once the resulting regression did not present a satisfactory result.

16 This sample consists of countries that have adopted some type of control measure of capital flows. Taiwan should be in this group. However, due to lack of availability of data this country does not make the list of countries in the IMF – it is not part of the selected sample.

References

Arellano, M. and Bond, S. (1991). "Some Tests of Specification for Panel Data: Monte Carlo Evidence and an Application to Employment Equations", *Review of Economic Studies*, 58: 277–297.

Ariyoshi, A., Habermeier, K., Laurens, B., Otker-Robe, I., Canales-Kriljenko, J.I. and Kirilenko, A. (2000). "Capital controls: country experiences with their use and Liberalization", *IMF Occasional Paper*, No. 190.

Baltagi, B.H. (2005). *Econometric Analysis of Panel Data*. Chichester: Wiley.

Bastos, P., Biancarelli, A. and Deos, S. (2006). "Controle de capitais e reformas liberais: uma comparação internacional", *Economia e Sociedade*, Vol. 15, 3(28): 545–576.

Blundell, R. and Bond, S. (1998). "Initial Conditions and Moment Restrictions in Dynamic Panel Data Models", *Journal of Econometrics*, 87: 115–143.

Cardarelli, R., Elekdag, S.A. and Kose, M.A. (2009). "Capital Inflows: Macroeconomic Implications and Policy Responses", IMF Working Paper.

Carvalho, F.C. and Sicsú, J. (2006). "Experiências de Controles do Fluxo de Capitais: focando o caso da Malásia", in J. Sicsú and F. Ferrari (eds), *Câmbio e Controles de Capitais*, Rio de Janeiro: Elsevier.

Clements, B. and Kamil, H. (2009). "Are Capital Controls Effective in the 21st Century? The Recent Experience of Colombia", IMF Working Paper.

Coelho, B. and Gallagher. (2010). "Capital Controls and 21st Century Financial Crises: Evidence from Colombia and Thailand", Political Economy Research Institute Working Papers Series, No. 213.

De Gregorio, J., Edwards, S. and Valdés, R. (2000). "Controls on Capital Inflows: Do They Work?", *Journal of Development Economics*, 3(1): 59–83.

Edwards, S. (1999). "How Effective Are Controls on Capital Inflows? An Evaluation of Chile's Experience", mimeograph, UCLA, June.

Edwards, S. and Rigobon, R. (2005). "Capital Controls, Exchange Rate Volatility and External Vulnerability", NBER Working Paper 11434.

Epstein, G.A., Grabel, I. and Jomo, K.S. (2005). "Capital Management Techniques in Developing Countries", in G.A. Epstein (ed.), *Capital Flight and Capital Controls in Developing Countries*. Cheltenham: Edward Elgar.

Forbes, K. (2007). "One Cost of the Chilean Capital Controls: Increased Financial Constraints for Smaller Traded Firms", *Journal of International Economics*, 71(2): 294–323.

Forbes, K. (2008). "Capital Controls", in L.E. Blume and S.N. Durlauf (eds), *The New Palgrave Dictionary of Economics* (2nd edn), New York, NY: Palgrave Macmillan. Available at: http://web.mit.edu/kjforbes/www/articles1.html (accessed 18 August 2009).

Grabel, I. (2003a). "International Private Capital Flows and Developing Countries", in H.-J. Chang (ed.), *Rethinking Development Economics*. London: Anthem Press, pp. 325–345.

Grabel, I. (2003b). "Averting Crisis? Assessing Measures to Manage Financial Integration in Emerging Economies", *Cambridge Journal of Economics*, 27: 317–336.

Ilzetzki, E., Reinhart, C.M. and Rogoff, K.S. (2008). "Exchange Rate Arrangements Entering the 21st Century: Which Anchor Will Hold?", mimeo. Available at: www.economics.harvard.edu/faculty/rogoᵒ/Recent_Papers_Rogoff.

Kawai, M. and Takagi, S. (2003). "Rethinking Capital Controls: The Malaysian Experience", Macroeconomics Working Papers No. 473, East Asian Bureau of Economic Research.

Ma, G. and McCauley, R.N. (2008). "Efficacy of China's Capital Controls: Evidence from Price and Flow Data", *Pacific Economic Review*, 13(1): 104–123.

Magud, N. and Reinhart, C.M. (2006). "Capital Controls: An Evaluation", NBER Working Paper 11973.

Ocampo, J.A. and Palma, J.G. (2008). "The Role of Preventative Capital Account Regulations', IPD Working Papers, Columbia University, January.

Oreiro, J.L. (2006). "Autonomia, fragilidade e equilíbrio: a teoria dos controles de capitais", in J. Sicsú and F. Ferrari (eds), *Câmbio e Controles de capitais: avaliando a eficiência de modelos macroeconômicos*. Rio de Janeiro: Elsevier.

Ostry, J., Ghosh, A., Habermeier, K., Chamon, M., Qureshi, M. and Reinhardt, D. (2010). "Capital Inflows: The Role of Controls", IMF Staff Position Note, 19 February, International Monetary Fund.

Palma, J.G. (2008). "De-industrialisation, Premature De-industrialisation and the Dutch Disease", in: L.E. Blume and S.N. Durlauf (eds), *The New Palgrave Dictionary of Economics* (2nd edn), New York, NY: Palgrave Macmillan.

Roodman, D. (2006). "How to Do xtabond2: An Introduction to Difference and System GMM in Stata", Center for Global Development Working Paper No. 103.

Valdés-Prieto, S. and Soto, M. (1998). "The Effectiveness of Capital Controls: Theory and Evidence from Chile", *Empirica* 25(2): 133–164.

6   Trade dimensions in the impact of the global financial crisis in developing countries

Are the policy responses overlooking them?

Aldo Caliari

In late 2008, as the financial crisis reached undoubtedly global and historical proportions, the leaders of several countries started talking about the need for a "Bretton Woods II", in reference to the foundational character of the reform that the crisis should trigger. In November 2008, the Group of 20 (G20) – a grouping that involves several emerging market countries and was created after the East Asian financial crisis as an informal forum to broaden the discussion on international economic affairs – was vested with a new mandate. The Heads of State of this group – which hitherto had met usually at Finance Ministers' level – gathered in the US for an unprecedented G20 Summit on Financial Markets and the World Economy that agreed on "Principles" and an "Action Plan for Reform". The Summit was followed by second and third ones, held in London (April 2009) and Pittsburgh (September 2009). A Summit on world financial and monetary reform was also held at the United Nations, 24–26 June. Its preparations were fed by a Commission of Experts on Financial and Monetary Reforms appointed by the President of the General Assembly. It was chaired by Nobel Prize-winner economist Joseph Stiglitz and featured former and current well-known economic policy-makers, besides experts from academia.

While much of the attention in developing a response to the global financial crisis focused on financial measures, the trade dimensions of the crisis tended to be overlooked, except for those measures intended to limit protectionism and restore trade finance.

In what follows, this chapter discusses the many trade-related channels by which the financial crisis affected – and continues to affect – developing countries. The next section offers a brief introduction while section 2 discusses the role of commodity prices. Section 3 addresses financialization and the regulation of financial instruments. Section 4 focuses on debt sustainability, and section 5 on investment. Section 6 addresses monetary policy and exchange rate problems, while Section 7 touches upon conditions for credit finance and access to credit. Section 8 summarizes the trade aspects as approached in the G20 Summit Declarations, and Section 9 offers some concluding remarks.

1 The role of trade in the impacts of the global crisis on developing countries

The global economic crisis had its epicenter in the US subprime mortgage market. As such, its origins were of a financial nature. The crisis rapidly spread to other financial centers. Amidst the flurry of responses to the crisis, trade issues tended to take a back seat to financial ones.

It can be argued that in the case of developing countries, while the crisis had undeniable implications for their finances, the main channels by which they felt the impacts were trade and trade-related ones. This is not surprising, based on the sheer fact that developing countries' exports-to-GDP ratio increased from being about a quarter of their GDP in 1995 to being more than half of their GDP in 2007 (UNCTAD 2009). A look at mainstream analyses of the crisis will reveal that trade was not ignored. In all fairness, several reports highlighted the trade impacts. Nonetheless they generally listed trade alongside a number of impact channels, such as investment, debt, exchange rate movements, fiscal, remittances, etc. There is quite a difference between this sort of analysis and the argument that this chapter makes: that is, that the trade structure of developing countries and the way it interlinks with a number of financial dimensions – debt, investment, and so on and so forth – were at the center of how these countries were affected.

The conclusion holds important differences for a response that would better address the interest of peripheral countries as compared to those of center ones. The conclusion also holds sway far beyond crisis times. The crisis was preceded by a period (2003–2008) of boom in trade and exports. During this boom it became apparent that no country can succeed in using trade to develop or reduce poverty without complementary and supportive internal and external financial structures. A clear example can be drawn from sub-Saharan Africa, where the period in question registered the best six-year export performance since the start of structural reforms in the 1980s. Yet, the current account balance was negative, except for one year – when quite a small positive balance was registered.

Coming after decades of reform in developing countries that placed export-led growth as the central paradigm, the behavior of trade and the role that it played in their economies during the boom and during the bust allow two observations to be made. One, a focus on an improved export performance without an equal emphasis on the mechanisms by which such exports would yield increased and stable financial gains to the source countries does not mean much. Two, the success of a trade-led development model hinges not so much on market access or on trade policy reforms per se, but on redrawing the role of trade in developing country economies and its linkages to a number of external and internal financial structures in those economies.

2 Limited diversification of export base and markets

A key trade-related channel by which developing countries suffered the crisis was their limited diversification of export products and markets. This explains the large impact of the fall in commodity prices. To put these impacts in perspective, it is necessary to highlight that between 2002 and 2007 the prices of all commodities, in dollar terms, increased by 113 percent (UNCTAD 2008a: 23). This average masks large differences between the minerals group (around 260 percent) and food and tropical beverages (60 percent). Nonetheless, the increases were all significant across the board, especially after decades of declining prices.

As the crisis hit, with a scenario of lower demand everywhere, commodity prices went down at, in some cases, shocking speed (for example, oil went down to a 50 percent of its price in two months). The only bright side to the slump in commodity prices was that some developing countries that until mid-2008 were trying to cope with rising bills for their food and fuel imports experienced some relief (IMF 2009a: 5).

But the prevailing side of the picture is the significant negative effects that lower commodity prices had on export revenues. The fact that the exceptional growth period experienced by developing country economies in the pre-crisis five years coincided with the surge in commodity prices was more than a mere coincidence. For all but two Latin American countries, commodities represent more than 50 percent of their exports. More than three-quarters of the growth in export revenue in 2007 was due purely to price increases of those commodities (ECLAC 2008a: 22). A similar trend is notable in Africa, which is in fact more dependent on commodities than Latin America. Primary commodities, including fuels, account for near 70 percent of the average exports in the period 1995–2006 (UNCTAD 2008b: 20).

What these numbers are saying is that what has been characterized as a boom actually hid meager progress – or even retrogression – in the export profiles of developing countries. Very few countries had been able to use the increased revenue from the boom in commodities to get higher up in the ladder of diversification and value-added. There is evidence that in some cases – such as African countries – the export diversification actually retrogressed (ibid.: 19).

In some cases the hindrance to diversification was that the rents of the boom were not captured at the country level, while in other cases captured rents were not devoted to invest in infrastructure and productive capacity but in either immediate consumption or long-postponed social needs. A few countries were merely able to take advantage of the access to the natural resources to expand into natural resource-based manufactures. As a result, trade profiles have not changed much, leaving no room for cushioning the impacts of the decrease in prices of commodities. The effective utilization of increased commodity revenue would have required a capacity that, after years of downsizing and withdrawal from economic planning, states were barely starting to re-build.

To the extent that some countries had developed some manufacturing capacity, they also faced a problem of lower demand in client countries, forcing adjustments that, given the small margins available to adjust in price (or, in some cases, even wage cuts), had to be done via downsizing. The scarcity in trade credit magnified the problems as integration in global production chains is the common expression of the export-led model in manufactures by developing countries.

The limited diversity of products was not the only issue that countries faced, but also that of markets. While South–South trade has been increasing, developing countries still experience high concentration in their export markets, making them largely susceptible to a recession affecting markets of the North. Even in Asia, a region apparently registering a very high share of South–South trade, there was a need to look beyond the surface to understand that a lot of the South–South trade was trade in parts for products that were ultimately finished and exported from China to Northern markets. This meant that the chain ultimately led to Northern markets, and the fall in demand from those markets was magnified across it.

3 Financialization and commodities

Attention should also be paid to another way in which the structure of trade in developing countries interacted with the financial system, and this is the growing impact of the financialization of commodities. When the concentration of the export base addressed in the previous section is around commodities, the conditions of the international financial system tend to make it an extremely difficult stage for developing countries to exit from.

A noticeable trend in the years before the crisis was that commodities had become an asset class to be included in asset allocation models of portfolio investment. With this shift, their prices are no longer determined by the demand for final use relative to available supply by producers, but rather by the demand to hold commodity-based financial assets and by those willing to supply them, without actually producing the respective commodity. There was, as a result, a sharp increase in non-commercial demand for commodities at a time when other fundamental factors caused prices to tighten (Kregel 2008).

By mid-2008 there were sixty commodities-linked US funds and notes tracked by Financial Research Corporation (only nine with records stretching back more than two years). In Europe, over 100 exchange-traded commodities were on offer, mostly from London-based ETF Securities. Goldman Sachs estimated that pension funds and mutual funds had investments of a total of approximately US$85 billion in commodity index funds, and that investments in its own index, the Goldman Sachs Commodity Index (GSCI), had tripled over the previous few years. Between end of 2005 and early 2008, index-linked commodity investment had doubled to US$260 billion, according to Citigroup.[1]

Just as these investments amplified price movements on the rise, they amplified their movement down in the collapse.

As put by Kregel,

> financial market conditions are producing real changes in the production and export structure of most Latin American countries – changes that are not sustainable and produce substantial disruption when they are reversed. In particular, the bubble in commodity prices is reflected in what should be considered a bubble in real exchange rates throughout the region.... It is

clear that the changes in relative prices have been produced by purely financial rather than real factors.... Yet they are having real consequences on the
structure of the economies with large primary commodity sectors.

(Kregel 2009)

Thus, it is crucial to the trade interests of developing countries that the volatility of these prices receives adequate treatment through a thorough regulation
of "innovative" speculative instruments that are traded privately (over-the-
counter). These are currently neither regulated nor reported to public authorities.

4 Debt sustainability measures

Debt in developing countries is also intimately intertwined with trade dynamics.
Alongside the deterioration of trade and fiscal balances brought by the crisis,
debt levels rapidly deteriorated, too. For the low-income countries that had ben-
efitted from the debt relief committed in the Heavily Indebted Poor Countries
Initiative (HIPC) and the Multilateral Debt Relief Initiative – HIPC's most
recent expansion, launched by the Group of 8 meeting in Gleneagles in 2005 –
this happened in spite of the implementation of such debt relief. Trade is a key
factor in that equation. It is clear that the debt levels of the countries in question
have been heavily affected by increased lending and less favorable financing
terms. The fact that many countries moved from a positive to a negative current
account is an important factor in the debt increases. Non-HIPC developing countries, excluding China, registered a current account surplus of only 0.8 percent of
GNI in 2007, and already in 2008 moved to a deficit of 0.3 percent of GNI
(UNCTAD 2010: 27). But debt indicators have GDP, exports and revenue in the
denominator, with exports being the most widely used of them. The deteriorating export revenue has therefore magnified the falls in all of these indicators. As
for HIPC countries, a significant number of countries that received all the relief
promised in the Initiative will continue to remain at what the World Bank and
IMF call a moderate or high risk of debt distress. Moreover, low-income countries continue to be highly vulnerable to export shocks.[2] An IMF study reports
that most HIPC completion-point countries remain weak in their export diversification and vulnerable to terms of trade shocks (Yang and Nyberg 2009).

But it is important to keep in mind that the assessment of risks and "sustainability" is according to the rather tolerant parameters of the Debt Sustainability
Framework adopted in 2005. Such reform resulted in a ramping up of the thresh-
olds at which borrowers are considered to be in trouble. Some substantial criticisms had been made of the methodology for measuring debt sustainability in
the past, which relied on over-optimistic projections of export and GDP growth.[3]
In spite of its attempt to address the problem with stress-testing methodologies,
the boom of the last years continued to boost the optimism of the projections.
The IMF/Bank staff asserted, referring to the situation of countries not in the
HIPC/MDRI program, that the situation is not worse because these countries
were having an export growth rate of 11 percent average in a ten-year average.

Export projections based on such trends could be rendered useless by the impact of the crisis, and so will the projections of debt ratios for many countries. A former US Treasury official who was heavily involved in the design of the Debt Sustainability Initiative reports found last year that both export and GPD projections embedded in the Debt Sustainability Assessments were still leaning towards the optimistic (Leo 2010). The very notion of "low" or "moderate" risk will certainly come under challenge.

The increasing debt problems were not confined to the low-income countries group. Commodity prices had a major impact on worsening export outlooks for several middle-income countries, such as Argentina, Mexico, Brazil, South Africa and Kazakhstan. When the current accounts of some countries showed signs of worsening, making more borrowing necessary, rating agencies such as Fitch proceeded to downgrade them (Oakley 2008). The downgrades fueled a vicious circle, increasing the costs for these countries to repay their existing obligations or refinance them.

Reciprocally, the need to direct more income to paying debt service can only contribute to accentuate the problems both low- and middle-income countries have in making the investment necessary to expand their production capacity or place them in tighter competition with pressing immediate social needs.

5 Foreign investment

There was another factor boosting the "boom" in developing countries right before the crisis hit, and it was record increases in foreign direct investment (FDI). Most of the investment was tied, in more or less direct ways, to the high rates of export growth.

For Latin America and the Caribbean, ECLAC reported that unprecedented volumes of FDI were largely attributable to the persistent worldwide demand for the natural resources in abundant supply in the region. With the change in the price trends for commodities, the FDI trends also changed, and ECLAC was forecasting that FDI flows to the region would fall between 35 and 45 percent during 2009 (ECLAC 2009a). A more recent report by ECLAC observed that even as plans for FDI in the natural resources sector take more time to backtrack, firms in the sector were already revising their plans (ECLAC 2009b). These trends were replicated in FDI in natural resource-based sectors that were also a significant factor in FDI growing inflows into Africa and Central Asia. In 2006–2007, 82 percent of foreign investment in Africa landed in ten countries, most of them oil- or mineral-producers (UNCTAD 2008c: 39). That year also marked a second year in growth of FDI inflows to the Least Developed Countries in Africa – growth clearly linked to the rise in prices of commodities, and therefore also set to go down as prices fall (ibid.: 41).

Though it is true that the natural resource-seeking investment was a high share of total FDI (ECLAC 2008b), if the analysis of investments whose reversal is affected by trade were to stop at this type of investment only, it would incur in an understatement. Efficiency-seeking investment has been even faster to retreat. Referring to the efficiency-seeking investment in Mexico and the Caribbean, ECLAC says "The recession in the United States slowed activity among the export platforms located in the sub-region, which had been set up mainly to serve the United States market, and this stemmed the flow of export-oriented FDI" (ECLAC 2009b: 3). Also tied to trade was a good part of market-seeking investment – investment that goes to a country trying to profit from the rise of purchasing capacity developed in some countries (ibid.). It was the boom of natural resource exports that was backing the increased income and purchasing capacity in several countries. Consequently, in the countries that had been riding the boom, such investment already started to suffer correlatively as a result of decelerated growth (ECLAC 2009a). Commodity trends are even associated with some FDI flows in manufacturing, as reported by UNCTAD in regards to resource-based manufacturing products in Latin America (UNCTAD 2008c).

Reforms to foreign investment frameworks in the developing world were introduced in the name of facilitating and attracting such flows which, the rationale goes, would bolster growth and development. But the rapid change in investment projections during the crisis tends to reaffirm that foreign investment is attracted by high levels of growth than being the cause of them. From a purely neutral balance of payments perspective, attracting more foreign investment cannot be considered always to have a positive effect because foreign investment that comes in good times leaves in bad times, generating a rather pro-cyclical effect for the balance of payments.

The finding would also suggest that the contribution of foreign investment to domestic capital accumulation should be a guiding consideration in reforms and negotiations to attract foreign capital flows. The attraction of foreign investment to export-oriented sectors should be geared to ensure that part of the revenues from increased prices will contribute to a domestic capital base in good times, so as to nurture the basis for greater stability in bad times.

6 Monetary policy and exchange rate movements

The global financial crisis also increased the volatility of exchange rates. For developing countries, again, it is the role of trade in their economic structure that arguably has most to do with their susceptibility to the impacts of exchange rate volatility. As espoused by a recent study, the volatility of the currency has important impacts for the competitiveness of companies (Dobbs *et al.* 2009). This is consistent with findings about the difficulties that exchange rate volatility poses for the evaluation of competitive advantages, the viability of domestic investment oriented to exports and the costs of finance for export-oriented firms in developing countries (Kotte 2009).

Contrary to that claim, in two studies the IMF had already argued that fluctuations of exchange rates do not have such a strong impact in trade performance and has advocated in favor of market-based hedging instruments as the way forward for developing countries that are affected (1984, 2004). Critics contended that this is only available to large companies, with the means and sophistication to pursue such hedging.[4] But the difficulties faced by companies in emerging markets should call into question whether, even for large companies in developing countries, this practice is a reliable safeguard or the most efficient use for the resources of both the private sector and the government. In countries such as Brazil, Mexico and South Korea, companies have reportedly lost huge amounts by taking the wrong side on derivatives to hedge against dollar movements (Fidler *et al.* 2008; Wheatley 2008). In Brazil, the government had to intervene to protect the companies affected by lending to them at below-market interest rates, in another sign of the costs that the problem may have for developing countries' public treasuries (ibid.).

In fact, Dobbs *et al.* offer a counter to the IMF's and other empirical literature, arguing that the costs of volatility are more substantial than captured in such literature (Dobbs *et al.* 2009: 33–34). A survey of executives revealed that exchange rates have an important bearing on expansion or relocation decisions, as well as impacts on market share, profitability and investment decision-making (ibid.).

In addition to the effects that the exchange rate movements have on the export chances of developing countries, it is important to mention that in several cases the currencies of commodity-dependent economies are especially affected. The currencies of these countries, in fact, tend to lose value in the face of declining commodity price trends that make their growth and export prospects more dubious and may prompt investors to withdraw capital. Some experts use the term "commodity currencies" to refer to the strong correlation between the prices of commodity exports and the currencies in countries such as Chile (copper) or Australia and New Zealand (agricultural products) (Slater 2008). Even if the direction of causality might remain open to question, the phenomenon means, by definition, that the export profile of the country has a strong impact on how its currency will fare. Though the research cited here focuses on commodity-producing countries, there are indicia that it could more broadly relate to undiversified export structures.[5]

Surely, it is not only in bad times that the lack of a sound international monetary system to provide currency stability disproportionately affects the trade prospects of developing countries. A floating exchange rate, Frenkel asserts, "has an important negative attribute: the volatility of capital flows is transmitted through the volatility of nominal and real exchange rates and relative prices, with adverse effects on growth and investment" (Frenkel 2004; Rodrik 2004; Agosin and Tussie 1993).

While exchange rate volatility does, of course, affect countries at any level of development, the connection between a stable exchange rate and industrialization makes for an asymmetrical effect in countries depending on whether they have or have not crossed a certain threshold in their path towards industrialization. Rodrik, go as far as saying that "a credible, sustained real exchange rate depreciation may constitute the most effective industrial policy there is" (Rodrik 2004: 24).

7 Access to trade finance

A lot has been said about the impact of the crisis through a worsening of the conditions for trade finance – that is, the different mechanisms by which typically a bank or financial institution, for a fee, guarantees payment of shipments by an importer or exporter. The deterioration of availability and terms of trade credit was already being felt earlier in 2008, but the situation significantly worsened after September of that year, with the collapse and defensive stances taken by major international banks. According to a statement made by Brazil in the WTO regarding that year:

> Exporters from developing countries who seek trade finance find themselves in the odd situation of being among the most creditworthy economic agents, but unable to access credit in a scenario with heightened overall risk perceptions that lead to more stringent requirements by the banks, or simply because funds are not available any longer.
>
> (Working Group on Trade, Debt and Finance 2008a)

A World Bank staff paper pointed out that trade credit was traditionally thought to be only relevant from a microeconomic point of view, but the paper argued this should no longer be the case (Raddatz 2008). The author explores the role of trade credit as a mechanism for the amplification of shocks at the macro level, and finds strong evidence for the hypothesis that an increase in the use of trade-credit along the input–output chain linking two industries results in an increase in their correlation (ibid.).

In addition, the scarcity of trade credit brought to the spotlight a sector little heard of but vital to the continued operations of supply chains: trade insurance. While large companies tend to take the risk that trade credits will not be honored, small providers could be so largely affected by the failure of a big buyer that they usually take insurance. Between 2008 and 2009, it is reported that, due to the drying up of credit, trade insurers saw their losses rise. Atradius, the UK's biggest credit insurer, saw its losses increase to account for more than 70 percent of revenues, up from a norm of 50–60 percent (Stacey 2008). In what some reports say was a panic reaction, they quickly blacklisted as non-insurable many companies, some of them large buyers such as General Motors, Woolworths and Ford. A commentator speaks of the formation of a vicious circle:

> insurers are cutting trade credit insurance because they believe that the scarcity of bank loans has increased the chances of businesses failing. Companies who use the cover are then more exposed to collapse themselves, because some lenders will not advance new funds unless credit insurance is in place.
>
> (Guthrie 2008)

In November 2008, the urgency of the situation prompted the WTO Director General to take the unusual step of hosting a meeting of main trade-finance providers. Estimates presented at that meeting put the liquidity gap in trade finance amounts at US$25 billion, and analysts at that meeting predicted that the situation would get still worse (WTO 2008). In a more recent report the WTO shared estimates of unmet demand for trade financing that range between US$100 and US$300 billion on an annual and roll-over basis (WTO 2009a:18).

This is an area where policy actions were rapidly mobilized. In some countries, like Brazil and India, governments have rapidly made available credit support for exporters – but it is unlikely that countries with lower levels of reserves will have that support forthcoming (ibid.: 19). However, other reported actions include the following: (1) regional development banks and the IFC roughly doubled the limits for their trade finance facilitation programmes, from US$4 billion to US$8 billion; (2) key export credit agencies started to intervene, namely Japan's NEXI, the US' Eximbank and other Members of the Berne Union; and (3) the idea of co-risk sharing between multilaterals and the private sector emerged, in particular in the form of the creation of an IFC Global Trade Liquidity Fund (WTO 2009b).

The view that trade finance was such an important factor behind the drop in trade is not a unanimous one, though. The IMF has uncovered some evidence that would indicate that the fall in trade finance was due to a fall in demand for credit (due to the fall in trade) rather than to a fall in supply. In its Asian Economic Outlook, the IMF states:

> First, according to industry sources, banks in the region continue to lend to established customers and have reportedly maintained broadly the same credit limits as in the first half of 2008, except for smaller high-risk customers.
>
> Second, a recent survey of 500 firms by the Hong Kong Trade and Development Council shows that a key concern among respondents is the lack of foreign demand, while the availability of trade credit is one of the lesser worries.
>
> Third, if Asia could not meet G-3 demand for goods owing to financing constraints, shortages would have developed and prices of imported goods in the G-3 would have gone up. There seems to be no evidence, however, that this is happening
>
> (IMF 2009c:10)

Should the IMF's claim be true, it would further ground the thesis of this paper. The notion that the reduced demand for trade credit is a consequence of reduced prices and volumes of exports triggered by the crisis would be consistent with the notion that the trade structures of the developing countries acted as the primary channel for the impacts of the crisis.

In particular, the role of trade in the structure of the economies of developing countries can be cited as an important factor that accounts for differentiated impacts of reduced trade finance. The demands of a globalized economy have meant success for developing countries was equated to their ability to insert themselves into global production chains where their contribution can be quite limited. The high susceptibility of such production chains to vulnerabilities in financial credit was unlikely given its proper consideration in undertaking such strategy. The problems both for providers who need cash, and also for buyers who face the threat that their cash-strapped providers may disappear because of the inability to hold up without such credit, are becoming more evident. As expressed above, the global production chains have become factors that magnify the scarcity of trade credit. An additional issue for developing countries, though, is that, as mentioned by Studart, in many cases the survival of producers and suppliers depends upon their ability to access trade credit (Studart 2009).

But the trade structure of developing countries may have been more than a mere channel that magnified impacts of the drought of trade finance. It may have become subject to deeper imbalances as a result. A by-product of the drought in trade credit will be its contribution to narrowing down the base of local suppliers and producers in favor of those that are embedded in transnational companies. It is known that around a third of global commerce is carried out within companies rather than between them. As put by an analyst,

> since another feature of the past year has been a rapid rise in the cost of trade credit, through which companies in effect insure their commerce with partners in other countries, those companies big enough to have an entire global supply chain in-house are likely to gain an advantage.
>
> (Beattie 2009)

The diversity and density of the local economy, as well as its capacity to extract value from its participation in global production chains, is therefore further compromised.

8 The official response: the Group of 20 summits in Washington and London

It would be unfair to say trade considerations were absent from the international community responses to the global financial crisis. But this chapter argues that, in the light of the structural trade dimensions of how developing countries came to experience the effects of the crisis, these response measures failed to lay the basis for resilience of developing countries in future crises.

The references to trade in the outcomes of the Washington G20 2008 Summit could be taken as a proxy of how the international policy agenda is addressing the trade question in the face of the crisis. The response can be grouped along two main lines: one about stopping protectionism and expanding market access, and the second about restoring trade finance.

As for the first, the references on paragraph 13 of the Declaration issued by the G20 leaders says that leaders "underscore the critical importance of rejecting protectionism and not turning inward in times of financial uncertainty" (Group of 20 2008). They commit to not raising "new barriers to investment or to trade in goods and services, imposing new export restrictions, or implementing World Trade Organization (WTO) inconsistent measures to stimulate exports" for 12 months (ibid.). Second, leaders say they "shall strive to reach agreement this year on modalities that lead to a successful conclusion to the WTO's Doha Development Agenda with an ambitious and balanced outcome", instructing Trade Ministers to achieve this objective (ibid.).

In spite of the hype surrounding the summit, there was general disappointment, in all quarters, with the results, which made inevitable the reference to the summit as a "first step in a process" and a call to a new summit. This one was hosted by the UK Government, in London, on 2 April 2009.

As far as trade issues are concerned, and contributing to the generalized skepticism about the G20, in between the summits the World Bank and WTO released reports showing a generalized increase in trade restrictions by several countries, including seventeen of the twenty countries that at the 2008 summit in Washington had pledged not to do so (Newfarmer and Gamberoni 2009). Likewise, there were no signs that the WTO Doha Round could be unblocked.

The London Summit Declaration chose to address the trade issues in similar way as the Washington Summit had done. In a section called "Resisting protectionism and promoting global trade and investment", leaders reiterate their pledge from Washington to refrain from raising trade and investment barriers but promise, in addition, to "rectify promptly any such measures" and extend it to the end of 2010 (Group of 20 2009a). Further to this commitment, they call on the WTO and other international bodies to "monitor and report publicly on our adherence to these undertakings on a quarterly basis" (ibid.).

G20 leaders also restate their commitment to reaching "an ambitious and balanced conclusion" to the Doha Development Round (ibid.).

In the Declaration, the leaders say they "will ensure availability" of US$250 billion for trade finance (ibid.).[6] Part of this was a new trade finance facility launched by the World Bank the day before the summit, and presented with much fanfare as a "$50 billion trade finance facility". The fine print of that announcement revealed that pledges amounted to scarcely US$5 billion, with US$50 billion being the amount of total trade that was expected to be financed by it (World Bank 2009). One of the annexes to the Summit Declaration puts actual voluntary bilateral contributions made at the summit at US$3–4 billion, to be contributed to that same World Bank pool (Group of 20 2009b).

Another commitment at the summit in regards to trade finance was to ask regulators to "make use of available flexibility in capital requirements for trade finance" (Group of 20 2009a). The negative impact that Basel II may have on trade flows, inter alia, through increased pro-cyclicality of trade finance, has triggered complaints from developing countries (Working Group on Trade, Debt and Finance 2008a). Balance-sheet exposure to least-developing countries costs banks apparently three times as much as exposure to developed countries, creating a large asymmetry in access to this type of lending (Working Group on Debt, Trade and Finance 2008a). Unfortunately, making use of "available flexibility" offers very little space for hope, and the work program that is dealing with reforms to banking supervision is taking place in a separate fashion from the issues of trade financing faced by developing countries.

9 Concluding remarks: trade as a tool for development finance and financial stability

Thus, while trade was addressed in the response to the global financial crisis, the areas where trade was taken into account by the Group of 20 were protectionism and trade finance. This focus was rather misplaced, as these were not the most significant aspects where vulnerabilities of developing countries had built up.

A striking fact is that sub-Saharan Africa delivered its peak export performance of the last three decades between 2003 and 2008 – a period that registered no movement in the WTO Doha Round. This would seem to suggest that lack of market access is not really the central issue it appears to be in official responses, except maybe at the margins. Similar conclusions apply to trade finance. Section 7 mentioned that there is some backing for the conclusion that trade finance may be merely a function of trade dynamics rather than a trigger to them. Even if this conclusion were dismissed, in the light of our analysis trade finance can hardly be considered the priority trade-related source of concern for developing countries.

On the other hand, the preceding sections have established the different ways in which the trade structure of developing countries, in its interlinkage with financial dimensions, was at the center of how these countries were affected during the crisis. The global financial crisis and the momentum generated for an unprecedented response would have been the time to pursue a rebalancing act. Trade can be a development finance tool and one that helps countries to weather, rather than place them at the mercy of, financial cycles. In this regard, the crisis could be seen as an opportunity to address longstanding issues that have prevented developing countries from a more beneficial trade engagement in the global economy, including during much more benign times.

The highlighted issues are not confined to crisis times. These insights bear important lessons for how to approach the incipient recovery. Should the recovery be a mere resumption of trade along the same bases present before the crisis, it is unlikely the global economy will be in a more stable and reliable footing. An accurate reflection of this failure was provided in the comments by the IMF Managing Director who, referring to the growth forecast reports that the IMF is gathering from countries, said such reports "will not add up" (Giles 2010). Because exports from some countries are not matched by exports in other countries, he stated, many countries will find exports and overall demand falling short of their expectations. As a result, it is expected that overall forecasts for growth will not hold.

The approach that countries choose to take with regards to the role of trade in their economies, individually and collectively, will be crucial to the strength, sustainability and equity of the recovery.

Notes

1 For more details and statistics, see Caliari (2008).
2 "On the whole, post-completion-point countries' debt sustainability remains vulnerable to shocks, particularly those affecting exports..." (UNCTAD 2010: 64). "The combined trade shock (Table 3) points to the vulnerability of LICs in our sample to the trade channel, where about a fifth of all countries were found to be highly vulnerable" (IMF 2009b: 46).
3 For a survey of these criticisms, see Caliari (2006).
4 See, for instance, Goh (2009).
5 As put by John Plender: "Growth rates can be very high – in China's recent case, as high as 12 percent or so in real terms – but cycles are more extreme than in the developed world. This is not just true of energy and commodity-related economies. It also applies to Asian countries that rely more on manufacturing. They lack the protective cushion of a large service sector when the manufacturing cycle turns down" (Plender 2008).
6 The ambiguous reference, however, is rather an estimate of all that would be spent – by countries and private sector – in trade finance in the next two years, than a new and additional pledge attributable to this meeting. This includes a new trade finance facility launched by the World Bank the day before the Summit and presented with much fanfare as a US$50 billion trade-finance facility. The fine print of that announcement revealed that pledges amount to scarcely about US$5 billion, with US$50 billion being the amount of total trade that is expected to be financed by it. In a similar spirit, one of the G20 annexes puts actual voluntary bilateral contributions made at the summit at US$3–4 billion, to be contributed to that same World Bank pool.

Bibliography

Agosin, Manuel and Diana Tussie (1993) *Trade and Growth: New Dilemmas in Trade Policy*, New York, NY: St Martin's Press.

Beattie, Alan (2009) "Collapse in Global Trade Proves Fleeting", in *Financial Times*, London, 25 November.

Caliari, Aldo (2006) 'The Debt–Trade Connection in Debt Management Initiatives. The Need for a Change in Paradigm", paper presented at UNCTAD Workshop "Debt Sustainability and Development Strategies," Geneva.

Caliari, Aldo (2008) *International Policy Aspects of Food Price Inflation: Some Remarks.* Online: available at www.coc.org/node/6148 (accessed 5 May 2011).

Dobbs, Richard, David Skilling, Wayne Hu, Susan Lund, James Manyika and Charles Roxburgh (2009) *An Exorbitant Privilege? Implications of Reserve Currencies for Competitiveness. Discussion Paper*, McKinsey Global Institute.

Economic Commission for Latin America and the Caribbean (2008a) *Economic Survey of Latin America and the Caribbean: Macroeconomic Policy and Volatility*, Santiago: ECLAC.

Economic Commission for Latin America and the Caribbean (2008b) *Foreign Direct Investment in Latin America and the Caribbean 2007*, Santiago: ECLAC.

Economic Commission for Latin America and the Caribbean (2009a) "FDI to Drop Sharply in 2009 After Record High Levels in 2008",*CEPAL News*, XXIV(5), May.

Economic Commission for Latin America and the Caribbean (2009b) *Foreign Direct Investment in Latin America and the Caribbean 2008*, Santiago: ECLAC.

Fidler, Stephen, Adam Thomson and Jonathan Wheatley (2008) "Mexico Attacks 'Unethical' Derivatives Selling", in *Financial Times*, London, 23 October.

Frenkel, Roberto (2004) " 'Right' Prices for Interest and Exchange Rates", in *Diversity in Development – Reconsidering the Washington Consensus*, The Hague: FONDAD.

Giles, Chris (2010) "IMF Chief Warns of Reliance on Exports", in *Financial Times*, London. January 30.

Goh, Chien Yen (2009) Contribution, in A. Caliari and V.P. Yu (eds), *Trade and Finance Linkage for Promoting Development*, Geneva: Center of Concern, South Centre and German Marshall Fund.

Group of 20 (2008) *Declaration. Summit on Financial Markets and the World Economy*, Washington, DC, 15 November.

Group of 20 (2009a) *London Summit – Leaders' Declaration*, London, 2 April.

Group of 20 (2009b) *Declaration on Delivering Resources through the International Financial Institutions*, London 2 April.

Guthrie, Jonathan (2008) "Companies feel Chill as Credit Cover Dries Up", in *Financial Times*, London, 15 November.

IMF (1984) *The Exchange Rate System: Lessons of the Past and Options for the Future*, IMF Occasional Paper No. 30, Washington, DC: IMF.

IMF (2004) *Exchange Rate Volatility and Trade Flows – Some New Evidence*, Washington, DC: IMF.

IMF (2009a) *The Impacts of the Global Financial Crisis on Low-income Countries*, Washington, DC: IMF.

IMF (2009b) *The Implications of the Global Financial Crisis for Low-income Countries*, Washington, DC: IMF.

IMF (2009c) *Regional Economic Outlook: Asia and the Pacific*, Washington, DC: IMF.

Kotte, Detlef (2009) Contribution, in A. Caliari and V.P. Yu (eds), *Trade and Finance Linkage for Promoting Development*, Geneva: Center of Concern, South Centre and German Marshall Fund.

Kregel, Jan (2008) "Systemic Issues – Background Document", paper presented at ECLAC Consultation in Preparation for the Financing for Development Review Conference, Santo Domingo, Dominican Republic, June.

Kregel, Jan (2009) "Financial Markets and Specialization in International Trade: The Case of Commodities", paper presented at "Financial Crisis and Trade: Towards an Integrated Response in Latin America and the Caribbean", seminar organized by UNCTAD, Sistema Economico para Latinoamerica y el Caribe and Hemispheric Working Group on Trade–Finance Linkages, Caracas, September.

Leo, Ben (2010) *Will World Bank and IMF Lending Lead to HIPC IV? Debt Deja-vu All Over Again*, Washington, DC: Center for Global Development.

Newfarmer, Richard and Luisa Gamberoni (2009) *Trade Protection: Incipient but Worrisome Trends*, Trade Notes No. 37, 2 March, Washington, DC: World Bank.

Oakley, David (2008) "Downgrades Emphasise Emerging Economy Risks", in *Financial Times*, London, 10 November.

Plender, John (2008) "Insight: Reality for Emerging Markets", in *Financial Times*, London, 11 November.

Raddatz, Claudio (2008) "Credit Chains and Sectoral Comovements: Does the Use of Trade Credit Amplify Sectoral Shocks?", Policy Research Working Paper 4525, Washington, DC: The World Bank.

Rodrik, Dani (2004) "Growth Strategies", Cambridge, MA: Harvard University.

Slater, Joanna (2008) "Bad Crop: Commodity Currencies", in *The Wall Street Journal*, New York, 11 November.

Stacey, Kiran (2008) "Credit Insurers are Well-Placed ... and Unpopular", in *Financial Times*, London, 17 November.

Studart, Rogerio "Presentation", delivered at "Financial Crisis and Trade: Towards an

Integrated Response in Latin America and the Caribbean", seminar organized by seminar organized by UNCTAD, Sistema Economico para Latinoamerica y el Caribe and Hemispheric Working Group on Trade–Finance Linkages, Caracas, September.

UNCTAD (2008a) *Trade and Development Report*, New York, NY: UNCTAD.

UNCTAD (2008b) *Economic Development in Africa*, New York, NY: UNCTAD.

UNCTAD (2008c) *World Investment Report*, New York, NY: UNCTAD.

UNCTAD (2009) *Global Economic Crisis: Implications for Trade and Development*, Trade and Development Board TD/B/C.I/CRP.1, Geneva: UNCTAD.

UNCTAD (2010) *Responding to the Challenges Posed by the Global Economic Crisis to Debt and Development Finance*. New York, NY: UNCTAD.

Wheatley, Jonathan (2008) "Brazil Assesses Impacts of Currency Crisis", in *Financial Times*, London, 28 October.

Working Group on Trade, Debt and Finance (2008a) "Communication from Brazil", WT/WGTDF/W/39.6, Geneva: WTO.

Working Group on Trade, Debt and Finance (2008b) Expert Meeting on Trade – Finance "Note by the Secretariat", WT/WGTDF/W/38, Geneva: WTO.

World Bank (2009) "New Trade Finance Program to Provide up to $50 Billion Boost to Trade in Developing Countries", Press Release No. 2009/291/IFC-EXC, Washington, DC: World Bank.

World Trade Organization (2008) "Lamy Warns Trade Finance Situation 'Deteriorating'", News Release, Geneva: WTO, 12 November.

World Trade Organization (2009a) *Report to the TPRB from the Director General on the Financial and Economic Crisis and Trade-Related Developments*, Geneva: WTO.

World Trade Organization (2009b) *Overview of Developments in the International Trading Environment. Annual Report by the Director General*, WT/TPR/OV/12, Geneva: WTO, 18 November.

Yang, Jie and Dan Nyberg (2009) *External Debt Sustainability in HIPC Post Completion Point Countries. An Update*, IMF Working Paper 09/128, Washington, DC: IMF.

7 Trade integration after the Great Recession

The case of Argentina[1]

Leandro Serino

1 Introduction

The Great Recession, as the current global economic crisis is known (see, for instance, Borio 2009), is not just another financial crisis. The crisis has led to the collapse of financial institutions, seriously affected the functioning of global financial markets and has also had significant real effects. Some of these are the collapse of investment, the contraction of GDP and the rise of unemployment, particularly in developed countries, and the large reduction of trade and industrial production worldwide (Eichengreen and O'Rourke 2009). More important, in contrast to previous financial crises which principally affected the developing world, is the fact that this crisis started in industrialized countries and has been the consequence of an explosive combination of lax financial regulations, the development of new (and risky) financial instruments and the rise of households' indebtedness to preserve their standards of livings in a more unequal world (Blankenburg and Palma 2009, Serino and Kiper 2009).

At the moment of the crisis developing countries were in a strong position. Many of them learned the costly lessons from previous financial crises and implemented macroeconomic regimes that reduced their exposure to volatile capital flows and the instability of financial markets. Economists coined the term "decoupling" and by the end of 2008 considered that developing countries were not going to be affected by the current world economic crisis. Unfortunately, they have proven not to be immune to it.

Although the crisis so far has not led to the collapse of macroeconomic regimes in developing countries, as happened during the financial crises in the 1990s, it has been affecting them through different mechanisms. Some developing countries, especially those implementing inflation-targeting regimes and more integrated into the web of global financial markets (such as Peru and Colombia), suffered from the reversion of capital flows, as uncertainty spread out and institutional investors decided to move to "safe" financial assets.

In an increasingly integrated world economy, the crisis has been affecting most developing countries through the trade channel – first via the collapse of world trade between the second half of 2008 and the beginning of 2009, and second through falling external demand as industrialized economies went into recession and, in spite of China, world output contracted in 2009.

An additional and "paradoxical" mechanism through which the recent transformations have been influencing developing countries has been the fast recovery (and sustained expansion) observed in primary commodity prices, which, after falling strongly, have increased by 20 percent in US dollar terms since March 2009, according to the Index of Primary Commodity Prices elaborated by Argentina's Central Bank. This a priori constitutes a positive external shock for natural-resource exporting countries, as many developing countries are, which is linked in part to expansionary monetary policies that rich economies have put in place to overcome the crisis.

This chapter discusses how the persistence of some of the abovementioned effects of the crisis will influence the economic performance of Argentina. This is an interesting case because the country first is a primary commodity exporter, and second has been implementing a stable and competitive exchange rate regime (SCER) in recent years. The strategy underpinning both these factors is to promote its non-traditional tradable sector and diminish the vulnerability of the economy to the moods of international financial markets. This analysis focuses on two connected transformations. One is the recovery of the expected 2010 world output growth on the basis of a continuous supportive policy stance and given that persistent vulnerabilities do not undermine the recovery process (United Nations 2010). The other transformation focuses on the rebound in primary commodity prices and associated improvements in the price of Argentina's traditional exports.

The analysis is performed using a structuralist Computable General Equilibrium (CGE) model and a stylized Social Accounting Matrix (SAM) of the Argentine economy. The CGE model and the SAM were especially designed to capture structural features of the Argentine economy (see Serino 2009a, 2009b), like, for example, the presence of a natural-resource exporting sector and other tradable sectors operating under different economic rationales. Most features of the model are embedded in the structuralist tradition (see, for instance, Taylor 1990, Gibson and van Seventer 2000a, Gibson 2005). The relevant ones for the analysis in this chapter are: fix–flex closure rules in commodity markets, endogenous productivity growth in the manufacturing sector and demand-driven output. This closure rules implies that Argentina's macroeconomic performance is linked to the dynamism of the external sector and thus to the swings in world output and the international competitiveness of the Argentine economy.

The analysis presented here shows that the recovery of primary commodity prices and GDP growth in Argentina's trading partners will be both expansionary, yet they have different mesoeconomic implications. The predicted recovery in world output is expected to contribute to GDP growth in Argentina and to provide an impulse to resume the process of productive and export diversification that took place in the country in the period 2003–2008. These stimuli, however, will be weaker than before the crisis, and therefore call both to encourage further economic integration among developing countries, which are the fastest growing economies today, and for expansionary fiscal policies. This chapter also shows that the growing primary commodity prices in Argentina, a wage-goods exporting country, will be expansionary, yet, depending on the exchange rate regime, may crowd-out non-traditional exports. It is shown that a competitive exchange rate policy (implemented in combination with export taxes) is necessary to partly counteract Dutch Disease adjustments, which are commonly associated with positive primary commodity shocks, and to encourage domestic savings and investment.

2 Argentina during the golden years: the Great Recession and beyond

2.1 The golden years: Argentina in the Period 2003–2008

The international crisis has brought Argentina's longest sustained economic expansion in decades to a halt. According to the Ministry of Economy and Public Finance (MEPF), seasonal adjusted output expanded for twenty-six consecutive quarters between mid-2002 and the third quarter of 2008, when financial problems in advanced countries turned global.

Figure 7.1 shows real GDP growth and the contribution of aggregate demand components to output growth between 2003 and 2009. It also shows how these variables are expected to evolve in 2010, whereas Table 7.1 displays aggregate demand figures in addition to other key macroeconomic data. As can be observed through these data, Argentina expanded fast between 2003 and 2008. Output grew on average more than 8 percent per year during this period; an expansion that has been promoted by the sustained growth of all components of aggregate demand[2] (which was only at first linked to the recovery from the 2001–2002 economic crisis in Argentina and the deflationary years which preceded it). Table 7.1 shows that investments (although starting from low levels) and exports (until the outbreak of the international crisis in 2008), which are two key variables for the sustainability of growth processes in developing countries, expanded faster than output during Argentina's *golden years*. Investment, it is worth noting, reached a historical peak in 2008, as the investment rate grew to 24 percent and accounted for 50 percent of expansionary demand impulses (see Figure 7.1).[3] Private consumption in these years grew at a similar rate of output and government consumption grew on average slower than other variables.

Economic growth in Argentina has been in part related to international conditions. It benefited from fast economic growth and trade in the world economy, but especially from the good performances in developing countries. As shown in Table 7.2, whereas advanced economies grew around 2.5 percent between 2003 and 2007, output levels in the developing world and in South America (the largest destination of Argentina's industrial exports) grew 6.8 percent and 5.2 percent per year, respectively. In addition to a growing export demand, Argentina in these years experienced a sustained improvement in the external terms of trade. The ratio between Argentina's exported and imported goods improved 2.7

Table 7.1 Growth in output and aggregate demand and external and macroeconomic balances (selected years and periods)

| | Billions of ARG $ at 1993 prices | | | | % of GDP/a | | | | | |
| | GDP | CONSUMPTION | | TOT INV | EXP | IMP | TRADE BCE | CC AA | GOV PR S | GOV FC S |
		Private	Public							
1998	288.1	197.6	35.2	63.4	30.8	38.9	-1.04	-4.8	0.2	
2003	256.1	168.0	34.3	39.0	35.1	20.4	13.2	6.4	2.3	0.5
2004	279.1	183.9	35.2	44.2	38.0	28.6	8.7	2.1	3.9	2.6
2005	304.7	200.3	37.4	58.3	43.1	34.3	7.2	2.8	3.3	1.8
2006	330.6	215.9	39.4	68.6	46.2	39.6	6.5	3.6	3.5	1.9
2007	359.2	235.3	42.3	78.8	50.4	47.8	5.1	2.7	3.2	1.1
2008	383.4	350.6	45.3	90.9	51.0	54.4	3.9	2.2	3.1	1.4
2009	380.6	248.2	46.9	80.2	47.4	42.1	4.8	2.7	1.7	-0.2
2010 (b)	397.8	258.2	50.1	85.5	53.3	49.3				
	Annual average growth rate						Period average			
2003–2008	8.41	8.34	5.69	18.43	7.77	21.7	3.9	2.2	3.1	1.55
2008–2090	-0.73	-0.99	3.79	-11.75	-7.08	-22.54	4.35	2.45	2.4	0.6
2009–2010	4.50	4.03	6.69	6.58	12.42	17.04				

percent per year between 2002 and 2005, and at an annual rate of 7.5 percent between 2005 and 2008 (see Table 7.2).

Improvements in Argentina's external terms of trade have been in part due to skyrocketing primary commodity prices. As shown in Table 7.2, mounting demands for food and raw materials from rapidly growing China and India and speculation in financial markets increased the dollar price of primary commodities at an annual rate of 23 percent in the period 2005–2008.

Although Argentina faced favorable international conditions before the crisis, economic policies also played a critical role in shaping the country's macroeconomic performance, improving socio-economic conditions and the encouraging of a more diversified export structure. Argentina's competitive exchange rate policy has been of particular importance in this respect. The policy regime, which included export taxes in addition to the Central Bank's interventions in the foreign exchange market, have since 2003 encouraged industrial production, exports and employment (see Table 7.3 and Tavosnanska and Herrera 2010). Together with the renegotiation of Argentina's external debt in 2005, the policy regime contributed to achieving surpluses in current account and primary and financial government accounts (see Table 7.1). In so doing, the regime limited vulnerabilities which had historically conditioned Argentina's economic development.

Argentina's economic authorities, it is also worth mentioning, imposed capital controls in 2005 to discourage speculative capital inflows and actively prevented Dutch disease-type adjustments during the recent primary commodity boom (Serino 2009b). This approach to dealing with external shocks, which differs from the one taken in other South American countries like Brazil and Chile, where capitals inflows have been encouraged and the exchange rate has been used as the adjustment variable, expresses Argentina's decision to integrate in the international economy that is based on trade – rather than financial flows.

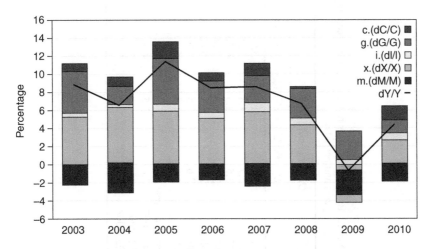

Figure 7.1 Output growth and contribution of aggregate demand components.

Table 7.2 External impulses to the Argentina economy: output and trade growth in the world economy and changes in international prices (selected years and periods)

	Output growth (1)					Trade growth (1)		TOT Arg. (2)	IPCP. (u$s) (3)
	GDP World	GDP Aced	GDP Dev	SAC	Arg. TP (EXP MOI)	Exp. World	Exp. Dev.	1993=100	1995=100
2001	1.7	1.4	3.0	1.00	0.93	-1.1	-1.9	105.5	70.6
2003	2.7	1.8	5.30	1.80	1.02	5.6	9.8	114.8	85.5
2005	3.5	2.5	6.70	5.10	3.13	8	12.7	113.8	100.9
2007	3.9	2.6	7.60	6.50	4.01	6.6	9.1	125	144.5
2008	2.1	0.5	5.40	5.30	3.27	2.8	2.1	141.2	189.1
2009	-2.6	-3.5	1.90	-0.10	-0.79	-12.6	-8.9	135.6	146.3
2010	1.6	1.3	5.30	3.70	2.67	5.5	6.5		150.0
Annual average rate									
2003–2007	3.6	2.5	6.8	5.2	3.2	8.08	11.4	2.2	14.1
2002–2005						7.47	10.9	2.7	10.7
2005–2008						6.7	8.6	7.5	23.3

This type of integration in the world economy differs from the one Argentina implemented in the 1990s and has diminished the country's vulnerability of the economy to the moods of international financial markets. It therefore has limited the negative consequences of the recent international financial crisis. In contrast to other developing countries, especially those implementing inflation targeting strategies, Argentina has not been hit by the sudden stops and massive reversions in capital flows after the collapse of Lehman Brothers. The country has, however, not been immune to the international crisis.

2.2 The Great Recession

The international crisis affected Argentina first through the contraction of world trade and Argentina's exports. As shown in Table 7.2, after growing at an annual rate of 8 percent (11 percent) between 2003 and 2007, the volume of world (developing countries') exports slowed down in 2008 and fell by 12 percent (9 percent) in 2009. Exported volumes fell due to lower primary commodity prices (an issue to which we turn to next) and due to the contraction of world output, following the great recession affecting advanced economies and some developing ones and the slowdown in output growth taking place in fast-growing East Asian countries. According to the UN's World Economic and Social Prospects (United Nations 2010), output in 2009 fell by 2.6 percent in the world economy and 3.5 percent in industrialized countries, while growing by less than 2 percent in the developing world (see Table 7.2). Although a large fraction of Argentina's exports goes to developing countries, output of Argentina's trading partners contracted by 0.7 percent in 2009.

Deflation in primary commodity prices, as mentioned above, has been the second mechanism through which the international crisis hit Argentina. According to the IPCP, prices in dollar terms rapidly deflated with the advent of the international financial crisis. Commodity prices fell 22 percent on average between 2008 and 2009 (see Table 7.2), and in March 2009 were down by 40 percent from the peak observed in June 2008. Two additional facts on this issue are worth noting. One is that primary commodity prices in March 2009 were, however, 50 percent higher than in 2003 and at the level of April 2007, before the run up that led to the international financial crisis (see Figure 7.2). The other fact worth mentioning is that, as the price of Argentina's imports also fell during the crisis, the country's external terms of trade fell 4 percent in 2009, which is less than the 22 percent adjustment observed in primary commodity prices (see Table 7.2).

Output in Argentina contracted in 2009, as the economic crisis unfolded and became global. As shown in Table 7.1 and Figure 7.1, the contractions of investment (down by 12 percent) and exports (down by 7 percent) have been the main negative demand impulses. Investment fell as the crisis increased uncertainty, rationed credit and limited demand. Exports, on the other hand, fell as a consequence of the crisis, but also due to internal factors. One is the political dispute between the government and agricultural producers over the distribution of the

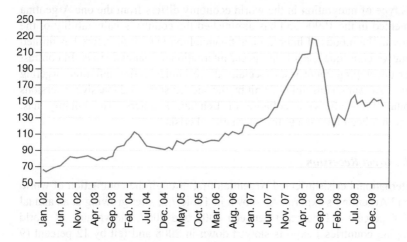

Figure 7.2 Index of primary commodity prices (US dollars, December 1995 = 100).

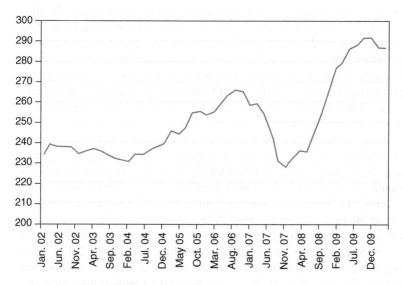

Figure 7.3 Multilateral real exchange rate (December 2001 = 100).

gains from growing primary commodity prices in 2008. The other is the severe drought that constrained agricultural production in 2009. Production in agriculture fell by 3 percent in 2008 and 10 percent in 2009, while exports of primary products, expressed in quantitative terms, were down by 10 percent and 30 percent each year; and agro-industry exports fell by 10 percent in 2008 but resumed growth in 2009 (see Table 7.3). Argentina's industrial exports, the fastest growing export group between 2003 and 2008, have been hardly hit by the international crisis. After growing 18 percent in 2008 (and at an annual rate of 14 percent during the golden years), industrial exports stagnated in 2009 (See Table 7.3).[4]

Imports and government consumption have been the two components of aggregate demand acting countercyclically in 2009 (see Figure 7.1). Imports were down by 22 percent in 2009, due to a decline in investments and private consumption, but also as a consequence of government administrative measures designed to discourage imports in 2009. In contrast to other variables (and other periods of crisis in Argentina), government consumption was up by 4 percent and different transfer mechanisms have been put in place to support employment and private consumption demand.[5] This has reduced the primary surplus by 50 percent and, for the first time in many years, turned financial government balances from surplus into deficit (see Table 7.1).

2.3 Future prospects

Although financial vulnerabilities have not disappeared, as can be seen from the recent crises in Dubai and Greece, and (probably sooner than later) the public sector in advanced economies may start devoting public income to repay debt rather than to encourage demand, the global economy is projected to move out of recession in 2010. According the UN WESP (United Nations 2010), which takes account of persisting vulnerabilities and therefore is less optimistic than projections from other international institutions, the world economy is expected to grow by 1.6 percent in 2010. Global GDP growth is explained in part because advanced countries (though not all) have been showing signs of recovery. After falling sharply, industrial production in the US, the EU and Japan has been recovering since mid-2009 and Japan had already achieved positive growth rates in December 2009. It is also the consequence of fast output growth in developing countries, with China and India in front, which are expected to grow more than 5 percent in 2010 (as they did in 2008).[6]

The recovery of global output will be accompanied by an expansion in the volume of trade, which is a process that has already started in the second half of 2009, and which will be more apparent in the developing countries (Table 7.2 above shows the projected expansion in the volume of exports). These projections are good news for Argentina's exporting sectors, but especially for its manufactures. Indeed, the dynamism of Argentina's non-traditional exports, and thus the prospects for further productive and export diversification, will be linked to the economic performance of Argentina's trading partners, trends in world trade and the competitiveness of the country's economy. All these factors are expected to provide positive impulses to Argentina's external sector, though smaller than prior to the crisis. The main impulses to Argentina's external sector are listed below.

First, output in the US, Brazil, other South American countries and two "small" European economies, The Netherlands and Switzerland, which are among the top ten destinations of Argentina's industrial exports and stand for nearly 80 percent of these exports, is expected to grow on average in 2010 by 2.7

percent (see Table 7.1). Second, world exports are expected to grow, although by less than in the 2003–2007 period, in which the overall volume of exports expanded at an average annual rate of 8 percent for the world and 11 percent for developing countries. Third, Argentina's price competitiveness has improved in the second half of 2009, as soon as exchange rates in Argentina's trading partners stabilized after the crisis (see Figure 7.3). The expected recovery in the production of Argentina's principal crops, which fell by close to 40 percent between 2008 and 2009 but are expected to expand by more than 45 percent this year, will provide an additional boost to Argentina's exports (Table 7.3).

Fast output growth in China and low interest rates in the developed world have promoted the recovery of primary commodity prices. After a large and fast adjustment between June 2008 and March 2009 (down by more than 40 percent), primary commodity prices have been growing again, and in February 2010 were close to 15 percent higher than in March 2009 (the lowest point in the aftermath of the crisis), according to the IPCP (see Figure 7.2 and Table 7.2). Although it is difficult to know how primary commodity prices are going to evolve, especially in a world of very volatile financial flows, prices have remained higher than in previous recessions. This has occurred in part because demand for food and raw materials from fast-growing economies persists (Brahmbhatt and Canuto 2010).

Argentina is, after a period of adjustment, expected this year (2010) to experience positive impulses in its external sector. It bears mentioning that these impulses will be weaker than those prevailing before the international crisis. The country will experience two different positive natural-resource shocks: one linked to the recovery of primary commodity prices and the other associated with the expansion of traditional crops and exports. Argentina is also expected to benefit from the recovery of the international economy and global trade. The effects of these positive changes are analyzed in the coming sections through counterfactual simulations run with the support of a structuralist CGE model.

3 A structuralist CGE model for Argentina

3.1 General remarks

I employ a structuralist CGE model and a stylized SAM of Argentina to explore how exogenous shocks after the great recessions may affect Argentina's macro- and mesoeconomic performance. Although the model is dynamic, simulations are based on a static version, due to uncertainties about the evolution of the world economy in the coming years.

The SAM and the model were designed to capture some structural features of the Argentine economy. The model draws on existing applied models and is embedded in the structuralist tradition.[7] Key characteristics of the model are: fix–flex closure rules in the commodity markets; mark-up prices and quantity adjustment in the industrial sector; the inclusion of wage, trade and investment equations; and the Keynesian closure rule for the saving–investment balance.

Table 7.3 Production and exports in selected sectors and main crops in Argentina (selected years and periods)

	Export Quantity Index (1) (1993=100)			Production (1) (1993=100)		Production of cereals and oil crops (million tonnes) (1)			
	PP	MOA	MOI	Industry	Agriculture	Soybeans	Maize	Wheat	Sunflower
2001	208.9	179.9	239.5	94	124				
2003	195.8	226.3	235.5	97	131				
2005	150.5	291.7	302.8	117	145				
2007	285.0	317.8	397.8	137	162				
2008	262.1	286.3	467.7	143	158	46.2	21.3	16.3	4.6
2009	178.5	296.3	472.8	139	143	31.0	13.1	8.4	2.4
2010						52.0	18.0	7.5	2.2
Annual average growth rate									
2003–2008	6.0	4.8	14.7	8.07	3.79				

Other relevant features of the model (and the SAM) are the classification of commodities and economic activities. I distinguish five commodity groups and five economic sectors that produce them:[8] primary products (PP); resource-intensive manufacturing products (MR); other manufacturing products (MO); producer services (PS); and consumer services (OS). Their key characteristics are summarized in Table 7.4 at the end of the section, together with other relevant features of the model.

Following the tradition for multisectoral models of the Argentine economy,[9] the sectors linked to Argentina's natural resources (PP and MR) are assumed to: (1) have a price competitiveness advantage; (2) operate at full-capacity; and (3) sell to the domestic or the international market depending on the relative profitability of one or the other product destination. Excess capacity and quantity adjustments, on the other hand, are the norm in the non-natural resource manufacturing sector MO and in sector PS; hence, output in these sectors is demand-determined and depends on domestic and world income and the price and non-price competitiveness (and the events affecting them) of these sectors.

Finally, the model distinguishes between producer-oriented services and consumer-oriented ones. The reason for this particular classification of the service sector is to distinguish the group of modern services which are key determinants of the overall competitiveness of the economy – as in, for instance, software, transportation and financial services, public utilities, communication and specialized services – from other services as commerce, leisure and informal services.[10]

3.2 The CGE model

The material balance equation and demand components

A synthetic description of the model is provided in this section, which highlights the features of the CGE model that are relevant for the applied analysis; the reader is referred to Serino (2009a, 2009b) for its full specification.

Together with the commodities and economic sectors (denoted with supraindices c and a), the model distinguishes ten factors of production (one capital and nine labor categories, characterized with supraindices k and l) and identifies three types of institutions: households (H), government (G) and rest of the world (W).

Equation (1) presents the material balance equation:

$$XC_{c,t} = AINTD_{c,t} + \sum_h CDH_{c,h,t} + IO_{c,t}{}^{priv} + IO_{c,t}{}^{gov} + CDG_{c,t} + E_{c,t} - M_{c,t} \quad (1)$$

In the above equation, XC_c is commodity c demand, $AINTD_c$ is domestic intermediate inputs; $CDH_{c,h}$ refers to household consumption, IO_c^{priv} and IO_c^{gov} to private and public investment, and CDG_c to government current expenditure; and E_c stands for exports and M_c for imports.

The external sector: exports supply and demand, and the competitiveness of the non-natural-resource tradable sectors

The economic rationale for exporting natural-resource products is different from that for other exports, and therefore they are modeled differently. Exports of natural-resource related products (PP or MR) are supply-determined and producers decide the destination of production according to relative profitabilities. The decision between exporting or selling to the domestic market is modeled using a Constant Elasticity of Transformation (CET) function that links exports ($E_{c,t}$) and supply to the domestic market ($QDDA_{c,t}$) to the relative price prevailing in the external and domestic market $\left(\dfrac{PE_{c,t}}{PDC_{c,t}}\right)$. This function is defined in equation (2).[11]

$$\frac{E_{c,t}}{QDDA_{c,t}} = \left(\frac{PE_{c,t}}{PDC_{c,t}} \cdot \frac{\left(1-\psi_c^{cet}\right)}{\psi_c^{cet}} \right)^{1/\rho_c^{cet}-1} \tag{2}$$

The exponent parameter depends on the elasticity of the transformation between the domestic and export supply, which captures the ability of producers to shift from one market to another. To reproduce the capacity of Argentina's natural resource sector to export its surpluses, the model assumes high elasticity of transformation. This permits an easy reallocation of production between the domestic and external markets, and increases the pass-through of international to domestic prices. It thus serves to evaluate the adjustment to positive terms of trade shocks in wage-goods exporting countries.[12]

Output in sectors MO and PS is assumed to be demand-determined. It depends, among other things, on the demand for exports and the competitiveness of production in these sectors. Equation (3) defines the export demand equation for MO and PS products.

$$E_{c,t} = E_{c,t-1} \cdot (RERE_{c,t})^{\xi_{EP}} \cdot (y^W)^{\xi_{EY}} \cdot \left(\frac{ID_{a,t}^{priv}}{ID_{a,t-1}^{priv}} \right)^{\xi_{ENP1_c}} \cdot \left(\frac{QA_{APS,t}}{QA_{APS,t-1}} \right)^{\xi_{ENP2_c}} \tag{3}$$

The export demand equation goes beyond traditional specifications.[13] Exports are the function of conventional factors, such as changes in world income (y^W) and the price competitiveness of the products concerned, as captured by the sector-specific real exchange rate (RER_c). Yet, in this CGE model, the competitiveness of exports depends on factors other than price.

Following Leon-Ledesma's (2002) Kaldorian growth model, the equation incorporates two non-price determinants of competitiveness. The first links the competitiveness of production to sector-specific private investment, $\left(\dfrac{ID_{a,t}^{priv}}{ID_{a,t-1}^{priv}}\right)$, which enters the equation to account for factors facilitating access to foreign markets, as embodied by technical progress and investment in machinery and equipment. The second one associates export competitiveness with output increases in sector PS, $\left(\dfrac{QA_{APS,t}}{QA_{APS,t-1}}\right)$. This is included to capture the contribution of the producer services to the competitiveness of exports, an effect emphasized in Ros (2001) and the analytical model developed in Serino (2009b: Ch. 3).

The price competitiveness of non-traditional exports is defined by the sector-specific real exchange rate, and depends on the nominal exchange rate and domestic prices in sectors *MO* and *PS* as defined in equation (4):

$$PDA_{a,t} = (1 + TAUV_{a,t})VC_{a,t} \tag{4}$$

Prices in these sectors depend on the mark-up rate $TAUV_a$, which changes according to sectoral output, and variable production costs (VC_a), which are a function of intermediate input prices and unitary labor costs, as defined by nominal wages W_l and labor productivity.

The model also assumes that the price of labor is institutionally determined, depending on the growth of labor productivity (*LPRODG*), the evolution of consumer prices (*CPI*), changes in the rate of unemployment (*UN*) and an exogenous policy variable (*wpol*) which accounts for changes in government wage policy.

$$WL_{fl,t} = WL_{fl,t-1} \cdot \left[1 + \omega_1 \cdot \dfrac{\sum\limits_{a} LPRODG_{fl,a,t}}{a} + \omega_2 \cdot \widehat{CPI_t} - \omega_3 \widehat{UN}_{fl,t} + \omega_4 wpol \right] \tag{5}$$

Labor productivity growth is assumed to be endogenous in the model and determined by demand and supply factors. Demand-determined productivity growth is referred to in the literature as the Kaldor-Verdoorn effect, and links productivity growth to learning and specialization economies that arise with an expansion in demand. Modeling-wise, productivity is linked to changes in economy-wide capacity utilization. Supply-side determinants of productivity growth (i.e. human capital accumulation) are assumed to be exogenous in the model.

The specification of imports resembles the export demand equation, but includes real output instead of world income.

Domestic demand

The specification of domestic demand, to a large extent, follows the traditional structuralist CGE models. Demand for intermediate inputs is based on a Leontief function, and consumption demand is defined according to a linear expenditure system (LES).

Output also responds to changes in investment and government expenditure, which thus are determined according to particular behavioral equations or are defined as exogenous and determined by economic policies.

Private investment is defined as:

$$ID_{a,t}^{priv} = ID_{a,t-1}^{priv} \cdot \begin{bmatrix} 1 + \gamma_{1a}\widehat{UAV_t} + \gamma_{2a}\widehat{ID_t^{gov}} \\ + \gamma_{3a}\widehat{PRFR_{a,t}} - \gamma_{5a}\widehat{RIR_t} \end{bmatrix} \cdot IADJ_t \tag{6}$$

The model defines an investment equation for each economic sector; each equation incorporates an accelerator parameter γ_1, linking capital accumulation to changes in economy-wide capacity utilization, and a crowding-in parameter γ_2 that relates private investment to changes in public investment. Investment is also a positive function of the profit rate $P<Rcirc>FR_{a,t}$ and is negatively linked to the real interest rate $R\hat{I}R_t$, which accounts for the cost of borrowing.[14]

Government consumption and public investment are the remaining components of aggregate demand. The benchmark specification of the model assumes that *government expenditure (consumption and investment) is exogenous* and changes according to a pre-defined rule (*cdgrule* and *idgrule* in equations (7) and (8)), but that can be modified so as to simulate the impact of alternative government expenditure policies. The model allows for alternative specifications of government spending, for this also can be endogenous and adjust to balance government accounts (*GCADJ*) and (*GIADJ*),[15] or can be a function of government income from export taxes (*CDGTC_{c,t}*) and (*IGTI_{c,t}*).

$$CDG_{c,t} = \begin{bmatrix} CDG_{c,t-1} \cdot (1+cdgrule) + CDGTC_{c,t} \end{bmatrix} \cdot GCADJ_t \tag{7}$$

$$ID_t^{gov} = ID_{t-1}^{gov} \cdot \begin{bmatrix} (1+igrule) + IGTI_t \end{bmatrix} \cdot GIADJ_t \tag{8}$$

In the model, public income is invested exclusively to improve the provision of infrastructure. It occurs, therefore, in sector *PS*.

Production and labor demand

In the model, supply depends on capital accumulation and, thus, on investment, as defined in Gibson and van Seventer (2000b) and equation (9). Based on the assumption of price adjustment in sectors PP, MR and OS, equation (9) determines effective output in these sectors. In sectors MO and PS, where output is demand-determined, the equation defines potential output

$$QA_{a,t} = \left(\kappa_a \cdot K_{a,t-1} + QA_{a,t-1} \right) \tag{9}$$

where (9) κ_a is the sector-specific incremental capital-capacity ratio, and $K_{a,t-1}$ and $QA_{a,t-1}$ respectively denote capital stock and output in the previous period. The rate of capacity utilization ($U_{a,t}$) equals:

$$U_{a,t} = \frac{XA_{a,t}}{QA_{a,t}} \qquad (10)$$

Capacity utilization equals 1 in sectors PP, MR and CS, the sectors for which the model assumes full-employment and price adjustment, and is defined as the ratio of demand-determined ($XA_{a,t}$) to potential output ($QA_{a,t}$) in the other two sectors.

Sectoral labor demand depends on the endogenous labor output coefficients and output, as shown in equation (11).[16]

$$LD_{fl,a,t} = LOCF_{fl,a,t} \cdot XA_{a,t} \qquad (11)$$

Macroeconomic balances, system constraints and closure rules

The final elements of CGE models are macroeconomic balances. These concern balances in government and external accounts, which define public and external savings, and the macro equilibrium relation between savings and investment. Table 7.4 summarizes the main characteristic of the CGE model: the main features of economic sectors, the *numeraire* to express relative prices and the closure rules[17] that define how the factor and commodity markets adjust to excess demand and how the economy achieves the various macroeconomic balances.

As shown in Table 7.4, the nominal wage for unskilled and informal labor is defined as the *numeraire*, and a fix–flex closure rule characterizes the commodity market, with mark-up sectors MO and PS showing quantity adjustments, and sectors PS, MR and OS adjusting to excess demand via price adjustments. Quantity adjustments are the regulating mechanism in the labor market – in 2009, unemployment affected 8 percent of Argentina's labor force.

In the case of macroeconomic balances, the benchmark specification of the model assumes a fixed exchange rate (an assumption consistent with the managed exchange rate regime implemented in Argentina), exogenous government expenditures and a Keynesian closure rule for the savings–investment balance, where output adjusts to ensure the savings required to finance the exogenously determined investment.

3.3 The model parameters

The model is calibrated to reproduce the initial equilibrium of the SAM using different parameter values. Average and distribution parameters are calibrated to the SAM,[18] values for exogenous variables are obtained from different official sources, as shown in Table 7.A1 (see Appendix), and parameters for behavioral equations and exogenous or policy variables are calibrated using available information, borrowed estimations or as defined on the basis of guesstimates. This section makes a short description of the calibration.[19]

The model assumes a high elasticity of transformation (sigma = 5) to capture the ability of the natural resource producers to sell their surplus on the international market. Although high parameter values may overestimate the economic

Table 7.4 Main features of the dynamic CGE model

| MARKET | MICRO CLOSURE | |
	ADJUSTMENT MECHANISM	OTHER PROPERTIES
Commodity markets		
PP (primary) & MR (resource intensive manufacture)	Price adjustment to excess demand	Price competition; full capacity utilization and CET function to determine export supply
MO (non-resource manufacture) & PS (producer services)	Quantity adjustment	Non-price competition; excess utilization and mark-up pricing
OS (consumer-oriented services)	Price adjustment to excess demand	
Labor Market	Quantity adjustment	Institutionally determined wages
MACRO CLOSURE		
Foreign Exchange Market	Fixed/Flex exchange rate regime	
Savings–Investment Balance	Investment driven/Savings driven	
NUMERAIRE		
FWLNP1	Nominal wage of unskilled and informal wage labour	

or sectoral response to changes in international conditions or trade policy (Vos 2007), a high elasticity of transformation is a realistic and relevant assumption to describe the behavior of sectors PP and MR in Argentina.

Demand for exports from sectors MO and PS is assumed to have unitary price elasticity, in line with figures from Catao and Falcetti (2002). The income elasticity of exports for these sectors equals 0.94, which is the short-run elasticity for Argentina's exports estimated by Senhadji and Montenegro (1999). Price and income import elasticities are calibrated, taking Catao and Falcetti's (2002) estimations into account. The short-term price elasticity of imports is 0.25, and the income elasticity of imports has the value 1.92. These values illustrate the strong connection between Argentina's imports and the economic cycle and their unresponsiveness to changes in relative prices, especially in the short term. Due to a lack of empirical estimations, the elasticity of imports and exports to the determinants of non-price competitiveness is assumed to have very low values (equal to 0.025).[20]

Labor productivity grows due to labor-saving technical change, which is assumed to be exogenous and increases by 2 percent per year, but also varies according to changes in aggregate demand. The Kaldor–Verdoorn parameter capturing this relationship equals 0.5, as commonly assumed (see, for example, Ros 2001, Leon-Ledesma 2002).

Price and income elasticities of household demand are taken from Berges and Casellas (2002), and are employed to calibrate the intercept and marginal propensities of the household linear expenditure system according to the Frisch methodology.

The parameters of the wage and investment equation were defined considering estimations from a structural macroeconometric model for the period 2003–2006 (see Panigo *et al.* 2009).[21] The calibration of the wage equation considers: (1) an intermediate response of wages to labor productivity growth, with the respective coefficient taking a value equal to 0.5; (2) an indexation parameter equal to 0.8; and (3) a moderate elasticity to the situation of the labor market, since the coefficient linking wage growth to changes in unemployment equals 0.28. Parameters for the investment equation suggest a weak response of total investment to output growth, public investment and increases in the cost of capital, and that profits are the main driving force behind investment (see Table 7.A1).

Together with parameter values and sources, Table 7.A1 shows the range of values for which the CGE model works. None of the model's parameters, as shown in columns 2 and 3 of Table 7.A1, is at bound, but rather is distant from the values that make the CGE model unstable. This suggests that the functioning and stability of the model do not depend on any particular parameter value and that the CGE model works for values close to those defined in this calibration.

4 Life after the Great Recession: positive (and moderate) external shocks and domestic adjustment in Argentina

4.1 Positive primary commodity shocks and macroeconomic policies

The chapter discusses first how recent trends in primary commodity prices may affect the Argentine economy. It is assumed that commodity prices will remain high, but will not increase as before the crisis. The first simulation therefore considers that the international price of primary commodities in 2010 will grow by 2.5 percent, which is the growth rate at which prices have increased on average between 2009 and the first months of 2010. Unless stated otherwise, all simulations are run using the benchmark closure rules described in Table 7.5: quantity adjustments in mark-up sectors and the labor market, exogenous government expenditure, and a managed exchange rate regime, where the nominal rate does not clear the foreign exchange market and the Keynesian closure rules for the saving–investment balance.

Simulation results for a selected group of variables are presented in Table 7.5, where figures refer to percentage changes to the base run (BR) simulation. The positive change in world prices for Argentina's exports has small expansionary effects. As shown in column (1), output expands 0.3 percent in relation to the baseline as the shock increases available income in the economy and with it consumption (up 0.5 percent from the BR); and higher domestic demand, capacity utilization and prices promote investment (up 2.5 percent from BR).[22]

The shock, however, reduces exports. Sales to external markets contract first as more natural resource products, particularly wage-goods, are devoted to the domestic market. Exports also decline because increases in primary commodity prices also augment domestic prices (as the assumption of an easy reallocation of primary production between the domestic and the international market implies that the pass-through between international and domestic prices shows a one-to-one relationship), jeopardizing the competitiveness of non-traditional exports, which contract 2 percent in relation to the baseline (see Table 7.5, column 1, rows 7–12).

The shock promotes employment growth, and in an economy with unemployment levels lower than in previous periods and with active wage negotiations, real wages will (despite rising domestic prices) grow. This, however, is not sufficient to improve income distribution, as the price shock increases incomes in the richest households more than in the poorest ones and reduces the wage share (see column 1, rows 13–16).

The response to this positive external shock is not neutral to the macroeconomic regime. Instead of trying to promote a competitive exchange rate, Argentina's economic authorities could have opted to allow market forces to determine the adjustment in the external market. This has, to some extent, been done in other Latin American countries, for example in Chile, during the primary commodity shock prior to the international crisis.

Column 2 in Table 7.5 illustrates the effects of the positive primary commodity shock under a flexible exchange rate regime. Although increases in primary

Table 7.5 (Moderate) positive primary commodity shocks and domestic adjustment, alternative exchange rate and closure rules

	(1) 2.5% inc. PW_{PP} & PW_{MR}	(2) 2.5% inc. PW_{PP} & PW_{MR}	(3) 2.5% inc. PW_{PP} & PW_{MR}	(4) 2.5% inc. PW_{PP} & PW_{MR} and 10% inc. Export Tax
	BM CR	FLEX ER	NCL CR	BM CR
	% change to baseline			
Macroeconomic variables				
1 Real GDP	0.31	0.23	−0.17	0.15
2 Private investment	2.54	1.88	−1.02	1.24
3 Total consumption	0.51	0.79	0.03	0.25
4 Total exports	−0.92	−1.53	0.03	−0.46
5 Current account deficit (% GDP)	−2.1	−1.98	−2.56	−2.29
6 Gov. Prim. Surplus (% GDP)	3.30	2.95	3.15	3.34
7 Consumer price index	2.53	−0.46	1.54	1.15
8 Domestic price (PP & MR)	2.42	−0.93	2.07	1.06
Variables external sectors				
9 Real exchange rate M-up sectors (MO+PS)	−2.1	−2.60	−1.13	−0.96
10 Output M-up sectors (MO+PS)	0.75	0.53	−0.40	0.36
11 Exports PP & MR	−0.3	−0.98	0.70	−0.21
12 Exports MO & PS	−2.0	−2.57	−1.23	−0.94
Socio-economic variables				
13 Total Employment	0.21	0.16	−0.07	0.10
14 Av. real wage	0.31	0.63	−0.49	0.16
15 Labor share	−0.23	0.05	−0.70	−0.10
16 Income (YHQ1)/YHQ5	−0.11	−0.05	0.04	−0.05

commodity prices remain expansionary, the economy may experience additional changes worth discussing.

As expected, the shock promotes a stronger exchange rate, and this has its positive and negative consequences. The good news is linked to the stability in domestic prices and the related improvements in real wages vis-à-vis the baseline and the adjustment to the shock in the context of a managed exchange rate regime (see Table 7.5, columns 1 and 2, rows 7 and 8). The negative aspects of the alternative exchange rate regime come from Dutch disease-type adjustments, as the stronger exchange rate further reduces non-traditional exports.[23] Although (in spite of lower exports) production in these sectors expands, this may change in the medium term. As shown in Serino (2009a), increases in primary commodity prices over various periods of time, such as those between 2005 and 2008, can lead to an absolute decline in industrial production. This could even potentially make the positive shock contractionary, if the adjustment in external accounts is left to market forces (Berges and Casellas 2002). This may happen as a consequence of stronger exchange rates, but also because productivity and non-price competitiveness tends to be procyclical in modern industrial sectors. Because, as mentioned in the previous section, attempting to foresee the evolution of exogenous variables beyond 2010 is neither advisable nor feasible, the analysis is based on static simulations and the abovementioned effects do not materialize.

Simulation results in column 2 also show that under a flexible exchange rate the primary commodity shock reduces the current account surplus. Although the exchange rate adjustment does not turn external accounts into a deficit that needs to be financed from abroad, the point is worth mentioning because, as happened in Argentina in the 1990s, strong exchange rates and positive foreign savings have not encouraged investment but rather led to unsustainable consumption booms. On the contrary, the competitive exchange rate regime in place between 2003 and 2008 – and to some extent preserved today – promoted consumption, but also household and government savings, and these have been pillars of the fast and steady expansion of investment and output in Argentina before the international crisis.

The negative association between investment and foreign savings observed in Argentina in the past twenty years goes against the propositions of neoclassical models. Whereas from a Keynesian perspective investment depends on profits, demand and financial costs, according to neoclassical approaches investment is function of available finance. Running current account deficits to receive savings from abroad, as international financial institutions once and again advise developing countries, is therefore a key mechanism to promote investment and long-term growth. By the same token, whatever improves external accounts will reduce investment. Hence, as shown in column 3, increases in primary commodity prices in simulations run using the neoclassical closure rule may reduce investment and be contractionary. As recent history has shown, reality may be rather different.

Turning back to the adjustment of Argentina's exporting sector, it is worth noting that Dutch disease adjustments may happen if the nominal exchange rate appreciates, but also if the *pass through* of international to domestic prices is large – a particularly relevant issue in Argentina, a wage-goods exporting country. Export tax to natural resource exports may contribute to limit this adjustment. Column 4 in Table 7.5 shows the results from a simulation where the government raises export taxes 10 percent to cope with the primary commodity shock. The policy puts a wedge between international and domestic prices and limits domestic price increases, particularly of natural-resource goods. In so doing, export taxes reduce the contraction in non-traditional exports (down by 0.9 percent instead of 2 percent in the alternative scenario without changes in export taxes) and diminish (but do not eliminate) the negative impact of the shock on income distribution.[24]

Argentina reintroduced export taxes in 2002, and until 2007 had made discrete adjustments to adapt to changes in the international environment. However, since 2008, after the political crisis over the distribution of the gains of primary commodity shocks, there has been no scope for adjustments in export taxes. This may not be problematic if prices remain high but expand slowly, as in the simulations, but may require rethinking the macroeconomic regime if, for instance, commodity prices expand at an annual rate of 20 percent (14 percent), as between 2005 (2003) and 2008 (see Table 7.2).

4.2 Positive external and internal shocks to Argentina's exporting sectors and government demand impulses

Since the end of 2009 the world economy has been showing signs of recovery, and international organizations, with varying degrees of optimism, are forecasting that output will expand in most economies. Although countries from the North, with the exception of China, have made the largest effort in terms of expansionary fiscal and monetary policies, global recovery in 2010 will be guided by developing countries (see Table 7.2).

This recovery is beneficial for developing counties not only because it has contributed to the recovery of primary commodity prices, but also because it is bringing about world trade on the expansionary path. To analyze how this may affect output dynamics in Argentina, I simulate that world output expands by 2.7 percent, which is the weighted average growth rate predicted for the top ten countries importing industrial products from Argentina.[25] The shock is expansionary, mainly because it stimulates exports of non-traditional export products. As shown in Table 7.6, industrial and service exports go up more than 2 percent vis-à-vis the baseline, but natural-resource exports contract because when the Argentine economy expands a larger fraction of wage-goods is devoted to the domestic market. The shock also increases employment, real wages and the wage share, but worsens income distribution (see column 1, rows 12–15).[26]

Larger trade integration between Argentina and countries from the South, other than Latin America ones,[27] as shown in Table 7.6 column 2 (which simulates that global output expands 5 percent in 2010,[28] which is the growth rate predicted for developing countries), will further expand industrial exports and

Table 7.6 Positive exogenous and supply shocks and alternative demand impulses from the government (%)

	(1)	(2)	(3)	(4)	(5)	(6)	(7)	(8)
Macroeconomic variables								
1 Real GDP	0.2	0.4	1.9	0.5	1.5	1.7	1.8	3.5
2 Private investment	0.04	0.1	13.7	2.6	4.5	4.8	5.0	11.3
3 Total consumption	0.2	0.4	3.0	0.7	1.8	2.9	2.1	3.9
4 Total exports	0.6	1.1	-4.2	-0.4	1.6	-0.7	-2.3	-0.2
5 Current account deficit (% GDP)	-2.1	-2.1	-2.7	-2.2	-2.4	-1.8	-1.6	-0.6
6 Gov. Prim. Surplus (% GDP)	2.9	3.0	5.0	3.3	3.6	2.7	2.7	4.2
7 Consumer price index	0.3	0.6	14.7	2.8	4.8	6.6	8.1	9.0
8 Domestic price (PP & MR)	0.1	0.2	13.7	2.5	3.0	3.7	3.8	4.5
Variables external sectors								
9 Real exchange rate M-up sectors (MO+PS)	-0.30	-0.60	-10.80	-2.35	-3.87	-5.08	-5.89	-7.57
10 Output M-up sectors (MO+PS)	0.45	0.89	4.52	1.18	1.62	2.11	2.22	6.04
11 Exports PP & MR	-0.33	-0.65	-2.14	-0.66	3.12	1.05	0.81	-1.07
12 Exports MO & PS	2.23	4.40	-7.96	0.16	-1.39	-2.61	-3.45	-4.74
Socio-economic variables								
13 Total employment	0.09	0.18	1.22	0.30	0.75	0.89	0.97	2.01
14 Av. real wage	0.27	0.54	1.68	0.57	1.67	1.83	1.82	5.00
15 Labor share	0.14	0.27	1.21	-0.10	0.17	0.17	0.06	2.19
16 Income (YHQ1)/YHQ5	-0.05	-0.10	-0.57	-0.16	-0.09	0.05	-0.01	-0.48

reinforce the process of export diversification that has been taking place in Argentina in the twenty-first century. This will certainly require active policies and efforts from the private sector, but need not be impossible as Argentina's industrial products are exported to the European and North American markets.

Although there is life after the Great Recession, impulses from the international economy will play a smaller role in determining the evolution of output than before the crisis. Columns 3 and 4 in Table 7.6 compare positive external shocks before and after the crisis. Column 3 summarizes the results from the simulations, assuming that world output increases by 3.2 percent and primary commodity prices rise by 14 percent, which are the average growth rates observed in Argentina's trading partners and primary commodity prices between 2003 and 2007. Column 4, on the other hand, illustrates the impact of the changes predicted for 2010 (world output growing by 2.7 percent, as in Argentina's trading partners, and commodity prices increasing by 2.5 percent).

As shown in Table 7.6, simulations of impulses such as those observed before the international crisis promote expansions in real GDP, investment and consumption, as well as employment and real wages, that are three times larger or more than impulses projected for 2010 (see Table 7.6, column 3 and 4, rows 1, 2, 3, 13 and 14). Certainly there are differences between the two periods, and other shocks may be necessary or expansionary fiscal policies may have to be designed to provide the missing demand.

After two years of stagnation for political and climatic reasons, traditional agricultural production will expand in Argentina in 2010 and therefore provide an additional expansionary impulse. Data in column 5 of Table 7.6 show simulation results of a 5 percent increase of output in the primary sector. This positive supply shock in Argentina's natural-resource sectors sponsors an expansion in all components of aggregate demand, and may expand output by 1 percentage point vis-à-vis the scenario of exogenous impulses but not from the domestic economy (see Table 7.6, columns 5 and 1 and 4, rows 1–4). The shock increases total exports due to larger sales of traditional products (up by 1.5 percent and 3 percent vis-à-vis the baseline, respectively). However, industrial and other non-traditional exports contract in relation to the baseline and the "post crisis" scenario due to the so-called Dutch disease spending effect.[29]

In addition, three alternative expansionary fiscal policies can be envisaged to provide demand impulses in the aftermath of the crisis: increases in government transfers to households, and larger government consumption or investment. To analyze how these policies can add to the previous impulses, I modify the closure rule governing public expenditure decisions. I assume in these three final simulations that the government's financial requirements are constant, and that changes in government revenues are used alternatively to increase transfers, consumptions or investment.

All three policies are expansionary, but financing public investment has the largest expansionary effect (see Table 7.6, columns 6–8, rows 1 and 2). In the context of a crisis, however, the economy may need policies focused on vulnerable sectors rather than on projects that take time to realize. The decision between implementing transfers to poor households and expanding government consumption (as, for instance, through an expansion of employment or increases in wages in the public sector) will be made depending on the objective of government authorities. If preferences are in favor of expanding aggregate demand with the lowest impact on domestic prices, transfers may be a better policy than government consumption.

5 Final thoughts

In 2008 and 2009, economists were busy comparing the adjustments in world trade and industrial productions with those in the 1930s. Due to large fiscal and monetary stimuli packages, but also thanks to the consolidation of Asia as the new engine of global growth, the crisis has not turned into a depression. Although financial vulnerabilities and the risks of a downturn remain, the world economy has returned to an expansionary mode of development. Having learnt from previous crises, this time Argentina, like many other developing countries, has been less exposed to the up and downs of financial markets. The country today is therefore in a condition to benefit from the moderate recovery of global growth and trade that is projected for 2010.

This chapter has discussed how impulses from the international economies may affect the economic performance of Argentina in the aftermath of the crisis, in particular the recovery of primary commodity prices and output growth in Argentina's trading partners. The counterfactual simulations performed with the use of a structuralist GCE model have shown that these two positive external shocks will be expansionary. Impulses from the international economy, however, have also been shown to be weaker than prior to the crisis. Argentina will therefore have to intensively promote trade with developing countries to preserve its process from previous years of export growth and diversification. It also would be wise to implement expansionary fiscal policies to provide the exogenous impulses that vanished with the crisis.

There is certainly life after the Great Recession. Yet benefiting from greater integration with the world economy is very much related to the macroeconomic policies, and in particular the exchange rate regime. This concerns the Central Bank interventions and other policies like export taxes, (particularly in wage-goods exporting countries) and capital controls – a policy which today is recommended even by the IMF (Ostry *et al.* 2010). A competitive exchange rate regime is critical to prevent Dutch disease adjustments, associated with positive external shocks, and to promote an environment favorable to investment. The latter can be achieved through demand impulses, increases in the profitability of tradable production and higher domestic savings.

Appendix

Table 7.A1 Parameter value of the CGE model: parameter values, stability ranges and sources

Behavioural Parameters	PV	Range of PV a/ Max	Min	Source
Elasticity of transformation CET Fn. (c=PP and MR)	5.00	0.10	55	Guesstimate
Export Equation (EE) Price Elasticity (c=MO and PS)	1.00	0.00	7.00	Guesstimate
EE Income Elasticity (c=MO and PS)	0.94	−5.00	5.00	Senhadji and Montenegro (1999)
Import equation (IM) Price Elasticity (c)	0.25	0.00	3.00	Guesstimate
IM Income Elasticity (c)	1.92	0.00	4.00	Catao and Falceti (2002)
EE/IM Elasticity to sector specific investment	0.025	0.00	1.00	Guesstimate
EE/IM Elasticity Infrastructure and productive linkages	0.025	0.00	3.00	Guesstimate
Labour Saving Technical Change	0.025	0.00	1.50	Guesstimate
Kaldor-Verdoorn Parameter 2004–2007 (2010)	0.5	0.00	1.50	Guesstimate
Intercept LES Consumption Fn				Based on Berges and Casellas (2002)
Mg. Propensity to Consume LES Fn.				Based on Berges and Casellas (2002)
Wage equation (WE), Productivity	0.50	−1.00	5.00	Based on Panigo *et al.* (2009)
WE, change in CPI	0.82	−0.75	2.00	Based on Panigo *et al.* (2009)
WE, change in unemployment	0.28	0.10	1.70	Based on Panigo *et al.* (2009)
WE, Wage Policy	1.00			
Investment equation (IE), response to changes in capacity utilization	0.03	−2.00	2.00	Based on Panigo *et al.* (2009)
IE, changes in public investment	0.13	−0.50	0.85	Based on Panigo *et al.* (2009)
IE, changes in the sectoral profit rate	2.05	−0.70	3.25	Based on Panigo *et al.* (2009)
IE, changes in real interest rate	0.01	−2.00	1.25	Based on Panigo *et al.* (2009)
Labor supply adj. to wage differentials	0.05	0	2	Guesstimate
Mark-up elasticity to changes in total demand for MO (PS) commodities	0.1 (0.085)	0	3	Guesstimate
Exogenous Variables				
Capacity output ratio (%)	74.83 (2008)		INDEC	
	74.03 (2009)			
Base run unemployment rates (%)	8.77 (2009)		INDEC	
Nominal interest rate (%)	16.44 (2009)		BCRA	
Labor force growth (%)	1.92		INDEC	
Depreciation rate (%)	8.8		MEFP	

Notes

1 A previous version of the chapter was presented at the Fourth Annual Conference in Development and Change, which took place in Johannesburg on 9–11 April 2010. The chapter benefited from comments from the participants at the conference. Any possible error is, however, the author's responsibility.

2 As a consequence of internal and internal factors, exports have not contributed to output growth in 2008.

3 In spite of representing 20 percent of total output in the period 2003–2008, more than 40 percent of changes in real GDP are linked to investment growth.

4 Indeed, Argentina's industrial exports fell dramatically during the first two quarters of 2009 and only resumed growth in the fourth quarter.

5 The most important policies in this respect are the employment program *REPRO*, through which the government subsidizes workers training as a mechanism to prevent layoffs, and the *Asignación Universal por Hijo*, a subsidy for children from households whose head is unemployed or an informal worker.

6 China is expected to grow close to 9 percent in 2010 and India 6.5 percent, according to UN WESP.

7 The model has many points in common with the models developed in Gibson (2005), Gibson and van Seventer (2000a, 2000b) and Taylor (1990).

8 Primary and industrial products are classified using the CTP-DATA taxonomy proposed by Peirano and Porta (2000), and follow the taxonomy proposed by Pavitt (1984), adapted by Gurrieri (1989, 1992, quoted in Porta and Peirano, 2000), and used in the SELA study (1994, quoted in Porta and Peirano, 2000) to analyze the pattern of trade specialization in Latin American countries. The classification distinguishes products and sectors according to their main competitiveness factors (endowments, economies of scale, economies of specialization, technological intensity, etc.) and their reliance on price and non-price competitiveness advantages.

9 For different analytical specifications of Argentina's agricultural sector as the main exporting sector operating at full capacity, see papers by Diamand (1972), Canitrot (1975), Kostzer (1994), Nicolini-Llosa (2007a, 2007b), Porto (1975), Serino (2009a) and Visintini and Calvo (2000).

10 As discussed in Ros (2001) and Serino (2009a: Ch. 3), Dutch disease adjustments to positive external shocks follow form the expansion of the consumer-oriented service sector but not necessarily from an expansion of sector PS, which can counteract such adjustments.

11 In equation (2), ψ_c^{cet} and ρ_c^{cet} respectively are the share and exponent parameters of the CET function.

12 The CGE model specification differs from the specification in Serino (2007). In that model, sectors producing natural resource base products are indifferent as to the destination of production since they can charge the international price in the domestic market and export their surpluses. Modeling-wise, this specification implies fixed price and quantity adjustments for the natural resource sectors. This specification, however, is not included in the CGE model since it would reduce its flexibility – with four out of five sectors adjusting through quantities to excess demand.

13 See, for example, Dervis *et al.* (1982: Ch. 7).

14 Variable IADJ is included to allow for alternative saving-investment closure rules: it is endogenous under the neoclassical closure and exogenous with alternative closure rules.

15 Changes in government closure rules are also applicable to transfers to households and the rest of the world.

16 The labor supply grows according to an exogenous growth rate and responds to the wage differential among labor categories. Because labor categories differ in terms of the skills of the labor force, which are acquired through working experience or

participation in the education system, the response to wage differentials is assumed to be slow.

17 See Robinson (1989) and Sánchez Cantillo (2004) for a comprehensive discussion of closure rules, and Taylor (1990) for an exposition of fix–flex closure rules.

18 Average and distribution parameters represent the largest group of parameters, and include household saving rates, household income and expenditure structure, input–output coefficients and tax rates, among others.

19 The reader is referred to Serino (2009b: Ch. 6) for a comprehensive discussion of the calibration and validation of the CGE model used in this chapter.

20 Low parameter values are consistent with Catao and Falcetti's findings that capital accumulation influences exports in the long run but not in the short run. They also reflect Argentina's structurally high import dependency.

21 Parameter values employed to calibrate the wage and investment equations of the model do not necessarily coincide with estimations from Panigo *et al.* (2009), for these have been taken as a benchmark for the calibration.

22 This is in part because investment in Argentina in recent years has been very responsive to the profit rate (see Panigo *et al.* 2009).

23 Exports fall 25 percent more than under the alternative exchange rate regime.

24 As they take income out of the economy and limit price increases, export taxes reduce the expansionary effects of the primary shock. This additional characteristic of the adjustment has been particularly relevant in Argentina before the crisis, a period of strong demand impulses (see Serino 2009b). However, during the crisis or recovery period, export taxes may be used to underpin the recovery of aggregate demand.

25 The first top ten destinations received close to 80 percent of Argentina's industrial exports in 2008. In order of importance, the largest markets for Argentine products are: Brazil, the USA, Chile, Uruguay, Mexico, Venezuela, Switzerland, Bolivia, Peru, and The Netherlands.

26 This is because the shock impacts on sectors where skilled and formal employment predominates, which tend to belong to the richest household groups.

27 Latin American countries represent approximately 70 percent of Argentina's industrial exports, and these countries were a very active source of external demand in the years before the crisis.

28 This is certainly an over-optimistic figure, but is useful to show the benefits of integrating with countries from regions that will be growing faster than Argentina's main trading partners in the coming years. According to UN WESP, Africa is expected to grow 4.3 percent and East Asia (excluding China) 3.8 percent in 2010.

29 The positive shock encourages household consumption and this leads to higher prices of non-tradable goods (the CPI expands 60 percent more than prices of traditional tradable goods) which limits the price-competitiveness of non-traditional exports vis-à-vis the baseline and simulations of positive external shocks but no supply shock (see Table 7.6, columns 4 and 5).

References

Berges, M. and K. Casellas (2002) "A Demand System Analysis of Food for Poor and Non-Poor Households. The Case of Argentina", доклад на 10 конгрессе; EAAE, Exploring Diversity in the European Agri-Food System (28–31 August 2002), Zaragoza (Spain).

Blankenburg, S. and J.G. Palma (2009) "Introduction: The Global Financial Crisis", *Cambridge Journal of Economics*, 33: 531–538.

Borio, C. (2009) "The Financial Crisis of 2007–?: Macroeconomic Origins and Policy Lessons", Mumbai, India: G20 Workshop on the Global Economy.

Brahmbhatt, M. and O. Canuto (2010) "Natural Resouces and Development Strategy After the Crisis". Available at: www.voxeu.org/index.php?q=node/4696.

Canitrot, A. (1975) "La Experiencia Populista de Distribución de Ingresos", *Revista Desarrollo Económico*, 15.

Catao, L. and E. Falcetti (2002) "Determinants of Argentina's External Trade", *Journal of Applied Economics*, 5: 19–57.

Dervis, K., J. de Melo and S. Robinson (1982) *General Equilibrium Models for Development Policy*. New York, NY: Cambridge University Press.

Diamand, M. (1972) "La Estructura Económica Desequilibrada Argentina y el Tipo de Cambio", *Revista Desarrollo Económico*, 45.

Eichengreen, B. and K. H. O'Rourke (2009) "A Tale of Two Depressions". Available at: www.voxeu.org/index.php?q=node/3421 (retrieved 8 March 2010).

Gibson, W. (2005) "The Transition to A Globalized Economy: Poverty, Human Capital and the Informal Sector in a Structuralist CGE Model", *Journal of Development Economics*, 78: 60–94.

Gibson, W. and D. van Seventer (2000a) "A Tale of Two Models: Comparing Structuralist and neoclassical Computable General Equilibrium Models for South Africa", *International Review of Applied Economics*, 14: 149–171.

Gibson, W. and D. van Seventer (2000b) "Real Wages, Employment and Macroeconomic Policy in a Structuralist Model for South Africa", *Journal of African Economies*, 9: 512–546.

Kostzer, D. (1994) *A Model of the Argentine Economy*. Buenos Aires: Mimeo.

Leon-Ledesma, M. (2002) "Accumulation, Innovation and Catching-up: An Extended Cumulative Growth Model", *Cambridge Journal of Economics*, 26: 201–216.

Nicolini-Llosa, J.L. (2007a) *Essays on Argentina's Growth Cycle and the World Economy*. Amsterdam: University of Amsterdam.

Nicolini-Llosa, J.L. (2007b) "Tipo de Cambio Dual y Crecimiento Cíclico en Argentina", *Desarrollo Económico – Revista De Ciencias Sociales*, 47: 249–283.

Ostry, J.A., K.H. Ghosh, M. Chamon, M. Quereshi and D. Reinhardt (2010) "Capital Inflows: The Role of Controls", IMF Staff Position Note SPN 10/04, IMF.

Panigo, D., F. Toledo, D. Herrero, E. López and H. Montagu (2009) *Modelo Macroeconométrico Estructural para Argentina*. Buenos Aires: S. d. P. Económica.

Pavitt, K. (1984) "Sectoral Patterns of Technical Change: Towards a Taxonomy and Theory", *Research Policy*, 13: 343–373.

Peirano, F. and F. Porta (2000) "El Impacto de las Preferencias Comerciales sobre el Comercio Intraregional. Análisis del Mercosur y los Acuerdos Bilaterales de Chile", *REDES*, 18.

Porto, A. (1975) "Un Modelo Simple sobre el Comportamiento Macroeconómico Argentino en el Corto Plazo", *Desarrollo Económico*, 59.

Robinson, S. (1989) "Multisectoral Models", in H. Chenery and T. Srinivasan (eds), *Handbook of Development Economics*, Vol. II. Amsterdam: North Holland, Ch. 18.

Ros, J. (2001) "Política Industrial, Ventajas Comparativas y Crecimiento", Revista de la CEPAL 73, Washington, DC: CEPAL.

Sánchez Cantillo, M.V. (2004) "Rising Inequality and Falling Poverty in Costa Rica's Agriculture during Trade Reform", PhD Thesis. The Hague: ISS.

Senhadji, A. and C. Montenegro (1999) "Time Series Analysis of Export Demand Equations: A Cross-country Analysis", IMF Staff Papers 46, Washington, DC, IMF.

Serino, L. (2007) "Competitive Diversification in Resource Abundant Countries: Argentina After the Collapse of the Convertibility Regime", ISS Working Paper No. 441 (May).

Serino, L. (2009a) "Positive Natural Resource Shocks and Domestic Adjustments in a Semi-industrialized Economy: Argentina in the 2003–2007 Period", ISS Working Paper Series 484, The Hague: ISS. Available at: http://biblio.iss.nl/opac/uploads/wp/wp484.pdf.

Serino, L. (2009b) "Productive Diversification in Natural Resource Abundant Countries. Limitations, Policies and the Experience of Argentina in the 2000s", PhD Thesis. The Hague: ISS.

Serino, L. and E. Kiper (2009) "El trasfondo macroeconómico de la crisis internacional", paper presented at 1st Annual Conference AEDA (Asociación de economía para el desarrollo de Argentina), Argentina.

Tavosnanska, A. and G. Herrera (2010) "La industria Argentina a comienzos del siglo XXI. Aportes para una revisión de la experiencia reciente", in A. Müller (ed.), *Industria, Desarrollo, Historia. Ensayos en homenaje a Jorge Schvarzer*. CESPA. Buenos Aires: CESPA.

Taylor, L. (1990) "Structuralist CGE Models", in L. Taylor (ed.), *Social Relevant Policy Analysis*. Cambridge: MIT Press.

United Nations (2010) *World Economic Situation and Prospects, 2010 (WESP)*. New York, NY: United Nations, DESA.

Visintini, A. and S. Calvo (2000) *Macroeconomía y Agricultura: una Propuesta Metodológica para su Análisis*. Anales de la AAEP.

Vos, R. (2007) "What We Do and Don't Know about Trade Liberalization and Poverty Reduction", DESA Working Paper 50; ST/ESA/2007/DWP, DESA.

Part III

The technology and innovation dimension

8 Is renewables a solution?

Ethanol and the environment – the missing point

Luiz M. Niemeyer

1 Introduction

The objective of this chapter is to assess, through the lens of the Brazilian ethanol production, the opportunity for developing countries to invest in the so-called renewables sector under the framework of the current world crisis. What we know from previous crises is that it tends towards a process of "creative destruction", where some sectors decline while others rise. One can infer that the new technology wave encompasses biotechnology, nanotechnology, bioelectronics and new energies.

Bubbles are about the installation of a technological revolution, and they concentrate investment in the radically new industries and infrastructures. They happen every forty to sixty years, and are essentially a grand experiment to select the products and the companies that will serve as engines of growth for the next few decades. They are an intrinsic part of the transformation of the economy by a wave of revolutionary technologies. They are about financial speculation on top of real investment in real innovation (Perez 2002).

In another paper Perez considers developing as learning to take advantage of changing in technology as opportunities. She argues that opportunities for development are like moving targets: they show up and change due to successive technological changes. These not only move constantly ahead but also shift direction about every half century (Perez 2003:114). Let us assess if investments in renewables supports this rule or if it provides the exception. Since Brazil is the biggest sugarcane producer, with the best production technology and smallest production costs, the evaluation of its experience as an ethanol producer can be of great help to other developing countries.

This chapter will discuss major environmental aspects of ethanol production in Brazil. Two important qualifying points should be noted at the outset. The first is that the analysis in this chapter focuses on the environment impact of ethanol production in Brazil. Many articles have discussed the benefits stemming from this production – for example, it is renewable, it is an alternative to gasoline, it saves hard currency reserves and so on. These are legitimate points, but these issues are not addressed here. The second is that this chapter only investigates the production of ethanol; other biofuels are not taken into consideration in the evaluation.

The analysis has as a starting point the Brazilian Program on Alcohol (Proalcool) – that reached its peak in 1985 – and related developments. Being consistent with the Kyoto protocol, ethanol production (Proalcool) has been touted as a solution for environmental problems. Yet our contention is that its production poses serious environmental threats.

The production and consumption of ethanol is always debated in Brazil during periods of energy crisis. In spite of the intensive lobby of car manufacturers and alcohol producers, the use of hydrous or anhydrous ethanol[1] in the country as an alternative source of energy is still not very pronounced. It varies along with oil price and the international sugar price. Currently, the question of ethanol use is back in the spotlight for the following reasons. First, in 2005, 57 per cent of the manufactured cars in Brazil were made with "flex" technology – i.e., the engines can run with either gasoline or ethanol. In 2007, 21 per cent of the Brazilian car fleet was running with flex technology and ethanol was responsible for 16.7 per cent of the consumed fuel (ECLAC 2009: 142). In April 2011, due to the rise of the international price of sugar, ethanol's "substitute" good,[2] the price of ethanol rose by 30 per cent. Brazil, an oil self-sufficient country, had to import US\$15 billion of gasoline.The production decision is related to the evolution of sugar's international price.

This chapter will emphasize the negative impact of ethanol production on the environment. These aspects have been almost completely ignored, both in the debate until 1985 when Proalcool reached its peak, as well as in the current debate involving flex car production.

The chapter is structured as follows. Section 2 analyses the current crisis in the light of Schumpeter's theory and considers the recent surge of renewables in this framework. Section 3 critically reviews cost–benefit (CB) analysis of ethanol, since it is a major tool involving its production decision. Section 4 presents a brief outline of ethanol production in Brazil. Finally, section 5 discusses important environmental aspects of ethanol production.

2 Schumpeter's creative destruction

Schumpeter's theory of development is a long-run theory. The pillar of his theory is the concept of a circular flow of production and consumption (Schumpeter 1961: 61). The circular flow could expand, but development is entirely foreign to what one observes in the circular flow; "it is just this occurrence of the "revolutionary" change that is the problem of economic development" (ibid.: 63); it is spontaneous and discontinuous change (ibid.: 64). In order for development to take place, the circular flow itself must jump to a higher level.

Development will happen only when an entrepreneur (ibid.: 78) decides to take a risk (ibid.: 75) and innovate. The innovation can be an introduction of a new good, the introduction of a new method of production, the opening of new market, and so on (ibid.: 66). Every concrete process of development creates the prerequisite for the next. Only through innovation can the circular flow be broken and jump to a higher level. This jump occurs through the process of creative destruction (ibid: 67).

Following the initial innovation the entrepreneur will, for a short period, receive monopoly profits. Later on, as the barriers to entry are eased, other producers follow and imitate the process of creative destruction, which then spreads throughout the economy. In this manner, resources earlier used to manufacture other goods, or in other productive processes, are guided to produce the new "combination" (innovation). In this process some businesses might go bankrupt as demand for their goods drop, further facilitating the transfer of resources to the new innovation (Taylor and Arida, 1988). The dynamics of the Schumpeterian theory are explained in the last chapter of Schumpeter (1961) and are further developed in his analysis of the business cycle (Schumpeter, 1939).

> Due to the double nature of the process of creative destruction, Schumpeter saw innovation not only as the force propelling progress but also as the cause of recurring recessions and in general of the cyclical behaviour of growth rates and other economic magnitudes (Perez, 2002: 23).... Thus each technological revolution brings with it, not only a full revamping of the productive structure but eventually also a transformation of the institutions of governance, of society and even ideologies and culture so deep that one can speak about the construction of successive and different modes of growth in the history of capitalism. The process of creative destruction occurs then, every 50 or 60 years.
>
> (Schumpeter, 1939: 25)

Credit will provide the means for the entrepreneur to break the circular flow through innovation. "'Financing' as a special act is fundamentally necessary, in practice as in theory" (Schumpeter 1961: 71); therefore finance, together with the concept of circular flow, the hole played by innovations, and the entrepreneur are the four main points of Schumpeter's theory of economic development.

In his book, Perez (2002: 5) argues that that there are recurrent phases that are inherent in the nature of capitalism. They obey the following order: (1) technological revolution; (2) financial bubble; (3) collapse; (4) golden age and (5) political unrest. Further, he suggests that the phases of each great surge follow this order:

1   Installation period. Following a big bang, this has two phases: (a) Eruption and (b) Frenzy.
2   Deployment period. This starts at what the author calls a turning point, when a crash occurs and an institutional recomposition begins, and has two phases: (c) Synergy and (d) Maturity (ibid.: 48).

> Financial capital plays a crucial role all along. It first supports the development of the technological revolution, it then contributes to deepen the mismatch leading to a possible crash, it later becomes a contributing agent in the deployment process once the match is achieved and, when that revolution is spent, and it helps give birth to the next.
>
> (Perez, 2002: xviii)

For the purpose of this chapter we are interested in the "Frenzy phase" and in the turning point (ibid.: 169) that follows. The early years of the 2000s, with massive speculation, could easily be considered a component of the Frenzy phase, with the crash in 2007. This can be regarded as the period of the financial bubble, intensive investment in the revolutionary technology, decoupling between financial and production capital, and so on. It is, as the author states, the time of finance and bubbles (ibid.: 50)

> Production capital, including the revolutionary industries, becomes one more object of the manipulation and speculation; the decoupling between financial and production capital is almost complete...
> Nevertheless, this is the time of innovation for production capital ... during this period financial capital generates a powerful magnet to attract investment into new areas, hence accelerating the hold of the paradigm on what becomes "the new economy".
>
> (Perez, 2002: 75)

One can infer that the new technology wave encompasses biotechnology, nanotechnology, bioelectronics and new energy sources. The renewables enter into this last category. According to ECLAC, the investment in biofuels was US$13.7 billion in 2004 and increased to US$25.4 billion in 2007 (ECLA, 2009: 130). Another set of data allows us to evaluate the huge amount of resources directed to the renewables. According to a Merrill Lynch (2008) report, Global Venture Capital Investment flow in clean technology, which includes renewables, jumped from roughly US$1 billion in 2000 to US$8 billion in 2008 – an eight-fold increase in the period.

3 Ethanol and the cost–benefit analysis

In this chapter, we will not evaluate the theory that informed the modifications made in the CB analysis to take into account environmental aspects. Instead, using the theory behind the criticism regarding important modifications made in the CB analysis by mainstream economists, the chapter will assess the important environmental aspects involved in ethanol production (Proalcool) in Brazil that were ignored.

There has been considerable debate among economists on the alternative ways of incorporating the environmental effects of projects in the conventional CB decision framework. On the one hand, we have the attempt to incorporate irreversibly lost environmental preservation values as a cost induced by projects to develop a natural area. On the other hand, there is the traditional practice of ignoring the preservation alternative in the evaluation of a proposed development project in a natural area. Both approaches have their drawbacks.

Ethanol (Proalcool) production in Brazil can be used as an example of conventional CB analysis that has disregarded important considerations related to the environment. In order to illustrate our point of view, some cost and benefit analysis on the ethanol will briefly be discussed.

The calculation of the CB ratio is normally presented in textbooks and by some financial entities, like development banks (whether national or multinational), as universal criteria for public project valuation. What is mostly debated on the subject among neoclassical economists is not related to the validity of its use vis-à-vis other alternatives, but to the improvement of auxiliary techniques (Farber *et al.*, 2006).

For Sagoff (1988: 75), by and large, CB analysis assigns prices only to goods and services of the sort that are typically traded in markets and thus that can easily be priced. Certain economists generally list other values as "intangibles". The "intangible" values associated with environment, health, and safety policy may often be more important than the "tangible" ones.

According to the author, the existence of legislation prohibiting CB analysis shows that citizens value the idea that policies should result instead from ethical deliberation and the rule of law. Examples where CB tests are not allowed are the Endangered Species Act and Clean Air. These statutes have worked rather well. One may say that citizens rejected a cost–benefit or "consumer surplus" approach to trade-off between health, safety or environment quality, and economic growth.

Martinez-Alier (1991: 119) observes that economic values assigned in the conventional way to externalities (such as exhaustion of non-renewable resources, global warming, or radioactive pollution) would be so arbitrary that they cannot serve as a basis for rational environmental policies. Externalities, defined as uncertain social costs transferred to other social groups or to future generations, must be perceived before they are valued in monetary terms.

As a backdrop of our analysis on the environment impact of ethanol production, let us take as an example the Brookshire *et al.* (1992) proposition. These authors point out that, as far as the environmental costs induced by a project are concerned, the CB analysis has traditionally focused on the use values of natural environments. However, other values should be included as part of the total value of the natural resource or environment. The authors have suggested the contingent valuations method (CVM)[3] for valuing non-marketed commodities, which can be successfully used in estimating values associated with retaining the option of future use and the existence of a natural environment (Brookshire *et al.*, 1992: 112).

Regarding the CVM approach, Sagoff (1988: 88) points out that insofar as it tries to make respondents express preferences rather than deliberate about ideas, the method denies to the respondents their status as thinking political beings. For Sagoff, ideas are different than consumer preferences and go even further. Political and ethical debates are different from CB analysis based on CVM. For him, this difference is possibly the major reason that respondents so often enter protest bids or otherwise resist this sort of experiment.

A public policy based on the willingness-to-pay approach like the CVM may be disastrous. According to Sagoff, economic analysis tends to limit conflict to those parties who have something at stake for which they are willing to pay. This approach would prevent the socialization of conflict that is crucial to the functioning of a democracy (Sagoff, 1988: 95).

Technocracy localizes the conflict so that it can be resolved by the application of some mechanical rule or decisions. One example is to present ethanol (Proalcool) production as viable alternative if the oil price is above US$50 bbl (barrel equivalent of oil), as has been argued by the Brazilian government and *The Economist*.[4] As we will see, the CB analyses of ethanol do not take into consideration serious environmental concerns. Cost–benefit approaches to public policy, if taken to their extreme, would do this, and thus they would substitute themselves for the process of democratic government. For Sagoff (1988: 97), the "ideological" genius of CB analysis is to localize conflict among affected individuals, and thereby to prevent it from breaking out into the public realm.

We will now review the CB analysis in the peak phase of the Proalcool (1980–1985). We choose this period because much of the literature on the subject is related to this period. For instance, in 1985 ethanol production reached a record level of 11 billion litres. Bearing in mind that we have progressed twenty years on, the points that will be raised will help us evaluate the environmental aspect of ethanol production. Our comments will be based on three studies, namely Motta (1987), Motta and Ferreira (1988) and Rocha Filho (1992). The data and conclusions of Rocha Filho extend up to 1990.

According to CB analysis, the economic viability of Proalcool strongly depends on oil prices. Despite some years of steady prices, oil prices doubled in 1978 and reached US$35–40 per bbl in 1981. This was the major economic justification for the emphasis on the programme from 1979 onwards. However, in 1982 oil prices started to decline reaching levels below those traded in 1980.

For Marjotta-Maistro (2002: 11) the period between 1971 and 1987, which forms the economic context of both of Motta's analyses, is very different from the current period. During that period, the concern was the preponderance of hydrous ethanol over gasoline. In the 1990s, the concern was with the permanence of ethanol as a fuel. Thus Motta's analysis follows the conventional CB methodology, and the CVM techniques discussed above were not incorporated.

Rocha Filho (1992) also specifically discusses the CB of ethanol production. His major concern was the permanence of hydrous ethanol as a fuel. The data from the study go up to the 1986–1987 crop; however, some data extend to 1990. The author concluded that ethanol is a feasible long-term alternative, and advocated that the program should be maintained and expanded through incentives. His conclusion is different from that of Motta and Ferreira (1988), who argue in favour of the programme in order to maintain jobs.

In the three studies, we have the barrel of oil equivalent (bbl) or barrel of gasoline equivalent (bgl) as the benchmark for the decisions related to Proalcool. We can now recall Sagoff's comments about the "ideological" genius of CB analysis. It localizes conflict among affected individuals by the use of some mechanical rule (i.e. ethanol is feasible if the oil price is above US$45 per bbl), and thereby prevents conflicts or discussions about the impact of ethanol production on the environment from breaking out into the public realm.

The studies do not take into account the environmental aspects. Motta (1987) and Motta and Ferreira (1988) follow the traditional cost and benefit approach, while Rocha Filho (1992) follows the CVM but does not take into consideration environment aspects. Regarding more recent analysis, we will refer to the influential Embrapa. This Brazilian state company has been disseminating ethanol viability and technology worldwide, with special focus in African countries. Embrapa's studies do not discuss or incorporate the environmental aspects of the ethanol. See, for instance, Goez and Marra (2008) or Embrapa (2011).

4 Ethanol production (Proalcool)[5]

The use of alcohol as a fuel in Brazil and in the world precedes the creation of the Brazilian National Alcohol Program (Proalcool) announced in 1975. A mixture of gasoline and alcohol – gasohol – has previously been used in many countries. Since the early 1920s, Brazil has pursued an official alcohol policy to overcome restrictions on imports and/or to stabilize the domestic sugar sector due to a crisis of overproduction.

The first aim of the Proalcool was to produce anhydrous ethanol for mixing with gasoline. In Brazil in 1977 terms, on an energy content basis, alcohol was five times more expensive to produce than gasoline was in the US (Rothman *et al.*, 1983: 107). However, after the 1979 oil shock, with its dramatic price increase, and later the Iran–Iraq war that cut off one-third of the country's oil supply, ethanol production was impressively expanded; emphasis was placed on hydrous ethanol, which allows for total replacement of gasoline. The success of this programme in terms of ethanol production was beyond doubt. From a level of 600 million litres in 1974, ethanol production in Brazil reached 11.8 billion litres in 1985. Between 1975 and 1985, US$7 billion was invested in all sorts of incentives for ethanol production (Calabi, 1983: 237). Moreover, in 1985, pure

Table 8.1 Ethanol production from 1970–1971 to 2005–2006 (millions of litres)

Crop	Production	Crop	Production	Crop	Production
1970/1971	637.2	1983/1984	7,864.0	1997/1998	15,000.0
1971/1972	613.1	1984/1985	9,244.0	1998/1999	13,400.0
1972/1973	681.0	1985/1986	11,820.0	1999/2000	12,770.0
1974/1975	625.0	1986/1987	10,516.0	2000/2001	10,622.0
1976/1977	664.0	1987/1988	11,454.0	2001/2002	11,059.0
1977/1978	14,470.3	1988/1989	11,713.0	2002/2003	12,623.0
1978/1979	2,490.9	1989/1990	11,881.0	2003/2004	14,808.0
1979/1980	3,383.8	1990/1991	11,783.0	2004/2005	15,416.0
1980/1981	3,742.0	1991/1992	12,681.0	2005/2006	15,946.0
1981/1982	4,240.0	1992/1993	11,736.0	2006/2007	17,719.0
1982/1983	5,824.0	1993/1994	11,278.0	2007/2008	22,527.0
		1994/1995	12,726.0	2008/2009	27,513.0
		1995/1996	12,689.0	2009/2010	24,000.0
		1996/1997	14,030.0		

Source: Until 1979/1980 Magalhaes (1991: 29); from 1980/81 to 2001/2002, Marjotta-Maistro (2002: 16); remaining years, UNICA (www.unica.com.br).

154   *L.M. Niemeyer*

alcohol-fuelled engines accounted for almost 90 per cent of new cars and 20 per cent of all passenger cars in Brazil. In 1982, alcohol fuels accounted for 10 per cent of total energy use in transportation compared to less than 1 per cent at the end of 1976.

By the end of the 1980s, due to the substantial reduction in international oil prices, Proalcool lost credibility with the Brazilian public opinion. The IAA[6] was extinguished in 1990 in the wake of World Bank's Berg Report. This marked the beginning of the process of deregulation and opening of the sugar-alcohol sector. Marjotta-Maistro (2002: 3) informs us that the sugar price was deregulated in 1990, anhydrous ethanol in 1997 and hydrous ethanol in 1999. Currently we are witnessing a new phase of euphoria regarding ethanol production for the following reasons: (1) in the first two months of 2006, 90 per cent of the new cars sold had "flex" technology; and (2) President Bush launched an extensive campaign on alternative fuel, and this has strongly affected the Brazilian market/ production.

We present below several environmental aspects related to the programme. If these aspects were taken into consideration in the CB analyses of the programme, they would cast doubts on its feasibility. Some of the points raised have already been disputed by the programme defenders (see Magalhaes *et al.*, 2001).

5 Ethanol and the missing aspects relating to the environment

We will divide the evaluation of the environmental impact into parts: Proalcool and ethanol. In this section, Proalcool refers to the Brazilian government's programme of ethanol that achieved its peak in 1985 and has a rich literature. Ethanol is circumscribed here to more current aspects of ethanol production. The goal here is to double-check the validity of the criticisms. Following the reasoning discussed in section 2, we describe below several "intangible" aspects that were missed in the conventional CB analysis, or in a future one that would try to account for the environment.

5.1 The production of ethanol and water

Proalcool

> Brazilian water quality has already suffered greatly from the rapid expansion of Proalcool, as 12 to 17 gallons of slops are produced for each gallon of sugarcane alcohol. The 1980 Brazilian production level of 4.1 billion gallons of fuel is a gargantuan pollution problem. Even worse, the slops are usually discharged into rivers and streams during the six dry months of the year in which sugar cane is harvested. At this time, shrunken streams and rivers are least able to assimilate the discharges. Carl Duisberg reported in his doctoral dissertation on the Proalcool program that several large river

systems in the state of Sao Paulo, including the Piracicaba, the Mogi-Guassu, and Pardo have been virtually poisoned to death by stillage.

(Berton *et al.*, 1982: 182)

Berton *et al.* (1982) report that among the worst threats to water quality posed by the development of the alcohol fuel industry is the enormous volume of stillage that is generated. Stillage, also called slops or vinasse, is the left-over liquid of the fermented mash after the alcohol has been distilled off and the solids separated for livestock feed. Slops contain from 1–10 per cent of dissolved minerals and organic materials. The compounds rapidly decompose when dumped into waterways, robbing the water of oxygen required for the survival of fish and other aquatic life. Even after all the oxygen in a waterway has been dissolved, a second-stage anaerobic (oxygen-free) decomposition process is set in motion, producing the noxious-smelling hydrogen sulphide gas.

Rotham *et al.* (1983: 137) stress the importance of the State of Sao Paulo as the most important sugarcane producer. At that time, with seventy-six sugar and alcohol distillers, it accounted for two-thirds of the production of ethanol. This represents a pollution potential equivalent to 2.02 million kg BOD[7] (biochemical oxygen demand) per day, of which 1.79 million kg BOD per day (88 per cent) are produced by the different systems of production of the various ethanol industries. The rest (12 per cent, or 0.24 million BOD per day) represents a pollution equivalent to that produced by 4.4 million people.

During the 1990s, the problem of vinasse disposal was addressed by "congestion" – i.e. using slops to irrigate the soil instead of discharging it into rivers. According to Silva and Simoes (1999), Brazil solved the problem of vinasse disposal by using this byproduct of the ethanol production as a fertilizer and for irrigating the soil. This technique is known as "fertirrigação" (fert-irrigation).

Corazza (2001) assessed the environmental impact of an alternative technique, i.e. the anaerobic treatment of sugarcane stillage vis-à-vis fertirrigação. She recognized the positive aspects of the latter. However, remembering that until 2001 no substantial progress was made in the reduction of litres of ethanol/litres of stillage, she also pointed out its negatives aspects. Some of these are: (1) increasing saltiness of the soil; and (2) risk (vulnerability) of soil and ground water pollution (Corazza, 2001: 217).

Regarding ground water pollution, she reports that in 1986, 40 per cent of the slops produced were not reused in the process of fertirrigação. Ethanol producers could dispose it in areas known as "sacrifice areas" (using impermeable wrap to protect the ground water basin). Apart from the fact that this can affect the surface springs, no study was made whatsoever to evaluate the impact of the residue on the ground water springs, and some researchers are worried about this risk (ibid.: 215).

The last point becomes noteworthy if we bear in mind that the biggest ethanol producer region of the State of Sao Paulo – i.e. between Campinas and Ribeirao Preto – is the recharge region of the Guarani aquifer, one of the major aquifers of South America (ibid.: 216).

Ethanol

There is a natural conflict between agricultural and human needs regarding the use of water. Sadeq (1999: 19) reminds us of the increasing competition among the different types of water consumers, and considers the urban environment, where necessities are immense, as being in the worst situation. According to the author, worldwide the agriculture sector captures 69 per cent of the water while industry's share is 23 per cent and household consumption is 8 per cent.

In the case of Brazil, Hespanhol (2003: 38) estimates the consumption for agriculture at 70 per cent, and for industries and household at 15 per cent each. He forecasts that the agricultural share will reach 80 per cent in the first decade of the twenty-first century. The author (ibid.: 37) observes that this activity is totally dependent on water supply. Irrigation became a key component of increasing Brazilian agricultural productivity. Therefore, on the main Brazilian hydrographic basin that serves regions with an intense urban and agricultural development, we will see an increasing conflict of use.

In another study, Hespanhol (2001: 150) reports frequent water rationing in the cities of Recife and São Paulo. Furthermore, the author, together with 5 Elementos (2005: 21), reveals that the São Paulo Metropolitan Region needs to import 50 per cent of its water consumption through the Cantareira Production System.

Using the 2001/2002 crop, the state of São Paulo produced 65 per cent of ethanol and sugar in Brazil (Marjotta-Maistro, 2002: 18). Sugarcane plantations take up 8.2 per cent of the entire area of the State (Arbex, 2001: 72). We have a clear case of conflict of use, and this has repercussions on the water supply for the metropolitan region of São Paulo.[8] This metropolitan region has water disputes with the Piracicaba basin region. The latter, apart from being a major producer of sugarcane, is also surrounded by other great cane- and ethanol-producing regions.

Galvão (2000: 29) observes that this metropolitan region, served by the Alto Tiête basin, shelters 47 per cent of São Paulo State's population. This region imports water from the basin of the Piracicaba, Capivari and Jundiai rivers. Thus the great São Paulo, with its 16 million inhabitants and responsible for 20 per cent of the country's GDP, has water disputes with the Piracicaba valley. The latter region (Campinas, Jundiai and Piracicaba), is also highly industrialized with a diversified agricultural sector. It shelters 4.5 million inhabitants and is responsible for 9 per cent of the country's GDP; it too is not in a comfortable position in terms of water supply.

One can argue that the need to import water by the São Paulo Metropolitan Region could be avoided by the adoption of strict regulation regarding pollution of the fountainhead (wellspring). However, there are two points to be considered: (1) the costs involving the treatment of highly polluted water are very high and would thus make the costs for the existing industry very high (Galvão, 2000: 29); and (2) this strict regulation may be very important but it is biased towards agriculture, and we have to bear in mind that this activity in Brazil already uses 70 per cent of the water!

Ethanol production is water-intensive. Based on the 1999 influential work *O Estado das Aguas no Brasil*, Galvão (ibid.: 31) reports that each kilogramme of sugar produced demands 100 litres of water. Another study from the IDEC (2000) stressed that the sugar distillers require seventy-five litres of water to produce one kilogramme of sugar. Sugar and ethanol are substitutes in the production process. Given that distillation of the alcohol comes after sugar production, we can assume that the production of one litre of ethanol requires more than 100 litres of water.[9]

According to Rebouças (1997: 76), the average water potential of the Southeast Region rivers (the biggest ethanol producer in the country, where São Paulo State is located) is 334.2 cubic kilometres per year (km^3/year), accounting for 6 per cent of the country's overall potential. The social disposal of water (5,333 cubic meters per inhabitant per year) is slightly superior to that of the Northeast Region (average water potential of 186.3 km^3/year), the lowest-ranked region and quite well-known for its droughts. The Southeast Region was responsible for 83 per cent of the sugar production and 77 per cent of the ethanol production in 2001/2002 (Marjotta-Maistro, 2002: 16).

5.2 The production of ethanol (and Proalcool) and air pollution

In Brazil the use of anhydrous ethanol as fuel for passenger cars or the mixture of 22 per cent of hydrous ethanol with gasoline brought gains for the environment and the health of the population, mainly to those living in big urban centres. A major benefit was the reduction of the emission of lead in the atmosphere due the replacement of lead in anti-detonating by a combination of hydrous ethanol and gasoline.

However, the large-scale use of ethanol as fuel for passenger car has resulted in a substantial increase of the land used for sugarcane predominantly in the State of São Paulo. In the regions where the sugarcane is produced and industrialized the quality of the air suffered due to the increasing amount of cane and straw burned resulting in increased pollution of the atmosphere.

(Arbex, 2001: 126)

Arbex (2001: 85) reports that dust resulting from the sugarcane and straw burned, which falls on the cities around the plantation, affects the health of its inhabitants. During the period of the burning of cane and straw he found an increase in the incidence of asthma and emphysema as well as in the number of deaths due to respiratory diseases among the exposed population.

The author points out that in 1998 sugarcane production was the agricultural sector's major employer in the State of São Paulo, employing roughly 90,000 workers. The trade union was very much against the State Law (42056 of 08/06/1997), which established that the burning of the dust and cane should be eliminated gradually in eight to fifteen years' time.

Arbex (ibid.: 70) notes that in São Paulo during the harvest of 1997/1998, 81.8 per cent of the cropland was harvested manually, with the cane leftovers and straw burned. In more recent research, Tolmasquim (2003: 76) noted that 75 per cent of the entire cane harvest in Brazil is manual. This type of harvest is followed by burning of straw.

Arbex (ibid.: 76) brings to light some alarming data regarding the estimation of air pollution levels from sugarcane plantation burning: (1) the amount per year of dried material burned in the sugarcane plantation per unit of area is fifteen times greater than the amount burned in the Amazon region ($0.5\,km^2$ against $0.03\,km^2$); and (2) the State of São Paulo, during the harvest period, burns 82 million tonnes/day of cane straw. This burning is responsible for 285 tonnes/day of particular matter and 33,342 tonnes/day of carbon monoxide (the total state area used for sugar cane production is 8.22 per cent). In contrast, the vehicle emissions of particulate matter and carbon monoxide in the metropolitan region of São Paulo (2.82 per cent of the area of the state) are 62 tonnes/day and 4,293 tonnes/day, respectively!

5.3 Energy crops and food crops

Proalcool

Brown[10] (1980: 28) noted that the decision in 1979 to turn more strongly to energy crops, to fuel Brazil's rapidly growing fleet of automobiles, was certain to drive food prices upward, thus leading to more severe malnutrition among the poor. In effect, the more affluent one-fifth of the population who own most of the automobiles would dramatically increase their individual claims on cropland from roughly one to at least three acres, further squeezing the millions at the low end of the Brazilian economic ladder. As the author points out, Brazil is a chronically grain-deficient country. For instance, in 1979 imports of grains soared to a record 5.7 million tonnes.

Calabi (1983) showed concern over the production goal of 11 billion litres of ethanol in 1985. His concern stemmed from the country's record with respect to food security in the past. Since the late 1960s, Brazil had placed a lot of effort in promoting agricultural exports like soybeans. As a result of this, food imports rose to US$2 billion in 1979 vis-à-vis US$1.2 billion in 1978. The emphasis on ethanol production could increase the country's food imports further.

> The possibility of large-scale biomass alcohol production has posed the question of whether, and to what extent, such a development is likely to compete for land and other agricultural resources that could otherwise be allocated for producing food.... The issue is complex and can sometimes be emotional. Basic considerations in assessing the extent of future competition for agricultural resources are the relative price movements for energy and food. As noted, on a global basis a sharper increase in energy prices than in food prices or most other agricultural products is plausible, at least over the next decade. Assuming this occurs, the potential land use conflict between

food, export, and energy crops will increase as economic forces increasingly draw resources into energy production.

(World Bank, 1980: 53)

To illustrate the lack of concern of economic authorities regarding the question of "energy cropping" and its trade-off with food production, we refer to the government's contention that the social cost of an ethanol industry based solely on sugarcane would ultimately prove to be unacceptable. They were hoping to develop second-generation feed stocks. The most important of these second-generation crops was thought to be manioc,[11] one of the world's five staple crops (together with sorgo, rice, wheat and corn).

According to Motta (1987: 178), in 1983, São Paulo State accounted for 50 per cent of ethanol production and, as opposed to other states 'energy crops' replaced other crops such as rice, beans and corn. Hence the state suffered reduction in food production. São Paulo State is by far the most economically vibrant state, and also has the largest urban population.

> Town dwellers (the towns are the seat of political power) are therefore relatively well protected against famine, at least in peace-time and its for this reason that, when supplies are scarce, there is a mass exodus of country dwellers towards the towns to which they are lured by the hope of finding cheap food or some way of earning money, no matter how little. For, although in rural areas food shortages and high food prices are generally accompanied by a reduction in the number of jobs available, such is not the case in towns, which are less affected by seasonal variations. This migration towards the towns may be organized to a greater or lesser degree by the population itself.
>
> (Spitz, 1978: 868)

According to Spitz (1978), the urban areas have more power to buy food, and this aspect is an important one in urban migration in developing countries. The power that São Paulo State, and other powerful and urbanized states, had in the food market also contributed to the massive migration[12] of the rural and poor states' population to big cities like São Paulo, Rio de Janeiro, Belo Horizonte, etc. Hence these cities have all sorts of urban environmental problems, from squatting around the areas of water and the consequent pollution of the water supply, to an astonishing increase in the numbers of slum populations with a severe degradation in sanitation and the urban environment. Of course this "social injustice" is not due to Proalcool alone, but one can say that it did contribute to it.

Ethanol

A recent report from OECD-FAO (2007) notes that debate on energy cropping versus food cropping is very current. The increasing demand for bio-fuel, such as ethanol, is leading to fundamental changes in the agricultural markets, which are currently witnessing price increases in various products. For instance, the report notes that the world costs of food imports in 2007 increased by 5 per cent due to this rising demand. It also stresses that this increase in cost will mainly affect developing countries.

Silva (2007) draws attention to the influential IEA's (São Paulo State Agricultural Institute) report that in the 2006–2007 period there was reduction in the agricultural area of thirty-two products in the state; among them were rice (10 per cent), beans (13 per cent), manioc (3 per cent) and tomato (12 per cent). They also report a reduction of more than a million cattle.

5.4 Ethanol production as a substitute of energy

Proalcool

> Sometimes it is said that agriculture might become a source of energy, by which it is meant that biomass might be used as fuel, not merely in the form of wood or dung. It is difficult to understand the physics (as distinct from the sociology) of simultaneously excluding sugar production from the "energy sector" and including ethanol from sugarcane. It is only an "urban bias" (or an "upper class bias") of the most potent sort, which allows people who are perhaps worried about an excess of calories in their diet, to exclude food production from the "energy sector" of the economy.
>
> (Martinez-Alier, 1987: 20)

Martinez-Alier (1987: 15), in his book, calls our attention to the fact that economics is unable to deal convincingly with ecological critique. Therefore, it is paradoxical that the renewed faith in the market coincided with the energy crisis of 1973 and its aftermath.

Unlike Pearce and Turner (1990: 120),[13] Martinez-Alier (1987: 21) states that because ethanol is used as a fuel for cars, one relevant comparison is between the energy efficiency of ethanol production and other types of agriculture. Another relevant comparison would be between the energy cost of ethanol and the energy cost of other sources such as coal, oil and hydroelectricity; in this sense, ethanol from sugarcane appears to be quite expensive.

Considering the ethanol industry as one branch of the so-called "energy sector" of the economy, the energy cost of ethanol could then be compared with other sources of energy (coal and oil extraction, hydroelectricity, etc.). In coal or oil extraction, transport and refining, an expenditure of one calorie would be needed to produce five to ten calories; in ethanol production, with the appropriate corrections, an optimistic estimation would be two or three calories produced per calorie spent (ibid.: 27).

For Martinez-Alier[14] (1987: 27), the energy requirements of ethanol production are an additional reason why it is misleading to present the ethanol programme as an oil-saving programme, which at the same time allows motorization. The production of ethanol is very energy-intensive compared with oil or coal.

According to Da Silva *et al.* (1978) – quoted by Martinez-Alier (1987: 26) – the breakdown of about 50 per cent of the energy input of 4.2 million kilocalories/hectare per year is as follows: 50 per cent for fuel for machinery, 30 per cent for fertilizer, 10 per cent for machinery and equipment annual depreciation, and the rest for seed, pesticides and human labour. The ratio between energy produced from ethanol and energy consumed in the agricultural stage of sugarcane is 4.53. For Martinez-Alier (1987), the data of Da Silva *et al.* (1978) are regarded generally as optimistic, since they might depend not only on the use of crop-residues but also on the low fossil-fuel energy costs of agriculture in Brazil. They neglect, for instance, the energy cost of the workforce.

As far as the energy balance is concerned, existing differences of opinion derive primarily from variations in energy assumptions and their interpretations. Part of the controversy appears to have begun when Chambers *et al.* (1979) calculated that the energy content of ethanol produced from farm crops was less than the fossil-fuel energy consumed in the process. It should be noted that. excluding the positive energy balance given by Da Silva *et al.* (1978). most studies show little real net energy gain, if any (Rothman *et al.*, 1983: 124).

For Martinez-Alier (1987: 22), Proalcool as an agricultural programme was extremely impressive. The production of ten billion litres (eleven billion in 1985) requires nearly three million hectares of cane – more than the area of cane in Cuba – and also represents 10 per cent of Brazil's cropland. This area converted for food production would add about 900 kilocalories per head per day, for a population of 150 million. The essence of the ethanol programme, however, is not that it will provide energy as food (or drink), but that energy will be provided specifically as fuel for cars.

Ethanol

Regarding the energy cost of the workforce, we refer to the study by Pereira (2007: 16), published in the weekly magazine *Carta Capital*. This study discusses the reports of two experts on the work time of sugarcane workers: Dr Maria Aparecida de Moraes e Silva from São Paulo State University (UNESP), and Dr Jose Novaes from the Federal University of Rio de Janeiro (UFRJ). Both suggest that the work-life of these workers was fifteen years. From 2000 onwards, it dropped to around twelve years. Dr Moraes e Silva, who has been researching migrant workers for more than thirty years, recalls that, up to 1850, the work-life of the slave was ten to twelve years! Dr Novaes reports that the productivity of these workers has been increasing substantially over the years; it increased from five to eight tonnes in the 1980s, to eight to nine tonnes in the 1990s and to twelve to fifteen tonnes in 2004. There has been no improvement in the technology used, and they are paid based on production. Since 2004, the Catholic Church has been keeping an account of suspicious deaths among these migrant workers; the number of deaths under investigation since 2007 is above twenty.

6 Conclusions

We divided the evaluation of the environmental impact into parts: Proalcool and ethanol. The goal here was to double-check the validity of the criticisms. Following the reasoning discussed in section 3, we describe below several "intangible" aspects that were missed either in the conventional CB analysis or in a future one that would try to account for the environment.

Ethanol is a project that affects the life of the top 20 per cent of Brazilians – that is, car-owners – in terms of personal income distribution. The use of CB analysis as a mechanical rule or decision-making procedure to justify ethanol production in Brazil only serves to deflect public opinion. It seeks to prevent the breaking out into the public realm of serious negative aspects associated with its production that involve, among others, water quality and distribution and air quality.

Ethanol is only a part of what is called "renewables". This chapter does not intend to cast doubt on the whole green economy but just attempts to present some negative aspects of it to be taken into consideration in developing countries' strategic decisions to face and cope with the current world crisis.

Notes

1 Anhydrous ethanol is used for blending with a gasoline in proportion of up to 20 per cent; hydrous ethanol is used directly as fuel for passenger cars.
2 The production plant of ethanol can also produce sugar. The production decision is related to the evolution of sugar's international price.
3 Turner *et al.* (1993) present details about the CVM method.
4 *The Economist*, 22 April 2006.
5 It is not our intention to go into a deep discussion of Proalcool's evolution; we are just interested in the environmental impact and the CB of this programme.
6 The IAA, Instituto do Acucar e do Alcool, created in 1931, worked as a Government Market Board, controlling and planning the production, consumption, price and exports.
7 BOD is a chemical procedure for determining how fast biological organisms use up oxygen in a body of water.
8 According to SABESP (2002), São Paulo State's share in the distribution of water in Brazil is 1.6 per cent. From this total, São Paulo Metropolitan Region receives 4 per cent. As previously stated, this region shelters 47 per cent of the entire population of the State.
9 The household consumption of water in Europe averages 165 litres per inhabitant per day (Sadeq, 1999: 20). In Brazil, SABESP estimates household consumption of water at 120 litres per inhabitant per day (5 Elementos, 2005: 15). For more information on water consumption during the different stages of sugar and ethanol production, see Silva and Simoes (1999: 359).
10 This author's major concern is the impact of ethanol on corn and the production of food.
11 During the decade of Brazil's "economic miracle", as the living standards of the rural poor began to drop many people turned to manioc for survival. By the end of 1977, small manioc plots occupied some 2.1 million hectares of land – more than the total sugarcane acreage at the time (Berton *et al.*, 1982: 157).
12 Obviously, structural factors such as rapid industrialization and great disparity

between rural and urban incomes and lack of land reform are some of the major aspects that "promoted" the massive migration. What we are saying is that Proalcool is partly responsible for this situation.
13 They are in favour only of money terms of unit of account.
14 He is extremely critical of "farming with petroleum", and his book reveals his concern regarding the technical progress in modern agriculture.

References

Arbex, M.A. (2001) "Avaliação dos efeitos do material particulado proveniente da queima da plantação da cana de açúcar sobre a morbidade respiratória na população de Araraquara-SP", Unpublished doctoral dissertation, São Paulo: University of São Paulo (USP) Medical School.

Berton, H., Kovarik, B. and Sklar, S. (1982) *The Forbidden Fuel: Power Alcohol in the Twentieth Century*, New York, NY: Boyd Griffin.

Brookshire, D.S., Eubanks, L.S. and Randal, A. (1992) "Estimating Option Prices and Existence Values for Wildlife Resources", in A. Markandia and J. Richardson (eds), *Environmental Economics: A Reader*, New York, NY: St Martin's Press, pp. 112–128.

Brown, L.R. (1980) "Food or Fuel: New Competition for the World's Cropland", World Watch Papers, No. 35.

Calabi, A. (1983) *A Energia e a Economia Brasileira*, São Paulo: Pioneira-Fipe.

Corazza, R.I. (2001) "Políticas públicas para tecnologias mais limpas: uma análise das contribuições da economia do meio ambiente", Unpublished doctoral dissertation, Campinas: Instituto de Geociencias – Universidade Estadual de Campinas – Unicamp.

Da Silva, J.G., Serra, G.E., Moreiã, J.R., Gonqalves, J.G. and Goldemberg, S.H. (1978) "Energy Balance for Ethyl Alcohol Production from Crops", *Science*, 201: 903–906.

5 Elementos, Instituto de Educação e Pesquisa Ambiental (2005) *Águas no Oeste do Alto Tiête: uma radiografia da sub-bacia Pinheiros-Pirapora*, São Paulo: 5 Elementos.

ECLAC (CEPAL) (2009). "Inovar para Crescer". Available at: www.eclac.org/ddpe/publicaciones/xml/2/37972/2009–763-Innovar_para_crecer-portugues-web.pdf (accessed April 2011).

Embrapa (2011) "Produção de etanol: primeira ou segunda geração". Available at: www.embrapa.br/im – 15/04/2011.

Farber, S., Robert, C., Childers, D., Erickson, J., Gross, K. *et al.* (2006) "Linking Ecology and Economics for Ecosystem Management", *BioScience*, 56(2): 117–129.

Galvão, L.E. (2000) "As Águas não Vão Mais Rolar", in *Rumos: Economia e Desenvolvimento para Novos Tempos*, 24(168): 26–33.

Goes. T. and Marra, R. (2008). "Biocombustíveis – Uma alternativa para o mundo, uma oportunidade para o Brasil". Available at: www.embrapa.br imprensa/artigos/2008/Biocombustuivel%202008%20PDF3.pdf (accessed March 2011).

Hespanhol, I. (2001) "Gestão de Água no Brasil". Available at: www.crmariocovas.sp.gov.br/pdf/pol/gestao_agua.pdf (accessed July 2007).

Hespanhol, I. (2003) "Potencial de reuso de água no Brasil: agricultura, industria, município e recarga de aqüíferos", in P.C.S. Mancuso and H.F. Santos (eds), *Reúso de Água*, Barueri, São Paulo: Manole, pp. 38–50.

IDEC (2000) "Água, Disponível". Available at: www.idec.Ed.br/biblioteca/mcs_agua.pdf (accessed July 2007).

Magalhães, J.P.A., Kuperman, N. and Machado, R.C. (1991) *Proálcol, uma avaliação global*, Rio de Janeiro: Astel, Assessores Técnicos.

Marjotta-Maistro, M.C. (2002) "Ajustes nos Mercados de Álcool e Gasolina no Processo de Desregulamentação", Unpublished Doctoral Dissertation, Escola Superior de Agronomia "Luiz de Queiroz", University of São Paulo (USP).

Martinez-Alier, J. (1987) *Ecological Economics: Energy, Environment and Society*, Cambridge, MA: Basil Blackwell.

Martinez-Alier, J. (1991) "Ecological Perception, Environmental Policy and Distribution Conflicts: Some Lessons from History", in R. Costanza (ed.), *Ecological Economics: The Science and Management of Sustainability*, New York, NY: Columbia University Press, pp. 118–136.

Merrill Lynch (2008) "The Sixth Revolution: The Coming of Cleantech", Industry Overview. Available at: www.responsible-investor.com/images/uploads/resources/research/21228316156Merril_Lynch-_the_coming_of_clean_tech.pdf (accessed April 2011).

Motta, R. (1987) "The Social Viability of Ethanol Production in Brazil", *Energy Economics*, July: 176–182.

Motta, R. and Ferreira, L.R. (1987) "Reavaliação econômica e novos ajustamentos do Proálcool", *Revista Brasileira de Economia*, 41(1): 117–133.

Motta, R. and Ferreira, L.R. (1988) "The Brazilian National Alcohol Programme: An Economic Reappraisal and Adjustment", *Energy Economics*, July: 229–234.

OCDE-FAU (2007) "Agricultural Outlook 2007–2016". Available at: www.oecd.org/dataoecd/6/10/38893266.pdf (accessed July 2007).

Pearce, D. and Turner, R.K. (1990) *Economics of Natural Resources and the Environment*, Baltimore, MA: Johns Hopkins University Press.

Pereira, R.R. (ed.) (2007) "O Colossal Brasil. In Retratos do Brasil no. 1", *Carta Capital*, August, 22: 1–20.

Perez, C. (2002) *Technological Revolutions and Financial Capital: The Dynamics of Bubles and Golden Ages*, Cheltenham: Edward Elgar.

Perez, C. (2003) "Technological Change and Opportunities for Development as a Moving Target," in J. Toye (ed.), *Trade and Development: Directions for the 21st Century*. Cheltenham, UK: Edward Elgar

Rebouças, A.C. (1997) "Panorama da Agua Doce no Brasil", in A.C. Rebouças (ed.), *Panoramas da Degradação do Ar, da Água Doce e da Terra no Brasil*, Rio de Janeiro: Academia Brasileira de Ciências e CNPQ, pp. 59–107.

Rocha Filho, J.P. (1993) "A Alcool como Alternativa Energética para o Brasil", *Encontros Nacional de Economia*, Belo Horizonte, Anais, pp. 361–381.

Rothman, H., Greenchild, R. and Rosillo, F.C. (1983) *Energy from Alcohol: The Brazilian Experience*, Lexington, KT: University Press of Kentucky.

SABESP (2002) "Processo de Gestao Operacional para Reducao de Perdas no Sistema de Abastecimento de Agua da Regiao Metropolitana de São Paulo". Available at: www.cendotec.org.br/aspef/arquivos/seminario2.pdf (accessed March 2010).

Sadeq, H.T. (1999) "A Demanda Aumenta, Oferta Diminui", *Correio da UNESCO*, April: 19–26.

Sagoff, M. (1988) *The Economy of the Earth*, New York, NY: Cambridge University Press.

Schumpeter, J.A. (1939) *Business Cycles*, two volumes, New York, NY: McGraw-Hill.

Schumpeter, J.A. (1961) *The Theory of Economic Development*, New York, NY: Oxford University Press.

Silva, G.A. and Simoes, R.A.G. (1999) "Água na Industria", in A.C.B. Rebouças, B. Braga and J.G. Tundisi (eds), *Águas Doces no Brasil*, São Paulo: Escrituras, pp. 339–368.

Silva, M.A.M. (2007) "Atrás das cortinas no teatro do etanol", *Folha de São Paulo*, 2 October. Available at: www.1folha.uol.com.br/fsp/opiniao/fz0210200709.htm (accessed October 2007).

Spitz, P. (1978) "Silent Violence: Famine and Inequality", *International Social Science Journal*, XXX(4): 867–892.

Taylor, L. and Arida, P. (1988) "Long Run Income Distribution and Growth", in H. Chenery and Srinivasan, T.N. (eds), *Hand Book of Development Economics*, Vol. 1, Amsterdam: North-Holland.

Tolmasquim, M.T. (2003) *Fontes Renováveis de Energia no Brasil*, Rio de Janeiro: Interciência.

Turner, R.K., Pearce, D. and Bateman, I. (1993) *Environmental Economics: An Elementary Introduction*, Baltimore, MA: Johns Hopkins University Press.

World Bank (1980) *Alcohol Production from Biomass in Developing Countries*, Washington, DC: World Bank, September.

9 Creative destruction and recovery in Latin America

An out-of-crisis roadmap centred on technology and industrial policies[1]

Elisa Calza, Mario Cimoli, Annalisa Primi and Sebastián Rovira

1 Introduction

The recent financial crisis is probably one of most important economic phenomena in the past decades. Although it is not the first crisis episode of the century (and parallels with the Great Depression of the 1930s and the oil shocks of the 1970s have been frequently cited), the current crisis has some peculiarities that make it different and under some points of view unique.

First, differently from other episodes, this crisis has not been generated by external shocks (as is the case of many externally driven crises that hit Latin America in past decades), but internally: its root lies within the US financial system, where it has grown and developed until its abrupt outset. Its transmission around the world has made it an "imported crisis" for many countries that were not directly involved in the financial collapse, but its origin coincides with the worst affected country – the US. Second, the crisis could be defined as the "first crisis of the economic globalization" as it rapidly spread its effects all over world: interconnections and linkages across and within producers, consumers, markets, lenders, borrowers and investors had become so strong and deep that this crisis did not take long to develop a global character. Third, the impact of the economic shock has not just been global, it has also been fast. The crisis has been transmitted so quickly across regions that this can reasonably defined as an "extremely synchronized" crisis, in the sense that it did not take long before becoming a worldwide problem.

Financial crises have always produced serious problems. This is particularly true in the case of generalized, global and synchronized crisis episodes such as the current one, which is likely to bring deep and persistent consequences to the world economy. Hence, strong persistency could be considered as the fourth peculiarity of this crisis. The persistency of the crisis is also deeply related to the existing productive structure, the nature of technological capabilities and technological learning. In fact, the crisis induces reconfiguration of the productive structure at the micro-level, leading to a re-adaptation of productions and processes, and challenging the redefinition of firm structure. The post-crisis recovery is likely to offer good opportunities to firms that were successful in the re-adaptation process, and mainly to those that are dealing with new technologies and the new technological paradigms.

Regarding Latin America, the region has not been affected by the crisis as dramatically as other regions (with the exception of Mexico and some Central American countries, given their strong relation with the US economy). However, some parallels have been drawn between the current and the numerous crises that have affected the region in past years, pointing out the similarities between the current behaviour of some macroeconomic variables and their past patterns. With a simple diachronic comparison across static macroeconomic values, the current crisis does not seem too dissimilar from past ones, thus it might be expected not to have much different outcomes. However, this weak syllogism relies on a superficial interpretation, which stops at the mere observation of macroeconomic variables without inquiring what really lies behind them, what drives their behaviour; once the scope of the analysis is widened, it becomes clear that the crisis is not a repeat of past history, and neither will its consequences be.

Observing that "all crises are the same" because macroeconomic variables seem to move in the same way diverts the attention from the core issue: this crisis will have persistent effects because it will have important microeconomic consequences on the strategies adopted by firms, the production structure, the re-adaptation of learning processes and the long-term accumulation of technological capabilities, leading to persistent changes at the deepest levels of the economic structure. Thus, the microeconomic structure is being affected at its roots; these impacts will in turn affect the macro-performances of the whole economy in terms of productivity, diversification and sources for long-term growth (ECLAC, 2007, 2008).

Also, the reaction to the crisis depends on the existing productive structure and its microeconomic interrelations. In fact, the previous existence of adequate technological and human capabilities enables the firms to tailor a flexible and adequate response to the crisis. Hence, initial conditions matter: differences in the existing endowments of capabilities will result in different impacts, since they shape a country's ability to produce different response strategies. This is true across heterogeneous countries, with different availabilities of human and technological capabilities, but it holds even across heterogeneous sectors: high-tech sectors, which own high-tech and advanced capabilities, will be able to design a better response and a better way out of the crisis. Thus, every sector and every country will be affected in a different way, according to its productive structure.

Given its global dimension, the speed and scope of crisis transmission have been deeply related to the degree of external exposure. Trade channels have been crucial in spreading the contagion, but it would be misleading to affirm that the changes in international trade flows are the only channel through which the crisis has been transmitted: the actual role of the international exposure is much more complex, and is deeply interrelated with the productive structure which – as already noted – plays a significant role in strengthening and amplifying the impact of the crisis. In other words, it is not just the exposure to external markets itself that weakens a country in times of crisis, but how the country is exposed: the productive structure matters, and its importance in defining the impact as well as the crisis response should not be underestimated.

In past months the strength of the crisis seems to have gradually diminished, up to the point that many analysts are persuaded that, even if it is probably not completely over, at least the worst has passed. However, this does not make things any easier, and does not mean that world economy has finally landed on a safe shore. The game is still open, and the modes and times of the post-crisis recovery have not yet been properly debated.

The characteristics of this crisis imply that quite a long time will be required before the re-establishment previous economic levels (this is particularly true in the case of employment). Prospective post-crisis scenarios are still very uncertain, and it is not yet clear which strategy could guarantee a rapid and sound recovery: which international economic relations will be defined after the crisis? Which changes in global production patterns? How will firms react and adapt to new economic conditions? What lies behind the ability to design a post-crisis reaction? More questions will probably arise in the near future about what kind of world will emerge in coming years.

On one side, Latin America has been so far relatively less affected by the crisis than other regions. On the other hand, Latin America is facing the crisis with a burdening heritage: the prolonged absence of any industrial policy led to the current lack of structural change, of productive diversification and of the development of more knowledge-intensive sectors and related technological capabilities. This represents a stringent constriction, given the importance of technological capabilities in determining the intensity and direction of post-crisis recovery. The crisis hits an economic structure already weakened by past economic fluctuations and whose technological capabilities have been atrophied and destroyed by decades of chasing "wrong" (in the sense that they were not in favour of technological capability development) market incentives. As in a self-reinforcing process, this constitutes a major weakness in addressing the necessary re-composition and re-definition of the productive structure at micro-level (Cimoli, 2009a). If taking immediate action is avoided, the main risk is that, once this "economic storm" has passed, the region will be running at a slower pace than the rest of the world, being unable to "keep in the same place": the "Red Queen Effect" will appear once again, as in the past (Cimoli and Porcile, 2008).

Many analysts argue that it is now necessary to reconsider the institutions and rules governing the markets, addressing how in this transition the role of the State should be redefined. It seems clear that the time has come to urgently rethink policies in the fields of technology and industrial diversification. Latin America should return to policies aimed at building up technological capabilities, and to clear industrial strategies that could reform the existing productive structure towards more competitive technology-intense sectors. This seems the only way to guarantee a sound post-crisis recovery that could lead the region towards a long-term path of endogenously originated economic growth, based on technological capabilities.

In fact, all the reasons that impose the need for intervention in the financial system are present in the industrial system too, and the importance of adopting policies for the development of technological capabilities cannot be neglected in times of financial crisis – on the contrary, they are more necessary than ever (Peres, 2009). This holds in particular for the development and diffusion of new technological paradigms, whose potentialities have not been fully explored yet and which need to receive financial support in order to address the uncertainty that may limit private financing.

This work aims at contributing to the debate about the crisis and possible post-crisis scenarios by offering a comprehensive overview of the dynamics underlying the post-crisis response, with a special focus on Latin America. In Section 2, the first subsection analyses the role of the productive structure in determining the effect as well as the response to a crisis episode. The second subsection describes the importance of technological capabilities in undertaking a post-crisis re-adaptation process, while the third subsection explains the specific difficulties faced by developing country in dealing with these restructuring processes, in particular in the case of natural-resources based economies. The fourth subsection brings the debate from a theoretical to a more concrete level, describing Latin America economic features before and after the occurrence of the crisis. The fifth, sixth and seventh subsections are dedicated to prospective post-crisis scenarios in Latin America: productive arrangements, emerging technological paradigms (ICT, biotechnologies and nanotechnologies) and a new possible role of the State. Section 3 concludes.

2 Seven points for an out-of-crisis roadmap

2.1 The self-enforcing role of the productive structure

The crisis entails more than a systemic impact on aggregate macro-variables. The impact of the crisis on the real economy is not neutral with respect to the characteristics of the microeconomic structure and the behaviour of the firms. Moreover, the crisis leads to a re-composition of this same microeconomic structure, which in turn shapes the response of the economy.

The impact of business cycles and financial crises on the real economy is usually analysed in terms of their effects on aggregate variables – mainly output, investments, employment and demand – which represent the most visible effects of crises, both in the in the short term and in the mid term. However, behind the patterns of the aggregate variables there are "invisible" but crucial factors related to changes in human and technological capabilities, and to the flexibility of the production structure, which contribute to explain these trajectories. From this it can be argued that the impact of the crisis on the real economy is not neutral with respect to the existing characteristics of the microeconomic structure. Moreover, while a crisis has strong effects on the productive structure, it is also true that the latter defines how the economy reacts to the crisis.

Productive structure and its sectoral composition are crucial in accounting for global crises' impacts and responses. Economies that have a more diversified structure and higher shares of technology-intensive sectors seem to have higher income elasticity with respect to global growth. This higher elasticity determines how these economies will be affected by positive and negative economic circumstances: they will respond more dynamically to global growth in normal times; they will suffer more during episodes of global economic contraction; they will recover more easily in the post-crisis stabilization phase. Thus, the way the world economy may affect economic growth in a specific country could be considered to be "filtered" by the degree of structural change occurring in the domestic economy.[2]

The following exercise is meant to provide evidence of the importance of the industrial structure – and its sectoral composition – in forecasting how countries react and tend to move out of the crisis. The idea is to show how cyclical fluctuations in the world economy impact the domestic economy, and how this impact may be "filtered" by the prevailing industrial specialization.

A model of economic growth is estimated, including the production structure specialization as one of the right-hand-side variables, along with the variables traditionally used in growth regressions (education, investment, openness and the rate of growth of the global economy). The productive structure specialization is measured in terms of the share of technology-intensive sectors in total manufacturing value added, accounting for accumulated technological capabilities. This variable enters the regression in the form of an interactive term, which aims at capturing the interaction between the production structure and global GDP growth. The estimations refer to a time span of thirty years (1970–2003, subdivided into five sub-periods), and both developed and developing countries are considered in the analysis.[3] The results are presented in Table 9.1.

The results of the coefficients for the initial GDP per capita, education and investment confirm the magnitude and sign of what usually reported by the literature. It is important to stress that the "interaction variable" (world growth and industrial structure) appears as positive and significant. In particular, the impact of a marginal increase in the world GDP growth rate over economic growth has two components, one direct and the other indirect, which correspond to the interaction term.

Formally, the marginal effect is estimated as:

$$\partial(\text{growth})/\partial(\text{worldGDPgrowth}) = 0.36 + 0.014*\text{Structure}$$

where the first component is the direct effect and the second one the indirect term, which depends on the economic structure.

This exercise enables us to compare different situations across countries and years based on the evolution of the industrial structure and the sectoral composition of each economy. In Figure 9.1, the cases of Argentina, Brazil and the Republic of Korea are represented in two specific years (1970 and 2007). The

Table 9.1 Estimation results

Estimations		
Dependent variable: GDP per capita growth	*(1)*	*(2)*
Initial GDP	−0.23 (2.21)**	−0.37 (2.88)**
Education	0.01 (1.73)*	0.01 (1.69)*
Investment	0.20 (8.98)***	0.17 (7.59)**
World GDP Growth	0.80 (7.81)***	0.36 (1.64)*
Openness	.	0.001 (0.45)
Structure* World GDP Growth	.	0.014 (2.32)**
Constant	−1.57 (1.63)*	0.07 (0.06)
Obs.	150	150
Number of countries	30	30
Time periods	5	5
Wald chi^2 (6)	186.8	204.69
Prob>chi^2	0.000	0.000

Source: Division of Production, Productivity and Management (ECLAC).

Notes
Preliminary results. The estimation uses thirty countries over the period 1970–2003 (subdivided into five sub-periods). A panel data and generalized least squares (GLS) estimation method corrected by heteroskedasticity and autocorrelation is estimated. All variables are defined as average for each period, excepting Initial GDP which corresponds to the initial year of each period. Remaining variables are defined as follows: Education: percentage of total population over twenty-five years old having completed secondary school; Investment: average of fixed capital investment rate; World GDP Growth: GDP per capita growth; Openness: exports plus imports over total GDP and Structure: percentage of technological value added industrial sectors over total industrial value added. *t*-statistics with robust standard errors in parenthesis, * significant at 10%; ** significant at 5%, *** significant at 1%.

x-axis represents a proxy for the technological intensity of production structure (the share of high-technology sectors in the total industrial value added), while the *y*-axis represents the country's growth elasticity to global growth. Argentina experienced a reduction in the industrial structure index and in its relative growth elasticity with respect to world performance. Brazil and the Republic of Korea experienced an increase in the participation of high-tech sectors in total manufacturing value added, and a consequent increase in their growth elasticity with respect to global growth.

This shows that, when the long-term evolution of the two types of countries is observed, on average those which have a more technology-intensive structure perform better than the others: countries with an industrial structure specializing in high-tech sectors have been able to virtuously capture world economic growth, while countries with a reduced share of engineering sectors benefited much less from this growth. This happened because the higher growth elasticity observed in countries with more complex production structure works in both directions: in turbulent times and during the crisis they suffer more than the rest, but they are more able to reach the previous growth path more easily and fully capture the benefits of the world economic recover (ECLAC, 2007).

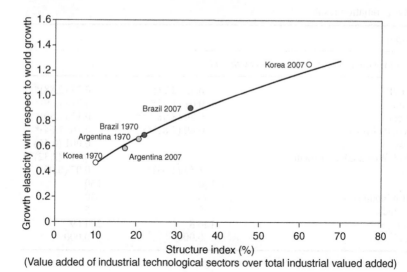

Figure 9.1 Growth elasticity with respect to world growth (source: Division of Production, Productivity and Management (ECLAC)).

Summarizing, the impact of a financial crisis and the response of the real economy suffer from strong sectoral effects: the technological specialization plays a crucial role in how countries respond to crises and it moulds their development trajectory. This confirmed what was observed also by Ocampo (2005): that a vicious circle arose from the interaction between the macroeconomic crisis and regressive structural change. Thus, the underlining changes in the sectoral structure of the economy and technological capabilities of the firms are the roots of different trajectories of aggregate variables.

But what lies at the root of the observed higher adjustment capacity of countries that present an industrial structure specializing in high-tech sectors? The answer is strictly related to their technological capability endowment. Thanks to the undergone pattern of structural change, these countries have accumulated the knowledge and the capabilities required to readapt strategies and structures to the new conditions that will shape the dynamics of the economy in the post-crisis scenario. This allows them to play a leading role in the definition of new technological paradigms that will dominate prospective patterns of economic growth, as well as to take part in the reallocation of economic powers. Thus, in order to understand the out-of-crisis response mechanism, it is necessary to look more deeply at the microeconomics of learning and at the process of accumulation of technological capabilities, and their relations with economic growth.

2.2 Technological learning and re-adaptation through global crisis

In crisis scenarios, firms and sectors readapt their capabilities, learning processes and production and investment strategies. The production structure undergoes processes of restructuring, which may imply the destruction of certain productive, technological and human capabilities.

Building, consolidating and relocating technological capabilities is not a straightforward process. Most of the difficulties that firms face in restructuring arise from the features of the technological capabilities, which in turn are related to the intrinsic nature of technological learning. Technological learning is characterized by a set of inter-related regularities that could be summarized as follows (ECLAC, 2007, 2008): first, it requires real time; second, it is accumulative, in the sense that the closer to the technology frontier, the faster the economy will be able to implement new processes of technology learning and move towards new technological paradigms; third, it is subject to path-dependency, which implies that the evolution of technological capabilities strongly depends on the sectors and directions of past learning; fourth, there is complementary across sectors, in such a way that externalities and increasing returns are crucial both at the industrial and economic level; fifth, there is irreversibility in the accumulation of technological capabilities, which most of times cannot just be abandoned or replaced.

These features of technological learning affect the nature of technological capabilities, which through this same process of learning are originated. A broad literature provides strong theoretical and empirical bases to the argument that the expansion or contraction of technological capabilities is not a linear, reversible process. As for human capital, relocating unused skills is not an easy challenge.

Building technological capabilities would require a continuous process of learning, time and resources; once certain capabilities have been obtained, they are not easy to reconvert in the short run, they are not reversible. These peculiar features allow us to define technological capabilities as "sticky".

Stickiness in capabilities and technologies characterizes the real economy, and it explains why the process of re-composition and re-adaptation of the microeconomic structure cannot be smooth and fast. Technological capabilities are also fragile, in the sense that their non-reversibility could make them "useless" or economically less attractive at the occurrence of negative shocks or particular economic episodes (such as a rise in commodity prices, as it will be analysed in the following section), becoming subject of sudden obsolescence, weakening and even destruction. The fact that technological capabilities are sticky, non-reversible and fragile implies that the effects of a shock or a crisis are less easily reversible in the real economy than in financial markets, and they may leave long-lasting marks in productivity growth and in the production structure.

An economic shock obliges the firm to readapt and redefine its technological capabilities, even through the destruction of the existing endowment. Some firms will have to restructure and redirect their investment planning and activities, even be forced to shut down given product lines and downsize production capacities.

Stickiness in capabilities implies that all these processes of re-adaptation may result costly and time-consuming. At the same time, going through a process of re-adaptation of the microeconomic structure is a mandatory path for firms in order to face new conditions and survive in the post-crisis scenario, and this is only possible if these same firms are endowed with an adequate amount of technological capabilities. In sum, technological capabilities are at the same time a burden to re-adaptation, given their stickiness, but also the only channel that make this restructuring really possible.

Not all firms will be able to respond swiftly enough and in any case the effects of the re-adaptation of capabilities and strategies on productivity will not be immediate: there will be a time-lag, and during this time, the economy will necessarily experiment a slowdown in productivity growth. The duration of this slowdown may itself depend on the kind of firms, its dimension and its sector, and this might represent a threat in particular for new firms, for firms with an increasingly diversified product mix, or might even lead a firm to disappear.

Although this re-adaptation encompasses the whole production apparatus, its impact has a strong sectoral component: firms which are operating on the technological frontier (and which are usually located in frontier economies) will probably reduce investments in new and risky projects, but they are likely to maintain investment in core activities, especially those based on R&D capabilities and efforts. However, given their advanced technological capabilities, these firms are likely to be more reactive: in the effort of developing new capabilities that will suit prospective techno-economic post-crisis scenarios, some firms might even increase their investments in R&D due to technological foresight exercises indicating that certain technologies will maintain the leadership. Those firms might even bring about a process of creative destruction moving forward towards a new production mix.

Thus, in the best scenario, the re-adaptation of technological capabilities that follows a crisis may give rise to a new configuration of the microeconomic structure through the springing around of new competitive firms, new high-tech products, new production processes, new capabilities. After a slowdown in productivity growth (or even a transitory fall in productivity), the economy will experiment a rise in productivity, which might end up growing at the same rate or even at a higher rate than that prevailing at the moment of the shock. However, a negative scenario is also possible: firms that are unable to reform and modernize their structure and technological capabilities will end up loosing productivity, competitiveness, market share, and in the worst outcome will have to cut down production or disappear.

As already noted, firms endowed with better technological capabilities are more likely to end up in the first, positive scenario. Obviously these kinds of firms are more likely to be found near to the technology frontier and in more advanced economies. For firms in catching-up and peripheral economies the second, worst scenario seems the most possible outcome of a crisis episode. This may easily be the case of Latin America: the overlapping of past economic crises and the implementation macroeconomic policies that did not support the development of endogenous technological capabilities may have affected firms' ability in re-adapting and designing an adequate crisis response, leaving the region in a disadvantaged position in terms of post-crisis perspectives. The reasons at the root of the existing asymmetry between frontier and peripheral economies' possible post-crisis outcomes are analysed in the following section.

2.3 Crisis and catching-up: capability-building and the dazzle of commodity prices

Industrial and technological structures are no less systemic than finance: network and domino effects are present in the real economy as well. Stickiness in production and technological capabilities implies that these effects are less easily reversible in the real economy than in financial markets.

The potential disruptive effects of a financial crisis are especially risky for catching-up economies, since the destruction of capabilities would have a higher systemic impact at an early stage of development than in frontier economies, where the level of human and technological capital is higher.

Developing economies are in the process of creating endogenous technological and production capabilities. With the occurrence of the crisis, this process slowed down and was eventually interrupted, resulting in a weakening of real capabilities that might appear as less dramatic in the short run than the immediate burning of wealth caused by a financial crisis, but which affects the microeconomic structure since it reduces the technological base with which those economies face the post-crisis scenario. The consequences for productivity and growth may be less revertible and more costly in the long run.

In these circumstances, although industry rarely experiences sudden collapse, it may experience chronic decline due to a long-run gradual loss in capabilities, whose accumulated impacts on growth and welfare are no less devastating than financial crisis. A sort of lock-in process emerges, in which countries which should invest more in supporting the creation of endogenous technological capabilities are led to invest less as a result of short-term pressures. This implies less future growth and facing a stronger international competitiveness, rather than a response focused on technological learning and productive diversification. The short-term response would reinforce their backwardness and their marginal position in the global economy.

Together with a weak technological capability endowment, volatility and uncertainty are recurrent issues for many catching-up economies, in particular those in which primary commodities represent a large share of the economic activity. In fact, promoting economic specialization in primary commodities does not seem to represent a good strategy in the attempt to upgrade technological capabilities, or to reduce the degree instability that may hit the economy through the channel of international commodity markets. In other words, large primary commodity endowment may not help a catching-up country undertake a phase of economic take-off, since it does not provide incentives to after-crisis

re-adaptation processes and technological capability development. This statement could be supported by at least two sets of explanations.

First, rising commodity prices may be a disincentive to structural change
towards high-tech sectors and the consequent development of technological capabilities. Let's consider a shock such as a temporary rise in the price of commodities. A shock of this type favours sectors which are less technology-
intensive and whose stimulus to human capital formation is weak, impeding the
replacement of obsolescent technological capabilities and the emergence of
knowledge-intensive sectors, and favouring polarization in income distribution.
This causes a further loss of technological capabilities and inhibits the creation
of new ones, with the consequence that the economic structure will have in
aggregate less capabilities and fewer sectors (a loss of diversification) than it had
before. A loss of sectors and capabilities will reduce systemic learning and economic returns, compromising international competitiveness. Both effects
combine and reinforce each other, giving rise to vicious circles that will hamper
economic growth in the long run.

Second, volatility of commodity prices affects firm response capacity. At the
occurrence of a crisis episode, the overlap of a decline in the price level and the
contraction of economic activity (which involves a fast diminution of terms of
trade *cum* global recession) will induce firms to look for more flexibility (Ferraz
et al., 1999) and processes of re-adapting and accumulating technological capabilities. If shocks are recurrent and/or if uncertainty persists, the firm might
need either to constantly readapt its processes and product mix or to adjust at a
slower pace (waiting for the emerging structure of relative process to become
more transparent). This process will end up affecting not only the micro-side but
also the macro-performances in terms of productivity, diversification and the
sources for long-term growth and development: the evolution of firm's productivity with successive price or uncertainty shocks will show productivity as being
stagnant, while indeed it has been fluctuating in such a way that firms are unable
to find a stable path of productivity growth. Aggregate impact of shocks on productivity may result in more than the sum of the effects on each individual firm,
and more than short-term fluctuations: to the extent that all firms will have to
adapt, a general slowdown in aggregate productivity is the most likely outcome
of the productivity slowdown induced by price volatility.

The instability driven by speculative shocks, price volatility in commodities
and real exchange rate, and deep recessions may leave lasting marks in productivity growth and in the production structure. The systemic risk of a crisis could
be even stronger in the real economy than in the financial sector, because stickiness in capabilities and technologies characterizes the real economy and is more
pervasive in industry than in the financial sector. This implies that short-term
fluctuations in productivity may represent more than a temporary loss in the
quantities produced (given potential output): if fluctuations are recurrent, they
may represent a loss of capabilities and therefore a loss of future potential
growth. When a crisis hits the economy, it will be less able to respond to new
challenges or to increase productivity at the same rates as before (Figure 9.2).

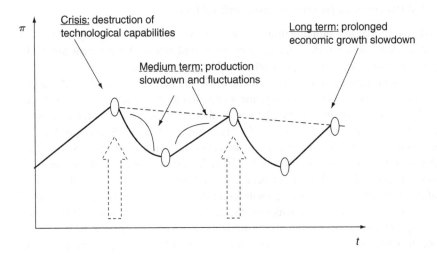

Figure 9.2 Stickiness in technological capabilities (source: Division of Production, Productivity and Management (ECLAC)).

Summarizing, abundant natural resources, even when combined with a well-developed human resource base, do not automatically lead to restructuring and diversification. Even through commodity processing may provide early industrialization opportunities, the possibilities of maintaining rapid development through deepening and diversification in the primary sector seem to be limited, and countries rich in natural resources can delay industrialization, but in general cannot reach adequate income levels without a strong industrial base that permits minimization of the risks of recurrent price fluctuations (ECLAC, 2007).

Moreover, in a globalized and polarized world, industrialization and technological development need policies and institutions that can mould them to current market incentives. If commodity-endowed countries design their productive strategies only on the base of market signals, in the case of rising commodity prices they will not have rationales to diversify their productive structure towards less commodity-intense sectors. Hence, they will not have incentives to develop more sophisticated processes of learning and to upgrade their technological capabilities, implying a risky vicious circle of lower capabilities and higher vulnerability to external shocks. This is even truer under crisis scenarios.

This poses a major challenge to the governments of the natural resource rich countries, which should be concerned with the long-run process of technological accumulation, and with the risks of its destruction, both in normal times and in times of crisis. Furthermore, in a post-crisis scenario the governments will play a fundamental role in supporting the development of new endogenous capabilities according to which new techno-economic paradigms will emerge and will shape future economic perspectives.

2.4 Latin America facing the crisis: stylized facts

After a "bonanza" quinquennium (2003–2008), where the aggregate GDP of Latin American countries increased by an annual rate of 5.5 per cent and GDP per capita increased by 4.2 per cent; a "cold shower" has arrived.

This five-year period of economic growth has been interrupted by the diffusion of the financial crisis through the global economy. Suddenly Latin America had to realize – as in a "cold shower" – that the economic "bonanza" experienced in recent years had basically been imported from abroad (as was its technological capital), and that once the economic engines of the US and other developed countries, constrained by financial turmoil and credit crunch, had slowed down, the region would need a good dose of realism to face the gravity of the crisis and to reconsider growth forecasts for the future. The recent years of economic growth had overshadowed the real economic conditions of the region, giving the impression that Latin America had finally caught the train of economic catching-up; the truth was that it was still suffering from the same unsolved economic issues and structural weakness as in the past.

The flip side of rising commodity prices

Thanks to a sharp rise in commodity prices, in the past five years many Latin American economies (particularly the southern ones, like Argentina, Brazil, Chile and Uruguay) have experienced substantial improvements in their terms of trade. This rise was in part due to normal fluctuations in the market and real variables, namely the steady expansion of international demand for commodities and raw materials, arising from the rapidly industrializing Asian economies (among which China was a key player). But it also responded to the influence of heavy speculation in commodity markets, heightened by increasing uncertainty.

At the same time, very little was done to upgrade technology and human capital. With the improvement in the terms of trade for commodities based on natural resources and the consequent appreciation of the exchange rate, the space for the diversification of technological capabilities and production had been dramatically reduced. A self-enforcing process of concentration in fewer activities took place, while the incentives to learn and invest in other sectors and activities were not diffused (ECLAC, 2007). Thus, following market incentives – such as rising commodity prices – led to a production pattern that inhibited the development of endogenous technological capabilities by favouring low-tech sectors and, consequently, by reducing the surge of endogenous demand for technology and technological knowledge.

Trade unbalances

In most countries, export and import coefficients have increased in recent years. In particular, the increase in the import coefficients between 2003 and 2007 in the case of the engineering (and high-tech) sectors was remarkable and showed the difficulties of the industrial structure in keeping pace with global demand for expansion of high-tech items and in competing in most (and new) sectors – an issue heightened by the rise of Asian competition.

Since the expansion of domestic demand has continued, what emerges is an industrial trade balance that presents a deficit or reduces drastically the surplus (see Table 9.A1 in Appendix A). Two cases are the exceptions: Chile and Brazil. The case of Chile is explained mainly by the rise of exports and prices of industrial copper until September 2008.[4] The case of Brazil is different, and is largely associated with higher competitiveness in different industrial sectors.[5] This competitiveness stems from a more diversified industrial structure, which in part reflects the persistence of industrial policy over the past twenty years.

Industrial production within the Global Value Chain

In Latin America, many production activities are integrated into the Global Value Chain (GVC). The position and relocation opportunities within the chain depend on the owned technological capabilities. For this reason, the process of learning and accumulating technological capabilities should be necessarily considered as the only way to facilitate upwards movements along the global value chain.

In Latin America, the positioning of within the GVC is still characterized by a concentration on traditional segments, as a consequence of foreign business strategies aimed at creating low-cost export platforms.[6] These sectors do not present relevant high-tech contents, and the degree of value added embodied by single output units is not large. Most of the multinational enterprises (MNEs), which delocalized some production stages according to the static comparative advantages some countries could offer, maintained the control over production nets and over R&D, keeping R&D activities in their home countries or moving them to dynamic emerging economies more specialized in high-tech industries and with an expanding potential domestic market, such as China. In this way, they did not help encourage technological capabilities accumulation at a local level (Cimoli and Katz, 2003) or lead to a significant increase in productivity (as will be shown in the following section). These elements contribute to make the positioning of Latin America within the global value chain extremely vulnerable to international competition, in particular coming from increasingly competitive countries such as China and other Asian low-cost producers.

But current threats to Latin America positioning within the GVC do not come just from international competition. Being part of the GVC means also becoming highly integrated into the world economy, including its boom and bust phases. In the region, the current crisis is reducing outer trade and cooling down foreign direct investment flows, which for the near future are expected to remain at a lower level than in previous boom years. This may reveal that the international value chain is under strain. Moreover, the increase in industrial production experienced by the region in recent years had been boosted mainly by the expansion of international demand, while internal markets remained underdeveloped and now are unable to act as a "spare wheel" in the face of shrinking exports.

Thus, despite years of industrial growth and diversification, when external engines of economic growth shut down – such as international demand and foreign investments – the region returns to being vulnerable to threats of downward relocation within the global value chain due to the previous (and still in place) destruction of endogenous technological capabilities and the inability (and lack of incentives) to create new ones.

Structural change and productivity

In the previous paragraphs, the importance of structural change for capabilities development and economic growth has been remarked on many times. But what kind of structural changes have Latin American countries experienced in the past two decades (1990–2007)? In order to answer this question, we analyse the evolution of the production structure by looking at the share in the industrial value added of high-tech, natural resources and labour-intensive sectors, and at their productivity in comparison with the United States – a mature economy used as a benchmark (see Figure 9.A1 in Appendix B). The general picture that emerges from the reported diagrams is that the growth episode experienced by the industrial sectors in the past five years has not coincided with a significant structural change in Latin American economies, and the above mentioned issues of low positioning in the GVC, trade unbalances, and weak technological capabilities are in part a consequence of this lack of structural dynamism.

Between 1990 and 2007, Latin America had fallen behind the technological frontier both in terms of technological specialization and productivity growth. In the US, the sectors that contributed the most to this productivity growth – the high-tech sectors – represented almost 60 per cent of the total manufacturing value added in 2007. These sectors are capable of producing abundant knowledge spillovers – in part also through network creation and local interactions – which contribute to fostering productivity in the whole industrial sector (including in those intensive in natural resources and labour), dragging upwards the overall industrial productivity growth. In other words, in the case of the US it is clear that the structural change has been associated with rising productivity throughout the economy as a whole.

Conversely, in Argentina, Chile and Colombia the increasing share of natural-resource sectors has not coincided with a process of technological upgrading, leading to the underdevelopment of those activities that have the peculiarity of spreading knowledge and improving technological capabilities throughout the industry. Brazil represents, to some extent, an exception, since its industrial structure has moved more clearly towards the inclusion of engineering and high-tech sectors. Still, this failed to produce a significant impact on aggregate productivity. Beyond the apparent restyling of the Brazilian manufacturing industry – where the majority of firms chose to follow efficiency and prioritized modernization through the increase of imports of capital goods and the introduction of new organizational techniques – the structural change was not as "radical" as would have been required (Ferraz *et al.*, 1999). The general attitude towards R&D investment remained generally cautious and the export profile of the country remained basically unchanged, still relying on basic and unprocessed industrial commodities. Thus, the overlap of a traditional macroeconomic management with a lack of coordination among different policies fostering industrial development and structural change contributes to explain the general stickiness in Brazil aggregate productivity growth.

The comparison of productivity levels between Latin America and the US gives an idea of the challenges that the region faces. Since the 1980s the index of relative productivity of Latin America with respect to the USA has been decreasing, and this fall has become especially intense in the past six years. This means that the productivity gap has been constantly increasing for more than two decades, even during the time span of recent economic growth. In fact, Figure 9.3 shows clearly that between 2003 and 2007 the performance of the region was the worst in the last thirty-six years, with the only exception being the 1980s (the lost decade).

On the contrary, the productivity of the US has increased at a rate of 5 per cent a year. Again, the "acceleration" of productivity growth is largely due to the transformation of the industrial structure and the incorporation of new paradigms – in particular the ICT – in the production process. This reinforces the idea that an incremental incorporation of technologies and elements forming the new paradigms is crucial in order to transform the production system and to keep on growing in the long run: new technological paradigms will bring along new and more sophisticated capabilities, contributing to a further increase in productivity

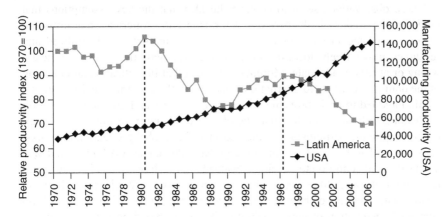

Figure 9.3 Latin America relative productivity index and USA productivity (source: Division of Production Productivity and Management (ECLAC). Authors' elaboration on the basis of PADI database).

Note
The relative productivity index of Latin America was calculated as the simple average of relative productivity index for four countries (Argentina, Brazil, Chile and Mexico).

182 E. Calza et al.

due to the fact that technological capabilities-intense sectors are capable of generating more positive spillovers towards the whole industrial sector. If the region loses ground in this field, it will face more difficulties in remaining competitive in the future.

As mentioned earlier, each shock – such as in price level – will be accompanied by a consequent productivity slowdown along the adjustment process. However, if technological capabilities and complementary assets are weak and/or have previously been destroyed, after the shock the productivity growth will slow down for a period of time that eventually becomes longer than the adjustment process. In other words, when the destruction of knowledge has occurred, each shock may depress the rate of productivity growth even after the adjustment for an indefinite time span.

This process, whose net effect is a destruction of knowledge, should be analysed in the context of the continuous moving ahead of the international technological frontier (here, the US). The effects of the crises that Latin America has been through in the past four decades are well visible in the diagram: a dramatic fall during the debt crisis of the 1980s, a moderate improvement in the late 1980s, and the new fall of the second half of the 1990s and early 2000s (Figure 9.3). Behind these fluctuations and the fall in relative productivity there are alternate periods of currency appreciation, trade liberalization and a mounting external debt, followed by major devaluations. Hence, the labour productivity path followed by Latin America in past decades has not succeeded in closing the gap with the frontier, or in reducing it significantly: in 2006, labour productivity was just half of the value observed in 1970. In short, the region has been clearly unable to overcome the "Red Queen effect": more than that, it has failed to keep pace with the technological leader and has fallen behind.

These observations seem to confirm the idea that the key assumptions that guided policy-makers in the period of reforms in Latin America – that firms and sectors adapt and produce more efficiently when markets are liberalized and resources move freely towards more competitive activities – were basically wrong or at least inadequate. Moreover, the idea that liberalization and opening of the domestic markets to international actors – such as international investors – would have led to an improvement of competitiveness and growth sounds a bit misleading in light of the fact that the observed downturn of productivity happened despite the participation of the region within global production networks. This means that the involvement in the global value chain (GVC) by itself was not a sufficient condition to develop advanced high-tech sectors and create sound technological capabilities, or to increase productivity. While capabilities in sectors with medium or high technological intensity were being destroyed, no symmetric generation of new capabilities in sectors based on natural resources took place.

To summarize, in the past five years Latin America had experienced a phase of economic growth without precedent in its recent history. However, the outbreak of the current crisis revealed the fragility of this growth, which turned out to have been mainly induced by foreign forces such as sustained international demand, rising international investments, remittances, and booming commodity revenues. Once these forces stopped pushing growth, Latin America had to realize that this "bonanza" had not brought any significant improvement to its long-term economic soundness, and the region was still stuck in the same situation of structural weakness as in the past: excessive dependence on exports (especially natural resources and traditional goods), chronic trade deficits in manufacturing, low positioning within the global value chain which impeded the attraction for quality foreign direct investments and advancement in endogenous capabilities generations, stagnation or even increase of the productivity gap, and progressive erosion of institutions meant to address the issues of structural change (ECLAC, 2002, 2007, 2008).

Hence, the region was not able to take advantage of the years of positive economic contingency and to turn them into a jumping-off point towards economic consolidation and production structure renewal. Latin America is now running the risk of facing the crisis from a disadvantaged perspective and without having developed the capabilities required to design an effective long-term response.

2.5 New productive arrangements

In this section the discussion turns to a firm-level analysis: what consequences is the crisis likely to bring to Latin America productive arrangements? Which strategic decisions are Latin American firms more likely to take? How will the firm size and demography be affected?

Strategic decisions and R&D investments

The first impact of the crisis on firms' operations is related to the sharp reduction of financial availability due to the collapse of the US financial sector. The "credit crunch" implied a generalized reduction in credit and investments, both from internal as well as from foreign sources. Foreign investors may perceive a higher level of risk from abroad investments and, given the evident financial restrictions they are facing, may prefer to divert their money towards domestic markets or markets perceived as safer, and cut investments in new plants. National investors who are indebted will struggle to repay the debts or to find new credit to sustain their existing business, forcing even established firms to shelve or postpone new projects. Hence, during a time of diminishing market prospects and financial constraints, allocating resources for adjustment and renewal becomes more difficult. Thus, the financial constraint may contribute to exacerbate the issue of scarce development of capabilities, in particular in a developing-country context.

Firms have to take decisions, even in the context of uncertainty such as in a crisis episode. This includes reorganizing production and reorienting their capabilities to increase efficiency as a response to changing conditions of demand and international competition. In this effort, some firms may prefer to close down some R&D departments; producer–user interactions may cease; public research agencies may go underfinanced; and human capital may drain out of the production structure. Thus, the ability of firms to realign their competencies and businesses for the benefit of further specialisation (e.g. moving up the value chain) and to improve productivity (e.g. investment in human capital, fixed capital or process innovation) could be severely hampered (OECD, 2009).

As in a vicious circle, this kind of response may pose a threat to the ability of industries to adjust to the crisis: in fact, it may lead to a loss of existing capabilities, with the consequence that the efforts to adjust to new shocks will become increasingly less effective, and the ability to learn and to restore productivity growth will be undermined. This outcome may occur particularly often in the case of developing countries, where technological capabilities and other strategic assets are already weaker and more vulnerable if compared with a more developed context. Here, new projects may be cancelled and foreign industries might migrate away, diverting their investments and cancelling prospective investments.

As firms seek to cut costs in response to the crisis and focus on core strengths, activities that are no longer considered viable are likely to be cut back, terminated or outsourced. The decision on what to cut back on and what to focus on will depend on the situation and business strategy of each firm. However, historical experience shows that firms in developed countries have tended to focus on activities that are highly productive and create high value added, in particular in sectors that are exposed to international competition. Activities that rely primarily on low-cost labour are the most likely to be cut back further, in particular where they are exposed to international competition from low-cost producers. For this reason, in the sectors in which technology mastery and specific technical knowledge are the core competences, the negative effects are likely to be less persistent, since the firms will foresee their way out through technological leadership. Thus, the crisis may increase the competitive advantage of research-intensive firms who seize the opportunity to reinforce market leadership through increased spending on innovation and R&D.[7]

This is not likely to be the situation for firms whose technological capabilities and other strategic assets are scarce and even weakened by the occurrence of the crisis, as may be the case in primary commodity specialized economies. As already noted, here foreign investors may be likely to cancel projects, activating a process of industrial migration and further contraction of local industrial production, aggravated by the eventual defaults of local producers.

Market structure and "firms' demography"

Past years of economic liberalization in Latin America have not only played a role in the weakening of technological capabilities; they also led to a progressive disarticulation of the productive structure through a double process of concentration in large international firms and pulverization of the small and medium enterprises in entities of minimum magnitude. There are good reasons to believe that the crisis will be particularly severe with the second type of enterprises, which are facing increasing difficulties in obtaining credit.

Small and medium enterprises (SMEs) experience specific difficulties in periods of economic crises. For small or young enterprises, the most important sources of financing are their own cash flow, retained earnings and bank loans. During the crisis, the contraction of international markets and the rising financial constraints both cause serious problems for this kind of firms. Banks not only restrict lending, but also attach more stringent conditions to loans, requesting collateral, assessing equity ratios and credit standing; short-term financing arrangements have become subject to higher costs and risk premiums since the beginning of the crisis. This implies that the cost of obtaining loans has risen considerably for SMEs, as the risk of default is taken into consideration more strongly. In addition, their earnings suffer as a result of a weaker economy and the delay in payment from customers tends to worsen in difficult economic times.

Furthermore, the "credit crunch" and the global economic situation also contribute to restricting the entry and speeding the decline of start-up firms that require financing or active exit markets. The growing aversion to risk and the lack of exit opportunities for investors are also drying up many sources of seed and venture capital.[8] This raises the issue of the urgency of instruments and tools that facilitate and enable renewal, such as seed capital funds; policies fostering entrepreneurship and start-ups; skills upgrading and training; and investments in capabilities for innovation.

Some data from the USA provide evidence of the fact that the crisis is significantly affecting firm survival. According to the bankruptcy-filing statistics released in March 2009 by the US Administrative Office of the Courts, the bankruptcies' basic liquidation for individuals and businesses in the United States increased by 43 per cent from December 2007 to December 2008; business bankruptcies increased by 54 per cent from 31 December 2007 to 31 December 2008, while non-business bankruptcies increased by 31 per cent for the same period. In Western Europe, the situation does not seem much better: more than 150,000 firms from seventeen countries filed for bankruptcy in 2008. The biggest increase in bankruptcies was in Spain, followed by Ireland and Denmark (OECD, 2009).

The crisis may also affect market concentration. A process of merger and acquisition represents a response that increases concentration, aimed at achieving economies of scale and stabilizing the market share. However, who is absorbed, who takes the lead in mergers, and how different players emerge from the crisis, all depends on their relative strength. It is likely that it will lead to an increase in merger and acquisition activity, due to the firms being unable to rely on their own financial resources and to the depreciation of the asset values, which may make these kinds of operations profitable.

Finally, it is necessary to stress the fact that the situation of state-controlled firms is very different. In this case, strategic decisions are still under local control. In this sense, policies of diversification and policies aimed at avoiding the destruction of local networks, clusters and districts should be sustained, since they clearly represent an anti-cyclical strategy.

2.6 New technological paradigms

Capabilities in new paradigms in science, technology and production will lead the resurgence from the current crisis, and will determine the repositioning in the global economy.

The process of capitalistic development entails a continuous transformation of production structures and organizational routines, a process that is characterized by given regularities and by unforeseen and random events. Among long-run regularities there is the appearance of new technological paradigms which recompose the way in which production and trade are organized. The process of application and diffusion of those paradigms is uneven and it is filtered by the accumulated capabilities of each firm (or, at the aggregate level, of each country). At the root of this process there is what Schumpeter called the process of "creative destruction" (Schumpeter, 1942).

At present we are facing a momentum of "crossing" new technological paradigms, which are about to reconfigure the way in which business is carried out. There is the information and communication technologies (ICT) paradigm, which has already reached substantial penetration (especially in frontier economies), and there are emerging paradigms – such as the bio- and the nanotechnologies and new materials – which are at their early stage of application. The full potential of these technologies, both individual and joint, has not yet been exploited and probably not even completely defined and understood. It is quite reasonable to expect that the potentialities of the new technologies will be at the basis of the new expansive cycle that will come about after the crisis. Those technologies will radically transform the way in which production, organization and trade are carried out; will create new products, services and processes; and will need different institutions to manage, apply and diffuse them.

Let's consider, for example, biotechnology (although the same applies to nanotechnology and new materials). It is possible to see a proliferation of genomics-based scientific discoveries and new biotechnology techniques. Some authors suggest that there have been no major impacts on production yet, and that the gains do not so far reflect the huge investment in R&D. These technologies are incipient, and firms have to deal with the persistent uncertainty surrounding these activities, the complex nature and the rapid rate of advance of basic scientific knowledge in this field. However, "gains" should not be measured only though current profits; they should also take into account the accumulation of capabilities that have been developed (in the US, in many advanced economies and in same emerging ones, such as Brazil and India). These countries are ready to master the new paradigms and have sound chances of leading the new post-crisis growth cycle based on these capabilities.

In this respect, those that have deeper understanding of the nature of this current crisis and who have capabilities that will lead the post-crisis scenario are business analysts and the CEOs of high-tech firms, who are urged to take decisions regarding which investments to maintain and which lines of business need to be shut down. It is highly probable that in the near future (and probably for quite some time) new profits and gains will emerge from investments in new technologies and knowledge, rather than from speculative behaviour in financial markets. This perception, which is diffused in some business sectors, determines that, for example, businessmen in IT-related business – a sector that has been and is still being strongly hit by the current crisis – are reconfiguring their portfolios of investments and are cutting down expenditures, maintaining invariant the investment in core high-tech activities and R&D.

This makes sense in the light of what has been said about technological capabilities accumulation: research and knowledge capabilities are difficult to reconvert and recover; and the perception that knowledge and technology mastery will be the assets that will determine the repositioning of powers in the post-crisis period justifies maintaining investments in these assets even in a crisis scenario. Of course it is not a matter of "spending for the sake of spending", as might be possible in a "bonanza" momentum – it is time for a "smart spending". But "smart" in this context is, more than ever, synonymous for technology, knowledge and intangibles assets, not for cost-effectiveness and efficiency in investment.

However, looking at the crisis as a "creative destruction" momentum in the current capitalistic development should not imply taking a naive stand viewing the crisis as straightforward opportunity. Opportunities in the post-crisis scenario will be strictly linked with capabilities in new paradigms and technologies: the accumulated capabilities in ICT, biotech, nanotech, new materials and new energies are a critical asset in the search for a way out of the crisis. Countries that master relevant knowledge in the new paradigms, countries whose human capital is concentrated in these areas, countries with big high-tech firms – all these will have an easier way out of the crisis than countries which were at the margins of the knowledge game in the pre-crisis scenario. Likewise, there will be windows of opportunities for all, but they will be understood and possibly profited by only by firms (and countries) which follow a knowledge-centred development strategy and which will prioritize the construction of scientific and technological capabilities in the post-crisis context.

For example, the US – the country where the crisis started and where its impacts have been dramatic – is still the big technological leader in many new core technologies, although this leadership is threatened by the rise of new potential technological powers, mainly South Korea and, to a certain extent, India and China. It is highly probable that in the future the basis for competitiveness of firms will be largely redefined; in this respect, the race to own the intellectual property of most of the basic knowledge in the areas of the new technological paradigms (bio- and nanotech), which has been led by the US since the 1980s, will play an increasing role in defining spaces and powers of agents in the knowledge game.

Regarding the accumulation of technological capabilities and the mastery of relevant knowledge, ranking some countries according to their technological production capacities and their innovative performance might help to clarify the point. In Figure 9.4, countries have been ordered along the horizontal axis

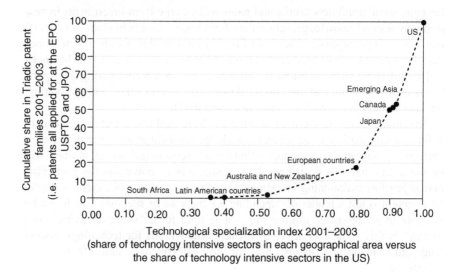

Figure 9.4 The knowledge curve: production stricture specialization and patenting (source: Cimoli *et al.*, 2009b).

according to the intensity of their technological specialization with respect to the frontier (which, in this case, is represented by the US). On the vertical axis, the cumulative share of all patents applied for at the three major world-patenting offices (European, Japanese and US) for each country or group of countries is plotted. The graph portrays what might be called a *knowledge curve*, showing the comparative technological intensity of production structures of countries and their relative patenting behaviour.

A clear differentiation between industrialized and industrializing countries can be observed. The US, Japan, Canada, emerging Asia and the European countries all show similar production structures, represented as the share of technology-intensive sectors within total manufacturing value added. The share of those sectors varies between 45 per cent in the case of the average of the European countries considered and 65 per cent in the US. Asian countries have been successful in fostering the development of technology-intensive industries by combining selective import substitution policies with an aggressive export-oriented strategy.

From Figure 9.4, it is evident that many emerging Asian economies have accumulated production capabilities in high-tech sectors, and in recent years have increased their patenting exponentially. On the contrary, in Latin America and in most African countries the opening-up process of the 1990s and the increasing exposure to external competition pushed to further specialization according to their static comparative advantages and products with low technological content. On the vertical axis, the graph shows the asymmetry in the ownership of innovativeness and capabilities – as measured by patent applications – which corresponds to and derives from the specialization pattern. Patenting results from the accumulated capabilities, especially in the new technologies. The leaders in the ownership of knowledge at the global level still are the same old players: the US, Japan and continental Europe.

Standard economists are arguing that the US economy will be able to adjust easily to the crisis. However, they affirm that on the basis of the "flexibility" of the economy. This work argues that the capacity of the US to respond to the crisis lies on different basis: as analysed in the earlier sections, it is the "stickiness" of the accumulated technological capabilities and the mastery of knowledge and technology which will determine the capacity of the economy to respond to the shock. Those economies that have accumulated the capacities and the "ownership" of relevant knowledge are now in a better position than Latin America for profiting from the revolution and the "creative destruction" process that the crisis is igniting.

2.7 The role of the state

Facing the crisis with a look at the future: the need "more than ever" for active industrial and technological polices. A smart policy mix: measures to avoid the destruction of production and technological capabilities and new incentives for the accumulation and adoption of new technologies.

The emergence of new technological paradigms entails a redefinition of *innovation and production*, how they are generated and through which means they can be diffused and appropriated. In new technological paradigms, primarily ICT, biotech and nanotech, innovation is increasingly incremental and cumulative in character, intensive in interrelations between firms (countries and institutions), and entails an increasing relevance of science. The concepts of replicability, usability and copying are constantly re-defined, the potential technological interrelations are multiple, and uncertainty regarding future possible outcomes is even higher than under past technological paradigms. This entails a renewed organization and definition of roles between the State and the Market. Will the line between them finally fall in the right place? Nowadays it seems that there is a new economic model taking ground "a public–private partnership" one in which the private sector gets the gains and the public sector gets the losses. For sure, this is not yet the right place where the line should be.

It is a fact that, recently, astronomic amounts of money have been dropped into the financial system to avoid its collapse, while resources and assets evaporate. For many analysts, it is time to rethink the institutions and rules governing the financial markets. We argue here that it is also urgent to rethink policies in the fields of technology and industrial diversification, particularly in catching-up economies. All the reasons that impose the need of intervention in the financial system are also present in the industrial system, and the importance of adopting policies for the development of technological capabilities cannot be neglected in times of financial crisis – on the contrary, they are more necessary than ever. And this is even more necessary if we think that the world after the crisis will be extensively shaped by new productive and technological paradigms.

In the past five years, many Latin American countries have experienced favourable terms of trade for their commodities. During these good times, very little was done to upgrade technology and human capital. Policy-makers looked at industrial policy suspiciously. Any step to promote an industry or to encourage learning had to be carefully explained and justified. Any industrial policy "picking winners" or protecting technological capabilities accumulated by previous generations had little support. And, when it was recognized that industrial policies are necessary, they tended to strengthen current exporting sectors (some times, with pro-cyclical implications) rather than developing new sectors in which technological learning is more intense.

What is going to happen with the already weak industrial and technological policies under the crisis? If they are simply abandoned, the production structure that will emerge from the crisis in developing countries will not be able to catch up with the new technologies and production paradigms. These countries will fall to a position still more distant from the technological frontier. The challenges from international competitiveness may become insurmountable, making economic recover more difficult. On the other hand, if a new set of policies is devised to develop and diversify productive and technological capabilities, the opportunities for catching up can be exploited, and therefore the influence and duration of the economic crisis will be milder.

A smart policy mix

In order to gain an understanding of learning dynamics and to take advantage of new technologies and the restructuring of production in the global scenario, it is necessary to look both at sectors dynamics and at the trajectories of individual firms. This means that it is necessary to adopt a variety of policies and instruments. Opportunities available in different sectors depend on their respective sectoral dynamics, and reflect the learning processes associated with the spread of technological paradigms (such as ICTs, biotech, nanotech and new materials).

Sectoral responses are heterogeneous. Sectors in which competitiveness depends on relative abundance of natural recourse – and export of natural resources and "commodities" – are mainly affected by prices and speculative forces in the financial market, and this crisis showed it clearly. Prices of commodities have increased in the past five years – improving the terms of trade of many developing countries – due in part to changes in global production and the increasing role of Asian countries. However, the sharp fall in prices and their increasing volatility since end of 2008 clearly indicate that the speculative dimension has been crucial in explaining the upward trend in commodities prices (see Figure 9.5). They may recover in the future, but it is highly unlikely that prices will again reach the levels previous to the crisis. In other words, as each reasonable observer knows, these prices are strongly affected by financial speculation. Such speculation probably contributed to a higher degree to the fall in prices and to price volatility than long-run demand patterns.

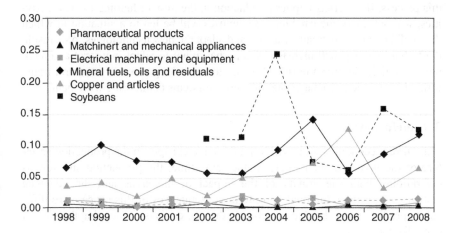

Figure 9.5 Variation coefficients (source: Division of Production, Productivity and Management (ECLAC). Authors' elaboration on the basis of Bureau of Labour Statistics).

Notes
2008 is estimated. Variation coefficient of the export price indexes (selected sectors, 1998–2008).
Index Type: HARMONIZED SYSTEM EXPORT INDEXES.

The variation coefficient reflects the fact that commodity goods prices are much more volatile than those of goods which are more technologically intensive. The low-tech sectors (textile/clothing, shoes) suffer the impact of falling demand and prices, but their volatility is lower than in commodities. Firms readapt their capabilities, reorganize production and reduce their scale. Policies are required to avoid the social impact (unemployment) of the contraction of these activities, so as to sustain a modernization process incorporating new technologies and human capital – and, in the case of medium and small firms, to sustain the dynamism of local networks, clusters and districts.

In the medium-tech sectors (mechanical engineering sector, chemistry), the competitive challenge is to learn how to adapt production and techniques. These processes are complex, and require human capital with high competences and resourses to exploit the opportunities arising from new technologies. The policy implications are similar to those in low-tech sectors, but technological assets assume a growing importance. In particular, a critical concern for policy-makers is to foster the adaptation process and the incorporation of new technologies (ICT, bio and nanotech), as well as to support R&D investment and the interaction with the public sector.

Finally, policies for the high-tech sectors require an important dose of courage, particularly in developing countries. Science is a crucial input, and attention should be given to all those research activities in universities and research centres, which are the vehicle for transferring technology and allowing the upgrade of the private sector. Private and public laboratories are central in this process. If the crisis implies a reduction in the flow of funding to these activities, without doubt the catching-up countries will be led to a situation in which they will be unable to "read", transfer and adapt the new technologies. As a result, the technology gap will increase. Again, the failure to adopt industrial and technology policies implies the risk of losing the next long wave of structural transformation and the advantages that the new paradigms could bring with them.

3 Conclusions

This current economic crisis will bring dramatic changes in the production structure of the involved economies. At the same time, the production structure is determining both the gravity of the impact of the crisis and the adequate response. Of course, the final, long-term consequences of this process are difficult to predict, as it is hard to discern whether the crisis is challenging the current capitalist paradigm.

Designing a sound forecast of the crisis major consequences is a complex exercise, since it is very difficult to grasp all the interrelations that are being affected by the crisis and what this will mean for the definition of future relationships. The spread of the crisis, the speed at which it is occurring, and its effectiveness in affecting world economies at a global scale are all phenomena that did not have such significant relevance in past crises; thus, there us no precedent from which to learn the better way to address them.

What is certain is that the deep changes that occurred at the micro-level will soon become evident on the surface of the economy, at the macro-level, resulting in the re-adaptation of the productive structure and the surge of new technological paradigms in industrial productions and processes, with the consequent redefinition of economic power across the economies involved in this development of new technological capabilities.

How deep and how persistent the impacts will be depends on the policy response that government is able to design. Of course, macro and financial policies play a central role in stabilizing and reducing the impact of volatility and crises, but the immediate counter-cyclical responses announced by some governments in the region are probably insufficient to avoid stagnation and contractions of economic activities. This is because current policy responses are avoiding tackling directly the necessity for new industrial policies that take into account the importance of the production structure and of the regeneration of firms' capacities and capabilities to drive the economy successfully out of the crisis. Furthermore, if it is assumed that all sectors are equivalent in process of technological accumulation (and diffuse knowledge thought in the economy), the design of policies which fix a roadmap to the out of a crisis will be incomplete.

Latin America is now facing a great challenge, which could turn into a great opportunity if properly managed. In this sense, regional leaders should reconsider the importance of industrial policy and macroeconomic policy that set "fair prices", in order to sustain the endogenous process of technological capability development and industrial structural change which is the only way that can offer the region a path of long-term growth in the post-crisis scenario. In particular, governments' support is crucial for the development and diffusion of incipient technological paradigms. As long as governments will not involve industrial policies in their reform plans, any resulting policy response will be insufficient.

Appendix A: industrial trade balance

Table 9.A1 Industrial trade balance

ARGENTINA	1970	1980	1990	1997	2003	2006
Technology-intensive sectors	−520	−4,214	−650	−12,250	−2,647	−11,644
TOTAL	−406	−4,441	5,379	−10,920	6,957	491
BOLIVIA	1970	1980	1990	1997	2003	2006
Technology-intensive sectors	−69	−294	−365	−979	−535	−969
TOTAL	−33	13	−362	−1,105	−713	−1,457
BRAZIL	1970	1980	1990	1997	2003	2006
Technology-intensive sectors	−1,051	−2,137	−948	−16,930	−3,027	−5,055
TOTAL	−362	3,514	9,622	−12,529	16,220	29,100
CHILE	1970	1980	1990	1997	2003	2006
Technology-intensive sectors	−438	−1,804	−3,274	−8,242	−6,188	−11,959
TOTAL	290	15	239	−4,660	−1,099	8,109
COLOMBIA	1970	1980	1990	1997	2003	2006
Technology-intensive sectors	−420	−1,793	−2,206	−6,493	−5,378	−8,095
TOTAL	−672	−2,939	−2,735	−9,474	−5,699	−8,678
COSTA RICA	1970	1980	1990	1997	2003	2006
Technology-intensive sectors	−98	−389	−554	−1,068	−958	−1,749
TOTAL	−205	−834	−966	−1,957	−2,498	−4,896
ECUADOR	1970	1980	1990	1997	2003	2006
Technology-intensive sectors	−110	−1,049	−715	−1,807	−2,429	−3,753
TOTAL	−176	−1,509	−1,311	−3,409	−4,241	−7,989
EL SALVADOR	1970	1980	1990	1997	2003	2006
Technology-intensive sectors	−51	−125	−233	−842	−1,128	−1,558
TOTAL	−88	−295	−356	−1,857	−2,699	−3,873
GUATEMALA	1970	1980	1990	1997	2003	2006
Technology-intensive sectors	−84	−378	−485	−1,284	−1,979	−2,980
TOTAL	−112	−535	−594	−2,299	−4,682	−7,071

continued

HONDURAS	1970	1980	1990	1997	2003	2006
Technology-intensive sectors	−77	−346	−262	−640	−791	−1,074
TOTAL	−148	−568	−611	−1,148	−2,433	−3,740
MEXICO	1970	1980	1990	1997	2003	2006
Technology-intensive sectors	−1,202	−8,238	−6,803	6,315	9,132	9,021
TOTAL	−1,431	−13,060	−12,197	−5,537	−17,959	−34,400
NICARAGUA	1970	1980	1990	1997	2003	2006
Technology-intensive sectors	−64	−151	−221	−409	−526	−736
TOTAL	−54	−470	−241	−917	−1,268	−1,848
PARAGUAY	1970	1980	1990	1997	2003	2006
Technology-intensive sectors	−28	−246	−686	−1,393	−759	−3,023
TOTAL	−11	−369	−947	−2,807	−1,572	−4,609
PERU	1970	1980	1990	1997	2003	2006
Technology-intensive sectors	−250	−1,090	−864	−3,619	−2,612	−5,170
TOTAL	242	−488	166	−2,605	−248	2,145
URUGUAY	1970	1980	1990	1997	2003	2006
Technology-intensive sectors	−76	−482	−437	−1,311	−344	−1,094
TOTAL	−19	−177	334	−1,032	166	−252
VENEZUELA	1970	1980	1990	1997	2003	2006
Technology-intensive sectors	−984	−5,948	−2,675	−5,983	−2,610	−16,913
TOTAL	−775	−4,950	2,058	−2,158	−3,531	−12,293
Latin America (16 countries)	1970	1980	1990	1997	2003	2006
Technology-intensive sectors	−5,522	−28,686	−21,378	−56,934	−22,779	−66,752
TOTAL	−3,960	−27,092	−2,523	−64,416	−25,299	−51,261

Appendix B: structural change and productivity

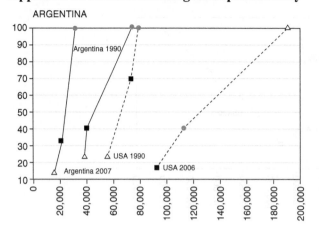

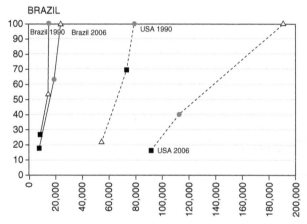

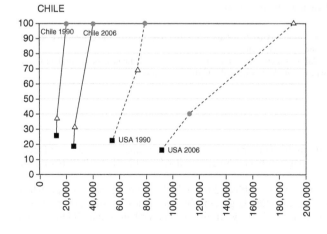

continued

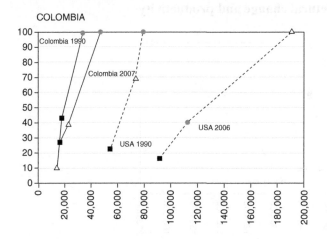

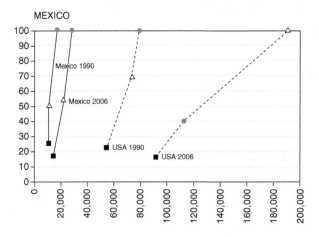

Figure 9.A1 Structural change and productivity.

Notes
Horizontal axes indicate labor productivity (Constant US dollars) and y axes the cumulative share in total manufacturing value added of each sector.
The black square indicates labour-intensive sectors; the grey circle indicates the natural resources intensive sectors, and the white triangle measures the high tech sectors.

Notes

1 The authors are grateful to the participants in the Fourth Annual Conference on Development and Change (ACDC), Johannesburg, South Africa (9–11 April 2010) for the useful comments.
   A first version of this chapter was published in the ECLAC document "La especialización exportadora y sus efectos sobre la generación de empleos. Evidencia para Argentina y Brazil", (LG/W.264), ECLAC y Ministerio del Trabajo (June 2009). United Nations publication.

2 There is an articulated theory behind the hypothesis that the economic structure allows for a better reaction and a more stable development path. According to this theoretical perspective, it is reasonable to expect that a structural change towards a higher partici- pation of technology-intensive sectors (thus, sectors that create more technological externalities, have higher technological opportunities and exhibit higher rates of innovation, also defined as possessing "Schumpeterian efficiency") would enable the economic structure to react better and exploit trade opportunities arising from changes in world demand (Dosi *et al.*, 1990), because these sectors imply a higher ratio between the income elasticity of demand for exports and the income elasticity of demand for imports. In the structuralist and evolutionary tradition, this ratio is related to the dynamic of innovation and international diffusion of technology, which determines the international competitiveness of a country and – according to the Keynesian theory of balance-of-payment constrained growth – it accounts also for differences in the rate of growth between different countries (Cimoli *et al.*, 2010).

3 The countries included in the analysis are: Argentina, Australia, Bolivia, Brazil, Canada, Chile, Colombia, Denmark, Egypt, Finland, France, India, Ireland, Israel, Italy, Japan, Korea Republic, Malaysia, Mexico, New Zealand, Norway, Peru, Philippines, Singapore, Spain, South Africa, Sweden, United Kingdom, United States and Uruguay.

4 If the contribution of this sector is subtracted from the manufacturing sector, the value of the deficits of Chilean manufacturing balance of trade becomes high and rising.

5 The sectors included are: food, leather goods, shoes, wood products and furniture, paper, iron and steel, non-ferrous metals, and automotive.

6 This statement represents very well the situation of Mexico and some Central America countries, whose productions are largely directed to US markets (almost 80 per cent of Mexican exports went to the USA in 2008), but of course there are huge differences across countries within the region.

7 There is evidence that many of today's leading technology firms, such as Samsung Electronics and Microsoft, strongly increased their R&D expenditures during and after the new economy bust of 2001 (OECD, 2009).

8 Recent trends show that total investment in venture capital in the United States is decreasing, and that the fall has been strongest for new ventures (OECD, 2009).

References

Cimoli, M. and Katz, J. (2003) "Structural reforms, technological gaps and economic development: a Latin American perspective", *Industrial and Corporate Change*, 12: 387–411.

Cimoli, M. and Porcile, G. (2008) "Volatility and Crisis in Catching-up Economies: Industrial Path Through the Stickiness of Technological Capabilities and *The Red Queen Effect*", Paper presented at Mount Holyoke College Development Conference, November 14–16 (2008), Mount Holyoke College, Springfield, MA.

Cimoli, M., Coriat, B. and Primi, A. (2009b) "Intellectual property and industrial devel- opment: a critical assessment", in M. Cimoli, G. Dosi and J.E. Stiglitz (eds), *The Polit- ical Economy of Capabilities Accumulation: the Past and Future Industrial Policies for Development*, Oxford: Oxford University Press.

Cimoli, M., Dosi, G. and Stiglitz, J.E. (2009a) *The Political Economy of Capabilities Accumulation: the Past and Future Industrial Policies for Development*, Oxford: Oxford University Press.

Cimoli, M., Porcile, G. and Rovira, S. (2010) "Structural change and the BOP-constraint: why did Latin America fail to converge?", *Cambridge Journal of Economics*, 34(2): 389–411.

Dosi, G., Pavitt, K. and Soete, L. (1990) *The Economics of Technical Change and International Trade*, London: Harvester Wheatsheaf Press.

ECLAC (2002) *Globalization and Development* (LC/G.2157 (SES.29/3)), Santiago: United Nations.

ECLAC (2007) "Progreso técnico y cambio estructural en América Latina y el Caribe", Project document, No. 136 (LC/W.136), Santiago: UN.

ECLAC (2008) *Structural Change and Productivity Growth 20 Years Later: Old Problems, New Opportunities* (LC/G.2367(SES.32/3), Thirty-Second session, ECLAC, Santiago: United Nations Publications.

Ferraz, J.C., Kupfer, D. and Serrano, F. (1999) "Macro/micro interactions: economic and institutional uncertainties and structural change in the Brazilian industry", *Oxford Development Studies*, 27(3): 279–304.

Ocampo, J.A. (2005) "The quest for dynamic efficiency: structural dynamics and economic growth in developing countries", in J.A. Ocampo (ed.), *Beyond Reforms: Structural Dynamics and Macroeconomic Vulnerability*, Palo Alto, CA: Stanford University Press, pp. 3–43.

OECD (2009) *Responding to the Economic Crisis: Fostering Industrial Restructuring and Renewal.* Geneva: OECD.

Peres, W. (2009) "The (slow) return of industrial policies in Latin America and the Caribbean", in M. Cimoli, G. Dosi and J. E. Stiglitz (eds), *The Political Economy of Capabilities Accumulation: the Past and Future of Policies for Industrial Development*, Oxford: Oxford University Press.

Schumpeter, J. (1942) *Capitalism, Socialism and Democracy*, New York, NY: Harper, 1975 [orig. pub. 1942], pp. 82–85.

Part IV

The gender and employment dimension

10 Economic cycles and gendered employment patterns in Turkey

Özge İzdeş

1 Introduction

Since financial liberalization in 1989, Turkey has been through three financial crises (1994, 1999 and 2001) and a significant economic contraction, in 1991. The crisis-prone structure together with a high and persistent unemployment problem contributes to the strikingly low female labor force participation and employment. The complex nature of women's participation in economic activity complicates the assessment of the gendered effects of economic crises in the labor market, yet various arguments reflecting various possibilities can be theorized under three main hypotheses[1]: (1) the *segmentation hypothesis* argues that there is a rigid sex-typing of occupations, and hence it is the changes in the composition of output that bring about changes in the gender composition of labor; (2) the *buffer hypothesis* implies that gender-specific characteristics of women's economic participation make women more disposable in times of crises; and (3) the *substitution hypothesis* suggests that the need for cost-saving strategies leads to more intensive use of female labor in both traditionally female and male industries.

Increasing female employment during the downswing of the economy or the relatively protected positions of women workers can be due either to women workers' concentration in less volatile jobs, or to substitution of cheaper female workers for male workers, or to a combination of both of these. Similarly, women may be disproportionately shed because of the vulnerable positions they hold in the labor market (unfavorable segmentation). Decomposition of changes in female employment across cycles allows us to distinguish segmentation (favorable and unfavorable) from the buffer and the substitution cases. Hence here the changes in female employment during economic cycles are decomposed to disentangle the multiple mechanisms behind those changes.

The remainder of the chapter is organized as follows. Section 2 gives a theoretical background on the impact of recessions on gendered employment patterns. Section 3 provides an overview of the structural characteristics of the labor market and women's employment in Turkey. The empirical analysis methodology and findings are presented in section 4. The final section reiterates findings and comments.

2 Theoretical background

Disentangling the effects of economic recession from those of structural adjustment on female employment is not straightforward. Some studies in the literature have analyzed this under the rubric of the labor supply decision of women under economic contraction, and used the "added worker" and "discouraged worker" framework. In this context, women either enter the labor force as "added workers" in order to compensate for loss of income in the family due to deteriorating employment prospects of the primary earner, or they may become "discouraged workers", given the reduction of employment opportunities under contractionary EOI regimes and during recessions. This chapter aims to focus on the employment outcomes of recessions in a broader context than the discouraged and added worker-effect framework can promise. The arguments on women's employment and recession can be categorized in three main hypotheses: (1) the *buffer hypothesis*, (2) the *segmentation hypothesis* and (3) *the substitution hypothesis*.[2]

The buffer hypothesis argues that women function as a flexible reserve, because they are less incorporated into the workforce compared to men. Their employment is pro-cyclical, and they have greater disposability. Hence they are disproportionately laid off during recessions. There are two main approaches to explain this phenomenon. The first is based on human capital labor market theories and dual labor market theories. The buffer role of women comes from their human capital endowments, which lower the incentive for firms to hoard women workers in a downturn.[3] The second approach, the Marxist one, argues that women constitute a *reserve army of labor*, whose size fluctuates with the business cycle because they are not fully integrated into the workforce. However, the reserve army concept is used with some reservation, as the peculiarities of female labor force participation should be taken into consideration. It is argued that the descriptive strength of the reserve army concept arises from the fact that women have been available as a reserve army in ways that men have not.[4]

What is expected to happen to female labor market indicators during recessions and booms, according to the three hypotheses reviewed here, can be discussed with the help of the predictions table presented below (Table 10.1). If the **buffer hypothesis** applies, it is argued that women are the first to be fired in recessions and first to be hired during booms. During downswings women's LFPR is likely to fall, since women who remain on the borders of production and re-production spheres have additional reasons to become discouraged workers. Moreover, we expect women's relative share of employment to increase during the booms and to decline in slumps.

The substitution hypothesis suggests that female labor is substituted for male labor during economic recessions, and that female labor is used more intensively in both traditionally male and female industries and occupations during recessions (Van Wagner, 1993). The Marxist framework argues that women tend to be more in demand especially during economic contractions as they constitute a cheaper, less organized and more controllable labor force. Hence, they consider this feminization process as capital's unwillingness to afford a proletarian work-force.[5] The neoclassical framework argues that recession periods create incentives for employers to break down the labor-market barriers and to correct the imperfections of the market which exclude women from certain jobs and crowd them into others (Becker, 1971).

In the case of the substitution hypothesis, women's employment is anticipated to be relatively stable and may even increase in the times of contraction (Table 10.1). If women replace laid-off men, and if this occurs by the reallocation of female labor across sectors, women's employment may remain stagnant. On the other hand, if substitution takes place without reallocation of labor or only partially with reallocation of female labor, then female employment may increase. The reverse of this trend is expected to be seen in the unemployment rates of women. However, the decline in female unemployment can be partly offset if women's labor force participation increases as a result of the survival strategy of the family to compensate for the loss in the male breadwinner's income. In this case, the female share of employment is assumed to increase and substitution possibilities vary inversely with women's share.

The segmentation hypothesis argues that there is a rigid sex-typing of occupations. Hence, it is the changes in the composition of output that bring about changes in the gender composition of labor. If women are concentrated in sectors or occupations that are less vulnerable to economic cycles, women are going to be sheltered from cyclical fluctuations (favorable segmentation) (Milkman, 1976). If they are concentrated in more vulnerable positions, the effects of the economic recession will be harder on them (unfavorable segmentation). This hypothesis argues that it is the secular trends rather than cyclical trends that determine female labor force participation.

According to the (favorable) segmentation hypothesis presented in the literature, due to their concentration in somewhat recession-proof industries, enterprises or occupations women are relatively protected from cyclical variation of total employment; hence we expect women's employment to be relatively stable (Table 10.1). On the other hand, the unemployment rate for women is expected to be lower when compared to their male counterparts. Overall, women's share in employment is expected to increase and the changing composition of total employment is expected to decrease the segmentation in the labor market, since the weights of predominantly male occupations are supposed to decline. However, as discussed above, this depends on what type of segmentation we are talking about. If the segmentation we are talking about is an unfavorable one, like women mostly holding jobs in cyclically vulnerable sectors, firms and positions, then labor market indicators are expected to move similarly with the buffer hypothesis.

3 An overview of the structural characteristics of the labor market and women's employment in Turkey

In 1980, Turkey incurred a dramatic shift from import substitution industrialization (ISI) to export oriented industrialization (EOI). The structural adjustment

Table 10.1 Predictions on employment indicators for women across economic cycles

Predictions on hypotheses	Women's participation rates	Women's unemployment rates	Women's employment	Women's relative share of employment	Employment segmentation
Segmentation	**BUST:** No prediction	**BUST:** Decreases relative to men's unemployment rates if women are protected or vice versa	**BUST:** Relatively stable if concentration of women is in less cyclically sensitive sectors or vice versa	**BUST:** Rises or falls depending on the type of segmentation in aggregate due to changing composition of total employment; stable within the sectors	**BUST:** Declines due to declining weights of predominantly male dominant occupations or vice versa
	BOOM: No prediction	**BOOM:** No prediction	**BOOM:** Same as the bust case	**BOOM:** Same as the bust case	**BOOM:** Same as the bust case
Buffer	**BUST:** May fall as the 'discouraged' women's worker's may leave the labor force	**BUST:** Rises relative to men's: but the increase in the unemployment may be smaller than the fall in the employment rates since discouraged workers leave the labor force	**BUST:** Relatively unstable; women are disproportionately shed	**BUST:** Declines in slump across all industries	**BUST:** Relative rise in segmentation due to declining relative numbers of women in one or more occupations as women workers are disproportionately shed
	BOOM: Increases relative to men's	**BOOM:** Decreases more than men's	**BOOM:** Increases relative to men's	**BOOM:** Rises across all industries	**BOOM:** Relative fall is segmentation as women's employment disproportionately increases
Substitution	**BUST:** May rise as households respond by 'adding' female workers	**BUST:** Reduced relative to men's though may be partly offset by rise in participation rate	**BUST:** Relatively stable or increases as women are disproportionately retained	**BUST:** Increases in the downturn, especially in the recession	**BUST:** If substitution possibilities vary inversely with the proportion of women, segmentation will fall due to sex composition change
	BOOM: No prediction	**BOOM:** No prediction	**BOOM:** No prediction	**BOOM:** Rises across all industries	**BOOM:** No prediction

Source: Based on Humphries, J. (1988), p.16 and author's predictions.

and macroeconomic stabilization policies adopted included trade liberalization, export promotion, cutbacks in agricultural subsidies, privatization, and repression of trade unions, which led to increasing insecurity for workers and lower labor standards, deterioration in real wages, and persistent and high rates of unemployment. There were two stages of structural adjustment: the first phase (1980–1989) was characterized by trade liberalization, smaller government, cutbacks in subsidies and social security, while the second phase (1989–present) began with full financial liberalization. In this study, we focus on the second phase. With full financial liberalization, Turkey has gone through four consecutive financial crises between 1989 and 2006 (i.e. the 1991 contraction, and 1994, 1999 and 2001 crises).

The differences between the adjustment ability of different social classes to financial liberalization and policies associated with it have important macroeconomic outcomes. High interest rates offered by government bonds and treasury bills resulted in the dominance of finance over the real economy. Big businesses adjust to high interest rates by transferring resources from real investment to financial investments. However, small and medium-sized companies try to adjust by passing on the increasing interest payments to the workers. Hence this new structure leaves the burden of the system on the working class by both limiting employment opportunities and decreasing the job security, and also by creating pressure on nominal as well as real wages. The increasing insecurity in the labor market has led households, especially poor households, to search for new coping mechanisms, which has had implications in terms of women's paid and unpaid labor burden.

The effect of the fragile economic structure on the real side of the economy, especially on the labor market, is the focus of this chapter. Before discussing the gendered employment outcomes of the recurrent financial crises, background information on the structural characteristics of the labor market and women's employment is crucial due to the interplay between secular and cyclical trends.

The labor force participation in Turkey was 47.9 percent in 2009, which is one of the lowest of the Organization for Economic Cooperation and Development (OECD) members. Labor force participation of men (70.4 percent) is close to the OECD average, whereas female labor force participation is as low as 26 percent (2009). Three out of four women do not participate in the market, and this leaves Turkey with an economy that keeps half of its working age population idle. The female labor force participation rate has increased in many developing countries from one-third to approximately 50 percent in the past few decades (Tzannatos, 1999). On the contrary, female labor force participation rate has been in a steady decline in Turkey since the 1950s – declining from 72 percent in 1955 to 24.8 percent in 2007.

There are several explanations to this dramatic trend (Tansel, 2000; Dayıoğlu and Kasnakoğlu, 1997; Onaran and Başlevent, 2003; Özar, 2000; Kızılırmak, 2005). The most important reasons are the decreasing role of the agricultural sector and the urbanization which began in the 1950s as a result of the industrialization policies and has intensified with the neoliberal policies after the 1980s.

Despite a significant transformation, one-third of the labor force is still in the agricultural sector. The rural economy is dominated by family-based production, in which all members of the family are considered as family workers. Once the rural economy is excluded, it is seen that urban female labor force participation historically remained below 20 percent in the 1990s and 2000s, until 2008.

The feminization U-curve hypothesis argues that at the initial stages of development female labor force participation is high due to the dominance of the agricultural sector; however, with economic development, urbanization leads to a fall in women's economic participation due to cultural values against women's work and lack of women's qualifications for the market's work. In later stages of development, as cultural norms change and women's human capital increases, once again female labor force participation is expected to increase. Tansel shows that Turkey has completed the first and the second phases of the feminization U-curve, and argues that the slight increase in female labor participation in the urban labor market in the 1990s shows that Turkey is on the edge of the third phase of the U-curve (Tansel, 2000). Nevertheless, there has been only a mild increase in the urban sector during the 1990s. The reason for low recovery and stagnant behavior in female labor force participation does not seem to be related to the skills and education levels of women, but more so with the gendered ideological context and the low employment creation of the export-oriented industrialization (EOI) strategy (Özar, 2000). The literature on women's export-oriented employment after 1980 shows that export growth has not led to an increase in women's economic participation or manufacturing employment (Çağatay and Berik, 1990; Toksöz, 2007; KEİG, 2009).

The dominant gender roles and gender ideology not only determine the participation of women in the urban labor market, but also where they work. The segregation measures show that "female work" is clearly defined in the urban labor market. The segregation measure dissimilarity index (DI)[6], demonstrates the decline in gender segregation in the urban labor market. The DI for the urban labor market decreased from 28.32 in 1988 to 25.13 in 2006 (see Appendix, Table 10.A1). However, this decline has been slow and not very significant when we consider the remarkable changes in the industrialization strategy.

Women are mostly employed in "Community, social and personal services" (33.8 percent), "Manufacturing" (23 percent), "Wholesale trade, restaurants and hotels" (19.7 percent) and "Finance, insurance, real estate and business services" (9 percent) economic activities (Table 10.A2). The decrease in DI is mainly due to the increasing share of female employment in "Community, social and personal services", "Wholesale trade, restaurants and hotels" and "Finance, insurance, real estate and business services", but not so much to a relative gain in "Manufacturing". The segregation trend clearly shows that a shift occurred from the agriculture and manufacturing sectors to the service-based sectors (İzdeş, 2010:114).

In the manufacturing sector, segregation measures show that there is significant gender segregation and women are over-represented in the food and textile industries (İzdeş, 2010). Within the two female-dominant sectors, women are usually employed as unskilled workers; when they become white-collar workers they do regular office work, having low representation at high-technical personnel level. On the other hand, in the sectors where women have low representation they are not employed as production workers; instead, they are employed in non-production positions. When they are employed as non-production workers they are generally not employed as high-level administrative personnel (Kasnakoğlu and Dikbayır, 2002).

The sectors in which women have a higher share of employment, such as wood products and food sectors, textiles and garment manufacturing, have lower average wages compared to the manufacturing sector average (Voyvoda and Yeldan, 2001). İlkkaracan and Selim (2007) have shown the female-to-male wage ratio in the manufacturing sector to be 70.6 percent. When they control for human capital variables and industry characteristics, there still remains a 10 percent difference between women's and men's wages, which is directly attributable to gender discrimination. Of the gender wage gap in the manufacturing sector, 57 percent can be explained by endowments and 43 percent remains unexplained; when the industry characteristics are included as well, 78 percent of the wage gap is explained and 22 percent is only explicable by gender discrimination. The big difference between 57 percent and 78 percent shows that a substantial portion of the gap is attributable to occupational and industrial gender segregation. Feminization of the job leads to undervaluation of the labor. For example, in the textiles industry the production tasks are divided between men and women, and this division of labor repeatedly leads to lower pay for women (Dedeoğlu, 2010).

As for the unemployment rate, we see that although it remained around 8 percent in most of the 1980s and 1990s, with the recurrent crises of 1994, 1999 and especially 2001 it has risen above 10 percent, and has remained in double digits ever since. The high and persistent unemployment problem despite high economic growth rates (jobless growth) continued when lack of decent employment prospects became more acute especially in the post-2001 crisis period. Despite the recovery in the economic growth rate, which has been 7.5 percent on average between 2002 and 2005, unemployment has remained as high as that in the crisis years, changing by −0.1 percent on average (Voyvoda and Yeldan, 2006). The deepening of the "jobless growth" phenomenon that was significant in 2004 and 2005, became even more significant especially after 2006, with a relative slowdown in economic growth rates. Persistent long-term unemployment is today a worldwide problem, faced by countries with all sorts of institutional and regulatory structures. The Global Employment Trends Report by the ILO (2008), as well as the 2007 report, addresses the problem of low job creation performance despite high growth performance on the world scale. Even though the average growth rate in 2007 was 5.2 percent on the world scale, the average unemployment rate was 6 percent. A more global-scale explanation argues that the hegemony of finance capital over industry has been leading to "job disappearances" in the world economy (ILO, 2008).

A better way to capture unemployment trends is to include those who are willing and ready to work if they could find a job, but have stopped looking for work due to low employment prospects. Especially in less-developed country contexts, remaining unemployed is a luxury since the coverage of unemployment insurance is usually not enough to provide real protection. This broad definition, as represented in Figure 10.1, demonstrates the jobless growth phenomenon more clearly. After 2002 the gap between the open unemployment rates and broadly defined unemployment widened, and by 2006 open unemployment failed to show almost half of the real unemployment problem.

Table 10.A3 presents the trends in basic labor market indicators between 1988 and 2007. Despite very low labor force participation rates for females, the trends in unemployment show that female unemployment has always been 2–2.5 times greater than male unemployment, ranging from 28 percent to 13 percent between 1988 and 2006. Moreover, very high and persistent urban unemployment of women leads to a significant discouraged worker phenomenon for women. Disaggregated trends demonstrate that the discouraged worker effect has historically been an important component of the labor market decision of women when compared to men. This can be traced either in the comparison of the official LFP rates and constructed (by including discouraged workers) broad LFP rates, or in unemployment rates (Table 10.A4). The average difference between official LFP rates for males and broad LFP rates is 3.9 percent, whereas it is 13.4 percent for females, which indicates that there is a significantly large group of women that functions as the latent reserve that is ready to step in depending on the employment prospects in the labor market. The difference on average between the two definitions of unemployment for female workers is as high as 5.46 percent, whereas the difference is significantly smaller for male workers (1.2 percent). After this brief summary of the structure of the labor market and gendered employment trends, next we focus on the cyclical behavior.

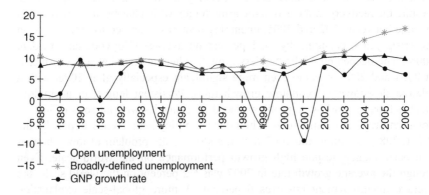

Figure 10.1 Trends in economic growth, unemployment and broad unemployment (source: drawn using TURKSTAT database, www.turkstat.gov.tr).

4 Empirical analysis

The purpose of this section is to analyze the impact of recessions on women's employment within the three-hypothesis framework (Rubery and Tarling, 1988). The three hypotheses are the flexible reserve or buffer hypothesis, the substitution hypothesis, and the segmentation hypothesis. These three hypotheses, presented above, are not necessarily exclusive or in competition; however, they co-exist with some tension. Rather than trying to identify a single causal explanation, Rubery and Tarling have developed a methodology that distinguishes between different influences. The change in women's employment during the economic cycle is decomposed in order to disentangle the multiple mechanisms behind such changes. Decomposition of changes in employment is applied for each economic crisis individually, which provides the opportunity to gather information on each specific crisis.

4.1 Data resources

The decomposition analysis on urban labor market employment is based on the Household Labor Force Survey (HLFS) database for 1988–2007, which is produced by the Turkish Statistical Institute (TURKSTAT). The HLFS has been carried out regularly since 1988, and the concepts and definitions used in implementations of the surveys are compatible with the International Labor Organization's (ILO's) definitions. Employment statistics in the rural economy are not as representative due to dominance of the subsistence economy, according to which any member of the household is counted as a laborer. Hence the study is based on urban labor market data in order to get a more accurate picture of the effect of economic cycles. Giving importance to the role of discouraged unemployment, variables such as broad labor force participation, broad unemployment and broad employment rate are calculated. The broad definitions are calculated by adding "discouraged" workers and workers "ready to work but not looking for a job".

4.2 The decomposition of changes in female employment

Decomposing the changes in female employment has three components. The first is the **growth effect**, which measures the contribution of employment growth to employment change, given the distribution of women across occupations. The second is the **share effect**, which measures the changes in the distribution of women across sectors, given total employment in each sector. In other words, the share effect shows to what extent women are gaining (or losing) employment vis-à-vis men's employment. Thus, the behavior of the share effect tests for substitution and buffer hypotheses. The third component is the **interaction effect** between growth and share effects.

Accordingly, if total female employment is

$$F_t = \sum T_{it} p_{it}$$

where p_{it}=proportion of female to total employment in industry $\underline{i}$ in time t, and T_{it}=total employment in industry i in time t, then

$$\Delta F_t = F_t - F_{t-1} = (T_{it} - T_{it-1})\, p_{it-1} + \sum (p_{it} - p_{it-1})\, T_{it-1} + \sum (p_{it} - p_{it-1})\,(T_{it} - T_{it-1}) \quad (1)$$

$$\sum (T_{it} - T_{it-1})\, p_{it-1} = \text{Growth effect} \quad (2)$$

$$\sum (p_{it} - p_{it-1})\, T_{it-1} = \text{Share effect} \quad (3), \text{ and}$$

$$\sum (p_{it} - p_{it-1})\,(T_{it} - T_{it-1}) = \text{Interaction effect} \quad (4)$$

The growth effect can further be broken into three components: scale effect, weight effect and a residual. **Scale effect** measures the effect of changes in total employment, given both the distribution of women across sectors and the weight of each sector. Second, given the total employment and distribution of women across sectors, the **weight effect** shows the effect of changes in the overall distribution of employment across sectors. It shows the effect of structural changes in occupational composition and the following outcomes in terms of women's employment. Since women's distribution across sectors is considered to be given, the weight effect provides a test of the segmentation hypothesis (Rubery and Tarling, 1988).

The growth effect can be rewritten and decomposed as follows:

$$\sum (W_{it} T_t - W_{it-1} T_{t-1})\, p_{it-1} = (T_t - T_{t-1}) W_{it-1}\, p_{it-1} + \sum (W_{it} - W_{it-1})\, T_{t-1}$$
$$p_{it-1} + \sum (W_{it} - W_{it-1})\,(T_t - T_{t-1})\, p_{it-1} \quad (5)$$

where W_{it}=the weight of employment in group i in year t, or $T_{it}/\sum T_{it}$, and $T_{it} = W_{it}\, T_t$ where T_t = total employment in year t

$$\sum (T_t - T_{t-1}) W_{it-1}\, p_{it-1} = \text{Scale effect;} \quad (6)$$

$$\sum (W_{it} - W_{it-1})\, T_{t-1} p_{it-1} = \text{Weight effect} \quad (7)$$

$$\sum (W_{it} - W_{it-1})\,(T_t - T_{t-1})\, p_{it-1} = \text{Residual} \quad (8)$$

The favorable segmentation hypothesis argues that women are concentrated in sectors and occupations that are less sensitive to short-term labor demand fluctuations resulting from economic cycles. Since those female-dominated sectors are expected to be more protected from the contractionary effects of the recession compared to other sectors, we expect the weight effect to be positive and significant during a recession. On the other hand, in a boom period we expect the change in the weight of those industries to be relatively small or even negative, as those sectors are unresponsive to short-run demand changes. Contrarily, if it is an unfavorable segmentation case, the weight effect is expected to be negative. If women are substituting men in recessionary periods, we expect the share

Table 10.2 Predictions on decomposition of female employment growth

Predictions	Buffer hypothesis	Segmentation hypothesis	Substitution hypothesis
Upswing	• Positive share effect	• Favorable segmentation: minor, even negative, weight dffect	• Positive relative minor share effect compared to the downswing
Downswing	• Negative share effect	• Favorable segmentation: positive, even substantial, weight effect	
		• Unfavorable segmentation: negative weight effect – buffer	• Positive significant share effect

Source: Constructed by the author.

of the women to increase, which will be reflected in a positive share effect. If the share effect is negative in the downswings and positive in the upswings, or if the share effect is relatively strong in booms compared to slumps, we conclude in favor of the buffer hypothesis (Table 10.2; see also Humphries, 1988: 29).

Findings of the decomposition analysis and reflections on gendered employment outcomes of 1991 downturn, 1994, 1999 and 2001 economic crises

The decomposition analysis enables us to evaluate each individual economic crisis in terms of buffer, substitution and segmentation (favorable and unfavorable). The economic cycles are defined in three different ways: (1) by using GNP growth to identify peaks and troughs; (2) by using GNP growth to identify troughs and lowest unemployment before the crisis to identify the peak; and (3) by using unemployment cycles to determine the peaks and troughs. Given the significance of the discouraged worker phenomenon, which is not reflected in the official unemployment numbers, unemployment rates are re-calculated with a broader approach that includes "discouraged workers" and "workers willing to work but not looking for a job". The cycles are re-determined based on this broad definition of unemployment. Tables 10.A5 and 10.A6 (see Appendix) reflect the economic cycles and the changes on labor market indicators. Tables 10.A7–10.A10 summarize the findings of the decomposition analysis for the urban labor market. In this section, each economic downturn will be evaluated in terms of three hypotheses in the light of the predictions table (Table 10.1) and results on the decomposition analysis.

GENDERED EMPLOYMENT OUTCOMES OF 1991 ECONOMIC
CONTRACTION

In all three versions of economic cycles based on official definitions, the relative changes in labor market indicators presented in Table 10.A5 depict a picture supporting the buffer hypothesis. Male unemployment increases by 11.57 percent as female unemployment decreases by 3.41 percent from 1990 to 1991. The relative change in employment rates shows that employment increases by 5 percent for men and there is no significant increase in women's employment. Hence we see that the decrease in female unemployment is not due to employment gains but to the relative decrease in women's LFPR, which is as high as 8.27 percent.

Using broad definitions gives us the same peak and trough years as the official unemployment numbers. The relative changes with the broad unemployment cycles are in the same direction as the official rates, and by using broad definitions we also see that 97 percent of the contraction in the female labor force is due to discouraged workers; hence, as the buffer hypothesis suggests, the primary reason of falling out of the labor force is low employment prospects in the market (Table 10.A6).

The findings of the decomposition analysis[7] of the 1991 recession show that even though the difference is not big, the magnitude of the growth effect is relatively larger than the share effect. The change in female employment is more related to the general employment change than female labor preference, since the growth effect dominates. However, even though the share effect is not the primary reason behind the change in female employment, it is very sizable. There is a very significant positive share effect in the boom and a very significant negative share effect in the slump; this suggests that the employment effects of the cycle are not gender-neutral. The sign and the significance of the share effect suggests the buffer hypothesis. The weight effect also supports this argument. When we ask whether the growth effect is due to a gender-neutral general employment increase in the labor market or whether it is related to the increasing weight of the female-dominated sectors, the negative weight effect suggests that the weight of these sectors decreases (unfavorable segmentation). Hence the decomposition analysis indicates that women are concentrated in sectors and/or positions that lose out in the 1991 economic recession, which reflects an unfavorable segmentation case.

GENDERED EMPLOYMENT OUTCOMES OF 1994 ECONOMIC CRISIS

When the official labor market indicators are used, only the first approach of determining economic cycles allows us to discuss the 1994 economic crisis (Table 10.A7). Looking at relative and absolute changes, we see that female unemployment declined by 10.5 percent, employment increased by 19 percent and female LFP increased by 11 percent (Table 10.A5). Thus, it seems that employment opportunities for women flourished during the 1994 economic crisis compared to that of men; and women also responded positively to increasing demand for female labor. Increasing labor force participation during a recession, especially under deteriorating or stagnant employment opportunities for men, suggests the added worker effect. The overall relative changes of employment opportunities of women vis-à-vis men during the 1994 recession reflect a mild substitution effect as well. This description is in accordance with the findings of Onaran and Başlevent (2003). Onaran and Başlevent focus on the 1994 economic crisis; they use microeconomic data and study the determinants of LFP decision of married women. They conclude that women whose husbands lost their jobs tended to participate in economic activity as "added workers" of the family.

The indicators based on broad definitions show that the change in female LFPR is 17 percent. This reveals the true size of the female population that is willing to work. During the 1994 crisis, the added worker effect coexisted with the discouraged worker effect, which limits the growth of the official female labor force participation rate (Table 10.A6). This is reflected in the difference in between the relative change of the two LFP definitions (17–11 percent). The comparison of the growth change in the official unemployment rate, which is −10.52 percent, with the change in broad unemployment rate, −5.61 percent, lets one see that once the discouraged workers are included the fall in female unemployment is only half of the very positive picture depicted by the official unemployment rates. These findings by broad definitions do not challenge the overall interpretation, but rather provide additional information to modify our prior observations.

Similarly, the decomposition analysis on the 1994 economic crisis proves that women had a relatively favorable position in this economic crisis. The share effect is positive in both the boom and the slump periods, and it has a greater value than the growth effect in the boom, and vice versa. This suggests an increase in female representation in the labor market. The second question is whether this increase is due to a favorable segmentation for women or whether it is due to the substitution of men with women workers. The negative weight effect in the boom is in contradiction with a favorable segmentation scenario, and is more in accordance with the substitution hypothesis, since it suggests that the answer for relative gains in this period cannot be found in sheltered female jobs.

GENDERED EMPLOYMENT OUTCOMES OF 1999 ECONOMIC CRISIS

When we use official unemployment rates and look at the first version of economic cycles based on GNP growth, we see that unemployment of men increases by 20 percent, whereas there is a slight decrease in female unemployment. Female employment and LFPR also mirror unemployment changes. They increase by 12 percent and, 5 percent respectively (Table 10.A5). Similarly to the 1994 economic crisis, women were in a relatively favorable position during the 1997–1999 downturn, which can be interpreted as evidence for the added worker effect that indicates the substitution or the segmentation hypothesis.

On the other hand, when we determine cycles according to broad unemployment rates, the percentage change in unemployment for both genders is significantly greater, and even more so for women. This indicates the important role of the discouraged worker phenomenon, and indicates that the added worker argument is not as significant as official numbers suggest (Table 10.A6). Hence the synthesis of six different ways of constructing cycles reflects the relatively favorable position of women during the 1999 economic crisis. This relatively stable and advantageous position can be interpreted as both segmentation and substitution hypothesis; in order to decide which of the two describes the changes in 1999, one needs to further investigate the change in female employment by decomposing the source of change in female employment. The decomposition of the change in female employment gives a positive and a significant share effect accompanied by no significant changes in the weight effect. This means that the relative gains of women in the 1999 recession are not due to their protected positions (favorable segmentation scenario), but to the substitution effect.

GENDERED EMPLOYMENT OUTCOMES OF 2001 ECONOMIC CRISIS

The absolute and relative changes demonstrate the severe unemployment cost of the 2001 economic crisis for both genders. If the economic cycle is determined according to economic growth cycles, Table 10.A5 shows that both genders' unemployment increases by one-third, and the percentage change in employment and LFP participation shows that the burden of the 2001 crisis is mainly born by men. However, indicators for female workers' are not positive enough to conclude for the positive segmentation or the substitution hypothesis.

Determination of economic cycles based on broad definitions gives 2000–2002 and 2003–2006 downturns that reflect the jobless growth phenomena after the 2001 economic crisis. The percentage change in broad unemployment across 2000–2002 downturn is as high as 51.68 percent for men and 19 percent for women, which shows that the first round of the burden that comes with 2001 crisis is mostly carried by men. Women are relatively protected from the first round of the negative effects of 2001 crisis on the labor market. However, very high unemployment rates make it difficult to argue for a substitution or (favorable) segmentation hypothesis. Moreover, 2002 reflects the second round of the negative effects of 2001 crisis on labor market indicators, and we see that this second round of the unemployment cycle hits primarily women; the change in unemployment is 52.24 percent for women and 11.35 percent for men (buffer hypothesis).

Findings of the decomposition analysis on 2001 crisis also support the buffer hypothesis. There is a negative share effect in the slump and a positive share effect in the boom. This means that women are employed more than their average share during the boom and, contrarily, women lose from their share of employment during the crisis period (buffer hypothesis). Besides, the negative weight effect in the boom shows that the gain in female share is not due to expansion of the female-dominated sectors but is linked to a general rise in female share of employment across all sectors. On the other hand, the very high weight effect in the slump together with a negative share effect indicates that even though women as a whole lose out in total employment, the lucky ones that keep their jobs are mostly employed in protected sectors and occupations (favorable segmentation hypothesis).

5 Conclusion

The aim of this research is to disentangle the gendered employment outcomes of the economic crises Turkey went through in the financial liberalization era, namely after 1989. With this objective, this chapter analyzed the gendered patterns in employment during the economic cycles of the 1991 downturn, and the 1994, 1999 and 2001 crises. The segmentation, buffer and substitution hypotheses provided the framework to theorize the three different possibilities addressed in the literature.

The decomposition analysis showed that the change in the gender composition during the 1991 contraction can be explained by the buffer hypothesis, which is due to unfavorable segmentation. On the other hand, the response in terms of gender composition of labor market indicators during the 1994 and 1999 crises reflect the relative gains in female employment in the 1990s, and supports a modest substitution hypothesis. The 2001 economic crisis represents a threshold in terms of persistent and very high unemployment in the labor market. The jobless growth phenomenon became persistent after the 2001 economic crisis; hence, using two different definitions of unemployment gave critically different outcomes. The broad definition gives us a 2000–2002 cycle accompanied by another round of unemployment fluctuation in 2003–2006. According to the decomposition analysis in the first round of the unemployment cycle following the 2001 crisis, the burden of the crisis fell on male workers. However persistent and high unemployment disproportionately affected women workers in the second round of the unemployment cycle that started in 2003. Overallm in the 2001 crisis women's share of employment decreased (buffer hypothesis) and women that preserved their jobs and the small employment gains were in those less cyclically sensitive sectors or occupations (favorable segmentation).

The results show that different hypothesis have dominated the labor market effects of crises over time. This can be due either to the changing structure of the crisis or to the changing demographic structure. The literature on secular trends in gender and employment addresses a demographic transformation in the urban setting during the 1990s. The increasing female employment in the urban setting in the 1990s is addressed in the feminization U-curve literature (Tansel, 2000; Tunalı, 1997; Bulutay, 2000), which is in accordance with our findings. Hence, the relatively better off position of women during the crises of 1994 and 1999 can be partially related to the positive secular trends.

In terms of the nature of the crisis, even though all crises in the post-financial liberalization era were financial crises which began with capital outflows, the responses to those crises in the labor market have changed over time. Gürsel and Ulusoy (1999) and Ansal *et al.* (2000) argue that the effect of crises in the 1990s was reflected in the underemployment rates, whereas crises after 1999 are reflected in unemployment and long-term unemployment rates which led to increasing discouraged worker phenomena (Taşçı and Özdemir, 2007). Hence, combining this information with the secular trends it is possible to argue that the relative gains of women in the 1990s have been lost, as the way employers cope with crises has changed in the 2000s. Increasing unemployment and long-term unemployment trends have hit women harder, who have a higher probability of staying long-term unemployed compared to men (Taşçı and Tansel, 2005).

Using different ways of determining cycles and different definitions of unemployment has been helpful at multiple levels. The replication of the analysis with broad LFPR and unemployment rates clarified the contribution of the added worker effect and discouraged worker effect in the crises. Especially after 2000, broad unemployment cycles were substantially different, and this addressed the structural change in unemployment in the jobless growth era.

Very low and further decreasing female labor force participation in Turkey is interpreted as a deteriorating development indicator, and hence has been a concern of scholars and international circles for a long time. The gendered patterns of employment during economic crises clearly show that crises contribute to the problem of low female labor force participation. Moreover, once we consider the highly vulnerable macroeconomic structure that has gone through four consecutive severe contractions since 1989 and has recently faced a global economic crisis, the effect of crises on long-term trends cannot be overlooked and, furthermore, should be considered as informative regarding the gendered structure in the labor market.

This study clearly demonstrates that labor force participation of women cannot be isolated from the high unemployment problem and jobless growth phenomenon that became unbearable in the 2000s. Hence it is not viable to think that policies towards increasing female labor force participation, such as provision of child-care services, increasing education and skill level of women, can alone help to solve the problem of under-representation of women in the paid economy. Unless high female unemployment and unemployment are addressed as the core of the problem, the policies towards increasing female labor force participation are unlikely to achieve the goal of greater representation of women in the labor market.

Appendix

Table 10.A1 Coefficient of Female Representation (CFR), Dissimilarity Index (DI) and Women and Employment Index (WEI) – Urban 1988–2006

	Agriculture, forestry, hunting and fishing	Mining and quarrying	Manufacturing	Electricity, gas and water	Construction	Wholesale and retail trade, restaurants and hotels	Transportation, communication and storage	Finance, ins., real estate and business services	Community, social and personal services	DI (urban)	WEI
1988	2.46	0.19	1.15	0.87	0.14	0.48	0.36	1.72	1.35	28.32	48.16
1989	2.52	0.13	1.10	0.60	0.10	0.51	0.39	1.72	1.42	28.11	47.36
1990	2.63	0.07	1.10	0.00	0.11	0.49	0.38	1.93	1.34	28.00	47.25
1991	2.09	0.32	1.10	0.00	0.10	0.52	0.43	1.88	1.47	27.36	46.52
1992	2.07	0.26	1.11	0.48	0.09	0.54	0.34	1.76	1.47	27.92	46.60
1993	1.77	0.15	1.22	0.33	0.13	0.56	0.49	1.74	1.51	28.36	47.95
1994	2.49	0.06	1.03	0.60	0.15	0.55	0.35	1.72	1.50	28.48	47.23
1995	1.99	0.10	1.04	0.42	0.15	0.61	0.31	1.82	1.56	27.45	45.49
1996	2.18	0.24	1.00	0.58	0.19	0.55	0.37	1.80	1.53	26.90	44.70
1997	1.95	0.19	1.03	0.69	0.18	0.64	0.34	1.75	1.54	25.27	41.76
1998	1.88	0.41	0.99	0.70	0.15	0.60	0.35	1.90	1.62	27.29	44.99
1999	2.06	0.25	1.02	0.58	0.13	0.62	0.32	1.67	1.53	26.55	43.31
2000	2.30	0.58	0.95	0.44	0.16	0.60	0.39	1.69	1.69	28.85	46.96
2001	2.51	0.14	0.96	0.45	0.13	0.60	0.39	1.56	1.64	28.56	46.43
2002	2.34	0.20	1.02	0.22	0.15	0.60	0.39	1.41	1.58	26.80	42.66
2003	2.24	0.32	1.01	0.35	0.19	0.62	0.38	1.42	1.57	25.52	40.80
2004	2.09	0.16	1.01	0.32	0.15	0.65	0.37	1.46	1.50	24.63	39.61
2005	2.07	0.16	0.96	0.36	0.14	0.67	0.40	1.40	1.58	25.49	40.73
2006	2.00	0.15	0.93	0.35	0.17	0.72	0.41	1.38	1.60	25.13	39.84

Source: Author's calculations based on HLS, www.turkstat.gov.tr.

Table 10.A2 Percentage distribution of female employment by economic activity 1988–2006 (urban)

Agriculture, forestry, hunting and fishing	Mining and quarrying	Manufacturing	Electricity, gas and water	Construction	Wholesale and retail trade, restaurants and hotels	Transportation, communication and storage	Finance, insurance, real estate and business services	Community, social and personal services
14.25	0.28	31.82	0.28	1.2	9.81	2.5	8.05	31.82
12.68	0.17	30.97	0.17	0.78	10.87	2.85	8.37	32.96
13.04	0.08	30.73	0	0.83	10.8	2.66	8.64	33.22
9.19	0.33	29.8	0	0.83	11.59	3.06	8.94	36.18
10.88	0.28	30.51	0.21	0.78	11.94	2.33	8.69	34.39
7.14	0.15	31.84	0.3	1.29	12.54	3.8	7.6	35.33
13.4	0.06	27.82	0.45	1.4	12.25	2.43	7.98	34.27
9.42	0.06	27.65	0.31	1.36	14.07	2.11	8.12	36.95
11.4	0.12	27.48	0.3	1.83	12.49	2.38	8.35	35.53
8.83	0.11	28.87	0.57	1.65	14.64	2.22	8.09	35.08
8.25	0.22	26.98	0.55	1.47	13.6	2.35	8.9	37.68
10.57	0.15	26.83	0.36	1.17	14.68	2.03	7.98	36.33
8.7	0.19	25.07	0.29	1.26	16.43	2.71	9.71	35.65
10.95	0.05	25.46	0.29	0.96	16.25	2.7	8.49	34.76
10.19	0.09	27.13	0.13	0.97	16.72	2.51	7.63	34.63
9.5	0.13	26.88	0.22	1.15	17.24	2.48	7.78	34.66
12.09	0.09	26.15	0.17	0.95	17.55	2.49	8.43	32.09
11.09	0.08	25.15	0.16	0.91	18.26	2.57	8.28	33.5
9.51	0.07	23.78	0.18	1.18	19.73	2.65	9.03	33.85

Source: Author's calculations based on HLS, www.turkstat.gov.tr.

Table 10.A3 Labor market indicators by gender (official definition) 1988–2006

Years	GNP (growth rate)	Male LFPR (urban)	Female LFPR (urban)	Share of FLF (urban)	Official unemp. (urban)	Official male unemp % (urban)	Official female unemp % (urban)	Share of female unemp. (urban)	Employed men (urban)	Employed women (urban)
1988	1.50	78.12	17.72	18.13	13.1	9.7	28.3	39.25	6,154	1,081
1989	1.60	76.82	17.78	18.54	13.1	10.1	26.2	37.16	6,201	1,159
1990	9.40	76.83	17.04	17.93	12	9.5	23.4	35.01	6,511	1,204
1991	0.30	76.97	15.64	16.93	12.7	10.6	22.6	30.19	6,839	1,208
1992	6.40	76.82	16.99	18.26	12.6	10.7	20.9	30.44	7,161	1,416
1993	8.10	75.17	15.67	17.43	12.6	10.5	22.8	31.58	7,235	1,316
1994	-6.10	75.34	17.40	18.89	12.4	10.5	20.4	31.09	7,567	1,567
1995	8	74.07	16.81	18.77	10.8	9	18.3	31.98	7,778	1,613
1996	7.10	73.21	15.98	18.04	9.9	8.7	15.4	28.01	8,044	1,641
1997	8.30	72.94	16.92	19.01	10	8.2	17.5	33.51	8,331	1,756
1998	3.90	72.78	16.77	18.79	10.5	9.1	16.5	29.47	8,608	1,831
1999	-6.10	72.16	17.76	19.77	11.4	9.9	17.4	30.14	8,709	1,968
2000	6.30	70.93	17.22	19.54	8.8	7.8	13	28.82	9,034	2,070
2001	-9.50	70.60	17.44	19.87	11.6	10.3	16.6	28.61	9,002	2,074
2002	7.90	69.77	19.07	21.51	14.2	13	18.7	28.20	8,844	2,267
2003	5.90	68.93	18.52	21.14	13.8	12.6	18.3	28.05	9,025	2,262
2004	9.90	70.83	18.33	20.65	13.6	12.5	17.9	27.11	9,519	2,325
2005	7.60	71.53	19.26	21.13	12.7	11.6	17	28.28	10,041	2,525
2006	6.10	70.77	19.93	21.79	12.1	10.9	16.4	29.41	10,368	2,712

Source: Household Labor Force Survey (HLFS) Data, www.turkstat.gov.tr.

Table 10.A4 Labor market indicators by gender (broad definitions) 1988–2006

Years	GNP (growth rate)	Male broad LFPR (urban)	Female broad LFPR (urban)	Share of FLF (broad) (urban)	Broad unemp.% (urban)	Male broad unemp % (urban)	Bemale broad unemp % (urban)	Share of female unemp. (broad) (urban)	Employed men (urban)	Employed women (urban)
1988	1.50	82.43	36.74	20.20	16.62	11.12	38.28	46.53	6,154	1,081
1989	1.60	81.01	37.05	19.22	14.24	10.55	29.78	40.18	6,201	1,159
1990	9.40	80.31	34.92	18.44	13.03	10.02	26.41	37.37	6,511	1,204
1991	0.30	80.87	34.86	17.59	14.06	11.34	26.65	33.33	6,839	1,208
1992	6.40	80.28	33.44	18.88	13.87	11.35	24.68	33.60	7,161	1,416
1993	8.10	78.60	27.39	17.96	13.86	11.16	26.19	33.94	7,235	1,316
1994	-6.10	79.09	32.09	19.64	13.87	11.22	24.72	35.01	7,567	1,567
1995	8.00	78.44	31.53	19.23	12.14	9.92	21.51	34.05	7,778	1,613
1996	7.10	77.96	31.21	18.59	11.38	9.59	19.24	31.43	8,044	1,641
1997	8.30	77.49	29.69	19.66	11.67	9.20	21.78	36.68	8,331	1,756
1998	3.90	77.63	30.22	19.60	12.53	10.28	21.72	33.98	8,608	1,831
1999	-6.10	76.81	31.28	20.79	13.85	11.28	23.63	35.49	8,709	1,968
2000	6.30	74.76	27.51	20.20	10.80	9.06	17.69	33.09	9,034	2,070
2001	-9.50	73.72	27.82	20.24	12.84	11.19	19.36	30.51	9,002	2,074
2002	7.90	72.39	28.62	21.90	15.38	13.74	21.18	30.16	8,844	2,267
2003	5.90	71.32	27.14	21.44	14.72	13.21	20.30	29.55	9,025	2,262
2004	9.90	74.87	27.75	22.23	17.79	15.05	27.41	34.24	9,519	2,325
2005	7.60	75.43	28.36	23.47	18.35	14.76	30.09	38.48	10,041	2,525
2006	6.10	75.31	29.10	24.41	18.66	14.72	30.90	40.41	10,368	2,712

Source: Calculated from Household Labor Force Survey (HLFS) Data, www.turkstat.gov.tr/.

Table 10.A5 Changes in labor market indicators across economic cycles (based on official definitions)

ECONOMIC GROWTH CYCLES: Peak and trough years are determined according to GNP growth

Official unemployment URBAN		Absolute change in official unemp. Rate		% Change in official unemp. rate		Absolute change in numbers employed (in thousands)		% Change in numbers employed		Absolute change LFPR		% Change in LFPR	
Peak year	*Trough year*	*Men*	*Women*	*Men*	*Women*	*Men*	*Women*	*Men*	*Women*	*Men*	*Women*	*Men*	*Women*
1990	1991	1.10%	-0.80%	11.57%	-3.41%	328	4	5.03%	0.33%	0.14%	-1.41%	0.18%	-8.27%
1993	1994	0%	-2.40%	0	-10.52%	332	251	4.58%	19.07%	0.17%	1.73%	0.22%	11.04%
1997	1999	1.70%	-0.10%	20.73%	-0.57%	378	212	4.53%	12.07%	-0.78%	0.84%	-1.06%	4.96%
2000	2001	2.50%	3.60%	32.05%	27.69%	-32	4	-0.35%	0.19%	-0.34%	0.22%	-0.47%	1.27%

HYBRID CYCLES: Trough years are determined according to GNP growth, peaks are determined by the unemployment rate

Official unemployment URBAN		Absolute change in official unemp. rate		% Change in official unemp rate		Absolute change in numbers employed (in thousands)		% Change in numbers employed		Absolute change LFPR		% Change in LFPR	
Peak year	*Trough year*	*Men*	*Women*	*Men*	*Women*	*Men*	*Women*	*Men*	*Women*	*Men*	*Women*	*Men*	*Women*
1990	1991	1.10%	-0.80%	11.57%	-3.41%	328	4	5.03%	0.33%	0.14%	-1.41%	0.18%	-8.27%
1990	1994	1.00%	-3.00%	10.52%	-12.82%	1056	363	16.21%	30.14%	-1.49%	0.35%	-1.93%	2.05%
1996	1999	1.20%	2.00%	13.79%	12.98%	665	327	8.26%	19.92%	-1.05%	1.77%	-1.43%	11.07%
2000	2001	2.50%	3.60%	32.05%	27.69%	-32	4	-0.35%	0.19%	-0.34%	0.22%	-0.47%	1.27%

Table 10.A5 continued

Unemployment numbers do not reflect growth cycles

UNEMPLOYMENT CYCLES: Peak and trough years are determined according to unemployment cycles

Official unemployment URBAN		Absolute change in official unemp. rate		% Change in official unemp. rate		Absolute change in numbers employed (in thousands)		% Change in numbers employed		Absolute change LFPR		% Change in LFPR	
Peak year	*Trough year*	*Men*	*Women*	*Men*	*Women*	*Men*	*Women*	*Men*	*Women*	*Men*	*Women*	*Men*	*Women*
1990	1991	1.10%	-0.80%	11.57%	-3.41%	328	4	5.03%	0.33%	0.14%	-1.41%	0.18%	-8.27%
1996	1999	1.20%	2.00%	13.79%	12.98%	665	327	8.26%	19.92%	-1.05%	1.77%	-1.43%	11.07%
2000	2002	5.20%	5.70%	66.66%	43.84%	-190	197	-2.10%	9.51%	-1.16%	1.85%	-1.63%	10.74%

Table 10.A6 Changes in labor market indicators across economic cycles (based on broad definitions)

ECONOMIC GROWTH CYCLES: Peak and trough years are determined according to GNP growth

Unemployment broad definition URBAN		Absolute change in unemployment rate		% Change in unemployment rate		Absolute change in numbers employed (in thousands)		% Change in numbers employed		Absolute change LFPR		% Change in LFPRe	
Peak year	Trough year	Men	Women	Men	Women	Men	Women	Men	Women	Men	Women	Men	Women
1990	1991	1.32%	0.25%	13.17%	0.94%	328	4	5.03%	0.33%	0.56%	-0.06%	0.69%	-0.17%
1993	1994	1.01%	-1.47%	9.05%	-5.61%	332	251	4.58%	19.07%	0.50%	4.70%	0.63%	17.15%
1997	1999	2.10%	1.85%	22.85%	8.49%	378	212	4.53%	12.07%	-0.67%	1.59%	-0.86%	5.35%
2000	2001	2.13%	1.67%	23.53%	9.44%	-32	4	-0.35%	0.19%	-1.04%	0.31%	-1.39%	1.12%

HYBRID CYCLES: Trough years are determined according to GNP growth, peaks are determined by the unemployment rate

Unemployment broad definition URBAN		Absolute change in unemployment rate		% Change in unemployment rate		Absolute change in numbers employed (in thousands)		% Change in numbers employed		Absolute change LFPR		% Change in LFPRe	
Peak year	Trough year	Men	Women	Men	Women	Men	Women	Men	Women	Men	Women	Men	Women
1990	1991	1.32%	0.25%	13.17%	0.94%	328	4	5.03%	0.33%	0.56%	-0.06%	0.69%	-0.17%
1990	1994	1.20%	-1.68%	11.98%	-6.36%	1,056	363	16.21%	30.14%	-1.22%	-2.83%	-1.51%	-8.10%
1996	1999	1.69%	4.39%	17.64%	22.81%	665	327	8.26%	19.92%	-1.15%	0.06%	-1.47%	0.19%
2000	2001	2.13%	1.67%	23.53%	9.44%	-32	4	-0.35%	0.19%	-1.04%	0.31%	-1.39%	1.12%

Table 10.A6 continued

Unemployment numbers do not reflect growth cycles

UNEMPLOYMENT CYCLES: Peak and trough years are determined according to unemployment cycles

Unemployment broad definition URBAN		Absolute change in unemployment rate		% Change in unemployment rate		Absolute change in numbers employed (in thousands)		% Change in numbers employed		Absolute change LFPR		% Change in LFPRe	
Peak year	Trough year	Men	Women	Men	Women	Men	Women	Men	Women	Men	Women	Men	Women
1990	1991	1.32%	0.25%	13.17%	0.94%	328	4	5.03%	0.33%	0.56%	-0.06%	0.69%	-0.17%
1996	1999	1.69%	4.39%	17.64%	22.81%	665	327	8.26%	19.92%	-1.15%	0.06%	-1.47%	0.19%
2000	2002	4.69%	3.48%	51.68%	19.67%	-190	197	-2.10%	9.51%	-2.37%	1.11%	-3.17%	4.03%
2003	2006	1.50%	10.60%	11.35%	52.24%	1,343	450	14.88%	19.89%	4.00%	1.96%	5.60%	7.22%

Table 10.A7 Female employment change according to official unemployment rates (economic cycles determined according to GNP growth)

Economic cycles determined according to GNP growth	Booms				Slumps			
Years	1988–1990	1991–1993	1994–1997	1999–2000	1990–1991	1993–1994	1997–1999	2000–2001
Ft-Ft-1 (thousands)	123	109	189	102	4	252	212	4
%								
Contribution of the share effect	43.12	69.11	16.75	99.08	–1,054.89	41.35	35.27	–1,051.86
Contribution of the growth effect	54.23	23.75	77.32	16.61	1,071.61	48.84	61.09	976.10
Contribution of the scale effect	107.75	293.19	112.06	474.33	160.17	72.55	78.82	–26.74
Contribution of the weight effect	–7.26	–181.76	–10.92	–359.93	–57.71	25.49	20.00	127.06
Contribution of the interaction effect	2.65	7.14	5.93	–15.69	83.28	9.81	3.63	175.75
Contribution of the residual	–0.48	–11.43	–1.14	–14.39	–2.47	1.73	1.17	–0.32

Source: Author's own calculations.

Table 10.A8 Decomposition of female employment change according to official unemployment rates (economic cycles are determined according to GNP cycles and unemployment cycles)

Economic cycles determined according to GNP growth and official unemployment rates	Booms			Slumps			
	1988–1990 ?	1994–1996	1999–2000	1990–1991	?–1994	1996–1999	2000–2001
Ft-Ft-1 %	123	74	102	4		327	4
Contribution of the share effect	43.12	−40.22	99.08	−1,054.89		42.32	−1,051.86
Contribution of the growth effect	54.23	143.41	16.61	1,071.61		52.55	976.11
Contribution of the scale effect	107.75	92.72	474.32	160.17		96.61	−26.73
Contribution of the weight effect	−7.26	6.86	−359.93	−57.70		3.07	127.06
Contribution of the interaction effect	2.65	−3.20	−15.69	83.28		5.13	175.75
Contribution of the residual	−0.48	0.41	−14.39	−2.47		0.31	−0.32

Source: Author's own calculations.

Table 10.A9 Decomposition of female employment change according to official unemployment rates (economic cycles determined according to official unemployment rates)

Economic cycles determined according to official unemployment rates	Booms			Slumps			
	1988–1990	1991–1996	1999–2000	1990–1991	1996–1999	2000–2002
Ft-Ft-1	123	433	102	4	327	197
%						
Contribution of the share effect	43.12	36.22	99.08	−1,054.89	42.32	71.34
Contribution of the growth effect	54.23	55.10	16.61	1,071.61	52.55	26.10
Contribution of the scale effect	107.75	103.23	474.33	160.17	96.61	2.54
Contribution of the weight effect	−7.26	−2.69	−359.93	−57.71	3.07	97.40
Contribution of the interaction effect	2.65	8.69	−15.69	83.28	5.13	2.55
Contribution of the residual	−0.48	−0.55	−14.39	−2.47	0.31	0.06

Source: Author's own calculations.

Table 10A.10 Decomposition of female employment change according to broad unemployment rates (economic cycles determined according to broad unemployment rates)

Economic cycles determined according to broad unemployment rates	Booms				Slumps			
	1988–1990	1994–1996	1999–2000	2002–2003	1990–1994	1996–1999	2000–2002	2003–2006
Ft-Ft-1	123	74	102	–5	363	327	197	450
%								
Contribution of the share effect	43.11	–40.21	99.07	1,079.34	39.36	42.31	71.34	17.92
Contribution of the growth effect	54.22	143.41	16.60	–998.75	53.70	52.55	26.10	80.36
Contribution of the scale effect	107.74	92.72	474.32	89.89	112.87	96.61	2.54	99.69
Contribution of the weight effect	–7.26	6.86	–359.93	9.95	–10.87	3.07	97.40	0.27
Contribution of the interaction effect	2.65	–3.19	–15.69	19.41	6.93	5.13	2.55	1.72
Contribution of the residual	–0.48	0.41	–14.39	0.16	–1.99	0.31	0.06	0.04

Source: Author's own calculations.

Notes

1 See Bruegel (1979) and Rubery and Tarling (1988).
2 See Humphries (1988), Bouillaguet and Gauvin (1988), Bettio (1988), Rubery and Tarling (1988), Baden (1993) and Van Wagner (1993).
3 See MacKay *et al.* (1971) and Jennes *et al.* (1975).
4 See Milkman (1976), Bruegel (1979), Enloe (1980), Goldthorpe (1983) and Wright (2000) for a discussion on the peculiarities of women's proletarianization and its relation to economic development.
5 See Mies (1998) and Milkman (1976).
6 The Dissimilarity Index was introduced by Duncan and Duncan (1955); it is the most commonly used measure of segregation. The DI has a minimum value of zero (no segregation) and a maximum value of 100 (perfect segregation). The index score can also be interpreted as the percentage of one of the two groups included in the calculation that would have to move to the other group in order to produce a completely even distribution.
7 See Tables 10.A7–10.A10 in the Appendix.

Bibliography

Ansal, H., Küçükçiftçi, S., Onaran, O. and Zekiorbay, B. (2000). *Türkiye Emek Piyasasının Yapısı ve İşsizlik*. İstanbul, Türkiye Tarih Vakfı.
Baden, S. (1993). "The Impact of Recession and Structural Adjustment on Women's Work in Selected Developing Countries". Brighton: Bridge Report No 15.
Becker, G.S. (1971). *The Economics of Discrimination*. Chicago, IL: University of Chicago Press.
Bettio, F. (1988). "Women, The State and Family in Italy: Problems of Female Participation in Historical Perspective", in J. Rubery (ed.), *Women and Recession*. London: Routledge, pp. 191–218.
Bouillaguet, B.P. and Gauvin, A. (1988). "Women, The State and The Family in France: Contradictions of State Policy for Women's Employment", in J. Rubery (ed.), *Women and Recession*. London: Routledge, pp. 163–191.
Bruegel, I. (1979). "Women as a Reserve Army of Labour: A Note on Recent British Experience", *Feminist Review*, 3: 12–23.
Bulutay, T. (2000). "Characteristics, Dimensions and General Trends of Women's Employment", in T. Bulutay (ed.), *Employment of Women*. Ankara: State Institute of Statistics.
Çağatay, N. and Günseli, B. (1990). "Transition to Export-Led Growth in Turkey: Is There A Feminization of Employment?", *Review of Radical Political Economics*, 22(1): 115–134.
Dedeoğlu S. (2010). "Visible Hands, Invisible Women: Garment Production in Turkey", *Feminist Economics*, 16(4): 1–32.
Duncan, O.D. and Duncan, B. (1955). "A Methodological Analysis of Segregation Indexes", *American Sociological Review*, 20: 210–217.
Enloe, C. (1980). "Women – The Reserve Army of Labor." *Review of Radical Political Economics*, 12: 42–52.
Goldthorpe, J.H. (1983). "Women and Class Analysis: In Defence of the Conventional View", *Sociology*, 17(4): 465–488.
Gürsel S. and Ulusoy V. (1999). *Türkiye'de İşsizlik ve İstihdam Cogito*, Istanbul: Yapı Kredi Yayınları.

230   *Ö. İzdeş*

Humphries, J. (1988). "Women's Employment in Restructuring America: The Changing Experience of Women in Three Recessions", in J. Rubery (ed.), *Women and Recession*. London: Routledge.

İlkkaracan İ. And Selim, R. (2007). *Kamu Sektöründe Kadın-Erkek Ücret Farklılıkları, Sıtkı Özlü'ye Armağan*. D. Bayraktar, F. Cebi and B. Bolat. Istanbul, Çağlayan Basımevi.

ILO (2008). *Global Employment Trends for Youth*. Global Employment Trends.

İzdeş Ö. (2010) "The Impact of Recessions on Gendered Employment Patterns in Turkey", PhD Dissertation, Department of Economics, University of Utah.

Jenness, L., Hill, H., Reid, N.M., Lovell, F. and Davenport, S.E. (1975). *Last Hired, First Fired*. New York, NY: Pathfinder.

Kasnakoglu Z. and Dayioglu M. (1997). "Kentsel Kesimde Kadın ve Erkeklerin İşgücüne Katılımları ve Kazanç Farklılıkları", *METU Studies in Development*, 24(3): 329–361.

Kasnakoğlu, Z. and G. Dikbayır (2002). "Gender Segregation in Turkish Manufacturing Industry", *METU Studies in Development*, 29(3–4): 333–353.

KEİG (2009) *Türkiye'de Kadın Emeği ve İstihdamı Sorun Alanları ve Politika Önerileri*. Available at: www.keig.org.

Kızılırmak, B. (2005) "Labor Market Participation Decision of Married Women – Evidence from Turkey", Policy Innovations – Policy Library.

Mackay, D.I., Boddy, D., Brack, J., Diack, J.A. and Jones, N. (1971). *Labor Market Under Different Employment Conditions*. London: George Allen and Unwin.

Mies, M. (1998). *Patriarchy and Accumulation On A World Scale*. London Zed Books.

Milkman, R. (1976). "Women's Work and Economic Crisis: Some Lessons of the Great Depression", *Review of Radical Political Economics*, 8: 71–97.

Onaran, Ö. and Başlevent, C. (2003). "Are Turkish Wives More Likely to Become Added or Discouraged Workers?", *Labour*, 17(3): 439–458.

Onaran, Ö. and Başlevent, C. (2004). "The Effect of Export Oriented Growth on Female Labor Outcomes in Turkey", *World Development*, 32(8): 1375–1393.

Özar, Ş. (2000). "An International Comparative Analysis of Gender Differences in Employment. Employment of Women", in T. Bulutay (ed.), *Employment of Women*. Ankara: State Institute of Statistics, pp. 153–176.

Özler, Ş. (2000). "Export-Orientation and Female Share of Employment: Evidence from Turkey", World Development, 28(7): 1239–1248.

Rubery, J. and Tarling, R. (1988). "Women's Employment in Declining Britain", in J. Rubery (ed.), *Women and Recession*. London: Routledge.

Tansel, A. (2000). "Economic Development and Female Labor Force Participation in Turkey: Time-Series Evidence and Cross-Province Estimates", in T. Bulutay (ed.), *Employment of Women*. Ankara: State Institute of Statistics, pp. 111–153.

Tansel A. and Taşçı M. (2005). "Determinants of Unemployment Duration for Men and Women in Turkey", IZA-Conference: Fourth IZA/SOLE Transatlantic Meeting of Labor Economists Buch/Ammersee, Germany; 30 June–3 July 2005.

Taşçı M. and Özdemir A.R. (2007). "Trends in Long-Term Unemployment and Determinants of Incidence of Long-Term Unemployment in Turkey", *Journal of Economic and Social Research*, 7(2): 1–33.

Toksöz G. (2007). "Türkiye'de Kadın İstihdamının Durumu Raporu", ILO.

Tunalı, İ. (1997). "To Work or Not to Work: An examination of Labor Force Participation Rates in Urban Turkey", 4th Annual ERF Conference, Beirut.

Tzannatos, Z. (1999). "Women and Labor Market Changes in the Global Economy: Growth Helps, Inequalities Hurts and Public Policy Matters", *World Development*, 27(3): 551–569.

Van Wagner, M.J. (1993). "Are Men's Jobs Becoming Women's Jobs? Substitution and Segmentation in the U.S. Labor Force", *Review of Radival Political Economics*, 25(2): 75–84.

Voyvoda E. and Erinc Yeldan, A. (2001). "Patterns of Productivity Growth and the Wage Cycle in Turkish Manufacturing", *International Review of Applied Economics*, 15(4): 375–396.

Wright, E.O. (2000). *Class Counts*. New York, NY: Cambridge University Press.

11 Comparative regional gendered impacts of the global economic crisis on international trade and production in the developing world[1]

Jason Jackson

1 Introduction

This chapter aims to provide a conceptual, analytic and empirical basis for assessing the gender-based impact of the global financial crisis in key developing regions and countries.

Economic crises often present opportunities for reconsidering the way in which economic policy is conceptualized, particularly from the standpoint of the effects of policies on societies that are poor and marginalized. In the wake of the crisis we have seen some initial, tentative discussions that challenge orthodox approaches to economic policy, even in key international organizations such as the IMF.[2] This chapter hopes to contribute to efforts amongst heterodox economists to engage in this debate by showing how the crisis differentially affects men and women based on a location in the economy that reflects deeply entrenched and longstanding gender-based inequities.

The tools and skills to do such advocacy are particularly relevant at this time, given the penchant for responses to the crisis to reinforce rather than undermine existing inequities. Instead, what is needed are efforts to directly address issues of poverty, inequality and social marginalization.

2 The gender effects of the crisis on international trade

The main channel through which the financial crisis is being transmitted to developing countries is international trade. Most low- and middle-income developing countries are dependent on goods and services trade with industrialized countries, and so have suffered from falling demand and depressed prices for their exports as industrialized countries grapple with the recessionary effects of the crisis.

As a result, the impact of the crisis has been felt through falling economic growth and increased formal and informal sector unemployment. This impact has been coupled with very real concerns about rising food prices beginning in the period leading up to the 2008 crisis, which have had a devastating effect on nutrition and consumption in poor households. Remittances have become a critical pillar of support for many middle- and low-income developing countries, both at the macroeconomic level as a principal source of foreign exchange earnings, as well as at the household level as a contributor to poor families' budgets. However, remittance flows have been affected by the crisis as migrants themselves face the effects of the recession through job losses or retrenchment in their host countries. This constrains the ability to send money back home. Finally, most low-income countries do not have the resources to launch the types of aggressive counter-cyclical 'stimulus' packages that have been put in place in the OECD as well as some large developing countries, leaving poor households with limited access to public support for basic foods and other necessities.

A brief summary of some of the principal channels through which the impact of the crisis is being felt is provided below:

1   reduced demand and lower prices for exports across manufacturing, agriculture and service sectors, such as apparel and tourism, and collapsing commodity prices in countries that are dependent on primary goods sectors and extractive industries;
2   declining remittances which provide critical support to household budgets, particularly amongst poor women-headed households;
3   rising food prices and concerns with domestic food security;
4   falling foreign direct investment (FDI) flows as projects are postponed or cancelled due to the global credit crunch;
5   uncertain overseas development assistance (ODA) flows, as rich countries grapple with the domestic effect of the financial crisis (Antonopoulos, 2009).

Across the world both men and women are feeling the effects of the crisis, but they are experiencing these crisis effects in different ways due to their differential location in the global economy, as well as their differential social rights and responsibilities. For example, the impact of the crisis on export demand affects women and men in different ways, as the composition of the labor market in different sectors varies by gender, as well as by country and region. In general, heavy industrial and mining sectors, such as automobile component manufacturing and assembly, or copper mining, tend to be industries that primarily employ men. By contrast, light industrial assembly activities such as textiles and apparel, leather and electronics principally employ young women. This gender division of labor also carries over to the service sector. While export services such as information and communication technology (ICT) based activities such as 'back office' work provides medium-income white collar jobs to both men and women, other service sectors such as tourism have a highly gendered structure, with mainly women earning low wages as housekeepers. Similarly, the construction industry is highly cyclical but tends to provide good wages, albeit mainly to men. Across all sectors of the economy flexible and casual workers as well as migrant workers are the most vulnerable to the effects of the crisis, as they have little formal labor market protection. In addition, men and women migrate to do different types of work, especially at the low end of the wage scale – for example, construction (South Asian men in the Middle East) or domestic work/child care (South Asian women in the Middle East, EU, Asia; Pacific Island women in Australia, New Zealand), so they are likely to face different vulnerabilities associated with the different types of work that they do.

This gendered division of labor matters not only for understanding the distributional effects of the crisis, but also for devising equitable policies that take into account existing gender-based socio-economic differences so as not to reinforce existing inequities. For example, capital-intensive manufacturing sectors as well as construction tend to be the areas of focus for counter-cyclical 'stimulus' policies. This general approach holds in both developing and advanced countries, as seen in the auto industry rescue package and green building retrofit plan in the United States (US), as well as in similar programs to boost the auto industry in India. Many of these programs effectively discriminate against women by focusing on areas of economic activity where men are primarily located. This reflects a longstanding 'male breadwinner bias' in economic policy-making that is based on conceptions of men as the principal earners in nuclear families – a view that is at odds with the empirical reality of most poor households in developing countries.

Contrary to common assumptions of women as wives and mothers whose daily activities primarily consist of managing households based on incomes provided by men, women in fact often are the primary income earners in large multigenerational households. This reality places an enormous strain on women, who face a particularly heavy burden during economic crises due to their societal role as caretakers. This is worsened by pervasive socio-cultural myths about the role or women and mothers who are expected to somehow 'make do' in times of need. This is reflected in major gender-based disparities in paid and unpaid work carried out within the household, as well as in the propensity for women to engage in insecure or high-risk activities, including various forms of transactional sex, in order to ensure the survival of the family. Children are also highly vulnerable either to being withdrawn from school, or to having to enter the labor market. There are other important mechanisms: reduced remittances not only constrain household spending but can limit women's poverty and autonomy. Similarly, tight credit markets associated with the global credit crunch can trickle down to the local community level by restricting the availability of microcredit, hence further reducing women's autonomy and power in the household (Antonopoulos, 2009).

In order to recognize and address the gender effects of the crisis, the macroanalytic frameworks employed by economic policy-makers must be enlarged to include all channels of transmission of economic shocks: trade, fiscal, monetary, foreign exchange and balance of payments. The critical dimensions from a gender perspective include the location of individuals with respect to paid and unpaid work, including household work, subsistence production, and care and volunteer work within the household and wider community.

If we analyze the economy using this type of expanded gender-aware framework supported by data on employment patterns, time use and the distribution of income and poverty, it allows us to see the extent to which men and women are located in different areas of the economy, have different responsibilities, and as a result face different vulnerabilities. For example, in many cases men tend to be located in higher-paid employment with more secure wages, whether in manufacturing or services. By contrast, women tend to be disproportionately located in low-paying services, agriculture and insecure manufacturing, especially forms of manufacturing tied to maquiladoras. Finally, women are often heavily concentrated in the informal sector and in unpaid work, while men tend to be in formal sector jobs, or when engaging in unpaid subsistence labor do so with greater ownership rights to the land that is being tilled than their female counterparts. However, while these gender-based differentials are widely applicable across country contexts, it is important to note that relative positions of men and women also vary within countries, by class, race, ethnicity and the urban–rural divide. All these dimensions need to be taken into account in order to have a true gender-aware picture of the global economy and to understand the full effects of the financial crisis.

With this gender-aware analytic framework in mind, we can move on to an empirical examination of the effects of the crisis across some of the major regions of the developing world.

3 Sub-Saharan Africa

Sub-Saharan African economies have been hard hit by the crisis. Many had benefited from steady economic growth throughout much of the 2000s, but this positive trend was largely reversed with the onset of the crisis in 2008. Much of the earlier economic growth was due to the rapid rise of commodity prices (Figure 11.1). This means that the sudden contraction in global demand hit at the precise drivers of growth that had fueled optimism in sub-Saharan Africa and exposed the persistent vulnerability of the region.

The global financial crisis has revealed multiple levels of vulnerability. At the same time the crisis struck, most poor sub-Saharan African as well as South Asian and Pacific households had already been grappling with the global spike in food prices, particularly basic food grains that comprise the majority of their food consumption basket. Women and girls often bear the brunt of this double burden, as women are expected to ensure that there is adequate food provided to the household, and when there is not enough food to adequately serve all members of the household girls are often provided with less than boys.

The main channel of transmission of the crisis on the real economy has been declining international trade flows. The African Development Bank (AfDB) reported that middle-income African economies have been particularly hard hit due to their relatively deeper integration into the global economy (AfDB, 2009a). The AfDB estimated that African countries faced a massive US$251 billion shortfall in export revenue in 2009, which is expected to be followed by an even

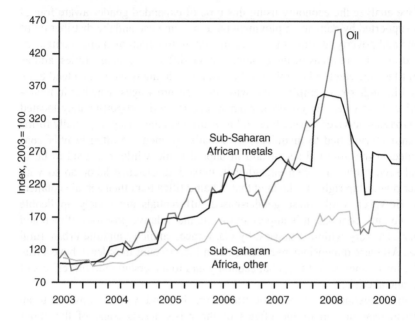

Figure 11.1 Sub-Saharan African commodity prices (source: IMF, 2009a, Figure 4).

Note
1 Other commodities (e.g. cocoa, etc.).

worse US$277 billion shortfall in 2010. In total, exports across the continent have been revised downwards by a massive 40 percent. Oil-exporting economies are expected to be worst hit, but other commodity dependent economies are also experiencing dramatic effects (ibid.).

Agricultural commodity exports have formed an important basis of economic growth and source of livelihoods for many sub-Saharan African countries. Coffee is a crucial commodity export in Uganda, as in other neighboring countries. However, coffee exports have suffered declines in both price and value, such that the value of coffee exports fell 24 percent in Q1 of 2009 relative to the same period in the prior year. In addition to the effects of the crisis, Uganda's coffee sector also faces significant internal challenges of drought and disease. Fisheries exports also suffered due to the recession, with Q2 exports falling by 37 percent. Like the coffee sector, fisheries also face important internal challenges that exacerbate the impact of the crisis, such as illegal fishing and over-fishing. High value-added export-oriented agriculture cut-flower exports have been one of the more resilient sectors in Uganda, but even this sector has seen declining albeit positive growth rates (ODI, 2010b). Women comprise more than 70 percent of the labor force in cut-flower production (Antonoupoulus, 2009). There has been good news: Uganda has seen informal cross-border trade (with its regional neighbors) grow strongly during the crisis, with non-traditional exports performing particularly well (ODI, 2010b). The value of this trade has increased by 45 percent, from US$1.07 billion to US$1.55 billion, in just one year, 2007–2008. These non-traditional exports have primarily comprised relatively high-value industrial products such as cement and steel (accounting for 65 percent), as well as some agricultural products such as beans and maize (less than 10 percent) (ODI, 2010b).

Along with agricultural commodity exports, mineral and metal commodities have been key drivers of African growth over the course of the past decade. Zambia provides an excellent case example of how some African countries have experienced rapid growth in the 2000s through metal commodity exports. Total merchandise exports increased from US$746 million to $5.1 billion. This six-fold increase was driven primarily by increased production of copper (which was privatized over the course of the decade) as well as a huge increase in the copper prices, which saw a fivefold increase from US$1,550/tonne in 2002 to US$8,714/tonne in 2008 – a clear reflection of the global commodities boom. While copper and copper-based exports are mainly headed for China and the EU, Zambia, like Uganda, has also been able to diversify its export mix to regional trading partners. Other non-traditional exports, such as sugar, cotton and tobacco, primarily serve regional markets such as South Africa and the Democratic Republic of Congo. These products are particularly important, as women comprise a much higher proportion of the workforce in these agricultural sectors than in mining.

African exports are not confined to agricultural or mineral commodities. Kenya is one of the more diversified economies in the region and has developed an important tourism sector, but tourism receipts were down 13 percent in the fourth quarter of 2008 as compared to the same period in 2007. The majority of lost employment in tourism, as well as other key sectors such as export agriculture, tends to be in low-paying jobs, such as housekeepers or informal sector farm laborers, most of which tend to be held by women. As will be seen in upcoming sections, Kenya's limited diversification and reliance on remittances, tourism and primary agricultural commodities is similar to a number of countries in other regions, such as the Caribbean and the Pacific, and women and men tend to be located in quite similar areas of the labor market and wider economy.

In addition to shocks to commodities and services exports, African countries have also suffered more direct effects of the crisis through the financial sector. Many African countries' fiscal and external account balance positions were already weakened by the food and fuel price shocks of 2007–2008 and have now been further hit by declining capital inflows from remittances, FDI and ODA (Figure 11.2).

Kenya has been hard hit by declining capital inflows. For example, in just three months, remittances in Kenya fell from US$61 million in October 2008 to US$39 million in January 2009. These have direct impacts both on macroeconomic stability, including foreign exchange reserves, as well as on Kenyan people's livelihoods, as remittances provide direct support to household budgets, particularly amongst poor women-headed households.

Vanishing liquidity in the international system has hindered governments' ability to raise capital, leading to delays (Kenya, Tanzania, Uganda, Nigeria),

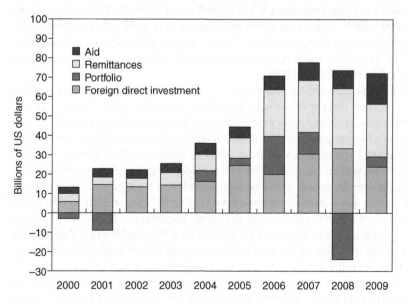

Figure 11.2 Selected financial inflows in sub-Saharan Africa, 2000–2009 (source: IMF 2009b, Figure 1.1).

cancellations (Ghana) and failure (South Africa) of various sovereign bond issues. This will have an immediate and negative effect on public expenditure programs, including infrastructure projects that would have been expected to provide significant direct and indirect employment to poor men and women. Worse, all this is happening at precisely the time when new domestic spending on jobs is most needed to counter the trade-related unemployment effects of the crisis.

The impact of government finances is particularly worrying. Overall, the Africa region is expected to move from a 2.8 percent surplus in 2008 to a 5.4 percent deficit in 2009 (AfDB, 2009a). This will have a massive and negative impact on the ability of governments to engage in counter-cyclical spending to alleviate the effects of the crisis on its people. This challenge highlights one of the key differences between most sub-Saharan African and other developing countries with limited fiscal resources, and better off developing and industrialized countries that can tap domestic resources for counter-cyclical 'stimulus' spending.

4 South Asia

The phenomenon of the feminization of the labor force is now well known and has been observed all across the developing world, but is still exemplified in many South and South-East Asian countries. The phenomenon reflects the expansion of jobs that women took up in light assembly, such as textiles and apparel, where, for example, in Malaysia and Bangladesh women comprise 78 percent and 85 percent of the workforce, respectively. However, with the crisis and contraction in global demand these are jobs that are hit hardest, and as a result women in these countries suffer disproportionately from the loss of income, as do their dependents, which often include children and the elderly.

Bangladesh is often cited as the epitome of feminization of labor, particularly in light manufacturing industry, and so provides an excellent case for under-standing the gender effects of the crisis on export manufactures. In general, Bangladesh's overall export performance in 2008 stood up well to the effects of the crisis, but the country's chief export sectors nevertheless were not immune. Export performance was volatile, and varied widely across sectors. While ready-made garment exports withstood the effects of the crisis better than expected, there were major declines in the export of other goods, such as tea, jute and especially leather, as well as smaller declines in footwear (Table 11.1). However, this performance in garments reflects strategic efforts by Bangladeshi exporters to cope with lower prices and profit margins as many tried to maintain relation-ships with powerful multinational firm buyers in developed countries. These measures include layoffs, as well as increasing working hours and lowering wages and benefits for many of the two million workers in the industry fortunate enough to keep their jobs. Most of these workers in the apparel sector are young women that already were considered to be facing difficult working conditions, and whose wages from the industry typically provide essential support to poor

Table 11.1 Declining export growth rate in major commodities in Bangladesh (2008–2009)

Export product	2008	2009	Difference 2008–2009
	%	%	%
Ready Made Garments (RMG)	31.1	2.5	−28.6
Woven RMG	25.4	1.4	−24.0
RMG	36.7	3.5	−33.2
Non-RMG	22.6	−13.2	−35.8
Raw jute	−0.7	11.7	12.4
Tea	26.9	−62.9	−89.8
Leather	−6.6	−34.3	−27.7
Jute goods	−3.5	0.8	4.3
Frozen foods	16.1	−27.5	−43.6
Chemical	46.2	−57.0	−103.2
Engineering products	−0.3	−2.0	−1.7
Home textile	15.8	0.1	−15.7
Footwear	36.9	−6.4	−43.3
Total Exports	29.0	−1.2	−30.2

Source: ODI (2010a, Table 3).

Note
* Note that these are changes in growth rates, NOT overall changes in exports by value/unit, etc.

families in rural areas. For these women, having to face the choice of reduced wages and benefits, or unemployment, reflects their weak and vulnerable position in the global industry.

Despite Bangladesh's initial resilience, by 2009 manufactured exports began to reflect the true effects of the crisis, falling by 11.7 percent in Q1 primarily due to a decline of 9.7 percent in apparel exports. Total agricultural commodity exports fell by 18.4 percent, with substantial variation by product: for example, frozen foods fell by 37.9 percent and tea exports were devastated by a 85.6 percent decline (ODI, 2010a). Bangladesh also lost export market share to major competitors, particularly China, which benefited from domestic 'stimulus' support of the type that poorer and fiscally weaker developing countries have been unable to afford. China's implementation of tax rebates and other export incentives along with price cuts and other domestic policy support allowed Chinese exporters to significantly gain market share in the EU and US at the expense of weaker producers. While Bangladesh was also able to raise its market share, it was forced to do so with far less domestic policy support to cushion the blow of lower prices and wage-cutting that characterized the response.

As in most other low-income developing countries, remittances are a major contributor to poor households' livelihoods. Bangladesh is a major exporter of labor, with the US, EU, India and especially the Middle East being the most important destinations and, as a result, the key sources of remittances. The total contribution of remittances to GDP more than doubled from 4 percent in 2000 to 11 percent in 2008. It is worth noting that these figures only account for official remittance flows transmitted through formal banking channels; they do not capture remittances sent informally, such as when persons send cash home or return with cash themselves. The greatest contributions to remittance flows by far, some 63 percent of flows in 2007, come from the Middle East. However, worryingly, this region attracts mostly low-wage workers, primarily men in the construction industry and women who engage in domestic work, and further is known for the worst treatment of migrant workers. The situation is being exacerbated by the fact that over the course of the last six to nine months there has been a marked decline in the number of Bangladeshis who are able to go overseas for work, as countries from the UAE, Saudi Arabia, Sudan, Singapore and Malaysia have cut back on visa offerings due to the slowdown in highly cyclical industries such as construction as well as other sectors that drove overall labor demand. Some countries have also begun sending Bangladeshi workers back home due to slowdowns in their economies and lack of work. Almost 40,000 workers were sent back in 2009, 97 percent due to retrenchment (ODI, 2010a). Growth in remittance flows reflected these dynamics in labor flows by showing volatile declines during the second half of 2008 onwards, before showing a small increase of 5.4 percent in the first half of 2009. It remains to be seen whether remittance flows return to their previous high growth trajectory as the slow but 'job-less' recovery proceeds in the industrialized countries.

A number of countries in South Asia faced the economic crisis in the context of serious domestic conflicts, adding a further dimension of vulnerability to women and children, particularly in poor rural households. In this respect, Sri Lanka faced a number of critical macroeconomic challenges in 2008. Like many other developing countries, Sri Lanka was hard hit by the rise in commodity and food prices in early 2008, and then was struck by capital flight with the onset of the crisis in the last quarter of the year. This period of macroeconomic instability saw the rupee coming under pressure, a sharp rise in inflation to 28 percent, and a loss of two-thirds of the Central Bank's foreign reserves. The real economy was also affected as exports declined by 5.2 percent between October 2008 and June 2009. All this was reflected in growth rates that fell sharply to 1.5 percent by the beginning of 2009.

This combination of a rapid increase in inflation and a sudden economic slowdown is devastating for poor households, as they face price increases alongside wage cuts and job losses. Better news in the form of the ending of the civil war provided a well-needed boost to the economy in mid-2009, leading to a significant capital inflows and greater stability in the foreign exchange market. However, these macroeconomic shocks occurred as the economic crisis was taking its toll on exports and production, and had a major impact on the Sri Lankan economy and livelihoods.

The Sri Lankan apparel industry faced significant uncertainty during 2008 and the first half of 2009, with some businesses appearing to avoid layoffs but most also not hiring new staff. However, given that the apparel industry is characterized by high turnover rates, this effectively meant that the industry experienced net job losses. As in Bangladesh and most other South and South-East Asian countries, up to 90 percent of Sri Lankan garment workers are young women, many from rural areas. Most of these workers already face very poor working conditions and are not unionized, illustrating how many young Sri Lankan women continue to face heightened vulnerability even when they manage to secure formal sector jobs in the cities. Men have also been disproportionately affected by industry-level effects related to the crisis. For example, the export-oriented service sector has been badly hit by the crisis, with the World Bank (2009) singling out the transshipment industry, which Sri Lanka had been trying hard to promote and which primarily employs men, as particularly hurt by the decline in international shipping. This variation in findings of the effects of the crisis on men and women highlights the need for gender-aware analysis of the crisis in order to design appropriate policy responses.

5 The Caribbean

Caribbean countries have felt the effects of the global financial crisis through the familiar mechanisms of declining export earnings, FDI, remittances and aid flows. These have been compounded by a general loss of trade credit as well as growing macroeconomic instability in some countries, particularly through increased pressure on inflation, domestic exchange rates and loss of international reserves. However, unlike many other natural resource-dependent developing countries, the Caribbean faces the crisis having seen very weak economic growth over the past ten years. The commodity price boom that many African and Pacific countries have enjoyed was not witnessed in the Caribbean. Instead, countries in the region saw generally weak and somewhat volatile growth from traditional agricultural exports, tourism, bauxite, petroleum and financial services.

Caribbean countries are highly dependent on international trade, with trade in most countries averaging up to 150 percent of GDP. Further, like most African and Pacific countries, most Caribbean member states have very narrow production structures, relying principally upon services exports such as tourism and offshore financial services, as well as agricultural and mineral commodities, principally sugar, bananas, bauxite and petroleum.

In addition, countries in the region are heavily reliant on three major trading partners – Canada, the European Union (primarily the United Kingdom) and the United States – which significantly increases their vulnerability to economic shocks. The region is also highly dependent on migrant remittances, both for supporting low-income households as well as for foreign exchange inflows and hence macroeconomic stability. As a result, the global financial crisis has had an immediate and strong negative impact on the region in terms of employment and income at the household level, as well as fiscal stability at the national level. Further, given that across the Caribbean women-headed households account for more than 50 percent of low-income households, and women tend to occupy the lowest paid and most tenuous positions in the region's main industries, the effects of the crisis have already begun to have a significant impact on women, children and the elderly.

As in other regions, women and men tend to be located in different types of activities in the Caribbean. For example, like many other middle-income developing countries, the export-oriented services sector is dominated by women. However, women are generally clustered around the lowest paying jobs, such as housekeepers in the tourism industry. Export-oriented light manufacturing in textiles and apparel was an important employer of women, particularly in Jamaica, but this industry has been on the decline in the region since the late 1980s, as the Caribbean suffered significant losses with the signing of the NAFTA trade pact between the US, Canada and Mexico, and later with the ending of the multi-fiber agreement. Similarly, export-oriented electronics assembly was an important employer of women in the Eastern Caribbean, but has also come under pressure from more competitive producers. The result of these trends in gender-based trade employment has been decreased formal sector job opportunities for low-skilled urban women, which in turn has led to greater concentration of female labor in the urban informal sector.

Education and skill level, however, remains an important feature that segments Caribbean labor markets, as skilled labor faces a significantly different opportunity set. Educational performance in the Caribbean is closely related to both social class and gender. Children from lower-income households consistently underperform their higher-income household peers. Further, despite significant gains for Caribbean women in educational achievements – women enjoy better secondary school achievement rates and now outnumber men almost two to one in tertiary educational institutions in the region – these gains have yet to be fully reflected in labor market outcomes in terms of both wages and occupational positions of women in regional firms. Services trade provides a useful example of this gendered dynamic.

Services trade is the most important area that the region has sought to promote, particularly in the context of declining income and employment in manufacturing and traditional agricultural sectors, and women have been quick to take advantage of these new opportunities. However, continued labor market discrimination has limited the gains that women might have been expected to make in newer export-oriented sectors such as offshore financial services, and has increased their vulnerability to job losses during time of crisis, despite their relatively high education and skill levels. The result is that skilled women workers in the export services industry paradoxically find themselves in a similar situation to unskilled women in export manufactures. Gender thus trumps skills in the international division of labor in important ways.

Tourism is the region's most important industry, and in fact the Caribbean is the most tourism-dependent region in the world. However, as elsewhere, the tourism industry felt the immediate impact of the recession in the industrialized countries. The region is highly dependent on the US, Canadian and European (especially UK) markets for tourism. According to recently released figures from the Caribbean Tourism Organization (CTO), every Caribbean country with the exception of Jamaica experienced sharp declines in tourist arrivals in 2009 as compared to 2008 (Table 11.2). Anguilla was the worst hit, with a devastating

Table 11.2 Caribbean tourist arrivals 2009

Destination	Tourist arrivals	Annual % change from 2008
Anguilla*	30,716	−22.6
Antigua & Barbuda	234,410	−11.8
Bahamas	1,326,722	−9.3
Barbados	518,564	−8.7
Belize	232,373	−5.2
Bermuda	235,860	−10.5
British Virgin Islands**	205,914	17.0
Cayman Islands	271,958	−10.2
Dominica***	64,402	−12.1
Grenada	113,370	−12.5
Guyana	141,053	6.2
Jamaica	1,831,097	3.6
Montserrat***	4,897	−17.1
St Lucia	278,491	−5.8
St Vincent & the Grenadines***	65,846	−11.2
Trinidad & Tobago**	251,975	−5.7

Source: Caribbean Tourism Organization, March 2010, Table 1

Notes
* Figures reflect January–June.
** Figures reflect January–July.
*** Figures reflect January–November.

24 percent drop in stay-over tourist arrivals, while several other countries in the region also experienced double-digit drops in tourist arrivals. However, in contrast to stay-over visitors, most countries in the region avoided major losses in cruise-ship passenger arrivals, though there was some important variation across countries. While Jamaica was the only country that managed to see slight (3 percent) growth in the number of stay-over visitors, perhaps due in part to an aggressive marketing campaign in its main tourism market, the United States, it nevertheless suffered the most regarding cruise-ship arrivals, which fell by 15 percent from 2008 to 2009.

These impacts have direct effects on employment in the tourism sector, which, as in other developing regions, is highly gendered, with women generally occupying the majority of positions, though these are concentrated in the low end of the income scale. For example, poor women in the tourism industry tend to be dependent on low-wage labor in the hotels, and so are highly vulnerable to fluctuations in stay-over arrivals. For example, Clegg (2009) reports that the Bahamas' largest private sector employer laid off 800 workers, amounting to 10 percent of its staff, the majority of whom can be expected to have been women housekeepers. By contrast, cruise-ship passengers primarily patronize taxis, restaurants and duty-free shops (as well as craft merchants), which are comprised of occupations with a much different gender balance. Most taxi drivers are low- to middle-income men, while restaurants and duty-free stores tend to be owned by the wealthy and hire low-middle income women and men as staff. There are few places in this part of the industry's structure for low-skill, low-income women who are similar to those who find opportunities in hotel housekeeping.

As in other developing regions, remittance inflows have also suffered due to the crisis. The region is highly dependent on remittances, with these flows amounting to 23 percent and 16 percent of GDP in Guyana and Jamaica, respectively (Clegg, 2009). As elsewhere, remittances play two key roles: first, they have become a critical source of foreign exchange and hence are pivotal in maintaining macroeconomic stability (in the case of Jamaica, remittances are the most important source of hard currency inflows); and second, remittances provide crucial support to poor households, the majority of which are women-headed in the Caribbean. Initial indications suggest that growth of remittance flows has been severely curtailed in the wake of the crisis. This is a major concern for countries like Jamaica, where remittances have been credited as one of the leading factors in the slow decline in poverty through the 1990s and 2000s. Once again, this is an area where women are expected to shoulder a heavy burden of adjustment arising from the economic crisis.

Caribbean countries have also suffered some direct effects of the financial crisis due to weak financial sector regulation and contagion. Notwithstanding the aforementioned gender-based biases in the industry, the growth of the Caribbean offshore finance sector represented something of a success story in the 1990s and early 2000s but began to come under pressure in recent years due to OECD tax avoidance measures. Financial services trade in this sector was directly impacted by the financial crisis in parent companies in Canada, the US and the UK, as well as well as by the collapse of major regional financial institutions in the Caribbean, such as the locally-owned Caribbean Life Insurance Company (CLICO), based in

Trinidad and Tobago, and the US-based Stanford financial empire, which had major operations in Antigua and Barbuda. The effect of the collapse of Stanford's operations on the Antiguan economy has been especially devastating, as Stanford was the largest private employer in the country, directly employing 5 percent of the country's labor force and indirectly supporting many more.

Finally, as elsewhere, the impact of the crisis on trade and the productive sector in the region, as well as on financial inflows, has negatively impacted the fiscal position of many countries. Further, most Caribbean countries are highly indebted and, with the exception of Guyana, have not been eligible for debt relief. For example, Grenada, Jamaica and St Kitts have public sector debt-to-GDP ratios of well over 100 percent and face severe fiscal constraints, while several other countries, such as Barbados, Belize, Guyana, St Lucia and St Vincent, have debt-to-GDP ratios that are dangerously close to the 100 percent mark. As a result, countries suffer from a significant debt overhang that acts as a major impediment for governments to engage in social sector spending, and in the context of the crisis severely limits the ability to engage in counter-cyclical spending (Lewis-Bynoe, 2009; CDB, 2008). The combination of this precarious fiscal position and the onset of the financial crisis has taken its toll on some countries, as Jamaica has been forced to enter into negotiations with the IMF, and other countries in the region have sought assistance through lending facilities from regional development banks. Past experience provides an ominous guide to the likely effects of IMF-led macroeconomic programs on poor vulnerable households in Jamaica, most of which are headed by women.

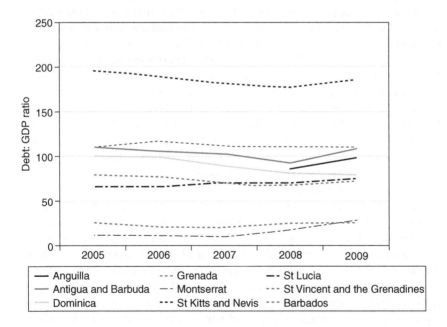

Figure 11.3 Public debt: GDP ratios in selected Caribbean countries (source: IMF).

6 The Pacific

As in much of sub-Saharan Africa, a number of countries in the Pacific have enjoyed relatively strong growth based on commodity exports, remittances and tourism over the course of the decade. However, as in other developing countries with narrow production structures, the vulnerabilities of this growth path and weak and uneven underlying social conditions is being exposed by the financial crisis. For example, the Solomon Islands has benefited significantly over the past several years from strong demand, but is expected to suffer heavily due to over-reliance on the logging industry, which provides a massive 70 percent of the country's export revenue and 40 percent of government revenue. Recent analysis by the Asian Development Bank (ADB) suggests that while some countries such as Papua New Guinea may be able to draw on resources accrued during the commodity boom, others such as Kiribati, the Solomon Islands and Tuvalu, with much weaker economic bases, are expected to be especially hard hit as they have limited ability to engage in domestic spending to boost growth or provide adequate social safety nets (ADB, 2009). As a result of the crisis and these existing weaknesses, UNICEF (2009) argues that in the Pacific region women and children are likely to be disproportionately impacted by declining income and rising food and fuel prices, given their heightened vulnerability.

It is important to note that wealthier Pacific countries have not been immune to the effects of the crisis. New Zealand and Australia both entered recession in Q4 2008, largely through the same mechanism that has affected developing economies: collapsing prices and demand for commodities. Besides major shocks to mineral exports in Australia, particularly coal and iron ore, both Australia and New Zealand also faced up to a 31 percent decline in prices of agricultural commodities such as milk and wool (UNICEF, 2009). As a result, the Pacific Islands' linkages with the larger economies of Australia and New Zealand often insulate the former countries from economic shocks, but the negative effect of the crisis on commodity-exporting Australia, for example, is likely to limit the extent to which the impact of the crisis on the region might be mitigated by its larger, more economically diversified neighbors. The effects of the crisis are likely to be compounded by the fact that many countries in the region have limited capacity to prepare for the crisis by adjusting macroeconomic policy and devising social safety nets, thus leaving poor households especially vulnerable to the effects of the downturn.

Most Pacific Island states, including the Cook Islands, Fiji, Samoa and Vanuatu, are heavily dependent on tourism receipts for foreign exchange earning, as well as for employment, incomes and supporting livelihoods. As in the Caribbean, however, the industries in these countries have been badly affected by the recession in the principal tourism markets of Australia, Canada, China, Europe, New Zealand, Taiwan and the US. Some tourism markets in the region have been further affected by their vulnerability to natural disasters. Samoa and Tonga both experienced tsunamis in 2009, which, in addition to reduced travel as a result of the crisis, further depressed tourism earnings. The loss of tourism earnings in the Pacific affects women in both the formal and informal sectors through retrenchment from hotels and other tourism-related service jobs, as well women's earnings from sale of handicrafts and other informal sector marketing activities that are associated with the sector (UNDP, 2010). The interaction of these countries' vulnerability to natural disasters and economic shocks, and the resulting effect on women and poor households, highlights the need for a holistic analysis of development challenges facing other developing countries. This is especially clear in Pacific, South Asian and Caribbean countries that have experienced major natural disasters over the past few years.

Food and nutrition has emerged as a particularly important issue in the region. In Papua New Guinea 85 percent of the population relies on agriculture, but at the same time 29 percent are undernourished. In the Solomon Islands and Vanuatu 80 percent of the population lives in subsistence, but with high reliance on rice, which has seen steady price increases. Low nutritional levels have important intergenerational effects that can lead to the persistence of poverty across generations, including stunting, lower cognitive ability and increased likelihood of under-performing or dropping out of school (UNICEF, 2009), which in turn has effects on future labor market prospects and, critically, the ability for households to transcend structural poverty. Further, in many Pacific Island countries up to 50 percent of household expenditure goes towards purchasing food, even in rural areas where most families are engaged in subsistence farming (ibid.). This suggests that the subsistence sector is no longer sufficient for nutritional, health or educational needs.

Urban migration does not appear to provide an easy route out of rural deprivation in the Pacific. Data on the Pacific Islands suggest that urban and rural poverty are at similarly high levels, as opposed to other developing countries, where rural poverty tends to be significantly worse. UNICEF (2009) suggests that urban citizens are not able to increase their standard of living given the available opportunities. As a result, urban and rural households are presented with limited options to escape poverty.

Prospects for young people hoping to improve their life opportunities by entering the formal labor market appear similarly dim. Many Pacific Island economies face high youth unemployment, of up to 20 percent, amongst both men and women. Much of this is due to unavailability of jobs but also, in some cases, to a mismatch of skills. For example, in Fiji every year half of the 15,000 school-leavers join the ranks of the unemployed; at same time, Fiji recruits 6,000 skilled workers because its own students lack appropriate skills and qualifications as schools do not train students to meet industry standards (UNICEF, 2009).

These challenges facing poor households raise important questions about sources of support, particularly in the context of the weak fiscal capacities of most governments in the region. This is becoming evident not only in terms of general social safety net support around food and nutrition, but also in the area of health. For example, the crisis is having an immediate impact on HIV/AIDS services. Papua New Guinea (PNG) reports a 75 percent cut in budget for HIV programs due to loss of ODA. Given the well-established role that women play as care-givers in households, especially when household members are ill, such a drastic cut in public sector support will almost certainly place an enormous burden on Papuan women, particularly those in poor and overcrowded house-holds. UNICEF (2009) notes that many Pacific Island societies boast strong local institutions based on care and redistribution within an extended family network that forms the basis of traditional social support systems. However, many of these systems rely on disproportionate contributions from women, as revealed in recent Pacific time-use surveys (UNDP, 2008, 2010).

Finally, even some apparently good economic news can have its downside. Inflation in the region is generally falling, mainly due to falling fuel costs. However, this general trend can mask important country-level developments. For example, the Fijian dollar was recently devalued by 20 percent in an effort to make the country more competitive in the tourism market. However, this strategy has potential costs, as devaluation may result in a rise in inflation that can negatively affect the poor through increased costs of food and fuel. Women are likely to be particularly affected, given their responsibilities for the household budget.

7 Summary and conclusions

This chapter has highlighted specific trade-related mechanisms through which the global financial crisis has affected countries across major regions of the develop-ing world, and how these effects have specific gender dimensions, many of which lead to women bearing a disproportionate share of the burden. It has further dem-onstrated that there are significant similarities across developing regions and coun-tries in the manner in which the economic crisis has affected local economies and livelihoods, and in particularly how it has affected – and will likely continue to affect – women and women-headed households. There are also, however, import-ant differences arising from the domestic economic structures and principal areas of economic activity, particularly as they pertain to trade.

The key trade-related mechanisms have been contracting demand and falling commodity prices, significant declines in tourism as well as reduced growth in remittances and weakened fiscal positions, the latter two of which undermine the scope for public sector support to poor and vulnerable households, most of which are headed by women. The chapter thus provides an initial conceptual and analytic basis for deeper discussion of the gender effects of the financial crisis across the developing world.

Notes

1 This chapter is a revised version of a draft presented at the Annual Conference for Development and Change held in Johannesburg, South Africa, in April 2010. This work is based on research conducted for the Commonwealth Secretariat and UN Women (Barbados and the Eastern Caribbean). I would like to thank Roberta Clarke, Esther Eghobamien, Donna St Hill and Aziza Ahmed for helpful comments and sug-gestions. The work represents my own views.
2 Note, for example, the issuance of a number of policy briefs by senior IMF economists along with the apparent reversal of the official IMF position on the use of capital con-trols. See Rodrik (2010) for further discussion.

Bibliography

African Development Bank (AfDB) (2009a) 'Impact of the Crisis on African Economies – Sustaining Growth and Poverty Reduction: African Perspectives and Recommendations to the G20', 21 March 2009. www.afdb.org (accessed 21 February 2010).

African Development Bank (AfDB) (2009b) 'Soaring Food Prices and Africa's Vulnerability and Responses: An Update', July, 2009. www.afdb.org (accessed 21 February 2010).

Antonopolous, Rania (2009) 'The Current Economic and Financial Crisis: A Gender Perspective', Working Paper No. 562, The Levy Economics Institute of Bard College.

Asian Development Bank (2009) 'Taking the Helm: A Policy Brief on a Response to the Global Economic Crisis', www.adb.org (accessed 20 February 2010).

Caribbean Development Bank (2008) 'Report on the Seminar on the Global Financial Crisis and the Caribbean: Impact and Response', Caribbean Development Bank.

Clegg, Peter (2009) 'The Caribbean and the Global Financial Crisis: Implications for Domestic Politics and Foreign Policy', 1 May 2009. http://americas.sas.ac.uk/events/docs/EconomicCrisisPapers/Clegg.pdf (accessed 19 February 2010).

Draper, Peter and Gilbert Biacuna (2009) 'Africa and the Trade Crisis', 27 November 2009. www.voxeu.org/index.php?q=node/4268 (accessed 21 February 2010).

International Monetary Fund (IMF) (2009a) 'Impact of the Global Financial Crisis on Sub-Saharan Africa', African Department. www.imf.org (accessed 21 February 2010).

International Monetary Fund (IMF) (2009b) 'Sub-Saharan Africa: Weathering the Storm', World Economic and Financial Surveys, Regional Economic Outlook. www.imf.org (accessed 1 March 2010).

Lewis-Bynoe, Denny (2009) 'The Global Financial Crisis and the Caribbean: Impact and Responses', 5 August 2009. www.caribank.org (accessed 18 February 2010).

Morrison, Dennis (2009) 'Impact of the Financial Crisis in the Caribbean: Tourism and Bauxite'. www.caa.com.bb/2009_Presentations/Impact_of_the_Financial_Crisis_in_the_Caribbean_Dennis_Morrison.pdf (accessed 16 February 2010).

Overseas Development Institute (2010a) 'Paper 12 Bangladesh Phase 2', Global Financial Crisis Discussion Series. www.odi.org.uk/resources/download/4719.pdf (accessed 22 February 2010).

Overseas Development Institute (2010b) 'Paper 21 Uganda Phase 2', Global Financial Crisis Discussion Series. www.odi.org.uk/resources/download/4719.pdf (accessed 22 February 2010).

Rodrik, Dani (2010) 'The End of an Era in Finance', Comment: Project Syndicate. www.project-syndicate.org/commentary/rodrik41/English.

UNDP (2008) 'Making Invisible Work More Visible: Gender and Time Use Surveys with a Focus on the Pacific and Unpaid Care Work', UNDP Pacific Centre, February 2008. www.undp.org (accessed 17 February 2010).

UNDP (2010) 'Economic Crisis and Unpaid Care Work in the Pacific', Pacific Conference on the Human Face of the Global Economic Crisis, February 10, 2010. www.undp.org (accessed 19 February 2010).

UNICEF (2009) 'Protecting Pacific Island Children and Women During Economic and Food Crises.' www.unicef.org (accessed 19 February 2010).

World Bank (2009) 'Sri Lanka Economic Update', September 2009. http://siteresources.worldbank.org/SRILANKAEXTN/Resources/233046–1237173995853/SLEconomicUpdateOctober202009.pdf (accessed 19 February 2010).

Part V

The scenario for big developing states

The case of South Africa

12 The impact of the global financial crisis on the South African economy

Seeraj Mohamed

1 Introduction

The South African economy was in a state of crisis before the global financial crisis. The official unemployment rate has remained well over 20 per cent over the past decade. Employment has declined in manufacturing, indicating de-industrialization of the economy. Services employment grew, but this growth was not due to growth in productive services but instead seems to have been driven by acceleration in debt-driven consumption, outsourcing and growth in private security services.

The South African gross domestic product (GDP) grew at around 5 per cent per annum from 2004 to 2007 (see Figure 12.1). This growth was accompanied by increased employment and investment. However, not all growth in GDP, investment and employment is good for a country. This chapter argues that an

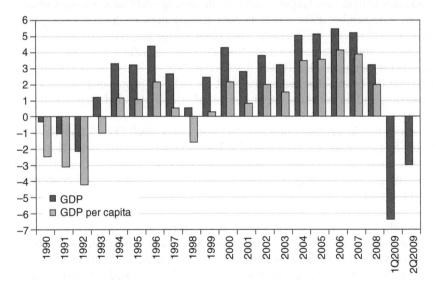

Figure 12.1 Annual percentage changes in GDP and GDP per capita (2000 prices) (source: SARB).

important lesson of this short period of relatively high economic growth in South Africa is that one has to consider the quality of economic growth and the type of employment and investment associated with this growth. In other words, we have to examine the causes of economic growth, the types of jobs created and investment. When we move beyond the assumption that all economic growth is good for an economy, we can begin to understand that an economy growing at 5 per cent per annum can be performing poorly. The South African economy was in crisis, even though GDP grew at around 5 per cent per annum from 2004 to 2007. The global financial crisis, which was set off by the collapse of the US subprime market in late 2007, hastened the onset of job losses and economic decline.

The global financial crisis and economic recession hastened decline in the growth rate to 3.1 per cent in 2008 and a recession in 2009. According to Statistics South Africa's *Quarterly Labour Force Survey*, there was a decrease of employment of 770,000 people (5.6 per cent) from the third quarter of 2008 to the third quarter of 2009 (see Figure 12.2). During this period the number of people classified as 'not economically active' increased by almost 1.1 million and more than half (0.56 million) of these were classified as 'discouraged work-seekers'. Manufacturing production decreased by nearly 20 per cent from April 2008 to April 2009, while services sectors, particularly retail trade, declined and lost jobs.

Home foreclosures and car repossessions grew substantially during the first half of 2009. The National Credit Regulator (NCR) reported in September 2009 that it expected 150,000 consumers to be under debt review by Christmas 2009. It said that there were about 100,000 consumers undergoing debt counselling in September 2009; these 100,000 consumers owed R20 billion, of which R12 billion was in home mortgages. Therefore, the average debt for consumers under review in September 2009 was R200,000. Clearly most of the people entering financial debt review were middle class, since a large proportion of poor South Africans do not have access to credit from the large financial institutions – and if they did they would not be allowed that level of debt.[1] It is also worth keeping in mind that the figures reported by the NCR are only for people undergoing debt counselling and do not show the true extent of middle-class indebtedness in the country.

So how did the economy manage to sink so low so fast? The *10 Year Review* put out by the Presidency in October 2003 sounded an optimistic note. This said that the government's economic policies had saved the economy from a fiscal crisis and put the economy on a path towards more investment and economic growth. It said:

> South Africa has achieved a level of macroeconomic stability not seen in the country for 40 years. These advances create opportunities for real increases in expenditure on social services, reduce the costs and risks for all investors, and therefore lay the foundation for increased investment and growth
>
> (The Presidency, 2003)

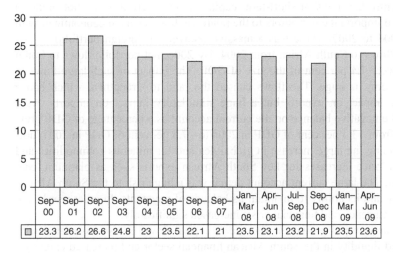

	Sep–00	Sep–01	Sep–02	Sep–03	Sep–04	Sep–05	Sep–06	Sep–07	Jan–Mar 08	Apr–Jun 08	Jul–Sep 08	Sep–Dec 08	Jan–Mar 09	Apr–Jun 09
☐	23.3	26.2	26.6	24.8	23	23.5	22.1	21	23.5	23.1	23.2	21.9	23.5	23.6

Figure 12.2 Official unemployment rates (source: StatsSA, drawing on their revised LFS 2000–2007 and QLFS 2008–2009).

The fact that the drafters of the *10 Year Review* believed that there was macroeconomic stability in the economy during 2003 shows that they had adopted a neoliberal perspective on economic policy. Within this perspective, macroeconomic stability is defined as maintaining a low government budget deficit (or preferably a surplus) and low levels of inflation. The authors of the *10 Year Review* seem to have forgotten the currency crisis during 2001, when the rand depreciated by 35 per cent relative to the US dollar. The South African Reserve Bank responded by pushing up interest rates by 4 per cent within a year. The impact of the increase in interest rates was increased unemployment. The official, narrow measure of unemployment grew from 23.3 per cent in September 2000 to 26.2 per cent in September 2001 and 26.6 per cent in September 2002. GDP annual growth dropped from 4.2 per cent in 2000 to 2.7 per cent in 2001, recovered to 3.7 per cent in 2002, and declined to 3.1 per cent in 2003. The authors of the *10 Year Review* let their neoliberal ideological blinkers blind them to all that recent macroeconomic instability.

The early 2000s were also remarkable because of the volatility in global financial markets as a result of the dotcom crisis. Capital fled equity markets in the US, and went in search of high returns in real estate, subprime and securitized debt markets to set up conditions for the next financial crisis. The impact of the dotcom bubble was felt in South African markets. The 2001 currency crisis was caused by the huge foreign investment portfolio outflows during 2000 that became panicked flight of capital in 2001. The volatility in the South African economy was a result of largely uncontrolled movement of short-term capital flows into and out of the economy. The massive depreciation of the rand to the US dollar had a huge impact on the inflation rate because of the higher rand cost of imports, such as oil. The SARB responded with interest rate hikes, and unemployment grew.

Uncontrolled flows of short-term capital (often referred to as 'hot money') were also important contributors to the relatively high levels of economic growth from 2004 to 2007. There was a massive recovery in foreign portfolio investment inflows to South Africa from 2004. By 2006, net portfolio flows to South Africa were 7.4 per cent of the size of GDP. The impact of such large flows in the economy is huge. The flows caused the rand to strengthen, which had a negative impact on exports but a huge stimulatory impact on imports. As a result, the negative balance on the current account as a percentage of GDP grew rapidly from −3.4 per cent of GDP in 2004 to −7.3 per cent of GDP in 2007, notwithstanding the large increase in global demand for minerals commodities and the large price increases for key South African exports such as platinum, coal and gold. The large current account deficit was a huge risk to the South African economy and its ability to maintain its balance of payments. In other words, the risk of a currency and financial crisis increased significantly.

The large, rapid growth in short-term capital flows is also associated with increased liquidity in the South African financial sector and increased extension of credit to the private sector. This increased credit was not used for long-term productive investment, but instead was associated with increased debt-driven consumption and speculation in financial and real estate markets. The huge increases in household debt (Figure 12.3) and the increased investment and employment in the retail and wholesale services sector were due to the increased credit extension made possible by increased hot money flows into the economy.

An impact of the process of global financialization was that events in financial markets shaped developments in the real sector. The debt-driven, consumption-led economic growth in South Africa was driven by increased inflows of short-term capital. At the same time, the South African financial

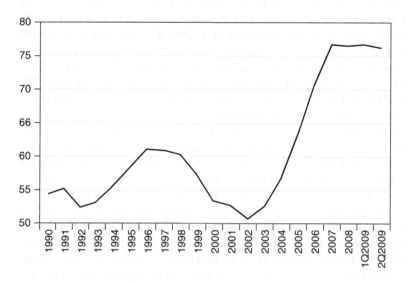

Figure 12.3 Household debt to disposable income (ratio) (source: SARB).

sector was emulating the behaviour of its US counterpart. It increased leverage and loosened lending conditions. It increasingly securitized debt and extended more debt for mortgages, car finance and consumption, and there was very rapid growth in derivatives markets. The South African large corporations had also become increasingly financialised. They seemed to follow the global trend where increasing product market competition caused many corporations to earn a larger share of their revenues and profits from financial activities and speculating in financial assets. The SARB's flow of funds data shows that the South African corporate sector was speculating more in financial markets than it was investing in fixed investment.

The broader context for these economic events in South Africa is the industrial structural weaknesses of the economy and massive changes in corporate structure that have occurred in the South African economy since the end of apartheid. The industrial structural weaknesses stemmed from the development of the economy around mining and minerals or the minerals and energy complex (MEC, as argued by Fine and Rustomjee, 1996). Much of the change in corporate structure occurred because of big businesses' responses to democracy. The global context was one of increasing financialization of non-financial corporations. This process led to massive global corporate restructuring and increased concentration of the global economy. The process influenced the change in South African corporate structure. The global process of concentration entrenched and deepened the existing global division of labour between the rich countries of the North and the developing countries of the South. In general, rich countries controlled global economic value chains and the design, engineering, branding and distribution of products. The developing countries were usually involved in either assembly manufacturing or providing low-cost agricultural or minerals inputs into the global value chains. The corporate restructuring in South Africa began a reversal of previous industrialization in South Africa. The economy was left more concentrated and more dependent on the mining and minerals sectors. These developments had a significantly negative impact on workers in South Africa.

The short period of growth at around 5 per cent per annum from 2004 to 2007 blinded many South African economists and economic policy-makers to the crisis that was unfolding. The current financial crisis provides an excuse for the poor performance and high job losses in the economy. On the whole, I believe that this short period of high growth from 2004 to 2007 has left the economy poorer. The decision to adopt neoliberal economic policies, particularly macroeconomic and financial policies, has had a huge negative impact on South Africa. It has allowed short-term financial flows to create macroeconomic instability that destroys industry and jobs. It has allowed the misallocation capital towards speculation and bubbles in financial and real estate markets, and away from long-term, job-creating productive investment. The relatively little fixed investment that has occurred is largely in services sectors linked to increased speculation in financial and real estate markets and the growth in debt-driven consumption.

2 Industrial structural weaknesses and corporate restructuring

South African economic development occurred around the mining and minerals sectors or a minerals and energy complex (Fine and Rustomjee, 1996). The state and mining industry supported growth of manufacturing sectors with strong linkages to the minerals and energy complex (MEC). According to Fine and Rustomjee, the formation of the MEC was a result of the political compromise between large English mining interests and the Afrikaner large business and political establishment. It was also shaped by the politics of oppression of black South Africans and the strict control over black workers.

Most manufacturing sectors with weaker linkages to the MEC have remained weak and have not received strong state support and adequate investment from the large mining finance houses that dominated the South African economy until the 1980s. With the exception of a few sectors, such as automobiles and components, manufacturing remains dominated by sectors with strong links to the MEC. These sectors, with the exception of engineering and capital equipment, are capital- and energy-intensive process industries, such as electricity generation, minerals beneficiation (iron and steel, aluminum) and the Sasol oil from coal processing and its chemical byproducts. Downstream, value-added manufacturing sectors have not been adequately developed and manufacturing remains relatively undiversified. The structure of the economy would undergo further change with the transition to democracy in South Africa and be shaped by changes in the global economy.

Many leaders of big business were uncomfortable with the democratic transition in South Africa.[2] The change in government was accompanied by massive restructuring of the South African corporate sector. I argue that the transition to democracy is one reason for the corporate restructuring. However, the shape of the corporate restructuring was influenced by important changes in the global economy.

Two significant changes occurred in the global economy during the 1990s. The first was the rise to prominence of institutional investors and the shareholder value movement.[3] The growth to prominence of institutional investors and the shareholder value movement was part of the process of financialization that had started in the 1970s.

Crotty (2002) says that the rise of institutional investors in the US led to a situation where on average US stocks are held for just one year. In addition, an increasing share of industrial company revenues is from financial, not productive, assets. The second change was the surge in merger and acquisition activity during the 1990s. There are a number of reasons for this global restructuring that concentrated global businesses and caused them to focus on core businesses. The prominence of institutional investors and the shareholder value movement was central to this restructuring, because institutional investors demanded simpler structures. Much of the funds for the new global giants was sourced from institutional investors, who invested most of their funds into big companies that have familiar brands, large market share, high R&D spending and focus on their core activities.

Both these changes to the global economy had profound impacts on the structure of the South African corporate sector. Since 1994, the South African corporate sector has engaged in the following activities:

- conglomerate unbundling and restructuring;
- consolidation within sectors by conglomerates as part of ensuring stronger focus and better strategic direction, which has also increased concentration;
- internationalization, mostly outward, by firms which moved their primary listing overseas, and foreign acquisitions by South African listed firms; and
- black economic empowerment deals, first, through special purpose vehicles for financing and second, more recently, in areas where government policy has provided a specific impetus.

Nolan (2003) points out that total global mergers activity grew from over US$150 billion in 1992 to over US$2,000 billion in 1998, when eight of the world's ten largest mergers took place. By 2000, it had peaked at over $3.4 trillion. Large South African companies were caught up in this process of global restructuring. The offshore listing of major South African corporations from 1997 can be seen within the context of this merger frenzy. The result was a spectacular growth in M&A activity in South Africa. According to Ernst and Young data, there was an increase from 136 M&A deals in 1994 to a peak of 605 in 1998. There was an average of 530 M&As from 1999 to 2002. According to Ernst and Young, in 1991 South African M&A activity was R12 billion and by 2001 M&A activity peaked at R502 billion (see Figure 12.4).

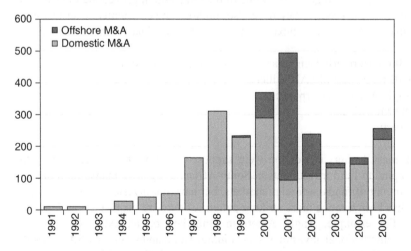

Figure 12.4 South African Mergers and Acquisitions (Rbn, current prices) (source: Ernst and Young (2006)).

Most of the pyramid structures, which were at the centre of the MEC as a system of accumulation and were used by the powerful families to control most of the South African economy, were restructured and disentangled. Global markets were restructured and market share was being reapportioned. The wealthy and powerful in South Africa did not want to be left out of this process. They wanted not only to ensure that they got their share of the international market in minerals by internationalizing their operations, but also to consolidate and secure the viability of their South African assets.

At the same time, South Africa was undergoing a transition from apartheid to democracy and there was contestation about the future economic policy of the country. The changes in South Africa meant that many of the wealthy and the large corporations wanted to move their assets out of reach of the new government. The restructuring of global assets and the transition to democracy provided important reasons for the move by a number of large corporations to move their primary listings. Studies show that capital flight had continued to be high throughout the 1990s, indicating that wealthy South Africans wanted to increase their wealth offshore.[4] A company that moved its primary listing offshore would be able to move a large amount of capital out of South Africa legally, because it would not be bound by exchange control restrictions on residents. Large amounts of capital could leave the country in the form of dividends or other payments.

A number of large South African corporations have moved their primary listing offshore to the London Stock Exchange since the late 1990s. This move has turned former South African corporations into foreign investors in South Africa. Some have opted for joint listings on the JSE and developed country stock markets. Common reasons provided for these delistings by the 'delisters' are that they allowed the companies to be valued in a hard currency, reduced the risk premium for changes in the value of the rand, and improved their expansion capability. In the process they have also modified the conglomerate structure to clear up cross-holdings. Companies that moved their primary listings include:

- Billiton (formerly Gencor and now part of BHP Billiton);
- SAB (Now part of SAB Miller);
- Anglo American Corporation;
- Old Mutual; and
- Liberty

The primary listings in London were supposed to allow the conglomerates to raise capital to fund investments in South Africa. They have managed to raise a large amount of funds in foreign markets, but have not invested in South Africa. There has been a much more striking pattern of outward acquisition and investments. For example, Anglo American embarked on an extensive drive to increase international investments in mining. Companies such as SAB, Sasol, Sappi and Kumba have also been involved in acquisitions of firms in Europe, South America, Australia and China.

The offshore listings have allowed the captains of industry that live and work as businessmen in both the global North and South Africa to change their power relationship with the new South African state. They are able to control the South African assets that they wish to control, but also have more control over the movement of their capital. The South African state has not interfered in these companies because they feared that they would lose credibility with other potential investors and financiers.

The changes also meant that the shareholder value movement in the North (including flighty institutional investors) and the business media that claim to present their views have had more influence over the major corporations operating in South Africa and also in the future direction of the economy. At the same time, the South African government has become hesitant about implementing progressive economic policies that could address unemployment and poverty for fear that these policies would drive down share prices and create a negative view of South African policies in international financial markets and business media.

The result of the offshore listings was that many large South African corporations were no longer South African, and that they were investing capital produced in South Africa over the past 150 years to expand their internationalized corporations. It is worth remembering that much of that capital was generated in exploiting the non-renewable mineral wealth of South Africa and in harsh exploitation of South African workers. Many of the businesses that listed offshore and become global corporations had been involved in extensive merger and acquisition activity. Through these M&As, their South African assets have decreased as a proportion of their total assets. They have diluted their South African identities and, with this, the size of their supposed responsibilities towards the new South Africa and development there.

These corporations strenuously advocated lifting exchange controls and argued for their right to list offshore. The central point of these arguments was that they would then be able to raise capital more easily to invest in South Africa. Clearly, the opposite was true. Roberts *et al.* (2003) correctly argue:

> In five of the last ten years outward direct investment has in fact exceeded inward FDI. Major foreign investments have largely been limited to the acquisition of stakes in state-owned utilities (Telkom and South African Airways) and the re-entry of firms such as Toyota and General Motors which had exited under sanctions, although specific examples exist of sectors where foreign companies have contributed to the resumption of growth.
>
> (Roberts *et al.*, 2003)

The unbundling of the conglomerates and the 'rebundling' should be considered within the context of both the political and the global factors affecting these businesses. The combination of the unease of white business with the changes in South Africa and the understanding of the leaders of big business that they had to signal a willingness to share future business activities with black people put two types of pressure on big business to restructure: the first was restructuring for political expediency; the second was directly linked to withdrawing from the South African economy. In other words, big business had adapted to the political changes by reducing its risk within the South African economy by internationalizing their operations. They also accepted a political compromise to maintain their control over much of the South African economy by sharing a portion of ownership with black businesses.

Goldstein's (2001: 15) interpretation of this process is:

> While the refocusing on core business has followed from the need to insure competitiveness against the background of the opening of the domestic economy to world competition and weaker gold and commodity prices, voluntary unbundling has been a expedient strategy to appease the possible rise of nationalization sentiments. The first such deal was Sanlam's sale of Metropolitan Life (METLIFE), an insurance company, to New Africa Investment Ltd (NAIL). In 1996 Anglo broke up its majority-owned sub-holding JCI (Johannesburg Consolidated Investment) into platinum (Amplats), a homonymous mining subsidiary, and an industrial arm.
>
> (Johnnic Holdings Ltd)

Goldstein recognizes that global and domestic factors shaped the behaviour of South African big business. Further, Goldstein's research indicates that the boom in merger and acquisitions in South Africa during the 1990s was different to those in other countries. He shows that there were particularly South African characteristics to the M&As. The restructuring in South Africa was more about dismantling pyramid structures than increasing the competitiveness of industrial sectors. Goldstein says:

> Of the twenty largest South African deals reported in 1992–1998, 75% corresponds to the simplification of the corporate structure; 10% to consolidation in the financial industry; 10% to foreign acquisitions; and only one deal – TransNatal's acquisition of Rand Coal to form Ingwe Coal in 1994 – is a "genuine" South African merger.
>
> Goldstein (2001: 17)

He makes the important point that it is remarkable that South African conglomerates have practically not made any large acquisitions in their own country. He points out that this lack of acquisition is true even in sectors such as utilities and Internet-related investments '...where family-controlled business groups in OECD countries have been active even while refocusing their portfolios on the core business' (ibid.).

The South African context for mergers and acquisitions was one where the MEC continued to stifle investments into diversifying the industrial base of the South African economy. Instead, the concern of big businesses that dominated the MEC was to restructure in order to appear more attractive to investors speculating in the markets where they had relisted.

3 Financialization of the South African economy

The South African financial system had developed along similar lines to that of the English and US systems, and can be described as market-based rather than bank-based (Roux, 1991). In other words, South African businesses that require finance for long-term investment would use retained earnings or seek finance in the securities markets. The state-owned Industrial Development Corporation does provide some industrial finance, but on the whole its lending is a very small share of total lending in the country and its main customers have been large, capital-intensive projects in the mining and minerals sectors (Roberts, 2007). The banks and other monetary institutions largely provided business with short-term operating capital and serviced the credit card, home mortgage, vehicle lease and finance, and other short-term lending for consumption.

Figure 12.5 shows that during the period 1990–2008 this form of credit allocation continued in the economy. One can see the growth in mortgage advances from 2003 to 2008, which supported the growth of a housing price bubble in the relatively more affluent real estate market in South Africa. South Africa has had average house price increases larger than the US during the period 2003–2007. For the period 1990–2008 we see that investment was a relatively very small share of total private sector credit extension.

An important phenomenon in the global economy and South Africa is financialization, as the size and influence of the financial sector grew from the 1980s

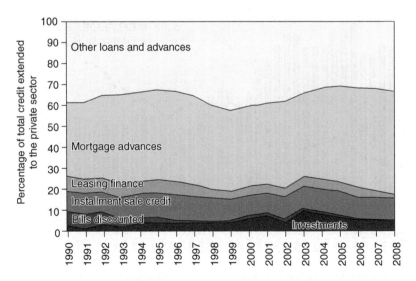

Figure 12.5 Private sector credit extension by all monetary institutions by type (percentages of total) (source: calculated using SARB data).

when financial markets and cross-border capital flows were liberalized. The market-based banking system and banking deregulation by the apartheid state during the 1980s seemed to have supported growth of the South African financial sector. Further, the political changes, the decline in MEC investments and trade liberalization led to greater private sector interest in financial assets from the mid-1990s. Figure 12.6 shows that value added of the finance and insurance services sector increased rapidly during the 1980s, when economic growth and investment as a percentage of GDP declined significantly. The finance and insurances sectors' contribution to GDP grew even more rapidly from 1994 to 2007, while overall investment levels remained relatively low. There was an improvement in investment levels from 2003, which included the impact of government's infrastructure investments from 2006, increased services sector investment linked to financial sector growth, increased household consumption, and more household construction and purchase of automobiles. In short, one sees that the growth of the financial sector and its increased share of GDP was not associated with higher levels of investment.

An important aspect of the financialization of the South African economy during the post-apartheid period was increased capital inflows, particularly short-term portfolio flows from developed countries. These short-term flows signalled not only the end of apartheid financial isolation but, more importantly, global financiers' change in sentiment about South Africa after ignoring it following its 1985 debt crisis. The slow liberalization of exchange controls by the South African government from 1996 may also have affected this sentiment. The more important reason for the increased flows to South Africa was the huge increase in global liquidity that was accompanied by large movements of short-term port-

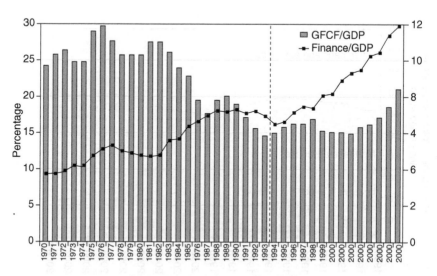

Figure 12.6 Gross fixed capital formation and finance and insurance sector value added as percentages of GDP (source: N. Zalk of Department of Trade and Industry, using SARB and Quantec data).

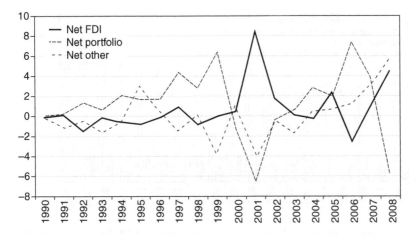

Figure 12.7 Net capital flows to South Africa as percentages of GDP (source: SARB).

folio flows into certain developing countries in Asia and Latin America, and South Africa in Africa.

Mohamed (2006) argues that the surge in net short-term capital flows to South Africa increased macroeconomic instability, with more volatility in exchange rates, interest rates and inflation associated with changes in capital inflows. A stark illustration of this volatility and instability was the sharp drop in the rand-to-dollar exchange rate of 35 per cent in 2001, which could be defined as a currency crisis. The 2001 currency crisis was caused by a rapid decline in net portfolio flows in 2000, which turned sharply negative in 2001 (see Figure 12.7). During this period, inflation increased sharply as a result of the weaker rand. The South African Reserve Bank, which follows an inflation-targeting policy, increased interest rates by 4 per cent. Net portfolio capital flows began recovering in 2002, and turned positive in 2003. They grew over the next few years to peak at nearly 8 per cent of GDP. This recovery in portfolio flows was accompanied by rapid reductions in interest rates that seemed to contribute to the house price and financial asset bubble during 2003–2007.

Mohamed (2006), in an examination of the period up to 2002, argues that the surge in portfolio capital flows to South Africa and the related increased extension of credit to the private sector during the 1990s was not associated with increased levels of fixed investment, but with increased household consumption, financial speculation and capital flight. Figure 12.8 compares the trends of total fixed capital formation, private business fixed capital formation, total domestic credit extension and total credit extended to the private sector all as percentages of GDP for South Africa for the period 1990–2007. Figure 12.8 shows that credit extension to the private sector increased about 22 per cent from 2000 to 2008, but that private business investment increased by only 5 per cent during this period. What can also be inferred from Figure 12.7 is that a part of the increase in capital formation from

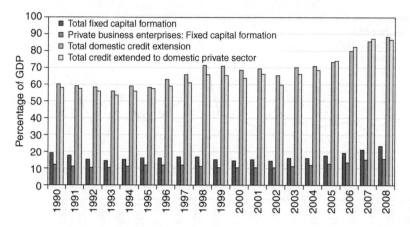

Figure 12.8 Credit extension and investment as percentages of GDP (source: calculated using SARB data).

2006 may not be due to private business capital formation but to state investment in infrastructure. The increase in private capital formation from 2003 to 2008 is due to investments spurred on by increased financial speculation and debt-driven consumption, not investment in long-term productive investment that may help redress the structural industrial weaknesses of the South African economy. I explain the process I describe as 'misallocation of finance', below.

Figure 12.9 draws on data from the SARB's flow of funds data to provide a trend of capital formation after depreciation by sector. We see that the foreign

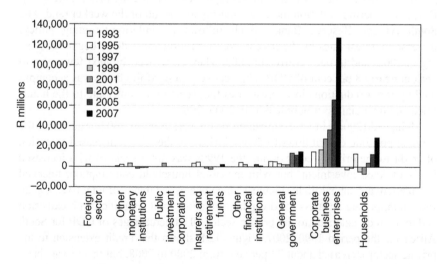

Figure 12.9 Capital allocated to capital formation by sector, Rbillions (source: calculated from SARB flow of funds data).

sector has very low levels of net fixed investment. The South African financial institutions' (the banks' and insurers') net investment in fixed capital formation turned negative from 2003. Figure 12.9 shows that there has been a huge increase in corporate business enterprise net investment from about R30 billion in 1999 to almost R130 billion in 2007. There has also been large growth in government and household net capital formation over that period.

Figure 12.10 shows calculations for trends of net acquisitions of financial assets by sector calculated from the SARB flow of funds data. The first stark difference between Figure 12.9 and Figure 12.10 is the scale of the different charts. The *y*-axis in Figure 12.9 goes up to R140 billion, and that of Figure 12.10 to R450 billion. The next stark difference is that every sector in Figure 12.10, except for general government, had large and increasing net acquisition of financial assets, whereas in Figure 12.9 we noted that it was only government, household and corporate business enterprises that had large increases in net capital stock. There was rapid growth in acquisition of financial assets in all the financial categories. The other monetary institutions category, which includes the commercial banks, had huge growth in acquisition of financial assets, which nearly tripled from just over R150 billion in 2003 to nearly R430 billion in 2007. Household net capital formation in 2007 at around R30 billion was a fraction of their net acquisitions of financial assets, which more or less doubled to R200 billion in 2007 from about R100 billion in 2005. The trend in acquisition of financial assets by corporate business enterprises increased up to the financial crisis (and the dotcom crisis) in 2001, and then declined until 2005. However, it had a sudden surge, and by 2007 had grown from the 2001 peak of about R100 billion to over R170 billion in 2007.

Figure 12.11 highlights an important fact about corporate business net acquisition of financial assets relative to net fixed capital formation for the period for

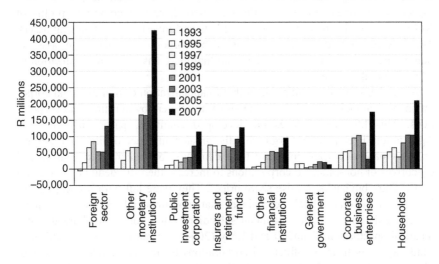

Figure 12.10 Capital allocated to financial assets, Rbillions (source: calculated from SARB flow of funds data).

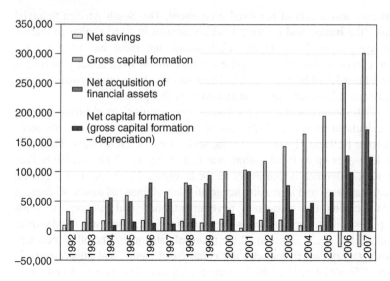

Figure 12.11 The main sources and uses of capital in corporate business enterprises, Rmillions (source: calculated from SARB flow of funds data).

which we have SARB flow of funds data (1993–2007). Corporate business enterprise net capital formation (i.e., gross capital formation less depreciation) was lower than net capital formation for all years between 1994 and 2007, except for 2004 and 2005. Corporate savings were low for the period, and turned negative in 2006–2007. Many of the studies of financialization in the US economy focus on the increasing financialization of non-financial corporations (NFCs). One aspect of this financialization is the increased share of income and profits of NFCs from involvement in financial markets and investment in financial assets. The flow of funds data on use of capital by corporate business enterprises in South Africa seems to support the notion that there has been financialization of NFCs in South Africa.

A number of recent studies show that financialization of non-financial corporations was associated with lower levels of investment by non-financial corporations. This literature focuses on developed countries, particularly the US. Aglietta and Breton (2001) argue that the greater influence of financial markets on non-financial corporations and their demands for higher returns influenced executives of non-financial corporations to increase their dividend payments and to use share buybacks to raise share prices. They were left with less capital for investment. Crotty (2002) explained that non-financial corporations have increased the sizes of their financial subsidiaries and gotten involved in more financial speculation. Duménil and Lévy (2004) showed that interest and dividend payments from non-financial corporations to financial markets increased. They argue that non-financial corporations, therefore, had less capital to invest in their own activities. Stockhammer (2004) uses regression analysis to show that financialization is associated with lower levels of capital accumulation. Froud *et al.* (2000) show the extent to which executives of non-financial corporations have become focused on the concerns of the financial markets for short-term high returns. They show, through case studies of global corporations, how this sensitivity to financial markets has created dysfunctional behaviour in large corporations. They argue that the narrative provided by CEOs of large corporations to financial markets is not supported by examination of the financial statements of those companies. Orhangazi (2007) uses firm-level data in the US to show a negative relationship between real investment and financialization. He argues that financialization of non-financial corporations may have caused a change in the incentives of management that led them to direct capital towards financial investments.

Much more research is required to understand the impact of financialization of NFCs on the South African economy and developing countries in general. Given the available evidence, I argue that the largest South African corporations have become more sensitive to the demands of the financial sector, particularly the shareholder value movement. Recent corporate restructuring and the content of annual reports of these giant corporations are indications of this sensitivity. Lazonick and O'Sullivan (2000) argue that the predominance of the shareholder value approach to corporate governance has been accompanied by a shift from patient to impatient capital. In other words, the increased influence of financiers and the shareholder value movement over corporate executives has caused a shift in management behaviour where investors and management are less concerned with building and nurturing businesses over a long period of time, but have become focused on short-term returns. This behaviour would be even more marked where big business had been making an effort to move capital out of South Africa and increasing its efforts to internationalize. Crotty (2002) says that this shift to impatient capital has led to management treating their subsidiaries not as long-term investments but as part of portfolios of assets. We have seen formerly South African giant corporations unload a huge number of South African businesses that they have decided are not part of their core businesses, and increasing their investments abroad. Froud *et al.* (2007) argue that this increased focus on short-term financial returns in NFCs is bad for labour because decreasing employment is good for increasing profits in the short run, even if losing experienced workers may be detrimental to these NFCs in the long run. South Africa requires capital that will make a long-term commitment to employment and building the skills of its workforce. Financialization increases short-term motives, where firms are less likely to invest in long-term skills development.

3.1 The South African economic crisis: financialization and de-industrialization

The process of financialization occurred on top of an industrial structure dominated by the MEC where the manufacturing sector was inadequately developed and diversified. The infrastructure and institutions of the economy had developed to support the MEC, and were not geared towards supporting diversified industrial development. Economic policy choices did not support investments in industry, but supported a preference for liquid, financial investments. The inflows of short-term capital to the economy from the mid-1990s led to increased private sector access to credit, but this increase in private sector access to credit was associated with increased debt-driven consumption by households, and speculation in real estate and financial asset markets.

Figure 12.12 shows acceleration in household consumption from the mid-1990s that speeded up even more from 2003. The impact of increased short-term capital flows and increased access to private debt seemed to be an important influence on household consumption. Obviously, the trade deficit was negative for years when net flows were positive, but we also see a large increase in the trade deficit from 2005. It grew to over 7.5 per cent of GDP in 2008. The ratio of household debt to disposable income grew from about 60 per cent in the mid-1990s to close to 80 per cent in 2008. Household savings turned negative in 2005, and remained negative through 2008. It is worth noting that a large proportion of South Africans do not have access to credit. Therefore, the average debt-to-disposable income numbers reported by the SARB may well underestimate the level of indebtedness of more affluent South Africans. Since late 2007, house foreclosures have grown to over R300 million per month and banks report over 6,000 car repossessions per month.

The impact of growth in net acquisition of financial assets and the increased level of household debt-driven consumption are shown with the next few figures. Investment and capital formation has been concentrated in the financial services sector and services sectors that benefit from increased consumption.

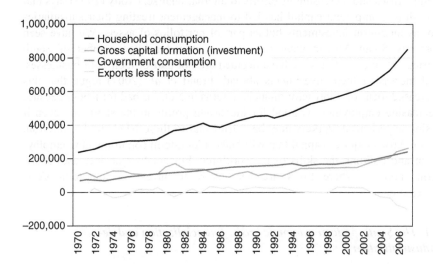

Figure 12.12 Trends in household consumption, government consumption, investment and trade, 1970–2007 (Real 2000, Rmillions) (source: SARB).

Figure 12.13 shows the top ten sectors by size of investments for 2006–2008. The year 2006 was an important year for increased debt-driven consumption, increasing minerals commodity prices and the growing house and financial asset price bubbles. During 2006, services sectors dominated investment. The other

2006 top 10 sectors by investment (as a percentage of total investment)

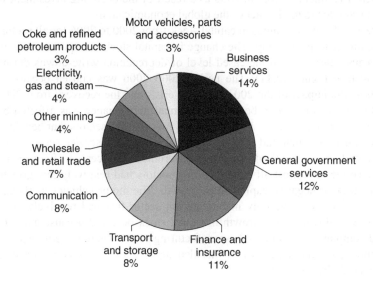

2008 top 10 sectors by investment (as a percentage of total investment)

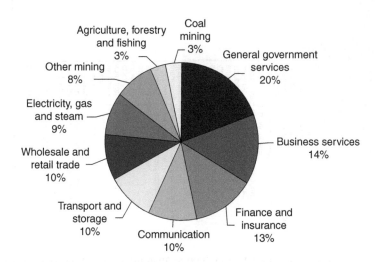

Figure 12.13 Top ten investment sectors for 2006 and 2008 (source: Quantec).

mining sector, which is largely platinum mining, makes it into the top ten. Two manufacturing sectors – automobiles and components, and coke and refined products (investments into Sasol, the formerly state-owned company that produces oil from coal) – make it into the top ten investment sectors. The automobiles and components sector was supported by increased private sector credit that led to a large growth in car sales. Manufacturing sectors do not make it into the top ten investment sectors in 2008 as a result of the declining investment in manufacturing due to the impact of the global economic crisis.

Figure 12.14 shows changes in capital stock from 2000 to 2006 for all sectors of the South African economy. The change in capital stock is important to consider, because there was an increased level of depreciation write-downs during the period (see Figure 12.11). The period 2000–2006 was chosen because it would show the impact of the 2001 currency crisis and the recovery from 2003 until 2006; 2007 is excluded because investment performance was affected by the start of the financial crisis. Figure 12.13 shows that the sectors that benefited from investment and that had growth in capital stock were service sectors. The largest capital stock growth after general government services was finance and insurance services. Almost all manufacturing sectors had relatively low growth in capital stock or negative capital stock growth. The motor vehicles, parts and accessories sector was the only manufacturing sector that had relatively large growth in capital stock. This growth in capital stock occurred because automobiles and components was the only manufacturing sector where government had implemented an industrial policy. It was also supported by the increased access to private credit by households.

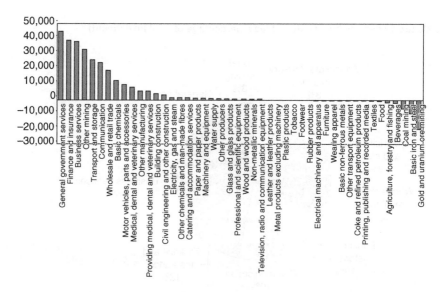

Figure 12.14 Change in capital stock from 2000 to 2006 for all economic sectors (Real 2000 prices, Rmillions) (source: Quantec).

The South African economy has not only emulated the increased levels of debt, house prices and household consumption in the US economy. Our financial sector has also copied the behaviour of its US counterpart. It has increased debt and increased securitization of debt. Figure 12.15 shows the rapid growth of the derivatives market (futures contracts) in South Africa from 2003. There was also huge growth in US and global derivatives markets during this period. Even though the South African financial sector has not had significant direct losses related to the collapse of the subprime market in the US, one sees that the South African financial sector could well have been heading to creating the conditions for a domestic financial collapse.

4 Conclusion

Big business worked closely with the apartheid state to prop up the economy during the politically turbulent 1980s, when community and labour struggles were advancing and international pressure and economic isolation of the economy intensified. The economy was dominated by diversified conglomerates. These large groups bought up the assets of foreign companies that left South Africa. In fact, there seems to have been a reversal of capital flight during this period (Mohamed and Finnoff, 2005). After democracy, there was huge restructuring of the South African corporate sectors. Many of the largest conglomerates embarked on a process to increase their international operations and to reduce their South African businesses. Obeying the demands of the shareholder value movement, they simplified their corporate structures and increasingly focused on core business activities when they restructured. In short, much of big business had diversified their businesses to reduce their exposure to the South African economy after 1994. At the same time, South Africa had a weak industrial structure focused around a MEC because of the political and economic historical

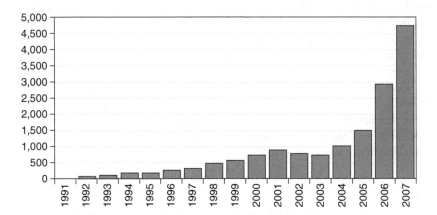

Figure 12.15 Derivative market futures contracts (Rbillions, current prices) (source: SARB).

processes that shaped its industrialization. The corporate restructuring further weakened the industrial structure of the economy.

The economic policies of the new democratic government were aimed to attract and appease foreign finance and investment. It was probably believed that foreign investment would pour into the new South Africa and reshape and modernize the industrial landscape. The economic policies were deliberately neoliberal because it was believed that foreign investors would be attracted to a country where the government is willing to show its credibility by ensuring low inflation and low budget deficits. The government did not adopt or implement an industrial policy to address the industrial structural weaknesses because of the fiscal implications, and because their neoliberal policies favoured less state intervention in the economy.

The neoliberal macroeconomic and financial policy choices of the government proved disastrous. The policy choices left them unable to deal with the effects of financialization and the corporate restructuring and de-industrialization crisis in the economy. These policy choices further integrated the economy into the global economy and opened the economy up to relatively uncontrolled hot money flows. The surges of hot money into and out of the economy led to volatility in macroeconomic variables such as exchange rates and interest rates, and had a huge impact on liquidity in financial markets. The effect of this volatility was to exacerbate the declining interest in long-term, productive industrial investment. Instead, there was a misallocation of capital towards speculation in real estate and financial markets and debt-driven consumption.

The integration into global financial markets has increased the risk of financial crisis and the vulnerability to contagion from financial problems elsewhere. The weak industrial structure and continued dependence on mining and minerals exports creates a balance of payments risk because imports for consumer goods and capital equipment for mining and infrastructure investment have increased. The large corporations and wealthy South Africans with their liquid and mobile capital are able to respond to macroeconomic volatility and the risk of financial crisis in South Africa by moving their money abroad. The government's policies have made this capital flight easier. Poor South Africans are forced to bear the brunt of the poor economic policy choices of their government. They have lost their jobs, or have had the quality of their jobs reduced through outsourcing. They have become more dependent on government grants, such as child support and old age pensions. Unless there is a huge effort to address the industrial decline in South Africa, and new economic policies are implemented to support industrial growth and transformation, the majority of South Africans will face an increasingly bleak economic future.

Notes

1 The NCR said in November 2009 that on average 80 per cent of new mortgages provided during June 2008 to June 2009 were to people whose gross income was over R15,000 per month.

2 See Terreblanche (2002) for an account of the response of white people and big business to the political changes.
3 For an interesting discussion on the growing influence of institutional investors and the emergence of maximizing shareholder value as a "new ideology for corporate governance", see Lazonick and O'Sullivan (2000). It is worth noting that the growth in importance of the business media industry and their influence over business structure and executive behaviour is also significant.
4 Mohamed and Finnoff (2005) show that capital flight from South Africa was higher during the period after the democratic elections (1994–2000) than it was before the election (1980–1993). They argue that misinvoicing of trade made up a significant share of capital flight, indicating that it was probably big businesses with large export and import volumes involved in misinvoicing of trade.

References

Aglietta, M. and Breton, R. (2001) 'Financial systems, corporate control and capital accumulation', *Economy and Society*, 30(4): 433–466.

Crotty, J. (2002) 'The Effects of Increased Product Market Competition and Changes in Financial Markets on the Performance of Nonfinancial Corporations in the Neo-liberal Era', Working Paper no. 44. Political Economy Research Institute, University of Massachusetts, Amherst.

Duménil, G. and Lévy, D. (2004) *Capital Resurgent*, Cambridge, MA: Harvard University Press.

Ernst and Young (2006) *Mergers and Acquisitions: A Review of Activity for the Year 2005*. South Africa: Ernst & Young (available at www.ey.com/ZA/en/Home).

Fine, B. and Rustomjee, Z. (1996) *The Political Economy of South Africa: From Minerals-Energy Complex to Industrialization*, Boulder, CO: Westview Press.

Froud, J., Haslam, C., Johal, S. and Williams, K. (2000). 'Shareholder value and financialization: Consultancy promises, management moves', *Economy and Society*, 29(1): 80–110.

Froud, J, Sukhdev, J., Leaver, A. and Williams, K. (2007) *Financialization and Strategy: Narrative and Numbers*, New York, NY: Routledge.

Goldstein, A. (2001) 'Business governance in Brazil and South Africa: How much convergence to the Anglo-Saxon model?', *Revista Brasileira de Economia Politica*, 21(2): 3–23.

Lazonick, W. and O'Sullivan, M. (2000). 'Maximizing shareholder value: A new ideology for corporate governance', *Economy and Society*, 1, 13–35 (www.informaworld.com/smpp/title~db=all~content=t713685159~tab=issueslist~branches=29-v2929)

Mohamed, S. (2006) 'Capital Flows to the South African Economy since the End of Apartheid', Presented at the Annual Conference for Development and Change, Brazil, December 2006.

Mohamed, S. and Finnoff, K. (2005) 'Capital flight from South Africa: 1980–2000', in G. Epstein (ed.), *Capital Flight and Capital Controls in Developing Countries*, Northampton MA: Edward Elgar.

Nolan, P. (2003) 'Industrial Policy in the early 21st century: The challenge of the global business revolution', in H.-J. Chang (ed.), *Rethinking Development Economics*, London: Anthem Press.

Orhangazi, O. (2005) 'Financialization and Capital Accumulation in the Non-financial Corporate Sector: A Theoretical and Empirical Investigation', Working Paper 149, Political Economy Research Institute, University of Massachusetts, Amherst.

Roberts, S. (2007). 'Patterns of industrial performance in South Africa in the first decade of democracy: the continued influence of minerals-based activities', *Transformation: Critical Perspectives on Southern Africa*, 65: 4–35 (www.transformation.ukzn.ac.za/index.php/transformation/article/view/978/793).

Roberts, S., Chabane, N. and Machaka, J. (2003). 'Ten Year Review: Industrial Structure and Competition Policy'. Report Prepared for the Presidency 10-year Review Project.

Roux, A. (1991) 'Financing Economic Development in South Africa', Unpublished mimeograph.

South African Reserve Bank, online data available from www.resbank.co.za.

Statistics South Africa, online time series data available from www.statssa.gov.za.

Stockhammer, E. (2004) 'Financialization and the slowdown of accumulation', *Cambridge Journal of Economics*, 28(5): 719–741.

Terreblanche, S. (2002) *A History of Inequality in South Africa: 1652–2002*, Pietermaritzburg: University of Natal Press.

The Presidency, Government of South Africa (2003). *Towards a Ten Year Review: Synthesis Report on Implementation of Government Programmes*. Pretoria: Policy Coordination and Advisory Services, The Presidency GSA.

13 Inequality and unemployment in the growth and recovery process

A case study of South Africa

Fiona Tregenna

1 Introduction

The global economic crisis has led to an increase in unemployment worldwide, and the recovery in unemployment is likely to be slower than the recovery in output. It is also likely to have short- and long-term distributional consequences, with previous evidence suggesting that inequality tends to rise during periods of crisis, as the poor are generally less able to protect their incomes than are the rich. Furthermore, inequality is tends to be 'sticky' in that after increases in inequality it is liable to remain at higher levels (unless there are strong interventions to bring it down).

One of the contributors to increases in inequality during periods of economic crisis is increases in unemployment. This would be particularly the case where low-income earners are disproportionately affected by job losses. Amongst those retaining employment, disproportionately high reductions in earnings at the lower part of the distribution would also tend to worsen inequality.

This study analyses the relative contributions of unemployment and earnings dispersion to earnings inequality in the case of South Africa. South Africa is known to be one of the most unequal countries in the world, as well as having amongst the highest rates of open unemployment. Although it is too early to fully analyse these dynamics for the current economic crisis, the findings are instructive and the methodology would be helpful in analysing other country experiences as well.

The next section presents the evidence on the patterns of unemployment and inequality across countries. It also reviews and critiques the (mainstream) international economics literature on the relationship between unemployment and inequality. Section 3 focuses on the case of South Africa. Static and dynamic decomposition methods are employed to quantify the relative contributions of unemployment and earnings dispersion to overall earnings inequality. Section 4 discusses the results and some possible policy implications, and concludes.

2 Inequality and unemployment internationally

Global trends in inequality prior to the crisis have been subject to debate, which is perhaps not surprising given the inherently political character of inequality as well as the complexities of data and measurement. The evidence seems to suggest that within-country inequality rose for most countries. When inequality is calculated across 'citizens of the world', this trend is mitigated by rapid rises in the incomes of relatively poor large countries, notably China and, to a lesser extent, India. In their review of the debate as to whether world inequality rose or fell in the era of globalisation, Capéau and Decoster (2004) attribute the divergent views concerning trends in overall world inequality primarily to how inequality within countries such as China and India (in particular urban–rural differences) are treated.

What does seem clear is that, by the onset of the crisis, within-country inequality was at extremely high levels by recent historical standards. This holds particularly for the major industrialised countries in which the crisis originated. Palma (2009) shows that income inequality in the United States rose dramatically between the election of Reagan and the outbreak of the crisis. By 2007, income inequality had reached the levels it was last at in 1929, not coincidentally just before the Great Depression. For example, the pre-tax income share of the top 1 per cent (including realized capital gains) was about 23 per cent in both periods. In fact, while the average income of the bottom 90 per cent remained practically stagnant during this near three-decade period, that of the top 1 per cent grew at an average real annual rate of 4.5 per cent, that of the top 0.1 per cent at 6.5 per cent, and that of the top 0.01 per cent at 8.1 per cent. Atkinson (2007) and Pikkety (2007) show, for the United Kingdom and France respectively, similar trends of significant pre-crisis increases in inequality, although these increases are not quite as dramatic as in the case of the United States.

Historically, at least in the twentieth century, crises and recessions have been preceded by spikes in inequality, and inequality has subsequently typically fallen for several years before climbing back up. Initial indications point to a small drop in inequality from before the crisis to the present in the United States, but it is too early to determine whether this fall will continue or will be reversed.

Since unemployment data come out more quickly than do inequality data, the impact of the crisis on unemployment is already clearly apparent (and in any case the impact of the crisis on unemployment is more predictable than the impact on inequality). Figure 13.1 shows the trends in unemployment in the major groupings of advanced industrialised countries since the onset of the global economic crisis. Unemployment rose by several percentage points, although it began to come down somewhat in 2010.

Of particular relevance to this chapter is the relationship between inequality and unemployment. Figure 13.2 shows inequality and unemployment rates for 127 countries. Measurement and reporting is not uniform internationally, and hence these data are not entirely comparable. The observations are not from the same year for each country (as suitable surveys are generally not conducted annually and there is a lag in reporting results), but those shown here are the most recent for each country. Separate series are shown for each of gross earnings, gross income, disposable income, and consumption or expenditure, with observations not being directly comparable across these series (for instance, as

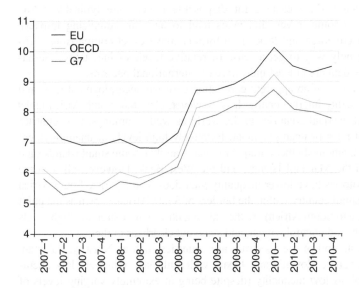

Figure 13.1 Recent unemployment trends in advanced economies (source: OECD Harmonised Unemployment Rates).

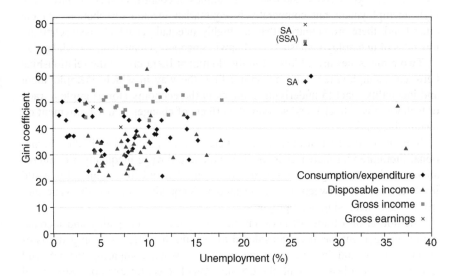

Figure 13.2 International comparison of inequality and unemployment.

Source: Tregenna and Tsela (2012).

Notes
The three points labelled 'SA (SSA)' use the most recent national data published by Stats SA, for both unemployment and three measures on inequality. The lower point for South Africa (marked 'SA') is based on the same international data sources as for the rest of the countries.
Data derived from WIDER World Income Inequality Database 2; ILO Key Indicators of the Labour Market; Statistics South Africa (2008a); and Statistics South Africa (2008b).

would be expected, the measures for disposable income are typically below those for gross income, given that taxes tend to have an equalising impact). While the poor coverage and lack of uniformity make exact comparisons difficult, this is the only way to get a sense of relative levels of inequality internationally, and the data are at least indicative of international patterns.

There is not much of an apparent correlation between unemployment rates and the level of inequality internationally. It is, however, clear that South Africa ranks among the most unequal countries in the world as well as amongst the countries with the highest rates of unemployment. Extremely high levels of unemployment are also found in, amongst others, Iraq, Armenia, Namibia, some small islands such as Reunion and the Marshall Islands, and the West Bank. However, all of these countries or territories have lower inequality than does South Africa. South Africa and Lesotho (a small country within the borders of South Africa, shown as the point on the chart close to South Africa) are the only countries with extremely high levels of both inequality and unemployment, and stand out clearly as outliers.

At the opposite end of the spectrum are countries such as Norway, Pakistan, Bangladesh, Hungary, Slovenia and Japan, which all have relatively low unemployment as well as low inequality (despite being at extremely varying levels of income per capita). Rates of unemployment and inequality are, however, not closely correlated (at least not when inequality is measured with the Gini). Albania, Slovakia, Croatia and Iran are examples of countries which are have very high unemployment but comparatively egalitarian income distribution. On the other hand, there are countries that are highly unequal yet which have relatively low rates of unemployment, such as Malawi, Singapore, Guatemala and Malaysia.

Two main issues are addressed in the dominant literature on the relationships between unemployment and inequality: first, the way in which unemployment and inequality react to underlying changes in the economy (for example a trade or technological shock); and second, the effects of changes in unemployment on income inequality.

In terms of the first of these issues, there is a prominent view in the international literature that increases in unemployment and wage inequality are 'alternative' results of changes in the structure of the demand for labour. This could imply a trade-off between increasing income inequality (specifically wage inequality) and increasing unemployment.

The notion of a trade-off between increasing income inequality and increasing unemployment has been considered to explain the differences in patterns of unemployment and income or wage inequality when comparing the US and Europe, and, to a lesser extent, the US and Canada (see, for example, Storer and Van Audenrode, 1998; Ayala *et al.*, 2002). Rates of unemployment tend to be lower in the US but wage dispersion considerably higher. Furthermore, in a dynamic sense, adverse shocks tend to result predominantly in increases in wage dispersion in the US, but primarily in increases in unemployment in the comparator countries. Unemployment also tends to be of longer duration in Europe than in the US. Countries in which wage inequality increased the most have tended to have lower and less persistent unemployment

Gottschalk and Smeeding (1997) summarise the 'stylised facts' emerging from the literature on the relationship between labour markets and inequality as follows. First, countries with centralised bargaining systems (such as Germany or Sweden) have greater equality of earnings than do countries with less centralised bargaining systems (such as the US or Canada). Second, earnings inequality increased in the majority of industrial countries during the 1980s, but most in the US and UK and least in the Nordic countries. Third, increases in demand for skilled labour and differences across countries in growth of supply of skilled workers explain a large part of the differences in trends in returns to education and experience. And fourth, institutional constraints on wages limited the increases in inequality, more so in countries with stronger constraints.

An adverse trade or technology shock may lead to some combination of lower wages in existing jobs; loss of some existing jobs and re-employment in lower-wage jobs; and/or loss of some existing jobs without replacement. Insofar as the jobs affected are disproportionately low-wage jobs, any of these outcomes will tend to increase inequality. The particular combination of these three outcomes that an economy experiences in response to an adverse shock depends on various institutional features.

In this type of approach in the literature, unemployment and inequality are essentially viewed as alternative equilibrating mechanisms to technological, trade or other shocks that affect the relative demand for different types of labour.

However, this apparent trade-off between increases in unemployment and inequality is not unidimensional or linear. There are also important exceptions, such as the UK, in which wage inequality widened yet unemployment remained high, whereas Germany has had relatively low wage inequality as well as unemployment.

Furthermore, to the extent that unemployment is a structural macroeconomic problem, and particularly to the extent that it is a product of problems in macroeconomic management, it cannot be considered in narrow labour market terms or as a result of excessive wages. In addition to the fact that the solutions to unemployment are not necessarily to be found in the labour market, attempting to deal with unemployment purely in this realm is likely to heighten inequality.[1]

The nature and extent of the perceived 'trade-off' between changes in unemployment and in inequality are also subject to policy interventions. The vulnerability of a country to a shock is affected by previous policy choices (for example, around financial and capital account liberalisation). In addition, the way in which a shock affects an economy is partially subject to policy mediation. The distributional impact of any exogenous shock is not predetermined. Even if the shock would have primarily or disproportionately affected low-income earners, some of these costs can be redistributed (through fiscal and other measures) such that the net impact on inequality is mitigated.

For instance, the effects of an adverse trade shock (in particular one that results in a reduction of demand for less skilled labour) on employment and distribution are subject to policy intervention in various ways. First, even given lower costs of production of labour-intensive goods in other countries, the degree of import penetration of such goods in the home market is contingent on the trade regime, and specifically on tariff and non-tariff barriers. Second, industrial and other policies mediate the degree and nature of the impact of increased or potentially increased import penetration on domestic industry. Third, skills levels are not static, especially in the medium to long term, and changing the skills profile of the labour force would influence the results of the shock. Fourth, the extent to which changes in relative labour demand actually translate into adverse distributional consequences is dependent on the distributional regime and subject to fiscal and other interventions. The fact that low-skilled labour may be directly affected by an adverse shock need not mean that this group actually bears the costs, although they are likely to do so unless there is specific intervention to the contrary.

However, in the absence of specific measures to counteract this, a change in relative labour demand in which the demand for unskilled or low-skilled labour falls is indeed likely to result either in higher rates of unemployment or in increased wage inequality, or more likely in a combination of these. The actual mix of increased unemployment and wage dispersion is likely to be mediated by institutional factors. These factors relate to labour market structure in particular, such as the bargaining system, the duration of contracts and of wage agreements, the system of unemployment benefits, a minimum wage, and so on.

We identified a second relevant issue in the international literature on the effects of changes in unemployment on inequality. The international literature consistently finds a negative causal relationship between unemployment and inequality. Time-series analysis of the effects of unemployment on inequality within countries generally finds that increases in unemployment worsen income inequality.

In their seminal paper, Blinder and Esaki (1978) find that unemployment had clear disequalising effects on income distribution in the US from 1947 to 1974. Reviewing the literature on the relationship between macroeconomic conditions and income distribution, Mocan (1999) concludes that 'the consensus has been that income inequality is countercyclical in behaviour, i.e., increases in unemployment worsen the position of low-income groups'. Mocan's econometric analysis of US data over the period 1949–1994 indicates that an increase in structural unemployment reduces the income shares of the bottom three quintiles, and may do so for the second highest quintile as well, but is associated with an increase in the income share of the top quintile.

Björklund (1991) finds that higher unemployment significantly raised the income share of the top quartile in Sweden between 1960 and 1973. In one of the few studies concerning developing countries, González and Menendez (2000) look at the effects of unemployment on labour income inequality in Argentina over the period 1991–1998. González and Menendez find that 43 per cent of the total increase in inequality can be explained by the increase in unemployment.

3   The case of South Africa

South Africa's exceptionally high rates on inequality are probably rooted in the country's partheid history. However, after seventeen years of democracy the high inequality has not come down, with some studies suggesting that inequality has actually increased during at least parts of the period of democracy.

Most of the other countries in the Southern African region also have very high rates on inequality. While Latin America is often regarded as the most unequal geographic region in the world, this is rivalled by Southern Africa. Within Southern Africa, inequality is extremely high in Namibia, Botswana, Lesotho and Swaziland (all neighbouring South Africa) and in Angola; the rates in all these countries are amongst the highest in the world.[2]

The empirical analysis that follows focuses on the relationship between inequality and unemployment in South Africa. After explaining the data used, a brief overview is given of inequality and unemployment in South Africa. The relative contributions of unemployment and other factors to overall earnings inequality are then investigated through static and dynamic decomposition analysis.

3.1 Data

The empirical analysis was undertaken using the full datasets of the Labour Force Survey (LFS), February 2001–September 2007. The LFS is a nationally representative biannual survey conducted by the country's official statistics agency, Statistics South Africa. All original datasets were accessed through the South African Data Archive.

There is a problem of non-response to the earnings question in the LFS, where some respondents refuse to disclose their earnings or indicate that they do not know their earnings, or no data are entered for other reasons. Since it is likely that the earnings variable is missing not at random, dropping of these observations could lead to bias in empirical analysis based on this variable. This problem was addressed by imputing earnings for missing observations. The method used was hotdeck imputation, in which a vector of respondent characteristics relevant to earnings was used to impute missing earnings, based on the characteristics of individual non-respondents and other individuals with similar characteristics who did disclose their earnings.

Various other steps of data preparation were undertaken prior to the empirical analysis. One of these steps related to the conversion of earnings reported in brackets to a continuous variable. Respondents unwilling or unable to state their actual earnings could instead indicate which of fourteen brackets their income falls within. This poses a problem for computations requiring income as a continuous variable. The mean income of people who reported actual incomes were calculated, by bracket, for each year. These were then assigned to the people in the same bracket who only identified a bracket.

3.2 Earnings inequality and unemployment in South Africa

Earnings inequality is extremely high: for instance, the Gini coefficient of earnings amongst the employed is 0.60.[3]

Figure 13.3 shows a Pen's Parade of earnings in South Africa. In this depiction of earnings inequality the height of each person denotes their income, with distribution represented by a 'parade' of people walking past in order from shortest to tallest (i.e. poorest to richest), shown on the *x*-axis of the proportion of the population from 0 to 1. The actual income (household per capita income) of a person at any point of the income distribution can be read directly off the *y*-axis. The curvature of the plot is astonishing, with an extremely steep rise at the top end.

In terms of trends over time, both earnings inequality and unemployment in South Africa peaked in 2002 and have since declined (at least until the onset of the global economic downturn), albeit at a slow pace given their severity. There has been a close relationship between unemployment and earnings inequality, both among the labour force and among all 'working age' adults, as evident from Figure 13.4. These relationships also hold when the 'expanded' measure of unemployment is used.[4]

These close relationships would be partially explained by the fact that higher unemployment means that a lower proportion of the labour force and of the working age adult population receive earnings, and hence inequality would be higher in a straightforward 'compositional' sense. Figure 13.5 therefore shows the relationship between earnings inequality *amongst the employed only* and unemployment. These series exclude the direct compositional effect of unemployment on labour force or adult earnings inequality.

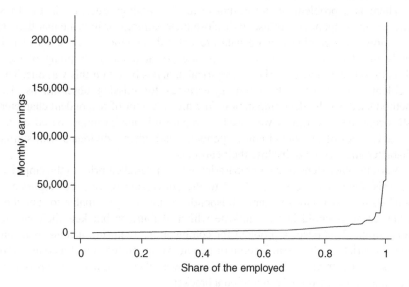

Figure 13.3 Pen's parade of earnings.

Notes
Labour force inequality refers to the inequality in earnings amongst all members of the labour force (employed and unemployed); working age inequality refers to earnings inequality among the population aged 19–65 (inclusive). Unemployment rates are for official unemployment. Data derived from LFS surveys 2001–2007.

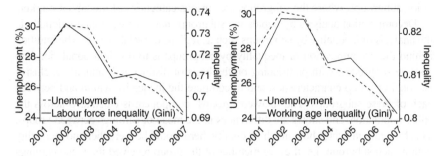

Figure 13.4 Unemployment and earnings inequality, 2001–2007.

Note
Data derived from LFS surveys 2001–2007.

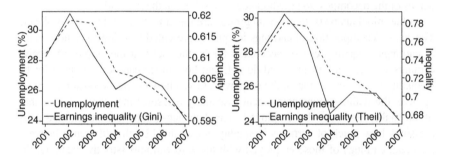

Figure 13.5 Unemployment and earnings inequality amongst the employed, 2001–2007.

Interestingly, there is still a very clear positive relationship between unemployment and earnings inequality amongst the employed. This suggests that there is a relationship beyond the 'compositional' channel. The relationship remains similarly close when other measures of inequality are used. In all cases, the correlation coefficient between unemployment and earnings inequality amongst the employed is over 80 per cent and is statistically significant.

It is remarkable how closely unemployment and earnings inequality have moved together over time. It would not be especially surprising to find a positive relationship between unemployment and overall income inequality (where this includes the unemployed), given that unemployment would directly affect income. What is found here, however, is a positive relationship between *earnings inequality amongst the employed* and unemployment.

3.3 Decomposition analysis

This and the next sections are based on Tregenna (2011). The effects of unemployment and of other selected dimensions of labour market structure on earnings inequality will now be investigated by decomposing earnings inequality by population subgroups, where the subgroups are various categories of the labour market.

Decomposition analysis by population subgroups has been used internationally in the analysis of inequality by subgroups such as regions or racial groups. The intuition behind the decomposition of inequality by subgroups is to divide a population into discrete subgroups, with partitioning on the basis of distinct and mutually exclusive personal or group characteristics, and to compute the inequality within and between each of these subgroups. The 'between-groups' component is calculated across the entire population, and shows the differences in the mean of earnings between groups. This basically indicates how much inequality there would be were there no inequality within each subgroup, i.e. if every member of the group received the mean earnings of the group such that inequalities between groups were the only source of inequality. The 'within-groups' inequality is a weighted sum of the inequality within each subgroup, and shows how much inequality there would be if there was no inequality between the groups. These two components sum to total inequality. The technical details of the decomposition methodology are set out in the Appendix.

In the initial analysis, the two subgroups are the employed and the unemployed. The static decomposition of earnings inequality presented here indicates how much of earnings inequality can be accounted for by the fact that the employed receive earnings whereas the unemployed do not, and how much can be accounted for by inequality in earnings amongst the employed. Given how the decompositions are set up here, the within-groups component essentially measures the relative importance of inequality amongst the employed. The between-groups component basically measures how much of earnings inequality is explained by the difference between the mean earnings of those employed with the zero earnings (strictly speaking, the imputed earnings of R0.01 per month for computational purposes) of those not working. While both components would be known to be positive a priori, the decomposition analysis can shed light on the *relative importance* of the two components.

The results are shown in Table 13.1, for decompositions on three alternative populations. These populations are the labour force – each of the official and expended definitions – and the working age adult population (between the ages of nineteen and sixty-five inclusive). For the two labour force populations, the two groups are the employed and the unemployed; and in the analysis of working age adults the two groups are those working and those not working

Table 13.1 Static decomposition of current earnings inequality by employment status (%)

	Between-groups	Within-groups	Total
Labour force – official definition	78.34	21.65	100
Labour force – expanded definition	87.02	12.98	100
Working age adults	92.98	7.02	100

Note
'All working age adults' refers to everyone aged between 19 and 65 inclusive. Earnings refer to annual earnings. Calculations based on September 2007 LFS data.

(i.e. including both the unemployed and those outside of the labour force) aged between nineteen and sixty-five inclusive.

A key finding from this part of the analysis is the importance of between-group inequality in accounting for earnings inequality (among the labour force or among the working age population). As would be expected, the relative importance of between-group inequality rises as the population being analysed expands, since the proportion of non-earners within the sample increases. The contribution of earnings inequality within the employed to broader earnings inequality – shown here by the within-groups component – ranges between just 7 per cent for the working age adult population and 22 per cent for the labour force (officially defined). This contribution is driven by very low earnings amongst some of the employed, and by the high degree of earnings inequality amongst the employed more broadly.

Next, a dynamic decomposition methodology is used to analyse the changes in earnings inequality between 2001 and 2007, in order to explain how much of these changes can be accounted for by changes in the particular aspects of labour market structure. Specifically, the analysis seeks to identify how much of the changes in earnings inequality can be accounted for by changes in the unemployment rate and by changes in the degree of earnings dispersion amongst the employed. The dynamic decomposition is based on the method pioneered by Mookherjee and Shorrocks (1982), and the details are contained in the Appendix.

This analysis allows for identification of the relative contributions to a change in earnings inequality of changes in earnings dispersion within each of the subgroups, of changes in the relative proportions of each of the subgroups, and of changes in the relative income of the subgroups. As with the static decompositions of inequality set out in the previous section, this analysis begins with a simple decomposition of inequality between just two groups – the employed and the unemployed. In this case, since the total population in the initial decompositions is the labour force, the second component (changes in the shares of subgroups) measures the relative (direct) contribution of changes in the rate of unemployment.

The results are shown for two periods: the episode in which both unemployment and inequality were increasing (2001–2002), and the episode in which both were falling (2002–2007). Applying the decomposition to these two periods separately avoids the high degree of volatility between individual years or between the biannual surveys, while also picking up the potentially different dynamics of these two distinct periods rather than mixing them together. The results are shown in Tables 13.2 and 13.3 (using the official and expanded definitions of unemployment respectively) in percentage form. The components sum to 100 per cent in the first period and −100 per cent in the second period, since inequality rose in the first period and fell in the second.

The most important result arising from this analysis is the importance of changes in the unemployment rate in explaining changes in earnings inequality within the labour force. During the first period, in which both unemployment and inequality rose, increases in the unemployment rate accounted for 77 per cent of the increase in earnings inequality within the labour force. Both unemployment and inequality fell in the second period, with the decrease in the unemployment rate explaining 72 per cent of the decrease in inequality. These results highlight the huge importance of the unemployment rate in explaining earnings inequality, during both rises and falls of inequality and unemployment.

Inequality *amongst* the employed contributed to a relatively small extent (16 per cent) to the increase in inequality amongst the entire labour force in the first period, and to a somewhat larger extent (40 per cent) to the decrease in inequality in the second. It is interesting that the contribution of inequality amongst the employed moved in the same direction as trends in overall labour force inequality as well as in the unemployment rate in both periods (as evident from the sign on the component 'effect of changes in earnings inequality amongst employed'). While decomposition analysis cannot discern causality between the components, it is noteworthy that the contributions of changes in the rate of unemployment and changes in earnings inequality amongst the employed moved in the same direction in both periods.

The third component of the decomposition is changes in between-group inequality. This captures the effect of the change in relative mean earnings of the employed and unemployed on changes in overall earnings inequality of the labour force, and is essentially a residual factor in this particular decomposition. This is the only component with the same sign (positive) in the two periods, indicating that it contributed to the rise in inequality in the first period and mitigated the fall in inequality in the second period. However, the contribution was relatively small.

The results are similar for the expanded definition of the labour force (including 'discouraged' job-seekers), as shown in Table 13.3. The main difference is that changes in the unemployment rate account for an even higher proportion (around 80 per cent) of total changes in earnings inequality, in the periods both of rising and of falling unemployment. This underlines the centrality of unemployment, not only in accounting for the greater part of earnings inequality in a static sense, but also in accounting for most of changes in earnings inequality over time.

Table 13.2 Dynamic decomposition of earnings inequality by employment/unemployment (official definition) (%)

	Effect of changes in earnings inequality amongst employed	Effect of changes on unemployment rate	Effect of changes in between-group inequality	Total
Period 1 (2001-1–2002-1)	15.6	77	7.3	100
Period 2 (2002-1–2007-2)	−39.8	−72.1	11.9	−100

Note
Calculations based on LFS data (February/March 2001, March 2002, and September 2007).

Table 13.3 Dynamic decomposition of earnings inequality by employment/unemployment (expanded definition) (%)

	Effect of changes in earnings inequality amongst employed	Effect of changes in unemployment rate	Effect of changes in between-group inequality	Total
Period 1 (2001-1–2002-1)	11.1	80.4	8.6	100
Period 2 (2002-1–2007-2)	−46.0	−77.9	24.3	−100

Note
Calculations based on LFS data (February/March 2001, March 2002, and September 2007).

4 Conclusion

Economic crisis is likely to affect the distribution of income. One of the channels of this would be through increased unemployment. The distribution of earnings amongst the employed would also be expected to change during and after economic crisis, and this would affect broader income inequality. This study analyses the contribution of unemployment and earnings distribution among the employed to overall earnings inequality. Although data availability does not yet allow for the analysis of these dynamics during the current crisis, the methodology applied here would be useful for subsequent analysis of this in South Africa and other countries.

The empirical results point strongly to the centrality of unemployment for understanding of inequality in South Africa. A surprisingly close positive relationship between the trends in unemployment and in earnings inequality amongst the employed over time can be observed, with a correlation coefficient of over 80 per cent (which is robust to the use of various alternative measures of inequality). This suggests that – at least for the period analysed and for the ranges of inequality and unemployment during that period – there might not be a trade-off between inequality and unemployment.

The relevance of unemployment to inequality is underscored and quantified by the results from the static and dynamic decomposition analyses of earnings inequality. Even insofar as a positive contribution of unemployment to overall earnings inequality might have been expected, these results are useful for measuring the relative contributions of unemployment and of other factors. The rate of unemployment is found to account for the bulk of earnings inequality. Furthermore, changes in the unemployment rate account for most of the changes in inequality, both during the initial rise in inequality and during the subsequent decline. Changes in the unemployment rate turn out to be much more significant than do changes in wage dispersion in accounting for changes in overall earnings inequality.

Together with the observed positive co-movement between the unemployment rate and the degree of earnings inequality among the employed, these results could suggest that rather than there being a trade-off between reducing unemployment and reducing inequality, similar policies might be able to address both. While this chapter has not specifically investigated the effects of earnings dispersion on the employed on unemployment, at the least the evidence discussed here does not provide support for the notion that greater earnings dispersion would be more conducive to reducing the level of unemployment, or, conversely, that reducing earnings inequality would worsen unemployment. Rather, the results suggest that addressing the crisis of unemployment is absolutely central to reducing South Africa's extremely high levels of inequality.

Earnings dispersion amongst the employed is an important though lesser contributor to inequality among the labour force and among working age adults. Having established the centrality of addressing unemployment for the reduction of inequality, it also cannot be said that just 'any jobs', however badly paid, would really be a solution to the problem of high levels of inequality in South Africa. An increase in the dispersion of earnings amongst the employed could erode the potential inequality-reducing effects of large-scale employment creation. A massive expansion of decent employment opportunities, particularly for the low-skilled and semi-skilled, could be the most important means of bringing down overall inequality in South Africa.

The effects on overall earnings inequality of the unemployed gaining employment would depend both directly on the earnings of those gaining employment, and indirectly on the effects of the reduced rate of unemployment and the new employment on the earnings distribution of those already employed. The unemployed are generally relatively low-skilled, and hence it is probable that, were they to gain employment, they would thus swell the lower end of the earnings distribution. Ceteris paribus, this would tend to reduce inequality. The indirect effects on the earnings of those already employed are less predictable. It seems most likely that reduced unemployment would tend to most strongly affect the earnings of those with whom the (previously) unemployed have the most similar profiles, by putting upward pressure on their earnings. In part, this could be through 'reserve army'-type effects of lower unemployment on the bargaining power of the employed. It thus seems credible that reduced unemployment could have indirect effects in pushing up the earnings of the lower part of the distribution of those already employed. This would also tend to reduce inequality (although the effects would be quite sensitive to which measure of inequality was used).

The most important dynamic underlying future distributional changes is likely to be through the labour market, in terms of both employment creation (or losses) and the distribution of earnings amongst the employed. It is improbable that South Africa's inequality could be brought down to 'normal' standards of inequality by international standards without increased demand for low- and semi-skilled labour, and to a lesser extent through a closing of wage gaps.

In light of the finding that unemployment accounted for the bulk of the changes in inequality (during periods both of rising and of falling unemployment and inequality), and given the fact that unemployment increased during the economic crisis, it seems likely that inequality also rose during the crisis. It seems unlikely that such increases in inequality would have been significantly mitigated by any other factors.

As well as being an outlier in terms of the extremely high rates of unemployment and inequality, some features of inequality and unemployment are distinctive to South Africa, associated in particular with the country's apartheid history. Nonetheless, there are also important commonalities between South Africa and some other middle-income countries in terms of inequality and labour market characteristics. These commonalities are especially pronounced with middle-income Latin American countries, with strong parallels between South Africa and Brazil in particular. South Africa and Brazil have until fairly recently counted as amongst the most unequal countries in the world.

An interesting difference, however, is that while inequality seems to have come down in Brazil in the past fifteen years or so, in South Africa the evidence – while inconclusive and contested – suggests that inequality has either remained stable or has actually worsened. A full and empirically-grounded explanation for these apparently disparate trends in inequality between South Africa and Brazil has yet to be advanced, and this would certainly be an interesting and valuable research avenue. The view of this author is that much of the explanation lies in differences in the labour markets of the two countries – in particular, the fact that the unemployment rate in South Africa is several times that of Brazil and that the unemployment rate in South Africa has not been significantly brought down. The empirical analysis of this chapter highlights the importance of this in accounting for inequality in South Africa. There are undoubtedly other important components of an explanation, including the impact of the *Bolsa Familia* and other social security programmes in Brazil; although South Africa has very significant social security programmes (especially a child support grant and old age pension), their impact on inequality may have been less than that in Brazil. But it is hypothesised that the primary difference lies in the two countries' labour markets. If this is indeed the case, it would have important implications for reducing inequality, especially in comparable middle-income countries. This would highlight the importance of minimising employment losses during periods of crisis if distribution is not to worsen further. It would also suggest that, even post-crisis, if a government seriously wants to reduce inequality then the maximisation of employment should be a central focus.

Appendix: Methodology for decomposition of income by population subgroups

Define: μ as the mean earnings of the population (with population as defined in each decomposition below); and y_i as the earnings of individual i for $i = 1, 2, \ldots n$.

The population can be partitioned into subgroups based on labour market status, with: N_k the subset of individuals in subgroup k; n_k members of subgroup

k; μ_k as the mean earnings of subgroup k; $v_k = \dfrac{n_k}{n}$ the proportion of the population in labour market subgroup k; and $\lambda_k = \dfrac{\mu_k}{\mu}$ the subgroup mean earnings relative to the aggregate population mean.

Earnings inequality (measured by mean log deviation) is then decomposed as follows:

$$I_0 = \frac{1}{n}\sum_i \ln\left(\frac{\mu}{y_i}\right) = \overbrace{\sum_k v_k I_0^k}^{\substack{\text{within-groups}\\\text{component}}} + \overbrace{\sum_k v_k \ln\left(\frac{1}{\lambda_k}\right)}^{\substack{\text{between-groups}\\\text{component}}}.$$

The between-groups figure is shown here as $\dfrac{100\sum_k v_k \ln\left(\dfrac{1}{\lambda_k}\right)}{I_0}$ and the within-groups figure as $\dfrac{100\sum_k v_k I_0^k}{I_0}$, showing the shares of earnings inequality accounted for by the between- and within-groups components respectively.

For the dynamic decomposition, further define: $\bar{v}_k = \dfrac{1}{2}\left(v_k^t + v_k^{t+1}\right)$ for time periods t and $t+1$, and similarly for $\bar{I}_0^k$ and $\overline{\log \lambda_k}$. Then the change in inequality can be decomposed as follows:

$$\Delta I_o \approx \overbrace{\sum_k \bar{v}_k \Delta I_0^k}^{\substack{\text{change in}\\\text{subgroup inequality}}} + \overbrace{\underbrace{\sum_k \bar{I}_0^k \Delta v_k}_{\substack{\text{effect on}\\\text{within-group inequality}}} + \underbrace{\sum_k \left(\bar{\lambda}_k - \overline{\log \lambda_k}\right)\Delta v_k}_{\substack{\text{effect on}\\\text{between-group inequality}}}}^{\text{change in shares of subgroups}}$$

$$+ \overbrace{\sum_k \left(\bar{\theta}_k - \bar{v}_k\right)\Delta \log \mu_k}^{\text{change in relative income of subgroups}}.$$

For ease of interpretation, the results show the relative contributions of the three components to the change in inequality in percentage form. That is, the contribution of the change in subgroup inequality is shown as $\dfrac{100\sum_k \bar{v}_k \Delta I_0^k}{\Delta I_o}$, the contribution of the change in the share of subgroups as $\dfrac{100\left(\sum_k \bar{I}_0^k \Delta v_k + \sum_k \left(\bar{\lambda}_k - \overline{\log \lambda_k}\right)\Delta v_k\right)}{\Delta I_o}$,

and the effect of changes in between-group inequality (i.e. the relative income of subgroups) as $\dfrac{100\sum_k \left(\bar{\theta}_k - \bar{v}_k\right)\Delta \log \mu_k}{\Delta I_o}$.

Notes

1 As Glyn (1995) puts it, if substitutability [between skilled and unskilled labour] is not high then it is clear that the distributional implications of relying on wage flexibility are highly inegalitarian – the worse-paid sections of the population have to bear the cost of reducing unemployment via substantial cuts in their wages while the better-off sections of society benefit from the cheaper services.

2 See Palma (2011) for discussion of the high rates of inequality in Southern Africa and Latin America.

3 Throughout the chapter, 'earnings inequality' refers to inequality in earnings on an individual basis.

4 The difference between the official and expanded definitions of unemployment is that the former excludes from the labour force people who have not looked for work or taken steps to start a business in the four weeks prior to the survey interview. Both measures are limited to people aged between fifteen and sixty-five who did not have a job or business in the seven days prior to the interview and were available to take up work within two weeks of the interview.

Bibliography

Ardington, C., D. Lam, M. Leibbrandt and M. Welch (2005) 'The sensitivity to key data imputations of recent estimates of income poverty and inequality in South Africa', *Economic Modelling*, 23(5): 822–835.

Atkinson, A.B. (2007) 'The distribution of top incomes in the United Kingdom, 1908–2000', in A.B. Atkinson and T. Piketty (eds), *Top Income Over the Twentieth Century: a Contrast between European and English-speaking Countries*, Oxford: Oxford University Press.

Ayala, L., R. Martínez and J. Ruiz-Huerta (2002) 'Institutional determinants of the unemployment-earnings inequality trade-off', *Applied Economics*, 34: 179–195.

Bhorat, H., M. Leibbrandt and I. Woolard (2000) 'Understanding contemporary household inequality in South Africa', *Studies in Economics and Econometrics*, 243: 31–52.

Birdsall, N. (2005) 'Rising inequality in the new global economy', 2005 WIDER Annual Lecture, *WIDER ANGLE*, No. 2/2005: 1–3.

Björklund, A. (1991) 'Unemployment and income distribution: time-series evidence from Sweden', *Scandinavian Journal of Economics*, 933: 457–465.

Björklund, A. and M. Palme (2001) 'The Evolution of Income Inequality During the Rise of the Swedish Welfare State 1951 to 1973', Stockholm School of Economics Working Paper Series in Economics and Finance, No 450.

Blinder, A.S. and H.Y. Esaki (1978) 'Macroeconomic activity and income distribution in the postwar United States', *The Review of Economics and Statistics*, 60: 604–609.

Capéau, B. and A. Decoster (2005) 'The Rise or Fall of World Inequality: A Spurious Controversy?', UNU-WIDER Discussion Paper No. 2004/02.

Casale, D., C. Muller and D. Posel (2004) ' "Two million net new jobs": a reconsideration of the rise in employment in South Africa, 1995–2003', *South African Journal of Economics*, 72(5): 978–1002.

Glyn, A. (1995) 'The assessment: unemployment and inequality', *Oxford Review of Economic Policy*, 11(1): 1–25.

González, M. and A. Menendez (2000) 'The Effect of Unemployment on Labor Earnings Inequality: Argentina in the Nineties', Princeton University, Woodrow Wilson School of Public and International Affairs, Research Program in Development Studies, Working Paper No. 216.

Gottschalk, P. and T.M. Smeeding (1997) 'Cross-national comparisons of earnings and income inequality', *Journal of Economic Literature*, XXXV: 633–687.

Hoogeveen, J.G. and B. Özler (2005) 'Not Separate, Not Equal: Poverty and Inequality in Post-apartheid South Africa', William Davidson Institute Working Paper Number 379, January, University of Michigan Business School.

Jenkins, S.P. (1995) 'Accounting for inequality trends: decomposition analyses for the UK, 1971–86', *Economica*, 62: 29–63.

Leibbrandt, M. and I. Woolard (2001) 'The labour market and household income inequality in South Africa: existing evidence and new panel data', *Journal of International Development*, 13: 671–689.

Leite, P.G., T. McKinley and R.G. Osorio (2006) 'The Post-apartheid Evolution of Earnings Inequality in South Africa, 1995–2004', International Poverty Centre Working Paper No. 32, October 1996.

Mocan, H. Naci (1999) 'Structural unemployment, cyclical unemployment, and income inequality', *The Review of Economics and Statistics*, 81(1): 122–134.

Mookherjee, D. and A. Shorrocks (1982) 'A decomposition analysis of the trend in UK income inequality', *The Economic Journal*, 92: 886–902.

Palma, G. (2009) 'The revenge of the market on the rentiers: Why neo-liberal reports of the end of history turned out to be premature', *Cambridge Journal of Economics* 33(4): 829–869.

Piketty, T. (2007) 'Income, wage and wealth inequality in France, 1901–1998', in A.B Atkinson and T. Piketty (eds), *Top Income Over the Twentieth Century: A Contrast between European and English-speaking Countries*, Oxford: Oxford University Press.

Statistics South Africa (Stats SA) (2008a) *Income and Expenditure of Households 2005/2006*. Pretoria: Stats SA.

Statistics South Africa (Stats SA) (2008b) *Income and Expenditure of Households 2005/2006: Analysis of Results*. Pretoria: Stats SA.

Storer, P.A. and M.A. van Audenrode (1998) 'Exploring the links between wage inequality and unemployment: A comparison of Canada and the US', *Canadian Public Policy/ Analyse de Politiques*, 241: S233–253.

Tregenna, F. (2011) 'Earnings inequality and unemployment in South Africa', *International Review of Applied Economics*, 25(5): 585–598.

Tregenna, F. and M. Tsela (2012) 'Inequality in South Africa: The distribution of income, expenditure and earnings', *Development Southern Africa*, 29(1): 35–61.

The scenario for small developing states

The Caribbean

Part VI

14 Factors impacting on whether and how businesses respond to early warning signs of financial and economic turmoil

Jamaican firms in the global crisis

David Tennant

1 Introduction

Much of the debate surrounding the recent global crisis is narrowly focused on respective governments' policy responses to the financial and economic downturn. Much less attention has been placed on the manner in which private sector businesses, the engine of growth in most economies, responded to the crisis. Pervasive credit crunches, recessions in numerous countries and drastic reductions in global consumption clearly indicated that most businesses would be affected by the crisis. As with most crisis situations, there were elements of high importance and immediacy that demanded a quick response by businesses, but also high uncertainty, which could translate to inertia or inappropriate responses if not handled properly (Calloway and Keen 1996: 18–19). It is therefore not surprising that studies conducted immediately after the crisis indicated that in numerous countries many businesses did not react to the crisis in a manner that made sense given their situations (see, for example, Heckmann *et al.* 2009, Banerji *et al.* 2009a). Surveys conducted with business managers in developed and emerging economies indicate that large proportions of businesses had not, at December 2008, initiated any response to the crisis, many hard-hit companies had not yet undertaken rationalization procedures designed to preserve cash, and numerous financially healthy companies were not taking advantage of the opportunities afforded by the crisis.[1] By contrast, other studies conducted during the same time period indicated that businesses were responding as expected, by cutting travel, communication and discretionary expenses, reducing inventories and receivables, instituting pay cuts, laying off staff if necessary and, where possible, aggressively pursuing new customers and opportunities (Raghavan 2005).

The early post-crisis literature focusing on business coping strategies warned of dire socio-economic consequences. As early as 2008, survey data from firms in the USA showed that 45 per cent of businesses had either laid off or were planning to lay off workers in the near future, while 55 per cent of American and 84 per cent of Latin American firms had or were planning to implement hiring freezes during the same time period (Watson Wyatt Worldwide, 2009b). Businesses surveyed in

Eastern and Central Europe indicated significant reductions in demand, and consequent decreases in sales, capacity utilization and employment (Ramalho *et al.* 2009). Firms in the rest of Europe and Central Asia highlighted similar effects, and were also observed to delay tax payments as a means of managing cash constraints (Correa and Lootty 2010). The ILO (2009a) notes that the consequences of such efforts to restructure enterprises are enormous, because 'in times of outsourcing and global supply chains, restructuring in one company affects many suppliers, their workers and localities all over the world.' Naude (2009: 7) thus predicted that:

> The possible combination of banking failures and reductions in domestic lending, reductions in export earnings, and reductions in financial flows to developing countries will end up reducing private sector investments and household consumption. This in turn will lead to reduced government expenditure, as governments will now face the higher cost of raising funds coupled with less tax income. Together, low investment, consumption and government expenditure could spell higher unemployment and poverty across the developing world.[2]

With this prevailing pessimistic outlook, the ILO (2009a) highlighted the need for appropriate government responses to the crisis which focused on managing how businesses adjusted to the credit crunch and reduction in demand. The appropriate design of such business-centred post-crisis management policies, however, requires rigorous analysis to enhance understanding of why businesses responded in the way they did and to predict the likelihood of similar responses occurring in the future. In previous economic crises affecting developing countries, Olukoshi (1996: 22–33) contributed to the literature by broadly categorizing business coping strategies as involving: rationalization of production and input use; changing managerial strategies and relations; economic diversification and export promotion; and changing marketing, procurement and financial arrangements. He also, however, correctly noted that the choice of coping strategies by different types of entrepreneurs is a varied and complex process impacted by numerous factors. The frequency with which businesses are required to adopt such crisis-coping strategies in an increasingly volatile global economy necessitates further investigation of the factors impacting on whether and how businesses respond to early warning signs of financial and economic turmoil.

The crisis management literature suggests that very few, if any, crises occur without warning signs that precede the acute and chronic crisis stages. Early signal detection and preparation or prevention activities are thus factors that impact on the eventual coping strategies used by businesses (Calloway and Keen 1996: 18–19). In the context of the recent global crisis, the early signals of the crisis outside of the USA were evidenced through international financial and trade transmission mechanisms.[3] Widespread credit crunches and reduced demand for imported goods and services in the USA and other developed country markets provided clear signals that were documented by authors such as Forbes (2000) and Boshoff (2006) in reference to the 'Asian Flu', 'Russian Virus' and 'Tequila Effect'. The extent to which those signals were evident to and properly interpreted by businesses in the current global crisis is an area that needs to be investigated. This will enable a determination of whether, for example, unresponsiveness or inappropriate response by businesses was caused, as suggested by Banerji *et al.* (2009a: 3), by paralysis induced by the sheer speed of the downturn and/or unwarranted optimism by businesses that misread the environment or their position in it.[4]

Even for those businesses that responded in the expected manner, further analysis is needed to determine whether there are clear differences between those that tended towards rationalization of production and input use, versus those that sought to diversify and expand. For example, were the experiences, expectations and basic business characteristics of businesses that felt compelled to lay off workers or cut wages different from those that sought new markets or alternative sources of finance as means of coping with the crisis? Did the size of the business, ownership structure, or sector within which it operated impact the likelihood of certain types of coping strategy? Or were coping strategies more heavily impacted by the type of international transmission mechanism most evident in the respective business environments?

Such questions, which have not to date been answered in the context of the current global crisis, are addressed in this chapter. Logistic regression techniques are used to analyse the results of a survey of 284 Jamaican businesses conducted in the first quarter of 2009, at a time when awareness of the global economic crisis was high, but the full impact on the country had not yet been felt. Jamaica is an interesting case study, as the smallness and openness of the economy and the heavy reliance on the USA in critical areas such as tourism and bauxite exposed the real sectors of the economy to significant external trade shocks. Financial shocks were also experienced as some Jamaican financial institutions were called upon by international banks to repay loans at short notice, commercial importers lost credit facilities, unfavourable reports from rating agencies adversely affected Jamaica's sovereign bonds, international capital markets remained closed to emerging market economies, and remittances significantly declined. Jamaica was unique in that in spite of negative economic growth in the final quarter of 2008, and official projections of further negative growth in the first quarter of 2009, a depreciating exchange rate prompted the Central Bank to implement tightened monetary policies (Table 14.1). Whereas other countries were responding to the credit crunch by reducing interest rates, the Jamaican government sought to defend the currency by increasing such rates across the spectrum of open market instruments.[5] An investigation of the expectations and responses of businesses in such conditions will be instructive, as will be an analysis of the factors most likely to precipitate respective responses.

Using the Jamaican case study, the existence of factors that predispose certain businesses to be unresponsive to the early warning signs of a crisis is first investigated. The factors impacting the choice of crisis-coping strategies are then

Table 14.1 Selected indicators of economic performance

Year	Economic growth (%)	Unemployment rate (%)	Inflation rate (%)	Average annual exchange rate J$ per US$	Adjusted central government balance	
					Fiscal Year	% of GDP
1992	1.7	15.8	40.2	23.01	1992/1993	3.7
1993	2.4	16.2	30.1	25.68	1993/1994	3.0
1994	1.0	15.4	26.7	33.35	1994/1995	3.1
1995	2.5	16.2	25.6	35.54	1995/1996	1.8
1996	0.0	16.0	15.8	37.02	1996/1997	−6.3
1997	0.0	16.5	9.2	35.58	1997/1998	−8.7
1998	−1.0	15.5	7.9	36.68	1998/1999	−12.3
1999	1.0	16.0	6.8	39.33	1999/2000	−8.3
2000	0.9	15.5	6.1	43.32	2000/2001	−5.5
2001	1.3	15.0	8.8	46.09	2001/2002	−5.7
2002	1.0	14.2	7.1	48.54	2002/2003	−8.0
2003	3.5	11.4	13.8	57.93	2003/2004	−9.9
2004	1.4	11.7	13.7	61.34	2004/2005	−8.6
2005	1.0	11.2	12.6	62.50	2005/2006	−4.8
2006	2.7	10.4	5.7	65.88	2006/2007	−4.7
2007	1.5	9.8	16.8	69.06	2007/2008	−4.8
2008	−0.9	10.6	16.8	72.92	2008/2009	−7.2

Sources: Bank of Jamaica Statistical Digest (various issues); www.boj.org.jm.

analysed for businesses that were responsive to the early warning signs of the crisis. The factors impacting on businesses' likelihood of rationalizing production and input use, adjusting staff and managerial relations, and diversifying markets and sources of finance were independently examined. Regression results are also presented for coping strategies of particular interest, to highlight factors which impact, for example, increased likelihood of laying off workers.

The results presented in this chapter are important, as in a world frequently beset by financial, economic and organizational crises, the speed and effectiveness with which a firm responds to a crisis often affects its 'reputation, credibility, integrity of operations and market performance' (Calloway and Keen 1996: 13). The effects are, however, not limited to firms, as in crisis situations affecting many firms the coping strategies chosen can have deleterious socio-economic outcomes. Understanding why businesses choose certain crisis-coping strategies and predicting how they are likely to respond in future crisis situations enables governments to be better prepared for future crises. This will involve the design of more appropriate crisis-response policies that are better targeted at businesses which are likely to adopt coping strategies with the most adverse socio-economic impacts.

The remainder of the chapter is organized as follows. The next section provides the contextual analysis by comparing the actual early responses of Jamaican businesses with how they should have responded in light of their degree of exposure to financial and trade shocks. This is followed by a description of the model, data and methodology used to identify the factors that impact on whether and how businesses responded to the early warning signs of the crisis. The results are then presented and analysed, and conclusions are derived.

2 How should Jamaican businesses have responded to the early signs of the global crisis, and did they respond in such a manner?

There is no one-size-fits-all business response to the global crisis. The early crisis-response strategy chosen by any business should hinge on its ability to survive a drastic reduction in sales volumes and prices for a prolonged period, and the strength of its market position – whether the business is a market leader or a marginal player (Heckmann *et al.*, 2009). Weak players should adopt a defensive approach in an attempt to survive or save as much value as is possible, while better positioned firms should aggressively and expeditiously seek to become as strong as possible, strategically capitalizing on opportunities (Branstad *et al.*, 2009). The strongest firms may seek to leverage their position to fine-tune their portfolio of businesses, pursue coveted assets that become available in the market, and enter key emerging markets (Heckmann *et al.*, 2009).

However, whether the businesses are strong or weak, there are two crisis-response principles that are generally agreed to by business experts. First, issues related to a crisis generally cannot wait and must be addressed quickly (ibid.). In this respect, preparedness is key. The ILO (2009a) notes that even though many firms did not foresee the consequences of the global crisis, they should have had early warning systems in place and should have utilized scenario planning so as to allow for speedy but strategic responses.[6] A study conducted by Penn, Schoen and Berland Associates (2009) has shown that businesses 'without a crisis plan can expect to be hit harder in terms of loss of revenue and layoffs than those companies that are better prepared'. Most businesses with a plan indicated that it saved them approximately a third of the average cost of the crisis, as it enabled them to recover from the crisis faster. Firms that act decisively and in a strategic manner in implementing appropriate early responses to a crisis typically fare better than those which suffer from early paralysis or implement panicked responses.[7]

The second general crisis-response principle is that in an imminent recessionary environment, preparations to weather the storm requires all firms to initially seek to stabilize and survive by securing funding and ensuring their cash flow (Heckmann et al., 2009). Branstad et al. (2009: 7) note that 'strong and weak companies alike may have too much capacity, too much manufacturing overhead, too much business overhead, and too much staff'. The crisis should thus precipitate businesses to respond by exiting underperforming businesses, cutting costs, paring working capital, and reducing exposure to operational and non-operational risk factors (ibid.). Business restructuring should thus have been pursued, involving a comprehensive evaluation of all costs. History has shown that the typical knee-jerk downsizing in response to crises has often not created the desired outcomes. Banerji et al. (2009b) note that when firms reduce expenses in a panic, or without an eye to strategy, harm is done to the business' competitiveness. *The Economist* (2009) illustrates by observing that

> during the 2001–02 recession, many firms quickly laid-off staff, especially in their lower ranks. These cuts made it challenging for executives to manage day-to-day execution and service or plan for further performance improvements that would enable them to emerge from the recession successfully. Furthermore, when economic growth picked up again, they found themselves poorly positioned lacking skilled staff to manage the expansion.
> (As quoted in ILO 2009a: 13)

Aguirre and Post (2009: 2) thus assert that the best businesses are 'avoiding across-the-board reductions that often destroy value and damage capabilities'.[8]

The ILO (2009a: 14) advocates a three-tiered strategic approach to cost-reduction that maximizes business gains, minimizes the hidden costs of restructuring, and gives adequate attention to the human and social side of enterprise restructuring during a crisis. The approach involves:

- Reducing non-staff costs first;[9]
- Second, aiming at staff-costs savings without making employees redundant;[10] and
- Finally, reducing staff-costs through layoffs and downsizing when

alternative sources of cost savings are exhausted, but doing that in a socially sensitive manner.[11]

An obstacle to the effective implementation of this strategy during periods of crisis is the need to not panic and to think beyond the exigencies of the moment. If businesses do not respond to crises in a timely fashion, and instead wait until they are forced to act, the suggested tiered approach is unlikely, as businesses believe that they lack the requisite time and money. Such businesses are also likely to 'underestimate the effort required to make these changes happen' (ILO, 2009b). The adoption of the second general crisis-response strategy is thus contingent on the implementation of the first.

Both principles were, however, particularly important in Jamaica if widespread adverse socio-economic consequences were to be minimized. By virtue of the country's size, the openness of the economy and the connectedness to the American financial and real sectors, the transmission of the crisis to Jamaican businesses should have been expected. An examination of CaPRI's (2009: 27) business survey results indicates that even though the majority (85.6 per cent) of Jamaican businesses surveyed have over 90 per cent of their total market located in Jamaica, just under half (41 per cent) of these businesses are suppliers of intermediate goods to medium-sized and large businesses. These larger businesses are more vulnerable to changes in the external demand for their goods and services, with over 40 per cent of medium-sized and large businesses having up to 60 per cent of their markets in foreign countries, particularly the USA.[12] Such vulnerability was evidenced by the fact that exports from Jamaica declined by 34 per cent between the second and final quarters of 2008 (see Figure 14.1).[13] In the most vulnerable sectors – tourism and bauxite – MNCs were major players, and were also the main customers of a number of small Jamaican businesses. However, in line with global trends, between 2007 and 2008 FDI inflows to Jamaica decreased by 9 per cent and the stock of FDI as a percentage of GDP decreased by 14.7 per cent.[14] Because of the high degree of interconnectedness within the domestic economy, there was considerable potential for contagion if certain businesses were adversely impacted by the crisis. The large number of small and micro-businesses that were not exporting at the time of the global crisis should therefore not have expected to be left unscathed, as it was clear that the effects could have spread very quickly throughout the economy through a small number of large and medium-sized businesses that were primary clients of many firms.[15] This was not considered a farfetched possibility, as although only 13 per cent of the respondents indicated a reduction in exports by the end of 2008, nearly two-thirds (61.1 per cent) reported declines in local sales between July and December 2008. Expectations were that local sales would continue declining in the medium to long term (CaPRI, 2009: 36). In such conditions, early preparations for the ensuing crisis were clearly necessary.

Lessons learned from the Jamaican experience with the financial crisis in the mid- to late 1990s ensured that financial institutions were largely protected from direct exposure to the sub-prime crisis by virtue of adequate capitalization, and

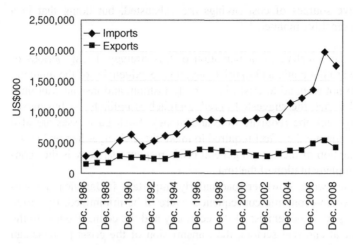

Figure 14.1 Trends in exports and imports (source: Bank of Jamaica, Statistical Digest, various issues).

strict regulatory requirements and oversight.[16] But, notwithstanding this, financial conditions in Jamaica and businesses' early experiences with lines of credit should have provided businesses with clear signals as to the likelihood of transmission of the global crisis through indirect financial linkages.[17] Even though a negligible proportion (8 per cent) of Jamaican businesses had credit with foreign financial institutions, Tennant (2010) notes that the importance of, and changes in the terms and conditions of loans from local financial institutions, and local and foreign suppliers, had greater relevance in businesses' choice of coping strategy. Almost a third (32 per cent) of the businesses surveyed at the time of the crisis had lines of credit with foreign suppliers, and more than half of these businesses considered such credit lines to be critical to the survival of their business. Approximately two-thirds of the respondents also had credit with local financial institutions and suppliers, and similarly regarded such credit lines to be important to their business operations. Considering the importance of credit to Jamaican business operations, any adverse conditions that would potentially affect the availability and/or terms and conditions of those loans should have precipitated early responses from the business community. The global crisis provided the adverse stimulus, exhibited by the fact that although most respondents indicated no changes in the terms and conditions of loans from foreign suppliers when surveyed in January–March 2009, significantly larger proportions expected worsening conditions in the medium to long term. Similar results were derived with respect to lines of credit from local sources, with the cost, availability and maturity of credit expected to worsen in the medium to long term (CaPRI 2009: 23–25).

These negative expectations were fuelled at least in part by the actions of the Central Bank, which implemented tightened monetary policies in response to a depreciation of the Jamaican dollar in the last quarter of 2008. There were also official projections of negative growth in the first quarter of 2009, with the Central Bank noting that 'the outlook for the economy remains surrounded by a high degree of uncertainty' (Latibeaudiere, 2009). With these ominous signs, early responses to the crisis by Jamaican businesses, similar to those suggested by the ILO (2009a), were expected. The results of the CaPRI survey, however, indicated that 20.4 per cent of the businesses surveyed noted that they did not plan to make any adjustments to their business operations in response to the global crisis. Such a high level of unresponsiveness to the global crisis is not uncommon, as the results of a 2008 survey of 245 Latin American companies indicate that 25 per cent of the respondents had not then implemented actions in response to the economic downturn. By 2009, however, this number had reduced to 11 per cent, highlighting the large number of firms that squandered the possible benefits of early response (Watson Wyatt Worldwide, 2009b: 3). In Jamaica, because of the high probability of transmission, such inactivity was inadvisable, and, as such, the factors precipitating unresponsiveness to early warning signs of crises clearly require careful examination to ascertain whether remedial measures are possible.

It is also instructive to note that of the businesses that indicated an intention to respond to the early warning signs of the crisis, most (91.3 per cent) did not see a need to shut down operations, 67.4 per cent were unlikely to lay off workers and 77 per cent were unlikely to reduce workers' wages. CaPRI (2009: 40) asserts that these results suggest that 'business owners and managers were attempting to shield their workers from the adverse effects of the crisis by minimizing adjustments that would directly affect staff'. This conclusion has, however, to be more rigorously examined in a regression framework that allows for the consideration of a range of possible explanatory factors. Other coping strategies that proved to be unpopular with Jamaican businesses were the reduced use of local and foreign inputs (with 62.6 per cent and 61.7 per cent of respondents, respectively, indicating that such responses were unlikely). The early coping strategies with a greater likelihood of being adopted by Jamaican businesses included reducing non-staff-related expenses (85.2 per cent), seeking alternative markets (67 per cent), seeking alternative sources of finance (52.2 per cent), and reducing 'other' benefits to staff (51.7 per cent).

Apart from the large number of Jamaican firms that were unresponsive to the crisis, the majority of firms seemed to have been attempting to respond in the manner generally advocated by the experts. Most sought to first reduce non-staff expenses and explore other options of weathering the storm before engaging in widespread layoffs. Notwithstanding this, the fact that one-third of the businesses surveyed intended to lay off workers should not be ignored, as this hints at significant adverse socio-economic effects that could ripple through the entire economy.

3 Economic model, data and methodology

3.1 The model

The model adopted in this chapter seeks to identify the factors which impact on whether and how businesses respond to early warning signs of financial and economic crises. As illustrated in equation (1), a number of different types of business responses (BUSres) are investigated.

$$\text{BUSres} = \sum (\text{UNRES, RATION, MANREL, DIVER}) \qquad (1)$$

In addition to the businesses that were unresponsive (UNRES), an adaptation of Olukoshi's (1996) classification of business coping strategies was used to broadly classify those that were responsive to the early warning signs of the crisis as being likely to rationalize production and input use (RATION), adjust staff and managerial relations (MANREL), and diversify markets and sources of finance (DIVER).[18]

Equation (2) theorizes the respective responses of businesses to be a function of managers' early experiences with the crisis (EXPer), their expectations in the medium to long term as economies and industries adjust to the crisis (EXPect), and certain basic characteristics of the business (BUSchar).

$$\text{BUSres} = f(\text{EXPer, EXPect, BUSchar}) \qquad (2)$$

Managers' experiences and expectations with regard to the impact of the crisis are influenced by their perception of the extent to which the crisis has been and will be transmitted to their business. In the context of the current global crisis, the literature on international transmission mechanisms is instructive, as the effects of financial crises typically cross borders via financial and/or trade linkages. Forbes (2000) and Boshoff (2006) both indicate that credit crunches, decreased exports and reduced competitiveness of exports are the most common manifestations of such transmission mechanisms.[19] Equations (3) and (4) thus illustrate this relationship by presenting managers' experiences and expectations as being dependent on credit (CREDlin) and trade (TRADElin) linkages. These transmission mechanisms are captured by a series of variables in which respondents were asked to indicate whether they experienced or expected changes in the following areas:

- Credit availability, Credit maturity, Cost of Credit, and Size of loans (CREDlin); and
- Quantity and Price of goods and services sold, and Availability and Cost of inputs (TRADElin).[20]

$$\text{EXPer} = f(\text{CREDlin, TRADElin}) \qquad (3)$$

$$\text{EXPect} = f(\text{CREDlin, TRADElin}) \qquad (4)$$

Finally, as indicated in equation (5), the basic characteristics of a business that are expected to impact on whether and how businesses respond to a crisis include those which influence the business' likelihood of being impacted by the crisis (CHARimp), and those which influence its ability to respond to the crisis (CHARres). The characteristics that were tested under CHARimp include:

- whether or not the business had deposits or investments with foreign financial institutions (as a proxy for direct exposure to the crisis);
- the importance of different sources of credit utilized by the business (including credit from foreign and local financial institutions and suppliers);
- the sector in which the business operates;
- the extent to which it relies on export markets (measured by the proportion of its total market which is outside of Jamaica); and
- the business' primary product line (classified as basic necessities, intermediate goods/services, medium-cost non-essential goods/services, consumer durables, or luxury goods/services).

The characteristics that were used as proxies for CHARres include:

- the size of the business (measured by both the number of employees and the value of total assets);
- the ownership structure of the firm (classified as sole proprietorship, partnership or limited liability company); and
- the number of years that the business has been operational.

$$BUSchar = \Sigma(CHARimp, CHARres) \tag{5}$$

When combined, these theorized relationships are captured in the preliminary econometric model outlined below:

$$BUSres = \alpha + \beta_1 \, EXPer + \beta_2 \, EXPect + \beta_3 \, BUSchar + \varepsilon \tag{6}$$

with BUSres representing the range of possible responses outlined in equation (1); EXPer and EXPect representing variables that highlight the theorized credit and trade linkages outlined in equations (3) and (4); BUSchar representing the two categories of business characteristics outlined in equation (5); and ε being a disturbance term controlling for all other unaccounted explanatory factors.

3.2 Data

Primary data, collected by the Caribbean Policy Research Institute (CaPRI), were used in the estimations. A survey of Jamaican businesses was conducted between January and March 2009. The target population was all businesses operating in Jamaica, stratified by size, sector and location (county). The sampling frame used was a database of all companies that are serviced by the sole provider of electricity in the country. This had the advantage of including both formal and informal businesses. A sample size of 400 businesses was targeted, and ultimately a random sample of 284 firms completed the survey.

3.3 Methodology

Many of the variables used in the model are derived from responses to Likert-Scale type questions, and as such, most are ordinal while a few are nominal. The dependent variables in all specifications of the model are binary, which necessitates the nesting of equation (6) within a logistic probability function, as follows:

$$F(Z_i) = p_i = e^{Z_i}/(1 + e^{Z_i}) \tag{7a}$$

Equation 7a can be transformed into the more intuitive functional form below:

$$\ln\left(\frac{p_i}{1 - p_i}\right) = Z_i \tag{7b}$$

where

$$Z_i = \text{BUSres}_i = \alpha + \beta_{1j}\, \text{EXPer}_{ij} + \beta_{2j}\, \text{EXPect}_{ij} + \beta_{3j}\, \text{BUSchar}_{ij} + \varepsilon_i \tag{7c}$$

and

> $\text{BUSres}_i = 1$ if the ith firm intends to or has undertaken the response under consideration or $= 0$ if it does not
>
> p_i = the probability that $\text{BUSres}_i = 1$. Therefore, $p_i/(1 - p_i)$ is the odds of the ith firm engaging in the response under consideration, and Equation 7b predicts the logarithm of the odds (referred to as the logit) for each value of the explanatory variables.
>
> EXPer_{ij} = the value of the jth explanatory variable relating to the experiences of the ith firm
>
> EXPect_{ij} = the value of the jth explanatory variable relating to the expectations of the ith firm
>
> BUSchar_{ij} = the value of the jth explanatory variable relating to the basic business characteristics of the ith firm
>
> ε_i = a disturbance term.

Before the model was estimated, tests of sampling adequacy and multicollinearity were conducted. Cross-tabulations were used to ascertain whether empty or extremely small cells are present in the dataset. Checks were made to ensure that cell frequencies were not less than one, and no more than 20 per cent of the cells in any estimation were less than five. So as not to risk instability in the logistic model due to sampling inadequacy, it was necessary in a few instances to combine the categories of categorical independents and to discard some variables. The approach used by Vandersmissen et al. (2004) and Menard (1995) was used to test for multicollinearity. Simple regression models were estimated using the dependent and independent variables under consideration. The Variable Inflation Factor (VIF) and the tolerance measure were used, with a tolerance of 0.2 or less and/or a VIF of 5 or more indicating problems of multicollinearity.[21]

Due to the large number of variables representing the experiences and expectations of managers and the characteristics of the businesses, it was not possible to include them all in the full model. In order to eliminate variables that did not have a significant impact on the response of businesses to the crisis, backward stepwise methods based on the likelihood ratio (LR) test were used to estimate a model that only included the constant and one explanatory variable. If the results suggest that there is no statistically significant change in the log likelihood ratio (−2LL) when the explanatory variable under consideration is dropped from the model (thus leaving only the constant), that variable is not included in the full model. This was sequentially done for each of the explanatory variables.

The full model for each of the dependent variables was then estimated using the explanatory variables determined in the manner described above. The Hosmer and Lemeshow (H–L) chi-square test of goodness of fit was conducted to determine the overall fit of the logistic regression model. If the H–L goodness-of-fit test statistic was insignificant (that is, >0.05), the null hypothesis that there is no difference between observed and model-predicted values was not rejected. This implies that the model's estimates fit the data at an acceptable level. While it does not suggest that the model necessarily explains much of the variance in the dependent, it indicates that what it does explain is significant.[22] The Omnibus Test of Model Coefficients was also conducted to test if the model with the predictors is significantly different from the model with only the intercept. When significant, it is concluded that there is an adequate fit of the data to the model, indicating that at least one of the predictors is significantly related to the dependent variable. The Nagelkerke's R^2 is reported for all models as a measure of strength of association, and two-by-two classification tables are used to match actual outcomes with predicted outcomes as an indication of the model's predictive precision of group membership. Additionally, outlier cases defined as three standard deviations about its mean were removed. Finally, the significance of each of the explanatory variables was reported. All variables that are insignificant at the 10 per cent level were removed from the respective models. This results in the more parsimonious reduced form models, which were then subjected to all the abovementioned tests. These models, along with the relevant test results, are reported in the subsequent section.

4 Results and analysis

Table 14.2 presents the frequencies of all the variables utilized in the reduced form models. Most of the businesses surveyed were small limited liability companies, with small businesses representing 53.2 per cent of the sample and limited liability companies representing 75 per cent. Notwithstanding this, there

Table 14.2 Description and frequencies of variables used in the reduced form models

	Code	#	%
BUSres			
RATION (Not Likely)	0	149	52.5
RATION (Likely)	1	135	47.5
MANREL (Not Likely)	0	80	28.2
MANREL (Likely)	1	204	71.8
DIVER (Not Likely)	0	101	35.6
DIVER (Likely)	1	183	64.4
UNRES (Not Likely)	0	226	79.6
UNRES (Likely)	1	58	20.4
EXPer			
ExperienceCreditAvailability (no change)	0	177	65.3
ExperienceCreditAvailability (decrease)	1	94	34.7
ExperienceCreditMaturity (no change)	0	182	69.5
ExperienceCreditMaturity (decrease)	1	80	30.5
EXPect			
ExpectedCreditAvailability (no change)	0	112	39.4
ExpectedCreditAvailability (decrease)	1	149	52.5
ExpectedCreditAvailability (increase)	2	23	8.1
ExpectedCreditMaturity (no change)	0	130	45.8
ExpectedCreditMaturity (decrease)	1	130	45.8
ExpectedCreditMaturity (increase)	2	24	8.5
ExpectedCreditCost (no change)	0	119	41.9
ExpectedCreditCost (decrease)	1	18	6.3
ExpectedCreditCost (increase)	2	147	51.8
ExpectedCreditSize (no change)	0	144	50.7
ExpectedCreditSize (decrease)	1	108	38.0
ExpectedCreditSize (increase)	2	32	11.3
ExpectedAvailabilityInputs (no change)	0	203	71.5
ExpectedAvailabilityInputs (decrease)	1	60	21.1
ExpectedAvailabilityInputs (increase)	2	21	7.4
BUSchar			
Ownership (Sole Proprietorship)	0	51	18.0
Ownership (Partnership)	1	20	7.0
Ownership (Limited Liability)	2	213	75.0
Number Employees (Micro 0–4)	Included as Continuous Variable	55	19.4
Number Employees (Small 5–50)		151	53.2
Number Employees (Medium 51–100)		43	15.1
Number Employees (Large over 100)		35	12.3

were sufficient numbers of respondents from all sizes and types of business to facilitate rigorous analysis, as all tests of sampling adequacy were satisfied.

Table 14.3 presents the logistic regression results for all the reduced form models estimated. Each model sought to predict the likelihood of one of the four categories of response under consideration. In each instance there was no multicollinearity, outliers were removed, and the Hosmer and Lemeshow and Omnibus tests indicated that the models' estimates adequately fit the data. The Nagelkerke R^2 for the respective estimations range from 0.149 to 0.325. Although this test statistic can range from 0 to 1, values above 0.3 are reasonable in studies of this nature. With the exception of the model with DIVER as the dependent variable, the Nagelkerke R^2 values are above or just below the average for models of this type. The classification tables for each specification indicate that the models predict between 68.3 per cent and 79.1 per cent of all responses correctly. The percentage of likely responses predicted correctly are fairly good for all the models (ranging from 59.2 per cent to 95.8 per cent), except for the model with UNRES as the dependent variable (for which only 9.3 per cent of the likely responses are predicted correctly). The models also perform well in correctly predicting the not likely responses, with the percentage of correct predictions ranging from 34.2 per cent to 98 per cent, and with less than 50 per cent of the unlikely responses being predicted in only one instance. The general model statistics thus indicate that the models perform fairly well in predicting the values of the respective dependent variables.

Most of the variables that remained in the reduced form models were significant at the 1 per cent level, with a few being significant at the 5 per cent level, and a maximum of two variables in any one specification being significant at the 10 per cent level. In most instances, the variables had signs that conformed to theory, with plausible explanations being proffered for the remainder in subsequent paragraphs.

The results from the first specification indicate that early experiences with reduced availability of credit increase the likelihood of responses to the crisis that involve rationalization of production and input use (RATION). A similar relationship is also exhibited with respect to expected reductions in the availability of credit. Conversely, firms which expect an increase in the availability of credit in the medium to long term are less likely to rationalize production and input use. These relationships clearly conform to theory, and highlight the critical impact that credit crunches and the threat thereof can have on an economy through the responses of businesses.

The relationships between RATION and the other explanatory variables are not as straightforward. There is, for example, a very significant negative relationship between expected decreases in the size of credit and the likelihood of firms' rationalizing production and input use, which is not easily explained. An examination of the logistic regression results of the models seeking to explain each of the specific responses which comprised RATION also does not clarify the issue. Table 14.4 indicates that a decrease in credit size does not have a significant relationship with any of the component responses under RATION. There is no plausible explanation as to why, when grouped, responses classified as involving rationalization of production and input use should be less likely to be adopted when firms expect a reduction in the size of the loans being issued.

A similar phenomenon is exhibited in regards to expectations about the maturity of credit. Although there is the expected positive relationship between an

Table 14.3 Logistic regression results – reduced form models

Variables	RATION			MANREL			DIVER			UNRES		
	B	SE	Exp(B)	B	SE	Exp(B)	B	SE	Exp(B)	B	SE	Exp(B)
EXPer												
ExperienceCreditAvailability (decrease)	1.017***	0.322	2.765	1.298***	0.411	3.664	0.575*	0.336	1.778	-2.142***	0.691	0.117
ExperienceCreditMaturity (decrease)										1.776***	0.682	5.908
EXPect												
ExpectedCreditAvailability (decrease)	1.106**	0.550	3.022				0.873***	0.309	2.393	-1.353**	0.591	0.259
ExpectedCreditAvailability (increase)	-1.576*	0.872	0.207				0.184	0.552	1.202	0.575	0.833	1.776
ExpectedCreditMaturity (decrease)	0.749*	0.432	2.115	1.194***	0.339	3.301				-1.187**	0.596	0.305
ExpectedCreditMaturity (increase)	2.534***	0.763	12.604	1.395**	0.692	4.037				-21.131	10886.941	0.000
ExpectedCreditCost (decrease)	1.626**	0.782	5.084									
ExpectedCreditCost (increase)	-0.037	0.365	0.963									
ExpectedCreditSize (decrease)	-1.415***	0.539	0.243									
ExpectedCreditSize (increase)	-0.996	0.685	0.369									
ExpectedAvailabilityInputs (decrease)										-0.431	0.529	0.650
ExpectedAvailabilityInputs (increase)										1.442*	0.796	4.228
BUSchar												
Ownership (Partnership)				-0.131	0.583	0.878						
Ownership (Limited Liability)				0.988***	0.355	2.685						
NumberEmployees							0.005**	0.002	1.005			
Constant	-0.941***	0.227	0.390	-0.644**	0.328	0.525	-0.277	0.206	0.758	-0.346	0.218	0.707
N	271			271			266			253		

Nagelkerke R-square	0.252	0.270	0.149	0.325
% of likely responses predicted correctly	59.20%	95.80%	76.80%	9.30%
% of not likely responses predicted correctly	76.00%	34.20%	54.10%	98.00%
Overall % predicted correctly	68.30%	77.90%	68.40%	79.10%
Hosmer & Lemeshow Test (sig)	0.888	0.077	0.731	0.641
Omnibus Test of Model Coefficients (sig)	0.000	0.000	0.000	0.000

Notes
*** 1% Significance, ** 5% significance, * 10% significance.

Table 14.4 Logistic regression results – ungrouped dependent variables: RATION

Variables	↑ Layoffs			↓ Use of Local Inputs			↓ Use of Foreign Inputs		
	B	SE	Exp(B)	B	SE	Exp(B)	B	SE	Exp(B)
EXPer									
ExperienceCreditAvailability (decrease)	1.193***	0.367	3.296				1.214***	0.321	3.365
ExperiencePricesGoodsSold (decrease)	1.376***	0.519	3.960						
ExperiencePricesGoodsSold (increase)	−0.148	0.376	0.862						
EXPect									
ExpectedCreditAvailability (decrease)	0.190	0.457	1.209						
ExpectedCreditAvailability (increase)	−1.793*	0.998	0.166						
ExpectedCreditMaturity (decrease)				1.15***	0.310	3.158			
ExpectedCreditMaturity (increase)				0.908*	0.522	2.480			
ExpectedCreditCost (decrease)	2.019***	0.686	7.528						
ExpectedCreditCost (increase)	0.121	0.413	1.129						
BUSchar									
Ownership (Partnership)	0.232	0.823	1.261				−0.274	1.198	0.761
Ownership (Limited Liability)	0.954*	0.502	2.596				1.474**	0.626	4.367
NumberEmployees				0.003***	0.001	1.003			
Constant	−2.689***	0.576	0.068	−1.874***	0.260	0.154	−3.115***	0.616	0.044
N	271			279			271		
Nagelkerke R-square	0.246			0.119			0.164		
% of likely responses predicted correctly	21.70%			8.00%			0.00%		
% of not likely responses predicted correctly	97.50%			98.50%			100.00%		
Overall % predicted correctly	78.20%			74.20%			79.70%		
Hosmer & Lemeshow Test (sig)	0.150			0.250			0.899		
Omnibus Test of Model Coefficients (sig)	0.000			0.000			0.000		

Notes
*** 1% Significance, ** 5% significance, * 10% significance.

expected decrease in credit maturity and RATION, there is a much stronger and more significant positive relationship with expected increases in credit maturity. Table 14.4, however, indicates that amongst those responses categorized as RATION, only the reduced use of local inputs is significantly impacted by expectations about the maturity of credit. Here, although expectations of an increase in the maturity of credit increase the likelihood of reduced use of local inputs, there is a stronger and more significant positive relationship with expected decreases in credit maturity, suggesting the converse relationship that conforms to theoretical expectations. This, however, does not explain why, when grouped, the responses classified as RATION exhibit relationships with the maturity of credit that do not conform to theory.

The results also indicate that firms are more likely to adopt responses to the crisis involving rationalization of production and input use when interest rates (i.e. the cost of credit) are expected to decrease. As indicated in Table 14.4, this result is strong and highly significant in regard to the laying off of workers, suggesting that when interest rates decrease, businesses are more likely to fire staff. This result also seems to be counterintuitive, as basic economic theory suggests that a future reduction in interest rates should allow businesses to borrow more and thus expand their operations. Prevalent Jamaican macroeconomic policies since liberalization of the economy in the early 1990s, however, provide a plausible explanation for two of the contrary relationships exhibited.

In attempts to combat inflation, finance the budget deficit and defend the local currency, the GOJ has for the past two decades consistently implemented high-interest rate policies and has issued high-yielding Treasury Bills. Even in response to the current global crisis, while other countries were reducing interest rates, the Bank of Jamaica increased interest rates across the spectrum of open market instruments. This has resulted in many Jamaican businesses developing an appetite for high-yielding and virtually risk-free government instruments, which is not limited to financial institutions, but extends to businesses and individuals across all sectors of the economy. Many entrepreneurs have thus made more profits from the returns on financial transactions than from productive ventures in the real sector. In this context, an expected reduction in interest rates may not be viewed positively by businesses, as it would imply a decrease in revenue from their portfolio of financial instruments, which would in turn necessitate the laying off of staff and other measures to rationalize production and input use.

When viewed in this light, an expected increase in maturities may also be cause for alarm for businesses heavily invested in financial instruments, as the turn-around time on financial investments would be prolonged, leading to cash-flow problems. The positive relationship between the likelihood of firms rationalizing production and inputs and such an expected increase in maturities is thus plausible in this context, as if cash flow is constrained by the extension of maturities on financial investments, businesses will be forced to cut costs at least until adequate liquidity is restored. The conflicting results for this explanatory variable may thus have been caused by the fact that some respondents interpreted the questions about the maturity of credit as referring to loans, while others may have thought about the implications of extended maturities on their portfolio of financial instruments.

For the first category of business responses to the crisis, it is also instructive to note that there were a few explanatory variables that were not significant for predicting the likelihood of rationalization of production or input use, but were significant predictors of one or more of the responses that comprised RATION. For example, Table 14.4 indicates that firms which experienced reductions in the prices of their goods/services early in the crisis period are more likely to lay off workers. Limited liability companies are also more likely to lay off workers and reduce use of foreign inputs than sole proprietorships. This is expected, as sole proprietorships often do not have as many cost-cutting options as do limited liability companies, and even when they do, limited liability companies tend to be more likely to exercise those options because the separation between owners, managers and staff of such companies, and the heavy emphasis on earning dividends, often increases the willingness to take unpopular decisions. The results also indicate that firms with a greater number of employees are more likely to reduce use of local inputs. This is instructive, as there may be considerable spin-off effects of the reduced use of local inputs by larger firms in an economy where many small firms are producers of intermediate goods and services.

In the second specification in Table 14.3, which sought to predict the likelihood of firms' responding to the crisis by changing staff and managerial relations, three variables are significant predictors. Firms that experienced a decrease in the availability of credit were more likely to engage in responses categorized as MANREL, again highlighting the importance of credit crunches in precipitating rapid responses by businesses. Limited liability companies are also more likely to engage in such responses than were sole proprietorships. The results presented in Table 14.5 further indicate that this relationship is particularly prevalent for businesses that are likely to reduce non-staff expenses in response to the crisis. This conforms to the results previously reported, as the organizational structure of limited liability companies better enables a wider range of cost-cutting measures in crisis situations.

Conflicting results for expected changes in the maturity of credit are also evident in this estimation, again highlighting the plausibility of the explanation previously given. That is, respondents which viewed an expected decrease in the maturity of credit as adversely affecting their outstanding loans were more likely to cut expenses by changing staff and managerial relations, while a similar response could also reasonably be expected from firms that perceived an expected increase in maturities as adversely affecting cash-flow positions through the impact on their portfolio of financial instruments. Table 14.5 further indicates that the unique relationship between interest rates and the nature of businesses' responses to the crisis also exists in this category of responses. In the last column it is shown that firms which expect interest rates to decrease are more likely to reduce staff benefits. This highly significant and strong relationship also supports the argument that the response of Jamaican businesses to

Table 14.5 Logistic regression results – ungrouped dependent variables: MANREL

Variables	↓ Non-Staff Expenses			Cut Wages			↓ Staff Benefits		
	B	SE	Exp(B)	B	SE	Exp(B)	B	SE	Exp(B)
EXPer									
ExperienceCreditAvailability (decrease)	1.13***	0.377	3.096				1.216***	0.292	3.374
ExperienceCreditSize (decrease)				0.964**	0.388	2.621			
ExperienceCostInputs(increase)				0.898**	0.437	2.456	0.713**	0.305	2.040
EXPect									
ExpectedCreditMaturity (decrease)	0.991***	0.323	2.694	-0.202	0.416	0.817			
ExpectedCreditMaturity (increase)	1.588**	0.698	4.893	0.999*	0.555	2.717			
ExpectedCreditCost (decrease)							2.403***	0.813	11.054
ExpectedCreditCost (increase)							0.075	0.291	1.078
BUSCHAR									
Ownership (Partnership)	-0.030	0.583	0.970						
Ownership (Limited Liability)	1.266***	0.352	3.546						
Constant	-0.928***	0.331	0.395	-2.500***	0.401	0.082	-1.421***	0.293	0.241
N	271			258			265		
Nagelkerke R-square	0.269			0.122			0.198		
% of likely responses predicted correctly	96.20%			10.60%			50.90%		
% of not likely responses predicted correctly	32.20%			98.60%			84.50%		
Overall % predicted correctly	75.60%			82.60%			70.60%		
Hosmer & Lemeshow Test (sig)	0.336			0.934			0.951		
Omnibus Test of Model Coefficients (sig)	0.000			0.000			0.000		

Notes
*** 1% Significance, ** 5% significance, * 10% significance.

changing conditions in financial markets is heavily influenced by their holdings of financial instruments, and thus may have different consequences from those expected by policy-makers.

There were also two explanatory variables that were not significant for predicting the likelihood of the grouped variable – changing staff and/or managerial relations – but were significant predictors of one or more of the responses that comprised MANREL. Businesses that experience early decreases in the size of loans issued are more likely to cut the wages of their staff as a coping mechanism. Increases in the cost of inputs have also been shown to precipitate a similar response, and will also increase the likelihood of businesses reducing benefits to staff.

The results for the third broad category of businesses' response to the crisis are presented in the penultimate column of Table 14.3. The model for DIVER is straightforward, as the variables which predict the likelihood of businesses seeking to diversify into new markets and financing arrangements all have the expected relationships. Firms that experience and expect a reduction in the availability of credit are more likely to seek to diversify. As highlighted in Table 14.6, this applies both to their likelihood of seeking alternative markets and new sources of finance. Table 14.3 also indicates that businesses with more employees are also more likely to diversify, again reflecting the greater capacity of larger businesses to engage in a wider range of responses in crisis situations. Smaller firms tend to be constrained in their ability to be similarly flexible. When the proclivities of firms to seek alternative markets and financing are independently modelled, the results presented in Table 14.6, however, show that the number of employees loses its significance, and instead the ownership structure of businesses becomes an important predictor of behaviour. Limited liability companies are more likely than sole proprietorships to seek alternative markets, while both limited liability companies and partnerships are more likely than sole proprietorships to seek new sources of finance. The limitations of sole proprietorships and very small businesses in responding to crises in an opportunistic manner are thus clearly seen. The resources needed to capitalize on opportunities presented in new markets are often not available to such businesses, and the likelihood of them attaining different sources of funds is very low due to the unavailability of suitably designed financing arrangements, such as venture capitalists, angel funds and junior stock exchanges.

Finally, the last column in Table 14.3 presents the results of the model that sought to predict the likelihood of a business being unresponsive to the early warning signs of a financial and economic crisis. The model, however, performed much better at predicting the likelihood of firms not being unresponsive, as significant negative relationships were exhibited with experienced and expected decreases in the availability of credit, and expected decreases in the maturity of credit. The relationships all suggest that a worsening of conditions in the credit market will lessen the likelihood of firms being unresponsive. Conversely, a positive relationship with expected increases in the availability of inputs suggests that firms which expect such an increase are more likely to be

Table 14.6 Logistic regression results – ungrouped dependent variables: DIVER

Variables	Alternative Markets			Alternative Financing		
	B	SE	Exp(B)	B	SE	Exp(B)
EXPer						
ExperienceCreditAvailability (decrease)	0.885***	0.271	2.423	1.101***	0.269	3.008
BUSCHAR						
Ownership (Partnership)	0.129	0.553	1.137	1.043*	0.566	2.837
Ownership (Limited Liability)	0.703**	0.335	2.020	0.699*	0.363	2.011
NumberEmployees						
Constant	−0.765**	0.305	0.465	−1.308***	0.338	0.270
N	271			271		
Nagelkerke R-square	0.091			0.116		
% of likely responses predicted correctly	45.00%			46.10%		
% of not likely responses predicted correctly	76.30%			80.10%		
Overall % predicted correctly	60.10%			65.70%		
Hosmer & Lemeshow Test (sig)	0.622			0.901		
Omnibus Test of Model Coefficients (sig)	0.000			0.000		

Notes
*** 1% Significance, ** 5% significance, * 10% significance.

unresponsive to the early warning signs of the crisis. Similarly, a decrease in the maturity of credit is likely to precipitate increased unresponsiveness. As previously explained, if such a decrease is reflected in a shortening of the maturities of financial instruments held by businesses, then improved cash flows may have resulted or have been expected, which would present a cushion against the adverse effects of the credit crunch and thus precipitate unresponsiveness.

5 Conclusions

Adverse external shocks from trade and financial linkages, along with government policies that worsened domestic credit conditions, clearly required Jamaican firms to prepare for the impact of the global crisis. Most businesses sought to quickly respond in a manner that would allow them to weather the storm while giving adequate attention to the human and social consequences of their restructuring efforts. The unresponsiveness of some Jamaican businesses to the early warning signs of the crisis, along with immediate reactions of other firms to lay off workers and reduce use of local inputs, however, contributed to a 21.7 per cent increase in the number of unemployed persons in the Jamaican labour force between 2007 and 2009. This, along with substantial underemployment, made it more difficult for the Jamaican economy to navigate through the downturn.[23] Jamaica, a country with negligible GDP growth over the past twenty years, could ill-afford significant job losses as a result of the global crisis, and is now even less prepared to absorb large numbers of unemployed citizens. In an attempt to aid the government in designing stimulus policies that will target businesses most likely to precipitate undesirable socio-economic effects, this chapter used logistic regression techniques to highlight the factors which impact on whether and how businesses respond to early warning signs of financial and economic crises.

The results indicate that businesses which are more likely to immediately resort to laying off workers are those which experience a decrease in the availability of credit and a reduction in the prices of their goods, highlighting the importance of traditional financial and trade linkages in the international transmission of crises. With respect to the former, temporary Central Bank support to the financial system to facilitate the flow of credit may be useful in reducing the likelihood of widespread layoffs. Expected decreases in interest rates were also shown to increase the likelihood of layoffs. This is because many Jamaican businesses had relatively large portfolios of financial instruments that had been more profitable than their productive real sector activities. The expected opportunities for borrowing presented by reduced interest rates thus paled in comparison with the immediate costs of lost revenues from financial investments. The government's current efforts to reduce interest rates will thus not immediately foster the expected expansion of economic activity, as businesses will have to gradually adjust to the new environment by reducing their reliance on financial investments and returning to productive activities.

The nature and size of businesses were also shown to impact the likelihood of workers being laid off and reduced local inputs being used. Limited liability companies are more likely than sole proprietorships to respond to crises by laying off workers, and larger companies are more likely to respond to crises by reducing the use of local inputs. These findings highlight the heightened proclivity of large listed firms to respond in crisis situations by scaling down operations, which clearly has economy-wide implications in a country where many small firms are producers of intermediate goods and services. This has significant implications for the design of future post-crisis stimulus packages in Jamaica. In the aftermath of the global crisis, the Jamaican government announced a package that emphasized support to micro- and small businesses in an effort to save jobs. This result suggests that widespread job losses would be better prevented if attention was placed on larger firms. This, however, does not suggest that sole proprietorships, micro- and small firms do not require support, as small businesses and sole proprietorships were shown to be relatively limited in their capacity to respond to crises in diverse manners. Not only do they lack the resources to respond to crises in an opportunistic manner, but they also often do not have as many cost-cutting options as do limited liability companies. Policies to support such firms thus need to be designed in a manner that will assist them to increase efficiency and identify and capitalize on opportunities presented in new markets.

Finally, it has also been shown that businesses without a crisis plan tend to be harder hit in terms of revenue losses and layoffs than better prepared firms. The widespread laying off of workers is less likely to be used as a last resort when businesses do not respond to crises in a timely fashion, and instead wait until they are forced to act. In addition to the suggested efforts at designing targeted post-crisis government policies to support businesses, pre-crisis public education thrusts encouraging preparedness and the development of business crisis plans are thus warranted.

Acknowledgement

Reprinted from *Journal of Economics and Business* (63)5, David F. Tennant, 'Factors impacting on whether and how businesses respond to early warning signs of financial and economic turmoil: Jamaican firms in the global crisis', pp. 472–491, Copyright (2011), with permission from Elsevier.

Notes

1 Based on a survey of 828 corporate managers in developed and emerging economies, Banerji *et al.* (2009a: 6) note that between a quarter and a third of hard-hit companies had not, at December 2008, accelerated their efforts to preserve cash – the most logical immediate course of action. Similarly, one-quarter of the financially healthy companies surveyed were not taking advantage of the opportunities afforded by the crisis.

2 The ILO (2009b: 22) estimated that 'global unemployment increased by eleven million people in 2008 and may increase by an additional forty million in 2009. In China, the steep decline in exports has resulted in the layoff of twenty million workers. The US economy lost 4.4 million jobs since the crisis there began in late 2007 and the Indian economy lost half a million jobs in the last three months of 2008.'

'Up to 200 million workers, mostly in developing economies, could be pushed into extreme poverty' (ILO 2009: 3a).

3 See Boshoff (2006) and Forbes (2000) for a discussion of the mechanisms through which financial crises are transmitted across countries.

4 This is supported by the results of psychoanalytic research in organizational crises which suggest that 'individuals in crisis-prone organizations, compared to crisis-prepared organizations, are seven times more likely to use defense mechanisms, such as denial, disavowal ... and ... grandiosity' (Pearson and Clair 1998: 62).

5 Latibeaudiere (2009) further notes that the statutory cash reserve requirement was increased from 11 per cent to 13 per cent.

6 'A McKinsey executive survey confirms that scenario planning is becoming a leading part of the strategic planning process. Over 50 per cent of the responding executives say that scenario planning is either playing a bigger role in their companies' strategic planning this year or has been newly added to the process.'

7 See, for example, Branstad *et al.* (2009). In Jamaica, timely responses to crises are particularly important for businesses because of relatively high redundancy costs. The Doing Business Report (2009) notes that Jamaica has a redundancy cost of sixty-two weeks of salary in comparison to an average fifty-three weeks in Latin American and Caribbean countries, and twenty-six weeks in OECD countries. This cost makes any strategy involving firing of workers (and possibly later re-hiring them) one which must be carefully planned for. If a business waits until concrete signs of a slowdown appear before reacting to the crisis, it may be forced to make redundancy payments at the time it can least afford to do so.

8 Heckmann *et al.* (2009) cite Germany's chemical giant BASF SE and Luxembourg's steel manufacturer ArcelorMittal as examples of companies that sought to cut costs by reducing working hours rather than laying-off staff. Dell Inc. and Honda similarly asked workers to accept mandatory unpaid holidays in an effort to save jobs while cutting costs. These businesses were all classified as being financially strong during the crisis.

9 This involves 'improving productivity, identifying wasteful practices, workplace cooperation, employee suggestion schemes, and cutting non-labour costs such as travel expenditures' (ILO 2009b: 14).

10 Including implementing a 'freeze on new hiring, work sharing, retraining and filling vacancies with existing employees, cuts in pay and bonuses, cutback on paid over-time, the introduction of different working patterns such as reduced hours and part-time solutions, and partial retirement as well as encouraged vacations or sabbaticals' (ILO 2009b: 17).

11 Efforts should focus on 'voluntary redundancy and early retirement, severance pack-ages, reducing casual staff, training to increase the employability of workers, assisting with job search, and support for self-employment' (ILO 2009b: 14).

12 Similarly, almost two-thirds of the respondents from the tourism sector have signific-ant proportions of their markets originating overseas (CaPRI 2009: 27).

13 Data sourced from the IMF's IFS (2009).

14 www.unctad.org/sections/dite_dir/docs/wir09_fs_jm_en.pdf.

15 'This is evidenced by the fact that although the primary client/customer base of Jamai-can businesses is spread across a wide array of mainly local clients, over a third (35 per cent) of the respondents noted that their primary clients were local large and medium-sized businesses, with the next most frequently identified category of primary clientele being local entrepreneurs and self-employed workers (14.8 per cent)' (CaPRI 2009: 36).

16 See Kirkpatrick and Tennant (2002), Tennant (2006) and Tennant and Kirton (2006) for discussion of the causes, consequences and legacies of the Jamaican financial sector crisis of the mid- to late 1990s.

17 See Boshoff (2006: 64–65) for a discussion of this type of transmission mechanism.

18 More specifically, RATION included laying off workers, reducing the use of local inputs and reducing foreign inputs; MANREL included cutting wages, reducing staff benefits and decreasing non-staff expenses; and DIVER included seeking alternative markets and alternative sources of finance.

19 Forced portfolio re-composition also forms part of Boshoff's (2006) financial transmission channel. Forced portfolio re-composition occurs as investors in the crisis country sell assets. If the assets to be sold are from countries other than the one in crisis, markets are unable to distinguish between countries in crisis and those not in crisis. Forbes (2000: 8), however, argues that the empirical evidence relating to this channel is ambiguous. This transmission mechanism is not included in this study, as early in the crisis there were no signs to suggest that it would have had a major impact in the Jamaican context. Also, there are no data to reliably measure its impact. Forbes (2000) and Boshoff (2006) also mention psychological linkages, wherein investor behaviour and information asymmetries can lead to herding or informational cascades. This linkage is also not included in this model, as difficulties were encountered similar to those highlighted by Boshoff (2006: 63) in testing the psychological phenomena associated with this channel.

20 Although the literature typically limits the credit linkage transmission of crises to decreases in the availability of credit, this chapter also includes other terms and conditions of loans as possible explanatory variables to capture less obvious ways in which the effect of volatility in credit markets may be transmitted to businesses. Similarly, although the trade linkage transmission of crises typically focuses only on reduced quantity and competitiveness of exports, the impact of the crisis on the cost and availability of inputs is also examined. The import dependence of the Jamaican economy necessitates such an examination as, if credit crunches and declining output in the overseas crisis economies cause input prices to increase and availability to decrease, adverse real sector outcomes are likely. The availability and cost of local inputs can also be impacted by the US crisis, as many intermediate goods are also import-dependent.

21 Gujarati and Porter (2009: 328) note that 'the speed with which variances and covariances increase can be seen with the variance-inflating factor (VIF), which is defined as $VIF = 1/(1 - r^2_{23})$. VIF shows how the variance of an estimator is inflated by the presence of multicollinearity. As r^2_{23} approaches 1, the VIF approaches infinity. That is, as the extent of collinearity increases, the variance of an estimator increases, and in the limit it can become infinite. As can be readily seen, if there is no collinearity between X_2 and X_3, VIF will be 1.' De Vaus (2002: 345) notes that 'as a general rule of thumb any variable that has a tolerance of 0.2 or less or a VIF of 5 or more could indicate problems with multicollinearity.' This is because such values indicate that the multiple r^2 among the independent variables is at least 0.8, which is generally considered to be too high.

22 www2.chass.nesu.edu/garson/PA765/logistic.htm.

23 Real GDP declined by 0.9 per cent in 2008 and a further 2.7 per cent in 2009 (Planning Institute of Jamaica 2008, 2009).

References

Aguirre, D. and Post, L. (2009) 'Building Talent Advantage in Recession and Recovery: A Memo to the Chief Human Resources Officer'. Available at: www.booz.com/media/uploads/Building_Talent_Advantage.pdf (accessed 19 August 2010).

Banerji, S., McArthur, N., Mainardi, C. and Ammann, C. (2009a) 'Recession Response: Why Companies are Making the Wrong Moves'. Available at www.booz.com/media/file/Recession_Response-FINAL2.pdf (accessed 19 August 2010).

Banerji, S., Leinwand, P. and Mainardi, C.R. (2009b) 'Cut Costs, Grow Stronger'. Available at: www.strategy-business.com/media/file/00001.pdf (accessed 19 August 2010).

Bank of Jamaica, *Statistical Digest*, various issues, Kingston: Bank of Jamaica.

Boshoff, W.H. (2006) 'The Transmission of Foreign Financial Crises to South Africa: A Firm-Level Study', *Studies in Economic and Econometrics*, 30(2): 61–85.

Branstad, P, Jackson, B. and Banerji, S. (2009) 'Rethink your Strategy: An Urgent Memo to the CEO'. Available at: www.booz.com/global/home/what_we_think/reports_and_white_papers/article/43229221?pg=all (accessed 19 August 2010).

Calloway, L.J. and Keen, P.G.W. (1996) 'Organizing for Crisis Response', *Journal of Information Technology*, 11: 13–26.

CaPRI (2009) 'The Effect of the Global Economic Crisis on Jamaican Businesses: An Analysis of Exposure and Responses', Report Prepared for the Department for International Development.

Correa, P. and Lootty, M. (2010) 'The Impact of the Global Economic Crisis on the Corporate Sector in Europe and Central Asia: Evidence from a Firm-Level Survey''. Available at: http://enterprisesurveys.org/documents/ECA-Note.pdf (accessed 19 August 2010).

Deutsche Bank (2000) 'Jamaica – Offering Circular', Mimeo, Deutsche Bank.

De Vaus, D. (2002) *Analyzing Social Science Data: 50 Key Problems in Data Analysis*, London: Sage Publications.

Doing Business Report (2009) 'Employing Workers in Jamaica'. Available at: www.doingbusiness.org/exploretopics/employingworkers/Details.aspx?economyid=97 (accessed 19 August 2010).

Forbes, K. (2000) 'The Asian Flu and Russian Virus: Firm-Level Evidence on how Crises are Transmitted International', National Bureau of Economic Research Working Paper 7807.

Forbes, K. (2001) 'Are Trade Linkages Important Determinants of Country Vulnerability to Crises?', National Bureau of Economic Research Working Paper 8194.

Gujarati, D.N. and Porter, D.C. (2009) *Basic Econometrics*, Boston, MA: McGraw-Hill Irwin.

Heckmann, P, Konik, F, Samakh, E. and Weissbarth, R. (2009) 'Restructuring in 2009: Understanding and Responding to the Crisis'. Available at: www.booz.com/media/uploads/Restructuring_in_2009.pdf (accessed 19 August 2010).

ILO (2009a) 'Micro, Small and Medium-sized Enterprises and the Global Economic Crisis: Impacts and Policy Responses'. Available at: www.ilo.org/wcmsp5/groups/public/--ed_emp/--emp_ent/documents/publication/wcms_108413.pdf (accessed 19 August 2010).

ILO (2009b) 'Responsible and Sustainable Enterprise-Level Practices at Times of Crisis: A Guide for Policy-Makers and Social Partners'. Available at: www.ilo.org/wcmsp5/groups/public/--ed_emp/--emp_ent/documents/publication/wcms_108420.pdf (accessed 19 August 2010).

International Monetary Fund, *International Financial Statistics*, various issues, Washington, DC: International Monetary Fund.

Kirkpatrick, C. and Tennant, D. (2002) 'Responding to Financial Crisis: The Case of Jamaica', *World Development*, 30(11): 1933–1950.

Latibeaudiere, D. (2009) 'Bank of Jamaica Quarterly Press Briefing'. Available at: www.boj.org.jm/news/news_htmls/governor_s_quarterly_press_briefing_feb_09.pdf (accessed 19 August 2010).

Menard, S (1995) *Applied Logistic Regression Analysis*, Thousand Oaks, CA: Sage.

Naude, W. (2009) 'The Financial Crisis of 2008 and the Developing Countries', UNU-WIDER Discussion Paper No. 2009/01.

Olukoshi, A. (1996) 'Economic Crisis, Structural Adjustment and the Coping Strategies of Manufacturers in Kano, Nigeria', United Nations Research Institute for Social Development, Discussion Paper 77.

Pearson, C.M. and Clair, J.A. (1998) 'Reframing Crisis Management', *The Academy of Management Review*, 23(1): 59–76.

Penn, Schoen and Berland Associates (2009) 'Crisis Preparedness and ROI'. Available at: http://issuu.com/burson-marsteller-emea/docs/crisissurvey2009 (accessed 19 August 2010).

Planning Institute of Jamaica (2008) *Economic and Social Survey of Jamaica*, Kingston: PIOJ

Planning Institute of Jamaica (2009) *Economic and Social Survey of Jamaica 2009*, Kingston: PIOJ.

Raghavan, A. (2009) 'The Economic Downturn: Coping Strategies and the Way Forward'. Available at: www.slideshare.net/achalraghavan/the-economic-downturn-coping-strategies-and-the-way-forward (accessed 19 August 2010).

Ramalho, R., Rodriguez-Meza, J. and Yang, J. (2009) 'How are Firms in Eastern and Central Europe Reacting to the Financial Crisis?' Available at: www.enterprisesurveys.org/documents/EnterpriseNotes/Note8.pdf (accessed 19 August 2010).

Tennant, D. (2006) 'Lessons Learnt by the Survivors of Jamaica's Financial Sector Crisis', *Savings and Development*, 30(1): 5–22.

Tennant, D. (2010) 'Global Financial Crisis to Real Sector Contraction: Transmission Mechanisms in a Small Open Economy – Business Coping Strategies in Jamaica', *Global Development Studies*.

Tennant, D. and Kirton, C. (2006) 'Assessing the Impact of Financial Instability: The Jamaican Case Study', *Iberoamericana Nordic Journal of Latin American and Caribbean Studies*, 36(1): 9–36.

Vandersmissen, M.H, Theriault, M. and Villeneuve, P. (2004) 'What About Effective Access to Cars in Motorised Households?', *Canadian Geographer*, 48(4): 488–504.

Watson Wyatt Worldwide (2009a) 'Current Economic Conditions Response Survey: General Industry Report'. Available at: www.watsonwyatt.com/asia-pacific/news/pdf/cecr_general-industry-report.pdf (accessed 19 August 2010).

Watson Wyatt Worldwide (2009b) 'Effects of the Economy on HR Programs – Latin America'. Available at: www.watsonwyatt.com/latin-america/media/LA_FinancialCrisisSurvey2009_ENG_08–04–2009.pdf (accessed 9 January 2010).

World Bank (2003) *Jamaica: The Road to Sustained Growth – Country Economic Memorandum*, Washington, DC: World Bank.

15 Crisis response

Beyond Caribbean remittances

Jessica Jones

1 Introduction

Remittances have become increasingly important to several small island developing states of the Caribbean, and the adverse impact of the global economic crisis on remittances is a critical issue for the region, given their significant contribution to the development of several economies in the area. Traditionally, remittances have had a tendency to increase after financial crises or natural disasters as migrants send more money home to assist their families. However, this crisis is different as, in the wake of the global economic crisis, for the first time since the 1980s remittance inflows to developing countries have fallen, by 6 per cent from 2008 to 2009.

For all developing countries, especially for those in the Caribbean where remittances play a large and evolving role, the global span of this crisis leads to several important questions, such as whether the current crisis will have a long-term effect on remittances to the region. With employment a lagging indicator of any sign of recovery from the crisis, unemployment and a lack of job opportunities will compel some workers to return home. Since return migration is one of the factors upon which remittance flows are dependent, it is also important to investigate if the Caribbean can benefit from return migration as a way to mitigate the slowdown in remittances. This study examines remittance data from several Caribbean countries, looking at the dynamics of migration in the region, with a view to answering these questions and providing policy recommendations. The results suggest that remittances, which declined across the board for the Caribbean Community (CARICOM) member states, fluctuating sharply for some countries after the crisis, have levelled off but are unlikely to stabilize at pre-crisis rates in the near future. Further, due to the global nature of the crisis, significant risks remain for remittance flows to the Caribbean. Policy options are therefore examined which go beyond remittances and examine other Diaspora engagement strategies.

The migration-development nexus forms the theoretical framework for this study, with remittances as the link. Migration is increasingly being treated as a development issue (IOM, 2002; De Haas, 2008; and the first Global Forum on Migration and Development held in 2007), with governments, international organisations and NGOs seeking ways in which to maximise the benefits which migration can have on development. Remittances are certainly not a panacea for development, as research suggests that, for most Caribbean countries, remittances may not compensate for the overall losses due to migration (Mishra, 2006).

Further, as shown in Table 15.1, the Caribbean countries for which remittances make the greatest contribution to the economy have the lowest human development index.

Nonetheless, several studies suggest that remittances can be leveraged to promote the benefits of migration for development (Agunias, 2006, provides a review of the literature on remittances, migration and development; see also Orozco, 2002; Nurse, 2004; Ratha, 2007, 2010; Ahortor and Adenutsi, 2009; Thomas-Hope, 2009; World Bank, 2006). At a macroeconomic level, remittances stabilise the balance of payments – an important consideration, especially in times of economic crisis, for those countries for which remittances contribute a large portion of GDP. Further, at a local development level, in contrast to other external sources of external finance such as official development assistance from developed countries, remittances go directly to families and individuals, who then decide how to disburse the funds and on what to spend the money. They therefore have the potential to have a more immediate impact on poverty alleviation. Remittances are playing an increasingly significant role in the development

Table 15.1 Remittances and HDI comparison

	Remittances as a share of GDP, 2008 (%)	HDI ranking (2009)	HDI value (2009)	
Barbados	4.9%	37	0.903	*High Human Development*
Antigua and Barbuda	2.1%	47	0.868	
St Kitts and Nevis	6.9%	62	0.838	
Trinidad and Tobago	0.5%	64	0.837	
St Lucia	3.1%	69	0.821	
Dominica	8.2%	73	0.814	
Grenada	10.0%	74	0.812	
St Vincent and the Grenadines	5.1%	91	0.772	*Medium Human Development*
Belize	5.7%	93	0.772	
Suriname	4.9%	97	0.769	
Jamaica	14.5%	100	0.766	
Guyana	24.0%	114	0.729	
Haiti	18.7%	149	0.532	*Low Human Development*

Sources: GDP% calculated by author based on World Bank 2009 remittances data; Human Development Report 2009 data.

of several small island developing states in the Caribbean, commanding an analysis of the impact of the global economic crisis on remittance inflows to the region.

Migrant remittances to the Caribbean are generally significantly underreported; however, several Central Banks in the region and international financial organisations are paying more attention to improving data collection in light of the considerable contribution that remittances make to the region. As this is a study with aggregate remittance data, one of the first issues is to determine the series of remittances to be used, given the difficulties in reporting informal flows and inconsistencies in reporting by Central Banks in different countries. For instance, remittances and compensation of employees are variously amalgamated or reported separately. With these difficulties in mind, and to allow for a consistent assessment, this study predominantly uses the broad estimate of remittances advocated by the World Bank's (2008) *Migration and Remittances Factbook 2008*. This gauge defines remittances as the sum of workers' remittances, compensation of employees, and migrants' transfers. The World Bank (2008) contends that to get a complete picture of the remittances flow, one has to assess these three entities together. World Bank data were available for most of the countries under consideration, for the 1990s and the last decade. Additionally, since 2000 the IDB-MIF has also contributed significantly to unearthing remittance channels, and an improved accounting of the volume of flows for several countries in the region. Wherever possible, the dataset is selected from the same source to allow for consistency of analysis, but it is at times supplemented with other sources to provide a more complete examination.

The global nature of the current economic crisis is crucial to this analysis, as it has severely impacted even the high-income countries to which most Caribbean migrants relocate. It is instructive to note that the 1997 Asian financial crisis resulted in a sharp, but temporary decline in remittances to Asia, with levels rebounding just one year later (Jha *et al.*, 2009). However, this was a comparatively localised crisis, and remittances from outside the region compensated for the drop in regional transfers. In this case, even the high-income countries outside of the region to which most Caribbean migrants relocate have been severely impacted. Unemployment in the USA and Canada, primary destinations for Caribbean migrants, continues to rise, reducing employment prospects for migrants as immigration policies tighten concomitant with the political reality of the need to allay the fears of domestic workers that a contracting job market is being saturated by immigrants. While some migrants may choose or have no option but to remain overseas, there is growing anecdotal and empirical evidence of increasing reverse brain drain to from the USA to China and India (Wadhwa *et al.*, 2007; Wadwha and Wucker, 2009). An analysis of this situation is policy relevant for the region, given that the Caribbean region has amongst the highest rates of brain drain in the world, with over 70 per cent of their highly-skilled population migrating in some cases (Carrington and Detragiache, 1998; Docquier and Marfouk, 2004; Mishra, 2006). In the face of the challenge of declining remittances, the Caribbean may be able to benefit from reverse brain drain, and return migration in general. The global span of this crisis raises several questions which are important for all developing countries (Jha *et al.*, 2009), especially for those in the Caribbean where remittances play a large and evolving role. Will the current crisis have a long-term effect on remittances to the region? Since return migration is one of the factors upon which remittance flows are dependent (Ratha *et al.*, 2009a), it is important to ask, can, and if so how, can the Caribbean benefit from return migration as a way to mitigate the slowdown in remittances? Should remittances continue to drop, how will the policies of remittance-dependent governments adjust to compensate?

This study examines remittance data from several Caribbean countries, looking at the present and future dynamics of migration in the region, with a view to answering these questions and providing policy recommendations. The rest of the chapter is structured as follows.

Section 2 provides a general discussion of the past trends of migration and remittances in the Caribbean. To elaborate on the significance of remittances to the Caribbean, section 3 takes a closer look at the growth pattern of remittances to the region and examines specific countries in the Caribbean. Section 4 examines the impact of the current global economic crisis on the remittance flows to the Caribbean from the perspectives of both remittance-receiving and remittance-sending countries. The final section provides conclusions and policy implications for the Caribbean, to mitigate the negative effect of the current economic crisis on remittances to the region, through and examining other Diaspora engagement strategies.

2 Major trends in migration and remittances in the Caribbean

Migration is a significant feature of the Caribbean, and, as Table 15.1 shows, the likelihood of migration increases with level of education gained. That more than 70 per cent of some of the skilled populations of the region migrate is indicative that the Caribbean has some of the highest rates of brain drain in the world (Docquier and Marfouk, 2004). Percentage-wise, Caribbean people show the highest propensity for migration in the world. As Table 15.2 shows, ten of the top fifteen countries in the world from which populations are most likely to migrate are members of the Caribbean Community (CARICOM[1]). Most Caribbean people migrate to North America, with the notable exceptions being Antiguans and Barbudans, for whom the most popular destination is Asia, and Surinamers, who tend primarily towards The Netherlands. The continued link which this Diaspora maintains with their home countries manifests in the money they send back home. As a share of GDP, the Caribbean is the largest receiver of remittances (IMF, 2009). On average, Caribbean migrants also send home almost twice as much per person as the average for Latin America and the Caribbean (US$114) as a whole (UNDP, 2009). This money contributes to these economies, often significantly, through consumption and/or investment.

Table 15.2 Select migration indicators for CARICOM countries

Global Emigration Rate Ranking and Origin of Migrants	US$ Rem per capita	Emigration rate (%) (2000–2002)	Migration Rate (%) (2000) Secondary Education	Migration Rate (%) (2000) Primary Education	Migration Rate (%) (2000) – Tertiary Education	Major continent for destination of migrants
1. Antigua and Barbuda	276	45.3	6.0	35.9	70.9	Asia 46.6% (Philippines)
2. St Kitts and Nevis	739	44.3	10.3	37.1	71.8	North America 37.3 (USA)
3. Grenada	524	40.3	9.9	69.5	66.7	North America 64.9 (USA)
4. Dominica	385	38.3	8.0	60.6	58.9	North America 83.3 (USA)
6. Suriname	305	36.0	17.5	43.9	89.9	Europe 82.2 (Netherlands)
7. St Vincent and the Grenadines	254	34.4	6.3	53.4	56.8	North America 51.9
9. Guyana	377	33.5	13.7	34.1	85.9	North America 78.6 (USA)
11. Barbados	476	29.8	9.9	24.3	61.4	North America 64.9 (USA)
12. Jamaica	790	26.7	8.3	30.0	82.5	North America 73.0 (USA)
14. St Lucia	188	24.1	2.6	32.1	36.0	Latin America and the Caribbean 40.4
19. Trinidad and Tobago	69	20.2	6.1	20.6	89.9	North America 81.4% (USA)
26. Belize	260	16.5	3.6	49.2	51.0	North America 83.3 (USA)
51. The Bahamas		10.8	1.5	12.1	36.4	North America 84.7% (USA)
71. Haiti	127	7.7	2.5	27.5	81.6	North America 64.3 (USA)

Sources: Human Development Report 2009 (UNDP, 2009). Global Migrant Origin Database updated March 2007 of the Development Research Centre on Migration, Globalisation and Poverty (Migration PRC) provides most popular destination country in brackets (). Tertiary Migration Rates 2000 – Migration Rate of Persons with Secondary and Tertiary Education to *OECD Extracted from Docquier and MarfouK (2004), showing emigration rates by educational attainment and country of birth.

Over the past two decades remittances have become increasingly important to several small island developing states of the Caribbean, and the adverse impact of the global economic crisis on remittances is a key issue for the region, given their significant contribution to the several economies in the area. Remittance flows are an important source of the region's foreign exchange, and Figure 15.1 allows a comparison of the extent to which they contribute in relation to other financial flows, including Foreign Direct Investment (FDI) and Official Development Assistance (ODA).

For most of the of the countries in the Caribbean, remittances contribute significantly more, and are more stable, than other external capital financial flows such as FDI and ODA. In 2008, remittances contributed 24 per cent to Guyana's economy and about 19 per cent and 15 per cent to Haiti and Jamaica respectively. And, as illustrated by Figure 15.2, formally recorded remittance flows to the Caribbean have generally increased over the past few years. The increases in the past decades are too impressive to be accounted for solely by improved methods of data collection and more competitive remittance costs, especially as these improvements are still ongoing, leaving the impression therefore that more money is being remitted.

Traditionally, remittances have had a tendency to increase after financial crises or natural disasters as migrants send more money home to assist their families (Clarke and Wallsten, 2003; Attzs, 2008; Mohapatra *et al.*, 2009). However, there has been a noted decline since 2008 (see Figure 15.2), when the Caribbean began to feel the effects of the global economic crisis. The impact has been broad and, for the first time in two decades, remittance inflows to developing countries as a whole were projected to fall, by 6.1 per cent, in 2009, in the wake of the global economic crisis (Ratha, 2009; Ratha *et al.*, 2009b). In the fourth quarter of 2008, investment has fallen by an average of 4.4 per cent in twenty-seven of thirty high-income countries (World Bank, 2009b). Although global ODA rose 10.2 per cent from 2007 to 2008, disbursements are likely to be

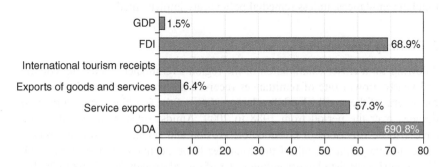

Figure 15.1 Latin America and the Caribbean (developing countries): remittance inflows as percentage of selected indicators (source: World Development Indicators (WDI) and Global Development Finance (GDF) database, 2008 data: Balance of Payments and Official Development Assistance for 2008, http://databank.worldbank.org).

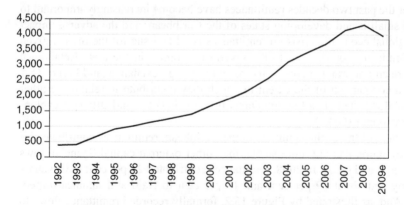

Figure 15.2 Aggregate remittance to CARICOM countries (million US$) (source: World Bank Remittance data (World Bank 2009a); 2009 is estimated. Excluded are the Bahamas, and Montserrat, as World Bank data are not available; and Suriname, as data are not available for entire series).

constrained, given the sharp rise in the fiscal deficits of the main ODA providers (World Bank, 2009b). While remittances are expected to regroup, the recovery is projected to be shallow, and significant risks lie ahead due to lagging job recovery, more restrictive migration controls and unpredictable exchange rates (Ratha *et al.*, 2009b). The direct consequence is that the economies of those countries which are heavily remittance-reliant and those which have become increasingly dependent on remittances will be more vulnerable to fluctuations in remittance flows. Even a small drop in remittances is therefore significant for the Caribbean. Falling economic growth in the current crisis, and the lack of fiscal and, to some extent, monetary policy space available to these economies will retard the region's poverty reduction strategies and achievement of the Millenium Development Goals (MDGs). Development will be further hindered by this downward trend in remittances, unless remedial policies are implemented.

3 Country case studies[2]

Allowing for a closer examination of the region's remittance trends, the volume and yearly growth rate of remittances received are presented here (Table 15.3) for several of the small island developing states of the Caribbean during the two decades over the period from 1988 to 2009. Amidst substantial growth, there have also been periods of considerable erosion and stagnation. Notably, remittances to many, but not all, of the countries listed declined from 2008 to 2009. The countries are listed in ascending order of rate of growth from 2008 to 2009.

Remittances to the Organisation of Eastern Caribbean States (OECS[3]) from citizens abroad, as well as the tourism industry (which is the main foreign exchange earner), have been adversely affected by the global economic crisis (Eastern Caribbean Central Bank, 2009). Similar results are being felt across the

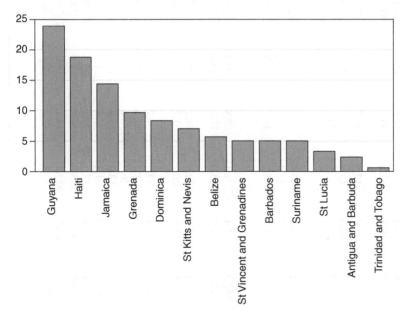

Figure 15.3 Remittances to CARICOM countries as a share of GDP, 2008 (%) (source: World Bank Remittance data, World Bank, 2009a).

region, and this study examines the significance of remittances to the Caribbean (as illustrated in Figure 15.3), examining the top three countries remittance-receiving member States of CARICOM, rated by remittances as a percentage of 2008 GDP: Guyana (24 per cent), Haiti (18.7) and Jamaica (14.5 per cent). Barbados, for which there is a growing awareness of the importance of the contribution of remittances to the economy, is also examined here.

3.1 Guyana

Figure 15.4 provides a comparison of the importance to Guyana's foreign exchange inflows with several other financial indicators, contributing appreciably more than FDI, ODA, tourism receipts and service exports. Until 2001, officially recorded remittances contributed only about 3 per cent of Guyana's GDP. This share has increased considerably, to about 24 per cent in 2008, indicating that the country has become significantly more reliant on remittances over the past few years. The increase is considerable, with the Central Bank of Guyana indicating that total transfers to Guyana increased from US$94.2 million to US$140.2 million, or by 48.8 per cent, over the five-year period 2000–2004 (Kirton, 2006: 8). Reasons for this increase may include:

1   improved remittance collection methods enhanced by the Bank of Guyana's participation in the IBD-MIF project geared towards strengthening the

Table 15.3 Caribbean remittance inflows (in US$ millions, % year-on-year)

Country		1988	1989	1990	1991	1992	1993	1994	1995	1996	1997	1998
Barbados	Volume	32.0	32.0	37.9	45.2	54.5	55.4	57.2	60.9	68.2	77.0	87.4
	% Growth		0.2	18.4	19.1	20.7	1.6	3.3	6.5	12.0	12.9	13.5
Trinidad and Tobago	Volume	1.7	3.2	3.4	5.2	6.6	19.5	26.8	31.5	28.1	30.2	44.6
	% Growth		89.1	4.3	52.8	26.8	197.8	37.0	17.6	-10.7	7.4	47.6
Belize	Volume	17.0	22.0	18.5	15.6	19.8	16.5	13.0	13.9	17.3	22.7	23.4
	% Growth		29.5	-15.9	-15.4	26.6	-16.5	-21.4	7.2	24.1	31.6	3.1
Haiti	Volume	124.1	122.8									
	% Growth		-1.0									
Grenada	Volume	23.5	16.9	18.0	8.3	8.6	18.4	26.2	37.8	41.3	41.3	42.4
	% Growth		-28.3	6.7	-53.9	3.8	113.6	42.5	44.3	9.3	0.2	2.5
St Vincent and the Grenadines	Volume	15.0	15.4	15.6	2.4	2.0	17.4	17.0	17.2	18.2	19.8	20.8
	% Growth		2.7	1.7	-84.3	-16.6	752.3	-2.4	1.1	5.8	9.1	4.9
Antigua and Barbuda	Volume	12.3	13.2	12.5	3.0	2.7	11.6	11.9	3.3	12.3	15.9	22.2
	% Growth		7.0	-5.0	-75.7	-10.9	328.4	2.7	-72.1	268.2	29.9	39.2
St Kitts and Nevis	Volume	12.2	19.2	19.3	1.5	1.5	15.1	17.6	20.2	21.2	22.5	24.6
	% Growth		57.9	0.4	-92.3	-1.0	925.9	16.4	14.9	4.7	6.0	9.7
Guyana	Volume					1.0	1.2	1.3	1.7	14.6	15.0	14.0
	% Growth						18.6	10.7	26.9	758.8	2.7	-6.7
Dominica	Volume	16.1	13.4	13.9	5.0	5.2	13.7	13.3	13.4	13.8	13.9	14.6
	% Growth		-17.0	4.1	-64.4	4.3	165.5	-3.3	1.1	2.4	1.0	5.3
St Lucia	Volume	15.9	15.4	16.1	17.7	2.1	15.4	21.8	23.1	27.4	25.2	25.9
	% Growth		-3.0	4.8	10.1	-88.4	649.3	41.2	5.8	18.8	-7.9	2.8
Jamaica	Volume	153.9	208.5	228.7	181.3	215.6	239.2	522.1	653.1	714.1	729.8	757.6
	% Growth		35.5	9.7	-20.7	18.9	10.9	118.3	25.1	9.3	2.2	3.8
Suriname	Volume											
	% Growth											

Country		1999	2000	2001	2002	2003	2004	2005	2006	2007	2008	2009
Barbados	Volume	99.4	115.0	131.2	125.1	130.5	130.5	134.8	138.6	141.2	101.2	113.3
	% Growth	13.7	15.8	14.1	-4.7	4.3	0.0	3.3	2.8	1.9	-28.4	12.0
Trinidad and Tobago	Volume	54.4	38.1	40.9	79.1	86.8	86.9	92.4	91.2	109.4	94.5	99.3
	% Growth	22.1	-30.0	7.3	93.4	9.7	0.1	6.3	-1.3	20.0	-13.6	5.1
Belize	Volume	26.2	26.4	30.5	28.4	33.8	35.0	46.1	65.5	74.8	78.1	80.5
	% Growth	12.1	0.7	15.6	-6.9	19.1	3.3	31.7	42.2	14.2	4.5	3.0
Haiti	Volume	422.1	578.0	623.6	675.7	811.0	931.5	986.2	1,062.9	1,222.1	1,369.8	1,375.5
	% Growth	28.9	37.0	7.9	8.4	20.0	14.9	5.9	7.8	15.0	12.1	0.4
Grenada	Volume	44.5	46.4	46.7	47.6	48.6	72.2	51.6	53.9	54.8	55.4	53.7
	% Growth	5.0	4.3	0.7	1.8	2.1	48.6	-28.6	4.6	1.6	1.0	-3.0
St Vincent and the Grenadines	Volume	21.2	22.5	22.7	23.1	23.5	25.5	26.5	29.7	33.1	31.1	29.9
	% Growth	1.7	6.2	1.0	2.0	1.6	8.5	3.8	12.2	11.5	-6.2	-3.9
Antigua and Barbuda	Volume	21.8	20.7	27.0	17.6	19.7	20.9	22.0	23.0	24.5	25.5	24.5
	% Growth	-1.6	-5.3	30.6	-34.9	12.1	6.2	5.1	4.6	6.3	4.3	-4.1
St Kitts and Nevis	Volume	26.1	27.1	27.8	28.6	29.9	31.3	33.5	36.4	40.3	44.1	40.5
	% Growth	5.9	3.9	2.6	2.9	4.7	4.6	7.1	8.6	10.6	9.6	-8.1
Guyana	Volume	20.5	27.3	22.3	51.0	99.3	153.0	201.3	218.1	282.7	278.4	253.0
	% Growth	46.4	33.2	-18.3	128.7	94.7	54.1	31.6	8.3	29.6	-1.5	-9.1
Dominica	Volume	15.6	16.3	17.1	17.4	17.8	23.2	25.0	25.4	25.9	26.1	23.1
	% Growth	7.0	4.2	5.1	1.5	2.3	29.9	7.9	1.6	2.0	0.9	-11.5
St Lucia	Volume	26.5	26.4	26.9	26.8	27.4	28.7	29.5	30.3	31.1	31.5	27.6
	% Growth	2.4	-0.4	1.6	-0.3	2.2	4.7	2.8	2.9	2.7	1.0	-12.2
Jamaica	Volume	790	892	1,058	1,260	1,398	1,623	1,784	1,946	2,144	2,181	1,912
	% Growth	4.3	12.9	18.7	19.1	11.0	16.1	9.9	9.1	10.1	1.7	-12.3
Suriname	Volume						50	55	102	115	120	103
	% Growth							10.0	85.5	12.7	4.3	-14.2

Source: World Bank Remittance data: World Development Indicators & Global Development Finance database (http://databank.worldbank.org/ddp/home.do) except for Suriname, which was sourced from IDB-MIF

recording mechanisms of Latin American and Caribbean Central Banks for information and statistics systems to better track remittances (Kirton, 2006: 11), allowing for wider capture by recording remittance data from post offices and migrants returning to Guyana;

2   lower costs of remittances due to global efforts and increased competition;
3   an ongoing dependency syndrome which is being manifested by an increase in the amount of remittances flowing into Guyana (Kirton, 2006; Khemraj, 2009.)

One study reveals that Guyana's remittance inflows are derived from altruistic motives (Agarwal and Horowitz, 2002). Also, in 2002, Manuel Orozco presented a study on remittances to Guyana, which identified four key findings:

1   The Guyanese Diaspora in the USA maintains significant contact with its home country and communities, focusing on various philanthropic projects.
2.   Although remittance flows to Guyana are high, officially estimated to be at least US$100 million annually, official figures underestimate actual transfers. Kirton (2006) estimates that 26 per cent of Guyana's remittance inflows are informal.
3   The cost of sending money to Guyana is among the highest in the Americas and the remittances market is largely uncompetitive, although global competition is driving the costs down.
4   Although some remitters use banks to transfer funds, formal remittances are hampered by the lack of international electronic fund capability in Guyana.

In the study, Orozco suggested various challenges that limited the development and growth opportunities resulting from significant remittance flows to Guyana, including weak remittance data collection and inadequate regulatory and public policy framework coupled with limited international connectivity of the financial sector.

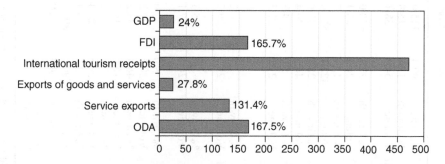

Figure 15.4 Guyana remittance inflows as a percentage of select indicators (source: World Development Indicators (WDI) and Global Development Finance (GDF) database, 2008 data: Balance of Payments and Official Development Assistance for 2008, http://databank.worldbank.org).

3.2 Haiti

Haiti ranks second in CARICOM in terms of the percentage contribution which remittance inflows make to the economy. Figure 15.5 presents a snapshot for comparison of the remittances to other financial inflows, showing the substantial contribution which remittances contribute to the country's inflow of foreign exchange.

Haiti is the only country in Latin America and the Caribbean to meet the low-income, human capital and economic vulnerability criteria for categorisation as a Least Developed Country (LDC), which recognises fundamental structural handicaps of relatively small economies. Unlike Guyana's relatively recent growth in the importance of remittance inflows, remittances have been a steady contributor to Haiti's economy for decades. A considerable number of Haitians are regular recipients of money sent to them by friends or relatives living abroad, according to a recent IDB survey (2007) which found that 31 per cent of Haitian adults (nearly 1.1 million people) received remittances in 2006. Although Haitians are statistically far less likely to emigrate than populations from the Caribbean (see Table 15.2), their movements, coupled with a long history of political instability, natural disasters and poverty, occupy a far higher global profile. Indeed, the earthquake which devastated Haiti on 12 January 2010 and left hundreds of thousands dead and millions homeless prompted global outpourings of aid and mobilisation of the vast Haitian Diaspora with monetary and in-kind contributions to their homeland. A disproportionately large 81.6 per cent of the tertiary-educated citizens emigrate (Docquier and Marfouk, 2004). Most of the people who have emigrated from Haiti take up residence in the USA (71 per cent) and Canada (14 per cent). Taking advantage of the language commonality, France and the French-speaking regions of Belgium are also popular destinations for students pursuing tertiary education (Eurostat, n.d.). In the Caribbean, following Jamaica, Haiti has the next highest rate of emigration of physicians in the region, with an emigration factor of 35.4 per cent (Mullan, 2005: 1814).

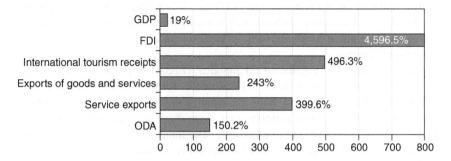

Figure 15.5 Haiti remittance inflows as percentage of selected indicators (source: World Development Indicators (WDI) and Global Development Finance (GDF) database, 2008 data: Balance of Payments and Official Development Assistance for 2008, http://databank.worldbank.org).

On average, Haitian remittance recipients receive monies from abroad ten times per year, or almost once per month, and the majority have been receiving remittances for more than five years, with the UNDP (2009) estimating an average of US$127 received. The Inter-American Development Bank (IDB) (2007) survey found that Haiti received approximately US$1.65 billion in remittances in 2006. This is more than the World Bank figure of US$1.06 billion reported for the same period, most likely reflecting the ability of the IDB survey to probe deeper into the informal inflows. How significant these informal flows are for Haiti is debatable, but they are undoubtedly understated. The IDB survey found that more than 80 per cent of Haitian remittance-receivers got their funds through remittance companies, with 3 per cent coming via a family member travelling to Haiti. On the other hand, Orozco (2006) found that remittances from the Dominican Republic travelled both formal and informal routes, in equal proportions, to arrive in Haiti.

3.3 Jamaica

With remittance flows making up 14.5 per cent of GDP for 2008, Jamaica stands third in CARICOM in terms of the contribution which remittances make to the group's economy. Stanford (2006) notes that in the case of Jamaica, having surpassed some of the key exports, remittance flows are typically used for debt financing. Jamaica continues to place greater emphasis on remittances in recognition of the significant increase that has occurred in the last decade, far outpacing FDI and ODA (see Figure 15.6). In light of this, the Bank of Jamaica revised its definition of remittances for greater clarity and to facilitate a wider capture of remittance flows. The new concept of personal transfers covers "all current transfers in cash or in kind made or received by resident households to or from non-resident households" (Bank of Jamaica, 2009), and the gap between the two definitions is steadily widening.

Net remittance inflows declined for 2009, representing a reversal of the increasing trend observed over previous years. This decreasing trend resulted from a reduction in remittance inflows (Bank of Jamaica, 2009). The Bank of Jamaica expects that these inflows will improve in ensuing quarters, although noting that the turnaround is directly related to the economic recovery of the main source countries.

Skilled migration is significant for Jamaica. Globally, Jamaica is the country with the highest emigration factor (41.4 per cent) for physicians (Mullan, 2005: 1816), above Ireland (41.2 per cent) and Ghana (30.0 per cent). Moreover, Docquier and Marfouk (2004) estimate that some 82.5 per cent of the island's tertiary-educated population are emigrants. The main destinations are the USA and the UK, which are also the main sources for remittance inflows (see Figures 15.7, 15.8).

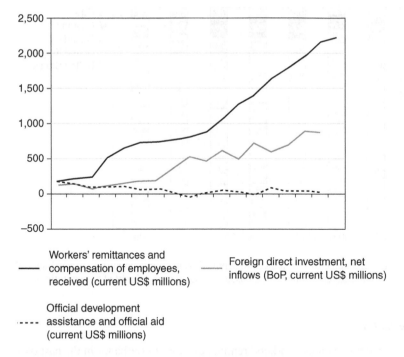

Figure 15.6 Remittance inflows, FDI and ODA to Jamaica (source: raw data from World Bank, 2009a).

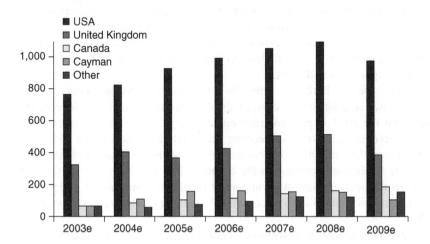

Figure 15.7 Remittances to Jamaica from source country (US$ millions) (source: Bank of Jamaica; e – estimates are based on information submitted by institutions).

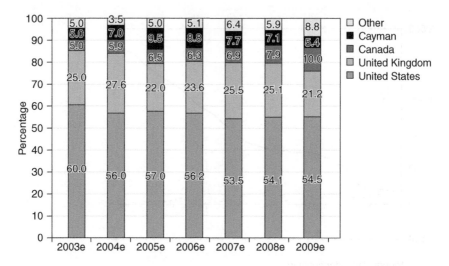

Figure 15.8 Percentage of remittances to Jamaica from source country (source: Bank of Jamaica; e – estimates are based on information submitted by institutions).

3.4 Barbados

Despite some fluctuations, workers' remittance flows to Barbados in the past two decades have grown steadily to assume greater importance in the reckoning of foreign exchange earnings in the country's balance of payments current account, especially in an environment of increasing trade liberalization, which has put its export sectors under greater pressure. Indeed, recognising the growing contribution of remittances to Barbados' economy, the Central Bank of Barbados is moving towards a more accurate capture of informal remittances. Comparatively, Barbados is one of the lowest remittance-receiving countries in the Caribbean (see Figure 15.3). Nonetheless, as illustrated in Figure 15.9, remittances have outstripped FDI and ODA.

Furthermore, for Barbados, primarily a remittance-receiving country, remittance inflows account for more than half of all private current transfer receipts and make the third largest contribution to foreign exchange earnings in the current account, after tourism receipts and total domestic exports (Stanford 2006). From 1987 to 2004, total remittance inflows represented more than four times the foreign investment into the country. And, at 5.7 per cent of GDP in 2008, remittances are almost as important to the economy as the agricultural sector, which accounted for 6 per cent GDP in 2000 (World Resources Institute, 2003).

In previous economic downturns (1990–1992 and 2001) remittances have proven somewhat counter-cyclical for Barbados, with remittance growth remaining relatively high in the crisis period (see Figure 15.10). However, it is notable that remittance growth dropped in the immediate aftermath. For instance, during

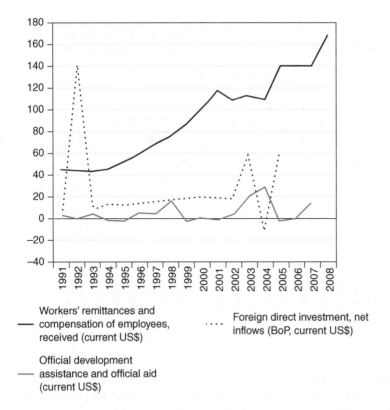

Workers' remittances and
—— compensation of employees,
received (current US$)

···· Foreign direct investment, net
inflows (BoP, current US$)

Official development
—— assistance and official aid
(current US$)

Figure 15.9 Remittance inflows, FDI and ODA to Barbados 1992–2009e (source: World
Bank, 2009a; 2009 data estimated).

the period of negative GDP growth from 1990 to 1992 remittances grew an
average of 19.4 per cent, and although they continued to exhibit positive growth,
the rate dropped sharply to only 1.6 per cent in 1993. The negative GDP growth
of 2001 was flanked by double-digit growth in remittances recorded that year,
plummeting to −4.7 per cent in 2002. Reversing this trend of increase in the rate
of maintenance inflows in periods of economic contraction, in this particular
crisis recorded remittance growth plunged by an all-time high rate in 2008.
However, although the contraction of the economy continued into 2009, with
negative growth (−2.8 per cent), remittances rebounded significantly. And,
despite the drop in remittances in response to the global economic crisis, these
monetary flows remain more resilient than FDI and ODA.

   Stanford (2006) argues that the maintenance of high remittance flows during
economic downturns, indicative of an inverse relationship between remittances
and the real GDP, could lead to the conclusion of an altruistic motive for Barba-
dians sending remittances, deliberately offsetting poor economic performance in
the home country; however, this conclusion should be tempered by the findings

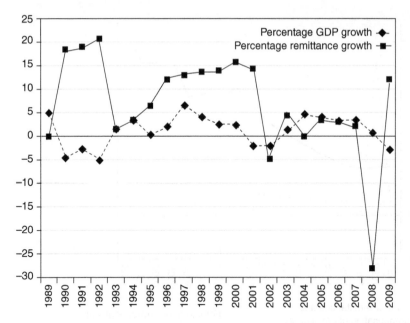

Figure 15.10 A comparison of Barbados' percentage GDP and remittance growth.

of Campbell (2005), which proffer a positive relationship between remittances and local real GDP. As the Barbadian economy grows, so does the propensity to migrate due to increased opportunities for education and training, and thus improved migration opportunities leading to an increase in remittances. However, in this global crisis, migration prospects as well as opportunities to remain in the host country are uncertain, and will be affected by the migration policies, employment prospects and economic fortunes.

4 The impact of the global economic crisis on remittance flows to remittance-receiving and -sending countries

4.1 Remittance-receiving countries

Global remittance flows have fallen in the wake of the global economic crisis, but remain more resilient than FDI and ODA. Remittances to Latin America and the Caribbean have been falling since September 2008, the point at which the IMF indicates that the global economic crisis hit the Caribbean. Jamaica is the only Caribbean country for which the World Bank collates monthly data. These data are derived from the Central Bank of Jamaica, which produces monthly reports on the status of the country's remittances. The monthly data for Jamaica are provided, in Figure 15.11, to allow a closer look at how the crisis affected that country. Remittances to Jamaica, which fluctuated sharply after the crisis,

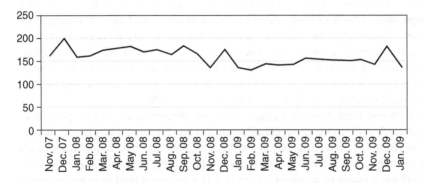

Figure 15.11 Monthly remittances to Jamaica (source: extracted from data compiled by Migration and Remittances Team, Development Prospects Group, World Bank from Bank of Jamaica, at www.boj.org.jm).

Note
Remittance estimates in the figure above only include workers' remittances, and not compensation of employees or migrant transfers. The latter two series are included in annual remittances data (see: http://siteresources.worldbank.org/INTPROSPECTS/Resources/334934–110315015165/Remittances Data_July09(Public).xls).

have levelled off, but have not regained pre-crisis rates. The flow of remittances will depend to an extent on the economic conditions of the sending countries. Notably, remittance inflows jumped sharply in December 2009 before plummeting again. The Bank of Jamaica (2009) reports that this sharp movement resulted from an augmentation in remittance inflows, as well as a decline in outflows. This underscores the significance of the Christmas period to the island, as this holiday is traditionally recognised as a time for family celebrations and household maintenance. December historically represents a strong month for remittances to Jamaica, regardless of activity throughout the rest of the year or previous months. Indeed, on average, from 2004 to 2009 remittances increased 31 per cent from November to December, dropping sharply by 23 per cent going into January. Historically, migrants continue to send money home regardless, even when they themselves endure income shocks.

4.2 Remittance-sending countries

Especially relevant from the perspective of the remittance-sending countries is an analysis of the impact on employment in high-income countries, especially the USA and Canada, which are the countries to which most migrants gravitate from the Caribbean countries for which remittances contribute most significantly. Evidence on return migration is inconclusive, pointing perhaps to return migration being a feature more so of skilled migration, and also dependent on the prospective economic growth and polices to encourage return migration in place in the home country. Ratha *et al.* (2009) suggest that there is negligible evidence of return migration as a result of the financial crisis in the US and Europe, due to fears of being denied re-entry as a result of tighter immigration controls. However, while some migrants may choose or have no option to remain overseas, there is growing anecdotal and empirical evidence of increasing reverse brain drain to from the USA to China and India, with skilled migrants leaving high-income countries and returning home to their developing economies (Wadhwa et al., 2007; Wadwha and Wucker, 2009).

The World Bank Poverty Reduction Group (Nieves et al., n.d.) reports that migration flows into major receiving countries are decreasing and return migration is rising, as governments worldwide are tightening visa requirements and encouraging return migration in response to the global economic crisis. In fact, in 2009 the number of applications for H-1 B visas for skilled migrants (temporary workers in specialty occupations) in the US fell sharply, due in part to the fact that the US stimulus package has made it increasingly difficult for companies benefiting from government assistance to hire foreign workers (Ratha et al. 2009). Many of these jobs are going overseas, especially to Asia – encouraging workers to return home, and work for US companies there (Wadwha and Wucker, 2009). Further, Ratha et al. (2009) recognise that as the crisis deepens, unemployment and a lack of job opportunities will compel some workers to return home. Continued economic growth for India and China, despite the crisis, provides motivating economic prospects for those who may be contemplating returning home. This is not the case for the majority of Caribbean countries. All of the Caribbean economies listed in Table 15.4 experienced negative economic growth in 2009, with the one exception of Trinidad and Tobago. This suggests that, by itself, the economic environment in these Caribbean countries is not sufficiently vibrant to lure often hesitant migrants back home. Policies specifically designed to take advantage of any return migration which may be occurring will be needed.

Some infrastructure is formally in place in countries in the region to manage return migration. As Figure 15.12 shows, from 2000 to 2007 the majority of returning migrants processed by the Barbados Facilitation Unit for Returning Foreign Nationals (FURN) were from the USA (43 per cent), with 40 per cent from the United Kingdom and about 10 per cent from Canada. After peaking in 2001, the number of nationals returning through FURN has steadily declined until 2007. An analysis of the data for 2008 and 2009, when they are released, will be warranted to gauge the impact of the global economic downturn on the decision of migrants to return home.

5 Conclusions and policy recommendations

Already contending with reduced fiscal options, a continued decline in remittances would create external financing gaps for Caribbean economies which are heavily dependent on remittances, particularly given already falling levels of FDI and prospective restricted ODA. IDB and Word Bank reports suggest that remittances will stabilise; however, this recovery will depend to a large extent

Table 15.4 Annual percentage GDP Growth Rates for CARICOM countries, China and India

Annual % GDP growth rates	2000	2001	2002	2003	2004	2005	2006	2007	2008	2009
Antigua and Barbuda	3.30	1.50	2.20	4.90	7.19	3.15	12.48	6.30	2.15	−0.94
Bahamas	5.00	−2.00	0.70	2.79	2.81	3.40	4.00	1.95	1.40	−3.22
Barbados	2.31	−2.06	−2.05	1.32	4.40	4.10	3.50	3.30	0.70	−2.80
Belize	12.28	4.87	4.24	9.40	4.20	3.60	5.80	1.57	2.50	−1.50
Dominica	1.31	−4.16	−5.08	0.10	1.10	2.10	3.10	1.60	2.30	−0.43
Grenada	6.93	−5.03	−1.10	5.77	−3.02	2.00	0.77	3.50	1.75	−0.90
Guyana	−1.42	2.25	1.05	−0.65	1.55	−3.01	3.30	5.33	3.47	−0.52
Haiti	0.85	−1.05	−0.50	0.40	−3.51	1.79	2.32	2.10	1.50	−1.75
Jamaica	0.76	1.47	1.09	2.26	0.90	1.40	2.46	1.43	−2.20	−0.70
St Kitts and Nevis	4.32	2.63	1.57	2.13	6.40	4.10	6.37	3.10	2.04	−0.65
St Lucia	−0.12	−4.30	0.40	3.00	3.50	5.40	4.04	0.50	1.60	−0.94
St Vincent and the Grenadines	1.15	−0.10	1.40	4.50	5.95	3.09	8.71	7.70	3.19	−0.72
Suriname	3.40	4.55	3.04	5.30	4.61	4.90	5.80	5.39	3.82	−2.24
Trinidad and Tobago	6.13	0.17	6.78	13.39	14.39	15.39	16.39	5.50	3.50	1.00
COMPARISON COUNTRIES										
China	8.40	8.30	9.10	10.00	10.10	10.40	11.60	11.40	8.90	7.20
India	3.94	5.15	4.09	8.61	6.90	8.43	9.69	9.03	7.00	5.00

Source: Adapted from World Bank World Development Indicators, International Financial Statistics of the IMF, Global Insight, and Oxford Economic Forecasting, as well as estimated and projected values developed by the Economic Research Service, all converted to a 2005 base year.

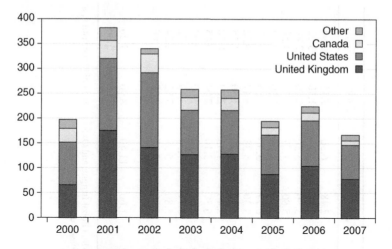

Figure 15.12 Barbados facilitation unit for returning nationals: statistics for 2000–2007 (source: Barbados Ministry of Foreign Affairs, www.foreign.gov.bb/ UserFiles/File/Statistics%202000%20-%202007.pdf, accessed 18 March 2010).

on the economic revival of the high-income countries to which Caribbean populations tend to migrate, and significant risks remain. Additionally, although migrants often surmount challenging circumstances to ensure money is remitted to their country of origin, the income and employment losses facing migrants in the current downturn, given emerging signs that the employment crisis will persist beyond economic upturn, suggest continued downward pressure on remittance flows to developing countries, including those in the Caribbean. Furthermore, the historical analysis provided by this study indicates that the depth of recovery will vary widely and country-specifically.

Even if remittances level off, further research is necessary to distinguish between remittances which are used for immediate consumption (for example, to provide food and clothing) as opposed to for business investment, since a reliance on remittances for consumption may indicate a failure of locally generated means to provide for the basic needs of a country's population. Governments would be challenged to step in and fill the gap, especially for poor families, and find innovative ways to continue their poverty-reduction strategies. They would be pressed to actively engage in maximising available remittance flows by concentrating on reducing the cost of sending remittances, and working with receiving countries to promote return or circular migration. Continued improvements in remittance data collection methods are also vital to providing a more accurate platform for decision-making.

The global nature of this economic crisis has shown that, given the policies which are currently being pursued, Caribbean countries are dependent to a large extent on the recovery of the high-income countries (which were also severely affected) to spur economic growth. Given the lack of policy space available to the governments in the region, there is a need to balance short-term economic stabilisation measures with long-term strategies for sustainable growth. One such strategy would be to take advantage of any return migration which may accompany the global economic downturn and recovery. This may be permanent or transnational, with the returned national maintaining a home overseas. Recouping maximum benefits from return migration will depend on the country's capacity to absorb this new labour into the workforce, and the extent to which any skills and knowledge gained overseas can be utilised. Even if the volume of return migration turns out not to be that substantial, the measures that would need to be put in place to encourage people to resettle would enhance the region's long-term prospects for research and development, facilitating easy investment by those who remain overseas, and may actually have a sustained multiplier effect on encouraging return migration. Skilled migration is a significant feature of the region, with more than 70 per cent of some tertiary-educated populations leaving the region. It would therefore be prudent for the region to position itself to benefit from any return migration that might occur due to the crisis, as many migrant-receiving countries tighten migration policies in the face of increasing unemployment. This study suggests that the Caribbean does not have the necessary policies in place, or prospects of economic growth, to benefit from reverse brain drain to the extent of China and India. However, there is significant potential in areas such as research and development, as 7–10 per cent of the Caribbean students undertaking tertiary education in the Europe Union are pursuing advanced research qualifications (Nurse and Jones, 2010). This is a key indicator of the research and development potential of the Caribbean, if this migrant population can be engaged to return to the region or contribute from the Diaspora.

Given the relatively large size of the Caribbean Diaspora, a successful Diaspora strategy is a key pillar in a development strategy seeking engagement beyond remittances. Table 15.5 summarises some of the fundamentals needed for a successful Diaspora strategy to encourage investment and maximise the resources to be gained from those who remain abroad and/or those who plan to return at some point. Importantly, there is a need to foster Diaspora networks in order to benefit more from return migration, Diasporic tourism and investment.

In evaluating possible Diaspora strategies, it is important to appreciate the differences between short-term remittance-driven plans and longer-term initiatives which focus on a Diasporic wider engagement. Table 15.6 summarises short-term strategies employed by the Philippines, Eritrea and Mexico.

Such initiatives are useful for maximising the benefits from remittances. However, remittances can only be used to lift people out of poverty for as long as the flows continue. The IDB (2007) survey on Haiti showed that remittances had a tendency to decline the longer a person spent abroad. Furthermore, should conditions emerge that prompt their decline, as has happened since mid-September 2008 with the global economic crisis, broader measures which have a sustainable effect beyond remittances merit consideration. Moreover, it is

Table 15.5 Fundamentals of a successful diaspora strategy

	Notes
1. Definition of Diaspora	Important factor determining who will be engaged and what kind of development the stakeholders are expected to contribute. Four conditions can be considered necessary for a group of people to be considered a Diaspora: 1. Have moved to more another country from an original country; indeed, perhaps dispersed across several countries. 2. A collective myth of an ideal ancestral home. 3. A strong shared ethnic identity. 4. A sustained network of social relationships with home country (Bakewell, 2009).
2. Rules of engagement for the stakeholders	Clarity of contributions sought from all parties.
3. Policy coherence with other national and international priorities.	Diaspora should be engaged with caution to ensure a win–win–win situation for governments, the Diaspora and those who have stayed home: to ensure that mobile populations are not privileged at the expense of all else.
4. Clear definition of role to be played by Diaspora.	Four major policy roles for the Diaspora can be identified: enabling, inclusionary, partnership, catalytic (Ionescu, 2006).
5. A focal point to ensure Diaspora (individuals, organisations or networks) have easy access to information.	Maintain updated database of Diaspora networks at home and abroad. [Several Caribbean governments have established Diasporic Units].
6. Country-specific implementation	Better chance of success if tailored to peculiarities of particular country and Diasapora.

evident that remittances are not a sufficient condition for development given the continued poverty and low economic growth found throughout the Caribbean, especially for those countries for which remittances contribute significantly to their economies. The region therefore also needs to consider broader longer-term strategies. For the Caribbean, lessons can be learnt from countries which actively court their Diaspora beyond remittances. For instance, India and China, for which remittance flows comprise a relatively low percentage of GDP (4.2 per cent and 1.1 per cent of 2008 GDP, respectively), have taken steps to engage their Diaspora to the benefit of the homeland. Table 15.7 outlines the main features of some of the alternative strategies, being undertaken by China, India and Taiwan, which adopt a more long-term perspective and offer an alternative

Table 15.6 Short-term diaspora strategies focusing on remittances

Policy	Country	Risks/challenges
Maximise income stream from remittances directly to households"	Philippines	Duration of migration dictates longevity of income stream; the remittance flow is therefore vulnerable to migration policies and economic conditions in the remittance-sending/host country
Pre-empt individual remittances into government channels	Eritrea	May erode some of poverty-reducing potential of Diaspora transfers
Use federal programs to promote collective remittances and to make the sum of individual household remittances greater than the sum of their parts	Mexico and similar systems arising in Central America and the Caribbean	While provides direct connection to the poor, outcome is dependent on improvement in macroeconomic conditions – systemic infrastructure problems including underdeveloped markets, corruption, poor investment

Source: Adapted from Newland (2004).

Table 15.7 Long-term diaspora strategies

Policy	Country	Potential benefits
"Brain trust" model, focused on attracting capital on attracting capital from the Diaspora	Taiwan	Positioned to benefit from any reverse brain drain (return migration) that may result from global economic downturn
Encourage Diaspora engagement in FDI and trade – "attract direct investment" and open trade opportunities through overseas Chinese communities	China	Long-term sustainable development
Multi-pronged approach – direct investment, portfolio investment, technology transfer, marketing opening, outsourcing opportunities	India	Diversity of approach spreads the risks

Source: Adapted from Newland (2004).

model for Diaspora engagement, with more potential for a sustained contribution to development. India has progressively adopted a more robust engagement with the Diasporas, moving away from a stance of "disapproving indifference" (Newland, 2004). Previously, India's Diaspora engagement manifested in the links between US and Indian high-tech firms was more a feature of the support provided by higher eduction institutions and general macroeconomic reforms. Private sector initiatives in tandem with government initiatives have succeeded in making a dent in India's poverty, and, while much work remains, it is important to note that "without the growth generated by India's Diaspora-led entry into the global economy (particularly the information economy) it would seem little more than a mirage" (Newland, 2004).

In addition to brain circulation (return migration and investment), there is also the potential for Diasporic tourism, given the propensity of Caribbean populations to migrate (see Table 15.1). In fact, heritage tourism is one of the fastest-growing niches in the industry. For 2004, 85 per cent of the stay-over visitors to Guyana were Guyanese on short visits from their adopted countries. Diasporic tourists are a significant proportion of the consumers of festival tourism. This is borne out in the case of Trinidad and Tobago, where as much as 70 per cent of the visitors for the carnival are from the Diaspora (Nurse, 2004). Potential benefits from Diasporic tourism include:

1   diversification beyond traditional tourism target markets;
2   Diasporic tourists investing more in indigenous goods and services;
3   the potential for higher levels of capital to be retained and circulate within the local economy, as compared with other tourism business models including all-inclusive hotels and cruise ships;
4   increase in trade in services as more small and medium-sized business are incorporated into the tourism sector.

The fall-off in international migration flows, and general economic and employment uncertainty, negatively impact the capacity of a household to mitigate the impact of the crisis via remittances and migration. Fortunately, remittances are not the only way for the Diaspora to assist in the development of their home countries. There is clearly scope for broader Caribbean Diasporic participation and contribution to both their home and host economies. What is important is to recognise the challenges but also the opportunities posed by the global economic crisis, to in effect broaden the Caribbean's development response towards a strategic approach to engage the Diaspora on a multitude of levels. Importantly, there is a need to look beyond remittances and implement programmes to build Diaspora networks in order to benefit more from return migration and Diaspora tourism and investment.

Notes

1 The Caribbean Community (CARICOM) is made up of several small island developing states of the Caribbean: Antigua and Barbuda, the Bahamas, Barbados, Belize,

Dominica, Grenada, Guyana, Haiti, Jamaica, Montserrat, St Kitts and Nevis, St Lucia, St Vincent and the Grenadines, Suriname, and Trinidad and Tobago.

2 For a rather detailed study of the Suriname–Netherlands remittance corridor, see the Unger and Siegel (2006) study.

3 The Organisation of Eastern Caribbean States is made up of Antigua and Barbuda, the Commonwealth of Dominica, Grenada, Montserrat, St Kitts and Nevis, St Lucia, and St Vincent and the Grenadines, which are also members of the Caribbean Community (CARICOM), as well as Anguilla.

Bibliography

Agarwal, R. and Horowitz, A. (2002) 'Are international remittances altruism or insurance? Evidence from Guyana using multiple-migrant households'. *World Development*, 30(11): 2033–2044.

Agunias, D. (2006) *Remittances and Development Trends, Impacts, and Policy Options: A Review of the Literature.* Washington, DC: Migration Policy Institute.

Ahortor, C.R.K. and Adenutsi, D.E. (2009) 'The Impact of Remittances on Economic Growth in Small-Open Developing Economies', *Journal of Applied Sciences*, 9: 3275–3286.

Attzs, M. (2008) *Natural disasters and remittances: Exploring the linkages between poverty, gender, and disaster vulnerability on Caribbean SIDS.* Helsinki: UNU-WIDER.

Bakewell, O. (2009) Which diaspora for whose development? Some Critical Questions about the Roles of African Diaspora Organizations as Development Actors. *DIIS Brief.* Copenhagen: Danish Institute for International Studies (DIIS).

Bank of Jamaica (BOJ) (2009) *The Balance of Payments: Remittance Update May 2009.* Kingston: Bank of Jamaica, pp. 12–13. Available at www.boj.org.jm/uploads/pdf/rem_updates/rem_updates_may2009.pdf

Campbell, T. (2005) 'The Long and Short-Run Determinants of Workers' Remittances to Barbados'. Central Bank of Barbados Working Paper.

Carrington, W.J. and Detragiache, E. (1998) 'How Big Is the Brain Drain?' IMF Working Paper.

Clarke, G. and Wallsten, S. (2003). *Do Remittances Act like Insurance? Evidence from a Natural Disaster in Jamaica.* Washington, DC: World Bank.

De Haas, H. (2008) *Migration and Development: A Theoretical Perspective.* Oxford: University of Oxford.

Docquier, F. and Marfouk, A. (2004) *Measuring the International Mobility of Skilled Workers.* Washington, DC: World Bank.

Eastern Caribbean Central Bank (ECCB) (2009) 'Report and Statement of Accounts for the Financial Year Ended 31 March 2009'. Available at www.eccb-centralbank.org/PDF/ar0809_forweb2.pdf, p. 10.

Eurostat (n.d.) Foreign students in tertiary education (ISCED 5-6) by country of citizenship. Available at http://appsso.eurostat.ec.europa.eu/nui/show.do?wai=true&dataset=educ_enrl8.

Inter-American Development Bank (IDB) (2007) *Inter-American Development Bank Haiti Remittance Survey, 6 March 2007.* Washington, DC: Inter-American Development Bank.

International Monetary Fund (IMF) (2009) *World Economic Outlook April 2009: Crisis and Recovery.* Washington, DC: International Monetary Fund.

International Organisation for Migration (IOM) (2002) *The Migration and Development Nexus: A Theoretical Perspective.* Geneva: International Organisation for Migration (IOM).

Ionescu, D. (2006) 'Engaging diasporas as development partners for home and destination countries: challenges for policymakers. In: *Migration Research Series.* Geneva: International Organisation for Migration.

Jha, S., Sugiyarto, G. and Vargas-Silva, C. (2009) *The Global Crisis and the Impact on Remittances to Developing Asia.* Philippines: Asian Development Bank Economics Working Paper Series No. 185.

Khemraj, T. (2009) *Are Remittances Pivotal to Guyana's Development?*, Stabreok News. Available at: www.stabroeknews.com/2009/features/07/08/are-remittances-pivotal-to-guyana%E2%80%99s-development/ (accessed 30 January 2011).

Kirton, C.D. (2006) *Unlocking the Potential of Remittances in Guyana: Remittances Mobilization through Microfinance Institutions.* Washington, DC: Inter-American Development Bank, June.

Mishra, P. (2006) *Emigration and Brain Drain: Evidence from the Caribbean.* Washington, DC: International Monetary Fund.

Mohapatra, S., George, J. and Dilip, R. (2009) *Remittances and Natural Disasters – Ex-post Response and Contribution to Ex-ante Preparedness.* Washington, DC: World Bank.

Mullan, F. (2005) 'The metrics of the physician brain drain'. *New England Journal of Medicine,* 353: 1810–1818.

Newland, K. (2004) *Beyond Remittances: The Role of Diaspora in Poverty Reduction in their Countries of Origin.* Washington, DC: Migration Policy Institute.

Nieves, C., Paci, P. and Sasin, M. (n.d.) *The Impact of the Economic Crisis on Migration and Remittances.* Washington, DC: World Bank Poverty Reduction Group.

Nurse, K. (2004) *Diaspora, Migration and Development in the Caribbean.* Ottawa: FOCAL Policy Paper.

Nurse, K. and Jones, J. (2010) 'Brain Drain and Caribbean–EU Labour Mobility'. Paper commissioned by by Observatorio de las Relaciones Unión Europea – América Latina (OBREAL) for the BRIDGES-LAC Project.

Orozco, M. (2002) 'Globalization and migration: The impact of family remittances in Latin America'. *Latin American Politics and Society,* 2: 41–66.

Orozco, M. (2006). 'Understanding the Remittances Economy in Haiti'. Inter-American Dialogue paper commissioned by the World Bank, 15 March.

Ratha, D. (2007) *Leveraging Remittances for Development.* Washington, DC: Migration Policy Institute.

Ratha, D. (2009) 'Dollars without borders: Can the global flow of remittances survive the crisis?' *Foreign Affairs,* 16 October.

Ratha, D. (2010). 'A conversation on migration and development' (1 February, K. Banerjee, Interviewer). Available at: https://blogs.worldbank.org/peoplemove/a-conversation-on-migration-and-development (accessed 2 February 2011).

Ratha, D., Mohapatra, S. And Silwal, A. (2009a) *Migration and Remittance Trends 2009: A Better-than-expected Outcome so Far, but Significant Risks Ahead.* Washington, DC: World Bank.

Ratha, D., Mohapatra, S. and Silwal, A. (2009b) *Outlook for Remittance Flows 2009–2011: Remittances Expected to Fall by 7–10 Percent in 2009.* Migration and Remittance Team, Development Prospects Group. Washington, DC: World Bank.

Stanford, S. (2006) 'Creating awareness about workers' remittance flows to Barbados: A note'. Presented at the 27th Annual Seminar Research Department Central Bank of Barbados. Barbados: Central Bank of Barbados.

Thomas-Hope, E. (2009). 'Perspectives on Migration and Development'. Presented at the joint launch of EC–UN Joint Migration & Development Initiative Jamaica Projects UNDP Human Development Report 2009, 14 October. Kingston, Jamaica.

Unger B. and Siegel, M. (2006) 'The Netherlands–Suriname Corridor for Workers' Remittances. Prospects for Remittances When Migration Ties Loosen'. University of Utrecht and The World Bank.

United Nations Development Programme (UNDP) (2009). *Human Development Report 2009: Overcoming Barriers: Human Mobility and Development.* New York, NY: UNDP.

Wadwha, V. and Wucker, M. (2009) Online radio show on reverse brain drain (M. Savidge, Interviewer). World Focus. Available online at: http://worldfocus.org/blog/2009/02/03/tune-in-online-radio-show-on-reverse-brain-drain/3904/ (accessed 30 January 2011).

Wadhwa, V., Jasso, G., Rissing, B., Gereffi, G. and Freeman, R. (2007) *Intellectual Property, the Immigration Backlog, and a Reverse Brain-Drain: America's New Immigrant Entrepreneurs, Part III.* Ewing Marion Kauffman Foundation.

World Bank (2006) *Global Economic Prospects 2006: Economic Implications of Remittances and Migration.* Washington, DC: World Bank.

World Bank (2008) *Migration and Remittances Factbook 2008.* Washington, DC: World Bank.

World Bank (2009a) Remittance data. Available online at www.worldbank.org/prospects/migrationandremittances.

World Bank. (2009b) *Global Development Finance: Charting a Global Recovery.* Washington, DC: World Bank.

World Resources Institute (2003) 'Economic Indicators – Barbados'. In: *Earth Trends Country Profiles.* Washington, DC: World Resources Institute (WRI). Available at: http://earthtrends.wri.org.

Index

356   *Index*

competitiveness *continued*
126–8, 132, 135; policy challenges
190–2; price factors 124, 126–8, 133–4;
South Asian economies 57–9, 179, 240
consumer demand 28, 51–4, 59, 123
consumption: Argentina 117–18, 123,
126–9, 133, 135, 138–9; South Africa
254, 256–7, 263, 264, 265, 266, 270–1,
273, 274, 278–9; use of remittances 346
contagion 77, 79, 167–8, 244, 274, 303
contingent valuation method (CVM),
externalities 151, 152–3
Corazza, R.I. 155
Corden, W.M. 23
core economies, and economic downturns
51–4, 59
Corn Laws, Britain 25, 26
corporate restructuring, South Africa
258–63
Correa, P. 298
cost reduction, businesses 302–3, 305
cost-benefit analysis, ethanol fuel 150–3
'COU-Ps-INs' 41
creative destruction 28, 148–50, 173–5,
186, 187
credit rating agencies 104, 299
crisis management literature 298–9
crisis plans, businesses 301–2, 321
Crotty, J. 258, 268, 269
Crowder, M. 63
currency crisis (2001), South Africa 255,
265, 272
current account balances 3, 5–6, 78, 86,
87, 100, 103, 104, 135, 256, 340
Curtis, M. 29
cut-flower exports

Da Silva, J.G. 161
Davis, M. 70
de-agrarianization, Africa 66–7
de-industrialization: Africa 14, 66; effects
of trade liberalization 21, 27, 30–4;
Mexico 58–9; South Africa 269–73
Deane, P. 26
debt sustainability measures 103–4
Decoster, A. 278
Dedeoğlu, S. 207
Delbeke, J. 48, 49
democratic transition, South Africa 258,
260, 261–2
derivatives market futures contracts, South
Africa 273
developed countries, trade policy towards
developing countries 26–7, 29–30

development finance, trade as tool for 111
development options, peripheral
economies 55–7
development policy implications, trade
liberalization 39–42
developmental state 64–5
Di Maio, M. 41
Diaspora strategy, Caribbean 347–50
Dikbayir, G. 207
direct instruments, capital controls 80–2
'discouraged worker' effect 202, 208, 209,
211, 212, 213, 214
Dobbs, R. 105, 106
Docquier, F. 329, 337, 338
domestic adjustment, Argentina 133–9
domestic demand 128–9, 133, 179
dotcom bubble 255
downsizing 101, 173–4, 302–3, 305
Duménil, G. 268
Dutch disease 76, 117, 119, 135–6, 138,
139
dynamic decomposition, earnings
inequality 287–9

earnings inequality and employment:
conclusions 289–91; global trends
277–82; methodology 291–2; South
Africa 282–9
Economic Commission for Latin America
and the Caribbean (ECLAC) 104–5
Economic Commission on Africa 70
economic downturns: analysis of impact
on gendered employment patterns
209–15; and peripheral economies 50–4;
theoretical background on impact of
gendered employment 202–3
economic expansion, Argentina 117–21
economic growth, emerging economies as
drivers of 57–9
Economic Partnership Agreements (EPAs)
24, 29–30, 41
economic performance indicators, Jamaica
299–300
economic power, shift in 2
economic recovery, prospects for 2–6
economic upswings and peripheral
economies 51–4
education, Caribbean 242–3
Edwards, S. 79
efficiency-seeking investment 104–5
emerging economies, as drivers of growth
2–6, 57–9
employment: Argentina 133–4, 138;
Caribbean 241–5; gendered structure of

Taylor & Francis

eBooks

FOR LIBRARIES

ORDER YOUR
FREE 30 DAY
INSTITUTIONAL
TRIAL TODAY!

Over 23,000 eBook titles in the Humanities,
Social Sciences, STM and Law from some of the
world's leading imprints.

Choose from a range of subject packages or create your own!

Benefits for
you

▶ Free MARC records
▶ COUNTER-compliant usage statistics
▶ Flexible purchase and pricing options

Benefits
for your
user

▶ Off-site, anytime access via Athens or referring URL
▶ Print or copy pages or chapters
▶ Full content search
▶ Bookmark, highlight and annotate text
▶ Access to thousands of pages of quality research
at the click of a button

For more information, pricing enquiries or to order
a free trial, contact your local online sales team.

UK and Rest of World: **online.sales@tandf.co.uk**

US, Canada and Latin America:
e-reference@taylorandfrancis.com

www.ebooksubscriptions.com

Taylor & Francis eBooks
Taylor & Francis Group

A flexible and dynamic resource for teaching, learning and research.

For Product Safety Concerns and Information please contact our
EU representative GPSR@taylorandfrancis.com Taylor & Francis
Verlag GmbH, Kaufingerstraße 24, 80331 München, Germany